P9-CJQ-483

PROPERTY OF
THE UNIVERSITY OF TEXAS

GIDEON LINCECUM

1793–1874

GIDEON LINCECUM

1793-1874

A Biography

By Lois Wood Burkhalter

UNIVERSITY OF TEXAS PRESS, AUSTIN & LONDON

Library of Congress Catalog Card Number 65–13515

Copyright © 1965 by Lois Wood Burkhalter
All Rights Reserved

Printed in the United States of America
by The University of Texas Printing Division, Austin
Bound by Universal Bookbindery, Inc., San Antonio

In Memory of My Father

IRA MACK WOOD
1882–1952

Who also cherished freedom

PREFACE

My interest in Gideon Lincecum began several years ago with a casual reading of a typescript of some of his letters. This brief but unforgettable introduction to the man and his writings led me to the Archives Collection, University of Texas Library, where eventually I read all the Lincecum Papers, deposited in 1930 and 1931 by Gideon Lincecum's grandsons, Clyde Bryan Doran and Frank Lincecum Doran, of Hempstead, Texas. The papers had been carefully preserved by their mother, Lincecum's beloved youngest daughter, Sallie Doran, who recognized her father's peculiar genius.

The collection is of monumental size and would have been at least 900 pages larger if dampness had not ruined documents buried during the Civil War to prevent theft or injury by vandals, who, Lincecum said, "destroyed the literary and scientific records of our country wherever they found them." This loss results in gaps in our knowledge of Lincecum's life and probably accounts for the unavailability of details of his early life in the South. With the notable exception of the Choctaw Indian notes and a journal of travel in Texas in 1835, the bulk of the material was written after his arrival in Texas in 1848.

Although Lincecum carefully filed all letters written to him, regrettably few survived. The result is a one-way correspondence, at times baffling. It was possible to quote from some of the missing communications because Lincecum often repeated passages from them in his replies or in letters to others.

During the years from 1850 to 1868, the most prolific period of his life, Lincecum used a letter press but discontinued this method of making copies of his correspondence while he lived in Tuxpan, Mexico. The only information available on his activities in Mexico is contained in letters to his daughters and in a series of autobiographical letters to a grandson.

When Lincecum was eighty years old he began writing another and more detailed autobiography, largely devoted to hunting and fishing adventures on various frontiers he had pioneered. This was published in nineteen weekly issues of the *American Sportsman* from September 12, 1874, to January 16, 1875, and has been used in this biography.

I have attempted to bring out of obscurity a remarkable and delightful American who deserves a place in the history of his country. In an endeavor to project the full force of his personality I have, wherever possible, used Lincecum's own words. In all cases, unless otherwise noted, quotations are from his writings, letters, or other documents. Since Lincecum frequently repeated himself to his numerous correspondents, in quoting him on any given subject I have sometimes combined the best sentences and paragraphs from different letters. In some cases I have taken the liberty of deleting some passages, for easier reading, from Lincecum's lengthier sentences, but in no case have words been changed. Some of his errors in spelling and grammar, obviously due to carelessness, have been corrected.

LOIS W. BURKHALTER

San Antonio, Texas

ACKNOWLEDGMENTS

In the course of researching and writing the biography of Gideon Lincecum, I gratefully accepted assistance and encouragement from a number of persons.

I am forever indebted to Dr. Andrew Forest Muir, of Rice University, for his patient instructions and criticism and for providing sources and facts from his inexhaustible knowledge of Texas history.

I was frequently heartened by the opinion of others who have been exposed to Lincecum's individuality—J. Frank Dobie, Dr. Samuel Wood Geiser, Dr. Pat Ireland Nixon, and Dr. T. N. Campbell. I am particularly grateful to Dr. Geiser of Southern Methodist University for his generosity in sharing notes on Lincecum and his scientific friends, and for reading and criticizing the chapters on natural history; and to Dr. Campbell, of the University of Texas, who made available his own writings on Lincecum's Choctaw material.

Additionally, I am indebted to the descendants of Gideon Lincecum: Dr. Addison Lincecum, his grandson; Andrew Bradford and Barney Lincecum, his great-grandsons; Mrs. Lucille Lincecum Reed, his gracious great-granddaughter; and Mrs. Willie Reed Rowe, his highly talented artist great-great-granddaughter.

The librarians of the Texas University Archives Collection and the Alamo Library have been unfailingly helpful and courteous.

Finally, I acknowledge my debt to Charles Ramsdell, whose transcript began this project, and to my other personal friends, associates, husband Harry Burkhalter, and family, who suffered through my obsession with Gideon Lincecum.

CONTENTS

ILLUSTRATIONS
(after page 130)

Letter from Lincecum to His Wife

Lincecum's Announcement of His Medical Practice

Receipt for Payment for Slave

Dried Hollyhock from Lincecum's Herbarium

Federal License To Practice Medicine

Cover for Lincecum's "Meteorological Journal"

Page from Weather Chart for February, 1861

Gideon's Account Book: "Good Notes and Accounts"

Gideon's Account Book: "Doubtful Papers, Now Notes"

Lincecum as an Old Man

GENEALOGICAL TABLES

GIDEON LINCECUM

1793–1874

CHAPTER ONE

GIDEON

Free thought? Oh, yes, holy free thought, I have cherished
ye a long lifetime and I promise myself and the world that
all my efforts either in word or deed shall be on "that side of
the blanket" so long as this old heart throbs. GID

GIDEON LINCECUM was endowed by birth and environment with certain traits and characteristics peculiarly timely in his era, the transitional span when an insecure young republic was struggling to maintain its national unity. The American nation of thirteen states was only three years old when Gideon was born on April 22, 1793, in a backwoods settlement in Warren County, Georgia. When he died on November 28, 1874, in Long Point, Washington County, Texas, this country had so changed that he was as anachronous as the frontier that produced him.

His ancestral background was typical.

My four grand parents were all Europeans—French, Scotch, English, Dutch. My father resulted from the conjugal union that took place between the French Huguenot, Gideon Lincecum, and the Scotch lassie, Miriam Bowie—own aunt to the celebrated desperado, James Bowie, the originator of the Bowie knife. If glory and greatness consist in the amount of throat-cutting performed, the Bowie knife was a greater invention than . . . Napoleon Bonaparte. . . .

My mother originated from the union of the Englishman, William Hickman, and the Dutch lady, Marie [H]Ornbeck. It fell my lot to be fathered and mothered by the last born of these two families. My father was raised

I. THE LINCECUM LINE

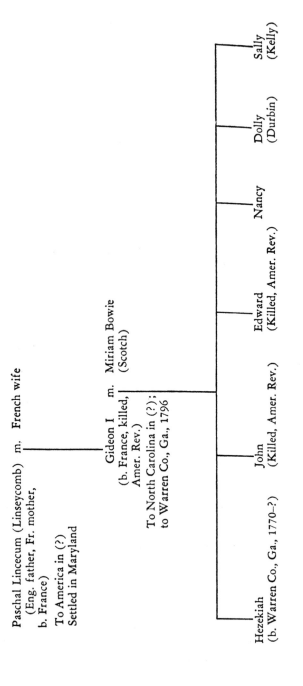

Paschal Lincecum (Linseycomb) m. French wife
(Eng. father, Fr. mother,
b. France)

To America in (?)
Settled in Maryland

Gideon I m. Miriam Bowie
(b. France, killed,   (Scotch)
Amer. Rev.)

To North Carolina in (?);
to Warren Co., Ga., 1796

Hezekiah
(b. Warren Co., Ga., 1770–?)

John
(Killed, Amer. Rev.)

Edward
(Killed, Amer. Rev.)

Nancy

Dolly
(Durbin)

Sally
(Kelly)

II. THE FAMILY OF HEZEKIAH LINCECUM

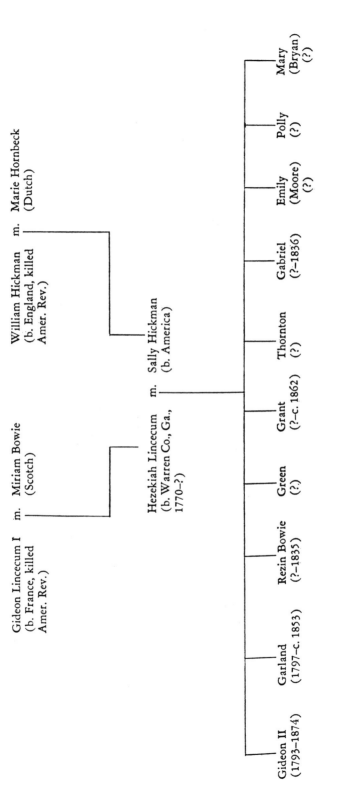

Gideon Lincecum I (b. France, killed Amer. Rev.) m. Miriam Bowie (Scotch)

William Hickman (b. England, killed Amer. Rev.) m. Marie Hornbeck (Dutch)

Hezekiah Lincecum (b. Warren Co, Ga, 1770–?) m. Sally Hickman (b. America)

Gideon II (1793–1874)

Garland (1797–c. 1853)

Rezin Bowie (?–1835)

Green (?)

Grant (?–c. 1862)

Thornton (?)

Gabriel (?–1836)

Emily (Moore) (?)

Polly (?)

Mary (Bryan) (?)

in the school of rebellion, and graduated on various battlefields during the American Revolution. He knew nothing of books, being able only to read tolerably. He was possessed of good, strong mentality, but owing to the unsettled state of the country and the turbulence of affairs generally, at the time he was forming character, it had been woefully misdirected. Being matchless in his physical powers, and having full confidence in his knowledge of their application and uses, he often repeated the remark that he "had nothing to fear." He delighted in a border life, and he reared his numerous progeny on the various boundary lines as they occurred from the frequent little treaties made with the Muscogee Indians on the western borders of the State of Georgia.

About my mother, there was nothing remarkable, except that she could outrun any body; was handsome, healthy, energetic, ingenious, industrious, frugal, but entirely illiterate.

I was the first-born of a mother not quite sixteen; was educated by the Muscogee Indians and hunters of a frontier country until I was fifteen, having the Muscogee children for my playmates and the bow and arrows and the blow-gun for my hunting implements.

Lincecum learned to read and write during a five months' term in a primitive and temporary school on a Georgia frontier, and as a teenage boy his mind and personality were forever marked by reading the works of Erasmus Darwin. Darwin's impact, to be reinforced in later years by the writings of his famous grandson, created a perpetual discontent with the imperfection of man and a more profound appreciation of nature. All the rest of his life was spent in an insatiable investigation of everything that crossed his path or came within range of his vision. Lincecum probed the minds of men, usually through correspondence, to learn their views on religion, politics, science, and a variety of other subjects.

A botanic physician, Lincecum had only scorn for the allopathic medical profession as a whole, regarding their remedies as more fatal than curative. Yet his dearest friends were among the early doctors who eventually legislated his type of practice out of existence. He long battled for medical reforms and high ethical standards, but his sense of freedom rebelled at legislation which protected incompetents and limited practice to one scientific theory.

Gideon found truth and logic only in science, a profession which he considered above religion, sectionalism, and politics and which, he felt, would someday prevail over the traps of ignorance and superstition, ultimately perfecting the human race.

His life was essentially a chronicle of one man's pioneering spirit and his search for freedom. At the age of seventy-five he still sought a new frontier, explaining: "I was not formed by nature for any kind of government. If I had the choosing I would not have preferred an agricultural community. Nature intended me for the forests but dropped me in a locality that was soon overrun and cut down by a race of world spoilers."

The desire for freedom was an old Lincecum tradition which began when Paschal, the son of a French mother and a British father, fled his native France for America. He brought with him his French wife and infant son, Gideon, and in the new country changed the spelling of the family name from *Linseycomb* to *Lincecum*.

The first Gideon grew up in Maryland, but when he married the lovely Miriam Bowie he thought it expedient to remove himself and his bride to North Carolina. The British-French Lincecums could find no common ground with a Scotch immigrant and the Bowies were not the kind to take an insult lightly.

This was a new, wilderness country and here the young couple plied their united efforts successfully. [Gideon Lincecum wrote to a grandson in 1871.] And now in 1769, hearing such good accounts of the territory of Georgia, they sold out their possessions in North Carolina and moved to Warren County. . . . They were a very industrious people and everything went well with them. They were not long in constructing comfortable buildings and a good farm upon which they produced in abundance all the necessaries of subsistence. Gideon Lincecum was captain of a company of rangers, one hundred strong under pay of the government, that had been organized for protection of the frontier against the incursions of the Muscogee Indians, who at that time were very troublesome on the border settlements of Georgia, being hired by the British to kill and scalp the people of Georgia. The Indians received from the British government, for each scalp of man, woman or child, a bottle of rum and $8.00 in money. . . . And now came the Declaration of Independence and the Revolution. . . . Colonel Nace Few sent an order to Captain Lincecum directing him to collect his rangers and meet his forces. . . . They had progressed about half the day when at a point a few miles of where Sparta, the county seat of Hancock County, Georgia, now stands, they came to a bunch of raw hide ropes that had been dropped in the path. Here they made a halt, and one of the men dismounted to get the ropes. At that instant the Indians, who were concealed in the switch cane that covered the ground in that new country, rose up and fired into the crowd. Except Captain Lincecum, who had received a shot in the thigh, Johnathan Hagerthy, and W. Higginbotham, all fell dead on the spot. . . . The captain and his two surviving companions beat a hasty retreat, the Indians pursuing with awful yelling and firing. They had not proceeded exceeding half a mile, when the captain, who was bleeding, and who seemed to be greatly excited, turned and faced the approaching savages. . . . His men urged him not to stop, for there was at least thirty Indians in sight. He seemed not to heed their earnest admonitions, but dismounted from his horse and made ready to fire on them as they came yelling towards him. . . . The captain fell mortally wounded and seeing that there was no possible chance to do anything more, they [his companions] reluctantly left the field. Higginbotham raised a company of men and went the next day to bury the dead. They came to the captain first. He was pretty badly mutilated, having had five scalp trophies taken from his head. . . . The widow of the late Captain Lincecum did not feel safe in remaining any longer in a country overrun with Tories, who had already abused her by whipping her with an iron ramrod, trying to make her tell where she had concealed her money. The negroes had all run away and left her in quite a helpless condition. Finally she concluded to move into South Carolina. A number of Georgia people were doing so and she too gathered up such things as she could carry and her six children and went into Edgefield District, where she remained until peace was made. In the meantime her two sons, Edward and John . . . were taken prisoners and shot soon after the battle of Cowpens. . . . as soon as peace was proclaimed, widow Lincecum returned to her home in Georgia. . . . She found only piles of charred wheat and rye where the barn stood when she got home. All the houses, fences, &c, having long since been consumed by Tory incendiarism. She had been absent seven years. Her stock of cows, hogs, sheep, & horses had all been appropriated. She had nothing but the bare earth that she could call her own, but there was Johnathan Hagerthy, Clabe Nusum, Nace Few, and David Criswell, old rebel neighbors, strong, good men who had passed through the stormy revolution unscathed and were home again, as good friends and neighbors as ever; and they lent a helping hand to the widow and orphans. Two of her negroes— a man and a woman, Africans, who had concealed themselves eight years in Williamson Swamp, subsisting on pigs, geese, frogs, snakes, fish—anything they could lay their hands on without exposure. They had been in America but two or three years when the war broke out . . . hearing no drums or any indication of war, Tom, the name of the male African, took it into his head to creep out in the night and go to his old home and see if Missus had come back. . . . He rushed into the little cabin exclaiming "Gord-a-blessy, gord-a-blessy, me Tom hi-ki-me glad," and he wallowed on the ground, put dirt on his head, and put his missus foot on it, and sobbed heavily. He then rose up and darted out at the door and was gone in an instant. Early next morning he returned with his wife, Hannah, both loaded with enormous packs of old pieces of quilts and other bed clothing they had picked up after the run away. So they got proudly back and were, as they were both young, a great help to the family.

A NOTE ON SOURCES

Facts concerning the ancestry and early life of Gideon Lincecum in the preceding chapter are drawn from three autobiographical sketches: "Personal Reminiscences of an Octogenarian," which was published in *The American Sportsman* in nineteen weekly issues, September 12, 1874, to January 16, 1875, and unfinished at the time of Lincecum's death (hereinafter cited as "Reminiscences"); a lengthy letter to "My Dear Bully Grandson" written in Tuxpan, Mexico, and dated November 3, 1871, the original of which is in the Lincecum Papers in the Archives Collection of the University of Texas Library (hereinafter cited as "Autobiography"); and a version of the letter to a grandson published as "Autobiography of Gideon Lincecum" in the *Publications of the Mississippi Historical Society,* Vol. VIII (1904) Oxford, Mississippi, pp. 443–519 (hereinafter cited as *PMHS*).

Additional biographical facts and quotations in Chapter I have been extracted from Lincecum's letters to Dr. R. P. Hallock, New York City, 21 [March, 1859]; to Joseph Lincecum, Orange County, Texas, February 24, 1863, and to Dr. A[ndrew] Weir, Harmony Hill, Rusk County, Texas, May 20, 1865 (Lincecum Papers).

CHAPTER TWO

GIDEON
AND HEZEKIAH

I knew before leaving my father's house at 15 years of age that I should meet a world of strangers and that the labor and fight for life would have to be done alone . . . but who will say that this long life of mine with so much to love and admire and so few actions to regret has been like a winter day? GID

IF HEZEKIAH LINCECUM had had the proper biographer or balladeer he easily could have become a legend of Southern folklore. He had all the makings of one. Many years after his death his first-born son, Gideon, reminisced about him with loving indulgence.

Shortly after the end of the American Revolution there appeared in a frontier settlement in Warren County, Georgia, an Englishman named Thomas Roberts, who had deserted from the British Army and had served the last three years of the war with the Revolutionary forces. He found Widow Lincecum struggling to restore her farm from war ravages and to support her three daughters with the help of only her strapping thirteen-year-old son, Hezekiah, the sole male Lincecum spared by the British.[1]

Roberts was educated, charming, bold, and given to profanity. When he came courting among the Lincecum girls they sent him on his

[1] Hezekiah's brothers, killed in the Revolution, were Edward and John Lincecum; his sisters, Sally (Kelly), Dolly (Durbin), and Nancy.

way. But Hezekiah, bored with being the pet of a household of women, was charmed by Roberts and easily persuaded to join him in enlisting in a Georgia regiment of Indian fighters. Roberts' influence had far-reaching results and were to shape the character and destiny of Hezekiah's unborn son, Gideon.

After being away three years, Hezekiah returned a giant of a man, handsome and roistering. He was a great fighter, as the men of the community discovered one by one when they crossed him. He could outdrink, outslug and outswear any man in Warren County. One of the feats of his colossal strength was to lift a 596-pound forge hammer and hold it on his arm. He was known widely as Ky.

Hezekiah had a voice that could charm the birds out of the bushes. Not only was his singing voice an experience to hear but his speaking voice was impressively eloquent and persuasive. Abram Brantley, the first Baptist preacher to appear in the Warren County community after the Revolution, assured Hezekiah that he had all the attributes for a great career in the ministry, provided, of course, he would curb his sinful tendencies and forsake his erring companions.

It was old Stephen Camp who, vividly and with great humor, told Gideon about the Sunday when Ky was converted. Gideon heard the story from Camp in 1843, when he found the old man living in the hill country in Alabama. Hezekiah, that great bulk of a man, confessed an imposing list of a variety of sins before an interested and awed audience in the Baptist Church and came out of the baptismal waters shouting the praises of God and urging his townsmen to renounce their sins and join him. Roberts, the first to feel the call, became Hezekiah's convert. There were many other converts, especially among the young ladies, who all seemed to want nothing more from life than to go to heaven with such a saintly and handsome man. He selected the most devout and beautiful of his converts, Sally Strange, to share his new life of humility.

The town folk predicted that Hezekiah would rank with the great ministers of the world until in a playful mood on a Sunday outing he applied the baptismal ceremony to an innocent and affectionate cat. This boyish prank was viewed with horror by his elders. The congregation was disturbed also by rumors of trouble between the young minister and his child bride. He and the saintly Sally had admitted that their marriage, while made in heaven, was an earthly failure, and Sally returned red-eyed and silent to her parents' home.

Presumably, Hezekiah and Sally Strange were divorced, but Gideon never records the fact. In all his accounts of Hezekiah, Gideon mentions only a separation, after which Sally becomes a lost figure in his chronicle.

More and more, Hezekiah was seen in the company of the back-sliding Thomas Roberts, whose conversion had failed to win the wholehearted acceptance of the church-going community. When all this damaging evidence came out at a church trial the good brethren voted Hezekiah out of the church.

Old man Camp recalled with an affectionate chuckle that Ky and his shadow, Roberts, walked out of the church together and retired to a near-by tavern, where they resumed their boisterous ways with far more enthusiasm than they had shown during their brief theological interlude. Gideon observed: "You may always notice that wherever you find a church in your life's journey, that it is not far from it to a liquor shop." Ky never went back to church, and his son Gideon to the day of his death had little regard for organized religion.

Hezekiah entered school after he left the church. It was his introduction to education, but his student life was of shorter duration than his ministry. His formal education ceased in 1791, when he married a fourteen-year-old schoolmate, Sally Hickman. Her father, William Hickman, an Englishman and a neutral during the Revolution, had been killed by plunderers at his home in Anson County, North Carolina. Her mother, Marie Hornbeck, whose Dutch ancestors had come to the new country in 1702, alone and with great difficulty and hardship, had taken her children to Georgia, where they were befriended by a relative, John Huckaby.

Hezekiah's guardian angel, Roberts, who in the meantime had married Elizabeth Kelly, was at the wedding reception and joined in numerous toasts to the happy event. Observing that the guests included the pillars of the Baptist Church and the minister and brethren who had voted them out of membership, Roberts assured Hezekiah that the occasion offered a glorious opportunity for retaliation. Hezekiah agreed and the two excommunicants charged into the guests knocking them down like ninepins. They moved on toward Parson Brantley, who had joined the couple in holy matrimony, but, unwilling to be a martyr, he retired hastily from the arena. Hezekiah demanded in a loud voice if there were any other damned rascals who wished to be fed from the same spoon but found only Roberts and his bride remaining.

Eventually Roberts drifted from Hezekiah's life, but Sally remained steadfast, uncomplainingly sharing his tempestuous life. Hezekiah was constantly on the move, seeking new frontiers.

As the years passed the rolling wagon became crowded with new babies whose care was assigned to Gideon's beloved grandmother, Miriam Bowie Lincecum, and to an ever-changing list of black mammies.

Shortly after Gideon was born Hezekiah moved to the Oconee River, near Scull Shoals in Georgia, but remained there only two years, because the Indians proved so troublesome. He then moved to Hancock County, Georgia, bought a place from Byrd Brazil, and lived there three years. Hezekiah raised the first cotton crop in that section of the state and sold it, hand-rolled and seed-picked-by-hand, for fifty cents a pound. While living in Hancock County, Hezekiah heard a report that a Yankee schoolmaster in Lincoln County named Whitney had invented an iron gin with thirty circular saws driven by horsepower and could clean a thousand pounds of seed cotton in a day. He and young Gideon saddled up and rode over to Lincoln County to see this remarkable invention.

Almost seventy years later Gideon recalled he had met the inventor and inspected the gin. He made no comment on Eli Whitney but described the machine: "It had thirty saws, crooked-breasting, and was every way like the best form of gins at the present day. The invention was perfect at the start and has not been improved, except perhaps a few alterations in the pulleys and running gear and it has been made larger."

Hezekiah's three brothers-in-law, Tyre Kelly and James and John Hickman, urged him to join them in Tennessee. "Three years of successful farming had tired him out and he sold everything that he could not carry with him, bought a good road wagon and four fine horses and set out for Tennessee."

When Hezekiah's mother became ill after the first day of travel

Hezekiah rented a house near his camp from a man named Morris. Hezekiah farmed here a year, sold his cotton for five dollars a hundred pound in the seed, and again headed for Tennessee. His wagon held a big chest, four beds, four children, his wife, his eighty–eight–year–old mother, and black Mammy Pat and her four children. Young Gideon, armed with a splendid bow and arrow, usually walked beside the wagon with his mother and Mammy Pat.

I shall never forget the exceeding gladness that filled my boy breast the morning we set out on our journey. I ran far ahead, shooting my arrows at every bird I could see. We rolled on four days and came to Vienna, a little dilapidated village on the banks of the Savannah River, just below the mouth of Broad River. There was another company ahead of us and we could not get our wagon into the flat till near sundown. Just as the wagon was turning to go down into the ferry boat, a quite handsome young lady came up and without asking any questions, threw a small bundle into the wagon and crossed over with us.

After getting over into South Carolina we only had time to get out into the timber before night. Here we camped. While collecting wood to make a fire, the young lady came up with a heavier log on her shoulder than a man could carry. My father said: "Cousin Asa (the oldest son of Aunt Sally Kelly . . . who had joined us a few days previous), relieve the lady of her tote," and he took it and threw it on the fire. The young lady observed to Cousin Asa, "Young man, I don't know your name but I can throw *you down*." Asa replied, "Neither do I know your name, but I can tell you that is a big banter, for I have not seen the *man* yet that can throw *me* down; and further, I will say as you are young and pretty and of an agreeable, jolly temper, I will agree to marry you if you throw me two best in three falls. On these conditions I accept your challenge." In reply to this the young lady remarked, "Young man . . . the proposition you have made . . . pleases me, and I have neither house nor home, kith nor kin, nor lover, nor aught of impediment or obstruction to prevent me from doing what suits me best; and that I am sound and in good health I will prove to you when we test the question." And turning to my father, said to him: "Sir, if you will see me fair play, I accept the conditions offered." My father assured her most earnestly that she should be fairly dealt with.

She threw Asa the first two falls and he declared she was as strong as a horse.

"I am clearly beaten, but I'll stick to it though I don't even know her name" and he went to where she was seated and making a low bow said:

"Madam, will you honor me so far as to communicate the name of her to whom I am indebted for the two severe upsettings I received just now?" She very distinctly and in a sweet musical voice replied, "Malinda Nevels. Now, Sir, will you return the compliment?" "With pleasure, Miss. My name is Asa Lincecum," and they approached each other and shook hands.

We remained at that camp three days and Malinda was so industrious and handy in helping about the camp that Mother fell in love with her. Father had been gone two days with an old drunken Irishman who came to our camp the next day after we got there. Mother was uneasy and said she didn't understand it, that it was mighty bad to lose three days pretty weather in such a long journey. But Father came back on the evening of the third day and astonished us all by informing us that he had rented an excellent house and farm on Calhoun Creek, Abbeville District, South Carolina. So we geared up and went there the very next day and sure enough found the house a good one and the land fine.

There were two good sets of houses on the farm. Asa agreed to crop it with my father, as there was plenty of open land on the farm. To make everything go more smoothly, Asa informed Malinda that he was ready to settle up what he had lost with her in the wrestle at camp. She was ready to receive it, and they sent for Parson Porter who witnessed the payment and fixed the papers legally and they were man and wife.

They had nothing but their health and strength to start the world with, not even a blanket, but they had courage and went bravely to work, cleaning up and fixing up the other set of houses. Mother lent them a bed stick and some blankets. . . . Asa made a fine crop of cotton and corn and Malinda spun and made cloth sufficient for clothing.

Hezekiah sold his cotton and went to visit his sister, Dolly Durbin, in Clark County, Georgia. When he returned he announced he had bought land one mile from Athens and twelve miles from his sister's house. Asa and Malinda remained in South Carolina.

Near Athens, Hezekiah raised a heavy crop of cotton and "as soon as it began to open every one that could pick out five pounds a day was forced into the field."

I could pick twenty pounds and father bragged of it to the neighbors. It made me think a great deal more of myself and exerted myself to get thirty pounds a day. It was not many days until I succeeded, when father got a blacksmith to make me a nice spike for my arrow, a thing I had long needed to shoot the pike that were found in great numbers in the little creeks and branches of that country. . . . no pen can portray the unspeakable delight I experienced on returning home with a string of fish a yard long. It took me until bed time to tell all about how I slipped up to the sleeping fish and darted my spike into them and how they fluttered but could not get off. Early Monday morning I pitched into the cotton field again and keeping myself half bent all day picked more cotton than I could carry home. Father said there was forty pounds of it and that I was a brave fellow and he intended to get me a new hat. . . . We all did our best to get the cotton out by Christmas. We succeeded and Father took it to the gin and got receipts for 4643 pounds, for which he received five cents per pound. He now again became restless and, selling out his place, put his wagon in good repair and set out on a third attempt to get to Tennessee. . . . Father did not like to drive a team of horses and he had hired a straggling old fellow to drive for this trip, and we rolled on bravely until we came to the Savannah River. There was a store and smith shop there and we stopped until the smith nailed a pair of shoes on the out-riding horse—and until Father and the teamster got themselves smartly intoxicated, and two bottles of whiskey to carry with them. The river was wide and swift, but shallow.

We forded it and in the course of a couple of hours were all safely landed on the border of South Carolina again. It was an excellent hard gravelly road and we had progressed about five miles when Father, being most deeply intoxicated, took a notion that he must go back and whip somebody that had insulted him there.

In his absence, the drunken teamster fell asleep and tumbled off the seat onto the wagon tongue, which frightened the horses so much that they ran off, leaving the driver asleep and unharmed on the ground. The running horses upset the wagon, scattering the children, Grandmother Lincecum, and the cargo about the woods.

Being the oldest Lincecum male present, Gideon took charge of the situation:

"Oh, my poor Grandmother," I cried, for I loved her more than all the rest of the world. I prayed that she might recover and put my hand on the bloody gash which was at least three inches in length and so deep that I could see the blue trunk of the great neck vein. I tried to close it up and stop the bleeding and was sitting holding the lips of the wound together when Father and Mother came up. . . . When my poor inebriated father . . . surveyed the disastrous scene—his wrecked wagon, wounded children and bleeding mother—he was so deeply smitten that he fell down on the ground and wept like a child.

This is Gideon's only recorded prayer and his first attempt at emergency treatment. His efforts possibly saved Grandmother Lincecum's life.

Three weeks later she and the injured children were able to continue the journey and on the first day they made twenty miles before camping. Hezekiah went in search of fodder, returned at length somewhat drunk, and informed his mother that due to her extreme age and in remorse and sympathy for her pain and discomfort while traveling, he had bought a place up the hill. This was near Pendleton, South Carolina. There he farmed and operated a tavern where he sold peach brandy.

Near the house were fifty trees said to be forty-four years old. They were certainly the largest peach trees I ever saw. They were full of fruit and he carried it oft to a still and had it made into brandy, which he sold to travelers. All his corn and fodder brought ready money at a good price. It was an easy place to make money in and Father seemed to be settling down to business. All the family were satisfied and willing to remain. But unfortunately about this time came Uncle Tyre Kelley, trapsing back from Tennessee bringing with him his seven motherless children. Aunt Sally had a carbuncle on the back of her neck that killed her, which was the cause of Uncle Tyre's returning to Georgia. He remained with us until the brandy was out and in the meantime had discouraged Father from going to Tennessee. Father became restless after Uncle left and sold out at the first opportunity. Soon we were on the road again. My brother Garland had grown large enough to run ahead of the wagons with me.

Hezekiah took his family back to Georgia, below Athens on the Oconee River. The land beyond the Oconee had been purchased by the U.S. government from the Indians but would not be open, according to the treaty, until the Indians had a twelve months' hunt. For five months, or until the Indians finished their hunt, the Lincecums lived in a settlement with others waiting for the new land to open. Gideon was fourteen, and here he attended school for the first and only time in his life. During Gideon's first days at school he "sat in a sea of burning shame" but very soon could repeat Webster's spelling book by "heart-brain." At the end of the five months he could read and write and do arithmetic to the double root of three. The schoolmaster,

Yound Gill, gave his class many poems to memorize and at the age of
sixty Gideon still remembered:

> Ah, few and full of sorrows are the days
> Of miserable man, his life decays—
> He like an empty shadow glides away,
> And all his life is but one winter day.

The land west of the Oconee River was surveyed into lots of $202\frac{1}{2}$
acres each and drawn in a general lottery. When the Indians departed,
Gideon and Hezekiah traveled west into the new land to select a location. Hezekiah chose a place on Little River. They then returned to
the Oconee to bring the remainder of the Lincecums to their new
home. When at last they arrived at the site on the Little River which
Hezekiah had marked as his own, Hezekiah found he was ineligible to
participate in the lottery because of his "moving and shackling about so
much." He was sorely disappointed to find a man named Thomas Mc-
Lellan in possession of the land he had selected. The good cabin which
McLellan had built there made Hezekiah even more determined to
have the location. After considerable bargaining, McLellan agreed to
take "all the money he had together with Mammy Pat and her two
children." The Lincecums' new home was on a timbered bank of a
beautiful clear creek, one mile from the present Eatonton, Georgia.

Great numbers of people flocked into the new country and the next year
after we came the county seat was laid off and named Eatonton. I was one of
the chain carriers, to survey the streets and lots. Though but 14 years old,
Simon Holt, the surveyor, said I was more exact in setting the sticks than
anyone he had tried. We had cleared and planted ten acres of ground before,
and this year we cleared fifteen more. Brother Garland and I grubbed it and
Father cut and split rails to fence it.

Here Hezekiah settled his family of seven sons—Gideon, Garland,
Grant, Gabriel, Green, Rezin Bowie, and Thornton—and his three
daughters—Mary, Polly, and Emily. And here in 1813 they buried
Grandmother Lincecum, the brave Miriam Bowie.

Hezekiah's notorious temper and Gideon's inherent resentment of
any doubt of his truthfulness caused their separation.

He was always very ill-natured when he had to work, and wanted every
body to be busy. I was very playful and could throw somersaults and

tumble like a show man, and in this exercise had hurt one of my hips. Next morning I was barely able to walk. Father was in a great bluster that morning and seeing me sitting on a stump on the way, for I had started with the rest of them to work, he asked me what ailed me. I told him that I had such a pain in my hip that I could hardly walk. He remarked that it was nothing but laziness and added several uncomely words that set awkwardly on the stomach of my pride, and in meaning of which I differed widely with him. I remained sitting on the stump till they all had gone to the field. Then I arose and went limping off up the road towards Eatonton. I intended to try to get some kind of work. I had on a coarse homemade shirt and pantaloons and an old wool hat. This completed the inventory of my worldly stores.

From that moment, Gideon was on his own. But his days of frontiering with Hezekiah were not over. Following his service in the War of 1812 and his marriage to Sally Bryan, Gideon returned to Hezekiah's farm.

I had two years previously bought and sent home a likely young negro man whose name was Dick, and this is all the record of the poor fellow's name in existence. He worked with me till September when he hurt himself lifting at a wagon wheel and died soon after. He was a good negro and was my friend. I hated to lose him. The next year I joined forces and farmed with Judge [Major Christopher B.] Strong. We made a good crop and that year cotton was worth thirty-one and a fourth cents per pound, but I had become restless and did not stay to help gather the crop, but sold everything to Judge Strong.

After the land west of the Tombigbee River was opened Gideon and Hezekiah sold out and were soon on the road to another new country.

We had proceeded about fifty miles when we came to the Ocmulgee River, which was the dividing line between the Georgians and the Creek Indians. A man by the name of Ferguson came to our camp and getting a little tight with Father, in a kind of frolic, sold him his lands and cattle. Satisfied that Father would not remain longer than a year, I concluded to do what I never did in my life, idle away the time until he was ready to move again.

Gideon did not idle long, but agreed to take over the school when the teacher, a Mr. White, left after the students gave him a ducking in the river.

These children had been borned and raised where I found them, among the cows and drunken cow-drivers and they were positively the coarsest specimens of humanity I had even seen. . . . At play time their conduct was indescribable and intolerable, the married and grown men being the ring leaders in the devilment. At the expiration of an hour I called them to books and one of the men . . . said . . . "You give short play time, Mistofer." . . . Before quiet was restored one of the men impatiently asked, "What's up now, Hoss?"

Gideon explained to his pupils that he planned to conduct school along the lines of a courtroom and when he finished his explanation asked if they were ready to vote on it.

"Yes, go it, Hoss. It's a good thing," exclaimed one of the married men. . . . One, [Elijah] Scatterwhite, as he handed over the pen to his successor exultingly exclaimed, "I tell you what, folks, this is going to be a big thing. We never had this sort of doings in these diggings afore. What next, old Hoss?" . . . The first case on the monitor's list was Stephen Heard, a grown man, charged with the offense of throwing a little girl's bonnet into the branch. . . . Stephen Heard was the first and last that received corporal punishment and he was also the first to advocate its abolition. He afterwards became one of the most solid lawyers in my school. Green Wheeler and George Clayton were the other two. All three became distinguished lawyers of the state.

As Gideon predicted, Hezekiah was ready to move on at the end of the year. While on the Ocmulgee River, Gideon's sister Mary married Joseph Bryan, the brother of Gideon's wife, and they joined the westward-bound party, which already included Hezekiah and his wife, their eight unmarried children, and their six Negroes, and Gideon and his wife, their two small sons, and their two Negroes. The large caravan started out on the morning of March 10, 1818. Their journey was through a wilderness rich in deer and turkey, with streams brimming with fish. "I felt as if I was on a big camp hunt," Gideon recalled many years later.

They stopped at Tuscaloosa, Alabama, a small log-cabin village which was daily swelling with arrivals from Tennessee. Here Gideon practiced medicine in Dr. Isbell's shop; joined John Weeks, whom he had known in Georgia, in a whipsaw partnership and cut planks for Peter Remington; operated a billiard table, and did other odd jobs while waiting for Hezekiah to continue his westward travel.

Hezekiah went alone on a long exploring trip, and when he returned to Tuscaloosa announced that at last he had found their final home. It was on the Tombigbee River, northwest of Tuscaloosa in the new state of Mississippi—"the wildest, least-trodden and tomahawk-marked country he [Hezekiah] had ever explored."

Gideon was delighted to leave Tuscaloosa, which was "full of people just landed—mostly from Tennessee—all felling timber and hastily building up a town of poles and clapboards and such people! I had never seen any of that type of the genus before. They were large men generally, full-fleshed and having the appearance of having been well-greased with hog's fat."

The three Lincecum families, with all their worldly goods, left Tuscaloosa on November 1, 1818. Gideon and Garland went ahead and hacked a road through the forest for the passage of the wagons. To Gideon the entire trip was "delightful beyond description." The weather was perfect. The deer, bear, small animals, turkeys, and geese were fat and plentiful. Berries and nuts were everywhere and the many clear streams were full of immense catfish.

Their travel ended on the banks of the Tombigbee River, three miles above the present location of Columbus, Mississippi. The country was as wild and beautiful as Hezekiah had said.

Still in the prime of life—he was only forty-eight years old—Hezekiah at last had found a frontier to calm his chronic restlessness. He had finally brought his large family into a wilderness where they were to assist in its rapid transition into a city which they would grow to dislike.[2]

---

[2] Grant and Gabriel Lincecum were among those who in 1831 gave depositions in the Choctaw Land frauds. Grant apparently was connected with Colonel William Ward, U.S. agent appointed to register Choctaws who did not wish to move to Indian Territory. Grant testified that Ward was drunk much of the time and failed to register numerous names. When Ward prepared to leave the agency Gabriel purchased some of his books and papers at a sale of his property. Among them was a book in which Ward entered names of orphans and neglected to transfer them to the main book (American State Papers, Public Lands, Vol. VII, pp. 630–631, 690–696, cited by Franklin L. Riley, "Choctaw Land Claims," *Publications of the Mississippi Historical*

Gideon's lifetime of reminiscing is strangely lacking in any reference to Hezekiah after their arrival on the Tombigbee. Presumably Hezekiah made his home there until his death in 1840.

But throughout the long years of Gideon's life Hezekiah was never far from his thoughts. Twenty years after Hezekiah's death Gideon lay in an exhausted sleep in his Long Point, Texas, bedroom. He had been in constant attendance at the bedside of his desperately ill wife and his troubled sleep was disturbed by the sound of Hezekiah's voice. Gideon returned to his worried sleep but again was awakened by Hezekiah's insistent voice and his command: "Gideon, go to Sally and mesmerize her and let her bleed." This time Gideon obeyed his father's voice. Sally responded to the treatment and Gideon considered the cure so miraculous that he wrote a report of it to the editor of the Galveston News.[3]

One of the many occasions during his life when Gideon recalled Hezekiah's words of wisdom occurred when he was seventy-eight years old and farming in Tuxpan, Mexico. Gideon longed for a cart or wagon to carry heavy loads, and considered himself fortunate when he found a man in the plaza with two wagon wheels for sale. Gideon built a cart around them and loaded it with wood. Immediately the wheels, made of pecan wood, twisted and as he watched each spoke break out of the hub, he remembered Hezekiah: "My father once told me impressively, never to buy an old mill, an old watch, an old rifle gun, nor an old wagon. I thought of my father and his precepts as I saw the cart fall."

Society, Vol. VIII (1904), pp. 345–395). Gabriel contributed to the growth of the area by building a bridge across the Noxubee River in the southern part of Oktibbeha County, Mississippi. In 1832 he bought out, for $500, the interest of Daniel Nail, a half-breed Choctaw, in a crossing of the Robinson or, as it was better known, the U.S. Government Road, built in 1826 from Columbus to Jackson. Gabriel's toll bridge was the first in the Choctaw Nation. Two years later he sold the bridge to McKinney Holderness for $1,000, later with Dr. John Watkins bought it back for $5,000, and eventually resold it for $20,000. Lincecum's Old Mill, long a landmark on the Noxubee River, was at the crossing of the Treaty Road (Wiilliam A. Love, "Historic Localities on the Noxubee River," PMHS, Vol. IX (1906), pp. 315–321). Gabriel died in 1836. Grant moved to Louisiana before 1848, later moved to Dallas County, Texas, where he died. Garland Lincecum was living in Caldwell County, Texas, in 1850 (Census, 1850). Rezin Bowie Lincecum lived in Somerville, Tennessee, in November, 1830 (Letter to him from George Shaeffer, Columbus, Mississippi, November 15, 1830; Lincecum Papers).

[3] The letter is in the Lincecum Papers but if printed can not be located in the *News.*

A NOTE ON SOURCES

The narrative of Hezekiah's life and travels is chiefly taken from "Autobiography"; Gideon Lincecum, Tuxpan, Mexico, to Sallie Lincecum Doran, Hempstead, Texas, March 14, 1871; Lincecum to Editor, Galveston *News,* n.d. (Lincecum Papers); and "Reminiscences."

CHAPTER THREE

GIDEON
AND THE INDIANS

Now if there could be born an honest, liberty-loving leader who would take things in hand, concentrate the Indian forces, capture all the praying white races and their allies, the mixed-blood cut throats, and chop off their damn heads, there would remain the most innocent, law-abiding people on earth—the pure Indian. GID

ROM GEORGIA to Mississippi and from Texas to Mexico, Gideon had a long and intimate contact with Indians. His first playmates were Muskogee Indian boys, from whom he learned native lore and methods of hunting and fishing. Gideon became an expert in the use of the bow and arrow and the more lethal blow-gun.

By the time I was five years of age, the use of these destructive implements had become a perfect passion with me. I vied with the best marksmen of my age among the Indian boys; could knock the picayune out of the split stick at ten paces distant as often as any of them. . . . During my eleventh and twelfth year I had five nice, good-natured fellows. . . . The prevalence of the basic rule of pure democracy secured the peace and filled our sporting hours with undisturbed delights. All strove manfully to excel; but superior skill or extraordinary success was never alluded to by the performer. This, however, is common with all Indians, previous to their being contaminated with the *is oon lush fillok chee*—the forked-tongue civilities of progressed society. . . . These boys could, and so could I, imitate the call notes of all the birds. . . . The most deadly and murderous deception practiced by us, and which was attended with the greatest success, was to take a blow-gun and plenty of arrows. . . . A good blow gun and strong healthy lungs can propel one of these arrows seventy-five yards. . . . it is certain and fatal as a rifle. I knew an Indian woman who killed her husband with a blowgun. Nobody blamed her, for he called her ugly. In Indian etiquette that is the most unpardonable offensive word that can be used. . . . My father retired before the unholy, intrusive tramp of civilization, and my Indian companions were frequently changed; but the new ones I came in contact with on the borders always seemed proud of me on account of my being able to talk with them, and my sports would be continued in my new life.

Later, Lincecum lived and traded with the Choctaw, Chickasaw, and Cherokee Indians on the Tombigbee River, in Mississippi. When he first arrived in that area Lincecum found the famous John Pitchlynn, his mother's second cousin, living in the Choctaw village. Pitchlynn, then in his sixties, had lived with the Choctaws since he was four years old. After George Washington commissioned him an interpreter among the Choctaws, Pitchlynn, on one of his trips to the capital, visited a month in Georgia with Gideon's parents.

One of Pitchlynn's half-breed offspring was destined to be among the Indian greats. He was Peter Perkins Pitchlynn, who became a chief after the removal of the Choctaws to Indian Territory.[1] Pitchlynn had another son, John, Jr., who had a trading post on the Indian side of the Tombigbee River. Opposite it Gideon erected what he said was the first structure on the present site of Columbus, Mississippi, and competed with John, Jr., as a trader.

Columbus soon grew into a sizable community. Gideon grew with it into numerous activities. He became chief justice and chairman of a school commission; he organized a county court and appointed officers; he surveyed and leased town lots; he organized a Masonic lodge and became its first worshipful master. But Gideon did not enjoy his role as a founding father; responsibilities and organizations restricted his freedom.[2]

---

[1] Frederick Webb Hodge (*Handbook of the American Indian*, BAE Bulletin No. 30, Washington, D.C., 1907–1910, Vol. II, p. 264) spells the name "Pitchlynn." Lincecum used only one *n*. George Catlin's portrait of Peter Perkins Pitchlynn (*Hatchoo-tuck-nee, Snapping Turtle: A Well-educated Half-breed*, 1836) is in the Smithsonian Institution.

[2] Gideon claimed that a mark he made with his knife on a tree on the present site

We were supposed to be in Alabama, but when the line dividing the states of Alabama and Mississippi was laid out, we found ourselves ten miles on the Mississippi side in a slip of country eighty miles long and averaging twenty miles wide. The Tombigbee River was the line betwixt us and the Indians. The legislature at length recognized us as a part of the state of Mississippi and named this long strip of land Monroe County. . . . About this time the people began to talk of sending me to the legislature and to avoid such a dilemma I went over the river and entered into partnership with John Pitchlyn Jr. . . . He was an educated man and a very clever fellow, but a most incorrigible drunkard. But that would make no difference, as according to the contract and to evade the intercourse regulations which forbid any white man with a family dwelling within the Nation he, Pitchlyn, was to have nothing in the management of the business. In the knowledge of all outsiders, I occupied the position of a superintending clerk. Pitchlyn had a good store house at the ferry landing opposite Columbus and four or five thousand dollars worth of goods. I had about the same amount and we put them together. . . . Pitchlyn's residence was two miles from the store, a circumstance favorable to our business for he was, when drunk, so abusive and so often drunk, that he was not popular with the Indians. I was known to most of the Choctaws. My Indian name was *Shappo-to-hoba*—White Hat. The first time they saw me, I had on a white hat. . . . I finished the large house Pitchlyn had commenced and on 8th of January 1822 gave a subscription ball, $5.00 a head for men, which from the novelty of such a thing in the Choctaw Nation was attended by a number of people. The ball money paid for the house. Great as was the situation for making money, we were so unhealthy that we were forced to leave it. Pitchlyn, without my knowledge, had gone up to Cotton Gin Port, rented a house and ordering his goods on the reputation of our Choctaw establishment had set up $5,000 stock of goods and engaged a drunken fellow by the name of [Andrew] Morrison to superintend the selling of them to the Chickasaw Indians. Pitchlyn spent most of his time there, where he could drink free of my interference. . . . After a while Pitchlyn came and told me that Morrison had made way with the greater part of the goods, and that he wanted me to go up and take possession and save what I could, and I finally consented. I rented houses for my family, but as we continued unhealthy, I went out into the hills and se-

---

of Columbus on the day of his arrival was the first evidence of the presence of a white man and that he built the first structure there. However, *Mississippi: A Guide to the Magnolia State* (Federal Writers Project, 1938, pp. 182–183) gives credit to a man named Thomas and to Spirus Roach. Lincecum is credited with founding, in 1821, Franklin Academy, the first free school in the state, an honor he never mentions in his letters or biographical notes.

lected a quarter section of public land, entered it and built houses and moved my family, as soon as possible. Here among the clean, uncropped grass, in high dry land we all recovered our health.

Lincecum spent many days in the Indian villages, recording the tribes' culture, traditions, and herbal medicines. He made friends with a number of Indians who became important figures not only in their own tribes but in the history of the United States. Later Lincecum wrote biographical sketches of some of them.

Among them were Mushalatubbee, a noted Choctaw chief and warrior who refused to join Tecumseh and his Shawnees in support of the British in the War of 1812, and Pushmataha, a distinguished Choctaw chief and orator who is buried in the Congressional Cemetery in Washington.

Gideon wrote of Mushalatubbee:

He was a handsome man, about six feet in height and quite corpulent. He possessed a lively, cheerful disposition, and as all fat men, was good-natured and would get drunk. He was not much of an orator, and to remedy that deficiency he had selected an orator to speak for him. His name was Aiaokatubi, and, except for Apushimataha [*sic*], he could deliver himself more gracefully and with more ease than any man I ever heard address an audience.

Mushulatubi[3] [*sic*] was a frequent visitor at my house, while I resided in the nation, for it was in his district I had my house, and but eighteen miles from his residence. He was good company, full of agreeable anecdotes and witty, inoffensive repartee, until he became too much intoxicated. Then he was nothing but a drunken Indian. . . . Mushulatubi resided on the military road, which, previous to the advent of steamboats on the Mississippi River, was the great thoroughfare upon which returned the hosts of flatboat men from Ohio, Kentucky, Tennessee and Indiana. . . . I have often heard those weary footmen while passing my house—I also resided on the military road —speaking of the friendly demeanor and the kind hospitality they had received at the house of Mushulatubi.[4]

---

[3] Accepted spelling is *Mushalatubbee*. George Catlin's portrait of him is in the Smithsonian Institution.

[4] An interesting sidelight on Lincecum's friendship with the chief is given by William Love ("Mingo Moshulatubbee's Prairie Village," *PMHS*, Vol. VII [1903], pp. 373–378, citing Major J. W. A. Wright of Alabama, "Southern Reminiscences," New Orleans *Times-Democrat*, n.d.): "The writer of this sketch remembers when a boy in Columbus, Miss., to have often seen the chief, who was generally called

Pushmataha was a frequent guest in the Lincecum house. Gideon wrote of him: "I always looked upon him as possessing the strongest and best balanced intellect of any man I had ever heard speak. . . . At their national councils quite a number of white men would attend, and I have seen them . . . chained to their seats for hours at a time, although they understood not a word of his language."

Gideon's curiosity about the origin of the numerous man-made mounds in the area led him to an ancient and wise old Indian, Chahta-Immataha, who was crippled and crusty but still bright of eye and mind. With him Gideon spent many hours over a period of years writing in Choctaw all that the wise man told him of the legends and traditions of the Chahtas, the ancient name of the Choctaws.

Lincecum learned Indian herbal medicine from a medicine man of great reputation who lived in Six Towns in the Choctaw Nation. Pierre Juzon, a half-breed, arranged for the two to meet "on the black rock bluff on the Noxubee River," seventy miles from Gideon's house. For six weeks the two were alone in the woods studying plants and their medicinal uses. Gideon wrote his notes in Choctaw. When the Indian doctor ended his instructions he looked at Lincecum's notes and said: "How strange that this small bundle holds all the knowledge I ever possessed."[5]

Gideon's prosperity as an Indian trader ended when a three-year illness, brought on after a strenuous bear hunt on a hot day, left him broken in health. Other misfortunes followed: his partner, John Pitch-

---

'Tubbee.' He invariably got drunk when he came to town. I once saw the noted old botanical doctor, Gid Lincecum, a great friend to the Indians, who claimed to have learned much of his art from them and who afterwards moved to Texas, give Tubbee to make him stop drinking, a small tin cup of a fearfully hot mixture of brandy and red pepper, known as 'No. 6.' The stoical old chief sat in the market house nearby drinking the fiery mixture, little by little, and though it burnt his mouth and made him slobber terribly, with his tongue lolling out, the old fellow, in common parlance, 'got away' with it and called for more."

[5] Lincecum's notes on Choctaw herbal medicine are apparently lost, but his herbarium of 305 pressed and annotated plants is in the Lincecum Papers. Accompanying data on some of the plants give their medicinal use by Indians. The plants have been studied and identified by Dr. Benjamin C. Tharp, Department of Botany, University of Texas (Dr. T. N. Campbell, "Medicinal Plants Used by Choctaw, Chickasaw, and Creek Indians in the Early Nineteenth Century," *Journal of the Washington Academy of Sciences,* Vol. 41, No. 9 [September, 1951], pp. 285–290).

lynn, Jr., was murdered; their store was robbed, and Lincecum found himself heavily in debt.[6]

I at length matured a plan that I thought would make money if I could succeed in getting it into action. The project was to raise a company of Choctaw ball players, travel with them and exhibit them in ball plays and war dances. I wrote my good friend, John Pitchlyn Sr., on the subject. Soon I received a reply by the hand of Fulahooma that forty choice ball players would assemble at the Oakshush [Okshash] spring on the next Monday, 29th November, 1829, and for me to come. We were on the ground in due time, and by 12 o'clock there were upwards of 400 ball players assembled. We built up a council fire and held a big talk. They were all hungry and I got my friend Pitchlyn to have three fat beeves driven to the place and slaughtered for them to eat. They thought 400 not too many to go, poor fellows. I did not know what to do so as not to give offense. Finally I proposed a draft. I would take every tenth man. Fulahooma had privately engaged forty brag players and given me their names. These names were put into a hat, a little boy called up and instructed how to draw. Then Pitchlyn explained that the draft would take only every tenth man, and to make it fair, the little boy had been selected to draw the names. There were 360 blank tickets put in the hat. . . . The Indians could not see into the deception, but calling it a lottery, directed by the Great Spirit, thought it exceedingly fair, and at the conclusion expressed satisfaction and went to cooking and eating the fat beeves. We were off by light the next morning, passing through Columbus and up the Military Road. I travelled with those Indians eight months, but made only money enough to feed and clothe them decently. I started without money and was so weak that the Indians would lift me on my horse. I camped out all the trip and my health improved. One of the Indians got crippled and I let him ride my horse and I walked. While I made no money the improvement in health was ample remuneration for the hardships I underwent. I brought all the Indians back, gave them five pounds of bacon apiece and disbanded them. They dubbed me *Hopiyeh Cheto*, Big

---

[6] John, Jr., known as Jack, served as first lieutenant under Pushmataha in the U.S. Army, March 1–May 29, 1814. He was married to a Colbert, member of a prominent Chickasaw family. He had the reputation of being an agreeable, quiet gentleman while sober, but when under the influence of whiskey, an exceedingly dangerous citizen. John killed his half-brother, Silas, and faced the Indian law of retaliation. Constantly trailed by other Indians, he was guarded by Garland Lincecum. One night when the two separated briefly, John was shot to death. His dying words were typical: "I am a man and a warrior" (Manuscript of J. P. Lincecum, of Lincecum, Louisiana, cited by Love, "Lowndes County," *PMHS,* Vol. VII [1903], pp. 365–366).

Leader, and we parted forever. I found my wife scuffling and fighting poverty; she had been spinning and weaving and had the children well clothed, and they still had corn and meat.

With deep sadness Gideon watched the first forced departure of his Indian friends and neighbors to new Indian Territory in Arkansas. On a bitter cold night in November, 1831, the Indians silently passed the Lincecum house, situated on what was to be known as the "Trail of Tears."

Thirty years later Lincecum wrote:

I remember now, though the time has long passed, with feelings of unfeigned gratitude the many kindnesses bestowed on me and my little family in 1818 and 1819 when we were in their neighborhood, before the country began to fill up with other white people. . . . It affords me pleasure, after the lapse of near half a century, to recall in memory the many happy days and hours I spent in the days of my young manhood in friendly intercourse with the innocent and unsophisticated people. We met often, hunted together, fished together, swam together, and they were positively and I have no hesitation in declaring it here, the most truthful, most reliable and best people I have ever dwelt with. While we resided in their country my wife had a very severe spell of fever that confined her to her bed for several weeks. During her sickness the good, kind-hearted Chahta women would come often, bringing with them their nicely prepared tampulo water for her to drink, and remaining by the sick bed for hours at a time would manifest the deep sympathy they felt by groaning for the afflicted one, all the time of their protracted visit. The time is long gone, and I may never have the pleasure of meeting with any of that most excellent race of people again. But so long as the life pendulum swings in this old time-shattered bosom, I shall remember their many kindnesses to me and mine, with sentiments of kindest affection and deepest gratitude, and my prayers for their elevation and progress as a people among the enlightened nations of the earth shall not cease.

A NOTE ON SOURCES

Lincecum's writings constitute a prime original source for an abundance of interesting anecdotes and lengthy accounts of events in the life of the mysterious Pushmataha. An article by Lincecum on Pushmataha's origin and oratory, published in the Houston *Tri-Weekly Telegraph* (November 24, 1865,

p. 7, Cols. 2–3), includes excerpts from one of the Indian's many remarkable speeches, the first to be printed, according to Lincecum.

After Lincecum's death, his daughter, Sally Doran, submitted a more detailed account of Pushmataha's life by Lincecum to the Mississippi Historical Society, which published it as "Life of Apushimataha" (*PMHS*, Vol. IX [1906], pp. 115–485). This account was cited by Hodge in his biography of the Indian, whose name Hodge spells "Pushmataha," the accepted version of a Choctaw word *Apushim-alhtaha*, meaning "the sapling is ready or finished for him" (*Handbook of the American Indian*, Vol. II, p. 329). Lincecum's spelling of the name is probably correct.

The Chahta Tradition is a long and involved Choctaw migration legend written by Gideon Lincecum from notes taken from 1822 to 1824 during interviews with a Choctaw sage, Chahta-Immataha. Lincecum's verbose account of the Choctaw traditions as related to him by this chief are in the Lincecum Papers, but the original notes written in Choctaw are apparently lost.

The aged Indian told Lincecum that for forty years his people had carried with them on their constant travels the bones of their ancestors. Finally a decision was made to deposit their burden in one place and to cover the bones with earth. Following Chahta-Immataha's direction, Lincecum found the mound, at Nanih Waiya, in the southern part of present Winston County, Mississippi, near the Neshoba County Line.

When Lincecum discovered that the mound was as the old man described it he was awed by the thought of what a rich field it offered to "a serious investigator." Nanih Waiya was made an historical site by the State of Mississippi in 1949 but has never been excavated. There are two theories concerning the site: one, that the Choctaws originated there; and two, that it was a stopping place in their migration. The aged Chahta told Lincecum that the first version was a false legend which began when some Choctaws, replying to a question about their origin, said "*Out* of Nanih Waiya." The proper reply was "Out *from* Nanih Waiya."

Throughout his life Lincecum was firm in the conviction that Chahta-Immataha was the only living Choctaw who knew the true tradition of their forefathers, and that he, Lincecum, was the only white man who had recorded the true version.

After obtaining the information Lincecum discussed it with elderly Choctaws and others learned in their tradition, including Pushmataha, and they all corroborated the facts of Chahta-Immataha's narrative, so far as they knew them.

The original notes, now lost, were in Choctaw. Lincecum put them aside and they were forgotten until December, 1859, when Lincecum received a letter from Willis H. Burnett of Aberdeen, Mississippi, who as a child had played with the Lincecum children. Lincecum was located through Burnett's sister, Martha (Mrs. Benjamin Knox), who lived in Brazoria County, Texas. Burnett remembered Lincecum's early interest in Indians and asked if Lincecum still had the Chahta Tradition. Their mutual friend, Davis H. Morgan, agreed to finance its publication.

The correspondence reminded Lincecum that he had never translated the notes and this he undertook to do. He finished the translation of 650 closely written pages in six months. Sallie Doran preserved during her lifetime the five quill pens used in writing the narrative.

Lincecum told Burnett that in his opinion the Tradition should be written in a manner dramatic enough "to seize upon and hold the public taste like a nightmare," but admitted that he was not capable of writing in such a style:

I could furnish the plain, unadorned facts as they were taught me by the last Indian who certainly knew the traditional history of his people. . . . To do justice to the . . . tradition of the noble race of red men and produce a book that would be acceptable to the reading community would require a writer with a fine taste and glowing descriptive power . . . clothed in the habiliments of truth . . . filled with interesting traditional history. . . . I am sure I am not capacitated to perform in a style that would either please the public or remunerate us for the labor. . . . If we could procure a writer of the proper type, I would be willing to make him an equal partner and deliver up my notes . . . but I never can consent to have my carefully and long-kept Chahta Tradition thrown off for the public criticism in a butchered up, uncomely style. . . . Don't be too easy pleased in the selection of the writer. If he is not endowed with the proper qualifications I shall know him as soon as I see his hands.

Burnett suggested as the possible writer Edward Goodwin, a professor of ancient languages and literature in Leighton, Alabama, and the author of *Lily White*. Goodwin was most eager to see the manuscript, as it "opens a field heretofore unexplored by the English and American antiquarian." He urged Lincecum to come to Alabama and work with him on the manuscript, assuring Gideon that "it will be for you and myself a monument more enduring than brass."

Publication plans were suspended with the Civil War. Later there were other proposals but nothing came of any of them.

Lincecum gave the manuscript to Sallie Doran. She once suggested that it be sent to Choctaws in Indian Territory, but Lincecum objected:

At this period, the Choctaws know no more about their traditional history than other people do. Some garbled scraps may yet linger with the old people but nothing reliable. Chahta-Immataha told me on my first visit to his house that even then they could tell nothing about it. He said they had all been drunk for forty years and had lost the truth. Any of the proud, aristocratic half-breed chiefs would look upon it as being too low in origin for his high blood and would take but little interest in it, if indeed he did not oppose and try to defeat it. But it makes but little odds what goes with it. In the hands of some people it would be valuable. Others again, would make a botch of it and it would turn out nothing.

Apparently Lincecum despaired of ever finding the "proper" writer and decided to "clothe [it] in my own language, which but poorly represents the original," as he said about his translation of Pushmataha's orations.

In 1889 Sallie Doran sent the Choctaw history to the Bureau of American Ethnology. There it was examined by James Constantine Pilling, who described it in his "Bibliography of the Muskhogean Language" (BAE *Bulletin*, No. 9, 1889, p. 53). A lengthy excerpt from the Chahta was published as "Choctaw Traditions about Their Settlement in Mississippi and the Origin of Their Mounds" (*PMHS*, Vol. VIII [1904], pp. 521–542).

Present-day ethnologists have made extensive use of Lincecum's voluminous Choctaw notes. John R. Swanton, who regarded the history as an authentic native document but was bemused by Lincecum's gradiloquent style, reprinted the *PMHS* article in his "Source Material for the Social and Ceremonial Life of the Choctaw Indians" (BAE *Bulletin*, No. 103 [1931], pp. 12–26). He pondered: "There can be no question that Lincecum knew the Choctaw thoroughly. . . . The core of the narrative is plainly a genuine Choctaw origin myth. The question is how much of the elaboration is native and how much due to Lincecum himself."

Dr. T. N. Campbell used Lincecum's notes in his "Choctaw Subsistence: Ethnographic Notes from the Lincecum Manuscript" (*The Florida Anthropologist*, Vol. XII, No. 1 [1959], pp. 9–24) and in his "The Choctaw Afterworld" (*Journal of American Folklore*, Vol. 72, No. 284 [1959], pp. 146–154). Dr. Campbell found the Chahta manuscript "surprisingly rich in reference to Choctaw foodstuffs and how these were acquired, preserved, stored, and cooked." Of the ten existing versions of the Choctaw origin and migration legend, Dr. Campbell judged Lincecum's the most detailed. His estimate was that "the ethnographic details in the Lincecum manuscript appear to be accurate in general, for it can be verified in most cases by comparison with the various descriptions of early Choctaw culture, most of which have been brought together by Swanton (1931, 1946). In many instances the Lincecum manuscript is much richer in ethnographic details than any other early source" ("Choctaw Subsistence").

The Lincecum version of the Choctaw afterworld, first used by Dr. Campbell, is not only the earliest on record but the most complete. It extensively supplements five other early nineteenth-century versions of Alfred Wright, George Catlin, H. B. Cushman, Israel Folsom, and David I. Bushnell, Jr. Dr. Campbell made a comparison of the versions and found that Lincecum's differed "mainly in its relative completeness and wealth of descriptive details" ("The Choctaw Afterworld").

Lincecum's "Autobiography," "Reminiscences," and botanical notes contain further choice bits of Indian lore. From a nonethnologist's viewpoint, the Lincecum Indian references are more interesting for gossipy and revealing items concerning such notable early American families as the Folsoms, Pitchlynns, and Colberts; and for other miscellaneous references, for example, to Itewamba Mingo's (Levi Colbert's) version of the Battle of Tollamatoxa (the Indian name for the site of Cotton Gin Port) between the Marquis de Vaudreuil and the Chickasaws in 1752, and which differs considerably from the accepted version; the trial of Mushalatubbee's brother, Atobi, for the murder of Luther Parker, Lincecum's hired hand; and the role of missionaries in the political life of the Indian. Gideon, of course, was on the side of the antimissionary Indians.

Supplementary material for this chapter was taken from the following Lincecum correspondence: to Prof. S. B. Buckley, Austin, Texas, May 12, 1861, September 25, 1866; to Willis H. Burnett, Aberdeen, Mississippi, August 10, December 21, 1859, July 22, October 28, 1860, March 25, 1862, July 30, 1867; to E. H. Cushing, Houston, Texas, April 7 and 15, 1865, November 7, 1867; to W. P. Doran, Houston, Texas, December 27, 1864, February 7, November 26, 1865; to Sallie Doran, Hempstead, Texas, May 22, 1871; to E. Durand, Philadelphia, Pennsylvania, May 27, 1861; to Professor Edward Goodwin, Leighton, Alabama, March 11, April 4, June 18, 1860; to R. B. Hannay, Hempstead, Texas, June 19, 1862; to Dr. A. G. Lane, Lockhart, Texas, October 7, 1863; to D. Boone Moore, Castroville, Texas, April 2, October 12, 1860, August 5, 1863; to Dr. William Byrd Powell, Cincinnati, Ohio, February 2, 1860; to Judge J. A. Rutherford, Honey Grove, Texas, January 20, 1862; and to H. M. Wright, New Orleans, December 12, 1860.

CHAPTER FOUR

GIDEON
AND THE TEXIANS

Old man Weaver said to me "Well, Gid, we have come to
the conclusion that we have seen enough of Texas. Have
you?" "No" said I, "I have seen nothing yet."

IN LATE 1834 the people of Columbus, Mississippi, beginning to
talk about Texas, organized an emigrating company of a hundred
persons. Lincecum was appointed physician to an exploring committee
to go to Texas and report back on conditions.

Gideon was prepared to leave on November 20 but not one of the
ten committee members appeared at the appointed place. Determined
then to go alone, he raised a traveling purse of $1,050. Five other men
volunteered to go along. They were Fred and Calvin Weaver, Benjamin
Nix, John Gwin, and G. Lincecum, possibly a brother. Fred Weaver is
identified only as a sixty-year-old Methodist minister and the others
only as "the four young men."

Let us return to 1832, when I had just finished and was clear of debt at
the final close of my ten years' mercantile career, but with nothing left. I
went to the practice of medicine, was quite successful, stuck close to it until
1835, when I was able to leave my family in good fix, and a thousand dollars in my pocket to defray the expenses of an exploring trip to Texas, which
was just beginning to be spoken of. There was a company of six of us, and
with two good pack horses we set out on the 9th of January, 1835. The

ground was covered with snow. Our first camp was twenty-five miles from home, in the wild woods of the Chickasaw country. . . .

Our pack horses carried meal, a little bacon, a six-gallon brass kettle, coffee pot, tin pans, and a pint tin cup a piece. We had a good double tent, which we never set up except when it rained. We camped out all the time, did our own cooking, and slept in the open air. . . . On our rifles we depended for our supplies of animal food and on the pack horses for bread, coffee, sugar, and soap.

We fared abundantly better than we could have done at the hotels, had there been any in the country through which we journeyed. We ate but two meals a day—breakfast and supper. Our supper consisted of fried venison or turkey, corn bread and coffee. Supper over, the six-gallon kettle was hung on [the fire] containing a proper quantity of the grits sifted from our corn meal —which we ground on a steel mill—salt, a little piece of bacon, and a venison ham or turkey, and plenty of red pepper, and as one or another of the company would be occasionally up during the night the fire would be mended and the kettle kept boiling all the time. Being boiled all to shreds the grits, as tender and much better than rice, with the holy glow of the cayenne regularly diffused through it, constituted one of the most digestible and healthy messes that could be made. We commenced on it at daybreak, and by sun-up breakfast was over and a good dog-bait left. We had a nice camp dog along.

Their route to Texas was through the Chickasaw Nation, the Natchez Trace through the Choctaw Nation to the Mississippi River, across the Ouachita, Little and Red Rivers. On February 3 the Sabine River was crossed and the expedition arrived "in the Spanish dominions."

After we got into Texas the game was very abundant, and I found but little difficulty in procuring plenty, especially after getting into the wide-spread prairie country. Hundreds of deer were to be seen in all directions, and wild geese everywhere—thousands . . . west of [San] Augustine [Texas] there were but few people seen. Once in forty miles you would perhaps find a family with a little corn patch and a log hut, with a cow or two. No Mexicans east of San Antonio, except at the mouth of the Brazos and La Bahía. No Indians, except a few straggling hunters west of the Brazos. There was green winter grass (*Stipa setigera* [?]) in abundance for our horses west of the Colorado, and, for our own consumption all manner of good game, fish and honey. . . . We slept as soundly and more sweetly by our camp fires in the balmy, dry climate—didn't rain on us in two months—than we would have done anywhere else in the world.

Once the Mississippians thought they saw six old bucks standing on the edge of the timber and the hunters crept down the creek beds, approached from behind. Instead of six old bucks they found six armed Indians. "They were standing erect with their heads turned toward the place where they had seen us last, and until we made a little noise in the dry leaves they had no idea of our new approach. They flashed their eyes around, and finding themselves nearly surrounded their flight was as abrupt as that of a gang of quail."

When the turkeys began to gobble, Gideon went out early one morning, hid in a large hollow stump, and "commenced yelping." Soon an old gobbler answered, but shied off. This puzzled Gideon:

I had the leaf of a wild peach (*Cerasus* [*Prunus*] *caroliniana*) and a most excellent leaf to yelp with, and I had been admiring how well I had been speaking turkey with it: had made no false or indifferent notes, and knew that on my part he had no grounds of suspicion. I began to suspect that there might be somebody else about and, as I have known several casualties of that sort to occur in turkey hunting, might yelp up an awkward hunter and get myself shot. So I sank down in the old hollow stump, ceased my yelping, whilst the old gobbler went roaring off through the swamp. After a reasonable time had elapsed, and I heard no noise, I peeped out through the slit in the stump where my gun lay. Soon I discovered the cause of the turkey's distaste to that vicinity. It was the first Texas leopard cat I had ever seen. It was, with its legs greatly shortened, creeping towards me, working its mouth and face and eyes in a very singular manner. It sometimes appeared very amiable and lovely; and, away back, the very end of his long tail, the black tip elevated a little higher than any other portion of the animal, was moving and flitting about like it belonged to somebody else, appearing to be twice as far off as it really was.

Gideon shot the cat, not in the face ("it being so pretty I disliked to spoil it") but carefully in the left eye "without misplacing a hair." He skinned and preserved the hide "claws and all" with its perfect jet-black tadpole markings. It measured $3\frac{1}{2}$ feet in length and 12 inches in height and weighed sixteen or seventeen pounds.

At their camp at Barton's Bluff on the south side of the Colorado

River, the young men found a bee tree and, while they were cutting out the honey, Gideon shot a deer for a "grand venison and honey supper." The narrow strips of venison were placed on rods of prairie dogwood and broiled over coals.

The most approved plan for eating is to take the piece of meat in your left hand, your hunting knife in the right, plunge one end of the meat into your cup of honey deep enough for a mouthful, thrust it between your teeth and hold it fast while you saw it off with your knife. . . . Neither bread nor salt nor coffee is used at one of these feasts; and for its easy digestive qualities and agreeableness in eating it is most certainly not surpassed by any dish ever set before mankind.

Lincecum indicates in his journal of the 1835 expedition that the men traveled no farther than Bastrop, but in his latter-day recollections he states that they continued up the Colorado "to where Austin now stands." He wrote: "Nobody lived near there then, and we found too many moccasin tracks to feel secure in regard to our horses. We stayed there but one night. We traveled over vast prairies southwardly; saw vast herds of wild horses, some buffalo, and countless deer."

Gideon's gun kept the group in fresh meat and, comparing his own prowess with the gun with that of the "young men," explained: "But I needn't to brag about it. I was born in the woods, and lived many a day on my hunt with the blowgun before I was seven years old. These boys slept in feather beds."

At Bastrop his companions decided they had seen enough of Texas and were ready to go home. But not Gideon. He told them:

It was to explore the country that I made my expensive outfit, left my family and came so far, and not having completed what I came for I am not satisfied; nor can I leave the country until I explore it enough to be able to describe its geography, and its most prominent features as an agriculture and grazing country. We have seen the Trinity, San Jacinto and Brazos and Colorado, but there is a vast district southwest that we have not seen. I shall not be satisfied until I explore that region."

His companions settled their accounts with Gideon and he bought one of the pack horses, an axe, one leaf of the tent, and one tin bucket. "All went quickly. We shook hands as affectionately as a set of good brothers would have done; and they left me sitting on a log, holding my horses, who were screaming and crying like two children to follow the company."

Feeling lonesome himself, Gideon rode to Jesse Burnham's house on the Colorado.[1] Gideon wrote:

He had the physiognomy of an honest, friendly man. Indeed, he made on me the impression of a familiar friend; and I very thankfully accepted his kind proposition to make his house my home. I unpacked and deposited my luggage, turned my horses out on the prairies, and I was at home. Burnham had lost his wife several years previous to my arrival, and he had a houseful of children: one daughter married and gone; three daughters and four boys at home. They were all good children, and the time I spent at his house was quite agreeable.

Burnham had lived on the Colorado for twelve years. His nearest neighbors, the Criswells, lived two miles away.

Written in the back of Gideon's journal, under date of March 10, 1835, is the following:

This day entered into an agreement to stop with Jesse Burnham. Board free on condition that I learn his son Hickerson bookkeeping &c. Have on hand in silver and United States paper three hundred and five dollars 99 ¾ cents—the amounts, numbers &c of the bills are on another page in this book. This I have recorded, for the purpose, should any accident befall me, to let the world know, all that is necessary for them to know about me.

My family resides in Monroe county Mississippi 10 miles north of Cotton Gin Port.

I am a Free mason; and by profession a physician.

Gideon Lincecum

Burnham and his children urged Gideon to linger with them but he was eager to explore. "I remained with them, receiving their kind attentions and doing everything I could to reciprocate their kindness. . . . Jesse Burnham . . . was as good a man as any country or situation could produce."

Burnham warned him that the Indians would kill him if he persisted in his lone travels. But he started out toward the coast, examining the mouths of rivers from the Brazos to Aransas Bay. Traveling

---

[1] Jesse Burnham, an early Texas settler, and Lincecum remained lifelong friends. Burnham and his large family later lived on Doublehorn Creek in Burnet County, Texas, where Lincecum visited him in 1867.

through a thicket he reached a coastal plain near the San Bernard River and, seeing cows grazing, moved toward them hoping to find the house to which they belonged. He needed salt for fowl and fish, his meat when he failed to get deer.

It was evening and before I got to the cows I saw a man come riding out from the Bernard timber towards them and we met at the cattle. He instantly invited me to go and stay all night or a week with him if I had time. I went with him. His name was Churchwell. His dwelling was on the south bank of the Bernard, had resided there twelve years; had a *lady* wife and six children. Had a neighbor fifteen miles toward Brazoria. . . They treated me very kindly; the good lady made me a pocket that held a pound and half of salt, and gave it to me. Morning came and I asked for information for the purpose of steering clear of getting hemmed in among the lakes and bayous, he could give me none. Said it was eleven miles to the sea beach, but he had never been there in his life. Said he should be afraid of Indians. I set out, found no difficulty or Indians; but fowls endless. There were a great many swans. . . . It was drawing towards sunset when I observed the swans were setting in a line, extending parallel with the shore as far as I could see either up or down the beach, half a mile out to sea. . . . There was no apparent commotion amongst them, no talking or noise going on . . . it seemed like everything but myself knew what was to take place. . . . It was near seven o'clock—deep twilight. . . . At that moment the shrill note of a small tin trumpet, down at the broad section in the drift of swans, waking sleeping echoes, breaking the dismal silence. At the sound of the second blast the note was repeated at measured distances, running along the vast belt of birds beyond the range of my ear-shot. At the same moment the threshing storm of wings commenced, which increased every instant, soon surpassed the din and uproar of the rushing hurricane. They passed square over at a height of not exceeding thirty feet. They were five minutes or more in getting past. I could feel the concussion of their wings; and somehow or other they seemed to devitalize the air. My breathing was painfully oppressed while the living tornado passed over me. I felt like there wasn't air enough; like the swans were using it all up to fly on. When they were gone and out of hearing, the disagreeable silence returned, and I sank to the ground feeling considerable exhaustion. I have witnessed the stampede of a thousand buffaloes; at another time six or eight hundred mustangs. I had a million wild pigeons pass over in a few minutes; but they all dwindle to insignificance when compared to the flight of the southern division of American swans, on the Texas Gulf Coast.

Gideon and his horse walked along the beach to the mouth of the Colorado and turned inland. For several miles they were accompanied by thousands of clamoring, swooping cranes. In a canebrake between Caney Bayou and the river, about fifty miles inland, Gideon found a worn path through the growth. Families living in the brakes invited him to remain with them but he explained he was in a great hurry.

The truth is, I did not like the appearance of those canebrake folks. I hurried onward, my path a wagon road now, and old Ned made the miles pretty fast. Night brought me to the house of a man by the name of Heard; and although I told him that I would prefer camping out, he said he could not permit me to do so; that there were Indians in the vicinity, and besides he had a use for me.[2] "So say no more about it, but alight, let the boy take your horse, walk in and let me introduce you to my family. Your name, Sir?" "Lincecum." "What state?" "Mississippi, but originally from Georgia."

We encountered his good lady at the door and he introduced me as a man from "our" state, but had forgot my name. I repeated it and she rejoined, "Walk in, Sir," with a very pleasant smile—and when we were seated she remarked, "I hope this is Dr. Lincecum of upper Mississippi. If so, I am almost acquainted with him. I have heard my dear father speak so often of him. Am I not correct in my surmise, sir?" "You are correct, Ma'am, but who was your father?" "Dr. Alexander." "Well, Ma'am, you are sure enough very near acquainted with me. Your father and I were close friends a long time.[3]

I had to stay with these people several days, and answer a thousand questions. They, too, were Georgians by birth. After washing up my shirts and mending the rents in my pants, they let me pass. Mr. Heard went out into the prairie a mile or so, and pointed out the tops of the timber growing around Eagle Lake, twelve miles distant. . . . I arrived about midway at one o'clock P.M. It is about six miles long and in some place four or five hundred yards wide, full of fish and alligators. It was such a pretty place I concluded not to leave it that day.

[2] William Jones Elliott Heard, a captain in the Battle of San Jacinto. His eye-witness account of the battle, countersigned by Eli Mercer, another plantation owner of Egypt, Texas, is in the *Texas Almanac, 1860* (p. 71). Heard was living in Chappell Hill, Washington County, Texas, in 1870 when the *Texas Almanac, 1871,* listed him as a surviving pensioner of the Texas Revolution. Apparently he and Lincecum never renewed their short friendship.

[3] A Dr. S. A. Alexander, "a steam doctor who wrote learned treatises on evolution and other scientific subjects," was an early settler of Clinton, Mississippi (Charles H. Brough, "Historic Clinton," *PMHS*, Vol. VII [1903], pp. 281–311).

As Lincecum prepared a fire for venison backstraps, he saw two Indians approaching. When he questioned them in Choctaw they answered that they came as friends, leaned their rifles against a tree, and came close to the fire. When Gideon invited them to supper they accepted and as their contribution to the meal went to get honey from a tree they had noticed a short way back. While eating, the Indians told Gideon they were farmers living with their tribe of 250 on a little river east of the Trinity. They had heard that a settlement on Old Caney had corn and was making sugar from cane. They hoped to get corn and learn to grow sugarcane.

The three camped together several days, eating venison, black bass, young bees in the comb, and honey. While the Indians fished and hunted, Gideon explored the lake for botanical specimens. Early one morning he heard in that vast solitude "the merry laugh of a lady."

"Very soon there dashed up two carriages containing three ladies, as many gentlemen, and some children with two out-riding negroes." They were the Heards and their neighbors on an outing. Gideon invited them to his camp. For supper, the Indians brought in more deer meat, honey, and black bass. One of the carriages was sent back to the settlement, which Gideon learned was called "Egypt," for a violin, blankets, bread, coffee, bacon, a basket of wine, and more neighbors.

The ladies ate the venison dipped in honey, "sawing it off at their pretty mouths" with Gideon's hunting knife. They were charmed by the two Indians, whom the men promised to supply with corn and to give instructions on raising sugar cane. On taking the violin from its case, Gideon found it a splendid one in excellent condition. He played Washington's *Grand March* so loudly he could hear it echo from across the lake. As the company danced on the grass, he played General Harrison's *March, Hail Columbia*, and the No. I Cotillion of the *Beggar's Set*.

The guests bedded down around the camp fire for the night and after a big breakfast "we all shook hands as affectionately as if we had been acquainted all our lives and parted, never to meet again."

When Gideon returned to Burnham's house he learned that Indians had been marauding in the vicinity.

He had been afraid the Indians had got me. That they had shot old Mr.

Ally full of arrows down at the corner of the field next to the river and killed him three days ago. . . . No one had seen them; and if old man Ally, who was dressing a deerskin down at the corner of the fence, had not been killed, it would not have been known that they were in the region. He thought there were six of them . . . the six arrows they had left sticking in the old man were all of a different style of workmanship.[4]

Gideon, eager to explore farther west, secured the services of a man named Keaton, who stopped by Burnham's place, to guide him for a dollar a day and food. They set out early one morning, over Burnham's protest, on the old San Antonio Trail. When Keaton proved to be an unpleasant and not very knowledgeable guide Gideon parted with him at a path he supposed led to Bastrop. Keaton took that path.

Gideon continued southwest to the San Marcos River, stopping to admire the view of the grass-covered valley and to watch the deer, wild horses, and buffalo grazing. An old she-wolf with seven whelps scampered into the timber. Gideon followed her and spent the remainder of the day exploring the river.

It was then in a perfectly natural condition. Not a hacked tree or other sign of human violence was to be encountered in any direction. The scar of civilization had never marred the beautiful face of that paradise valley with its ruinous tramp; nor had the supreme quiet of the birds and beasts ever been disturbed by the unholy clamor of the shouting saint.

Gideon continued south and, avoiding paths and signs of settlements, crossed the prairie between the Guadalupe and San Antonio Rivers, keeping clear of the town of San Antonio. Gideon paused to explore a large cave at the top of a cliff, thus startling thousands of Columbia turtle dove. A clear pool at the bottom of the cliff was full of large blue catfish but, since he again was without salt, he left them undisturbed.

Gideon found the San Antonio River too full to ford; so he constructed a raft of cottonwood poles secured with mustang grape vines, on which he crossed. Old Ned swam over. In the vicinity were "too

[4] Present Alleyton, three miles east of Columbus, Texas, was named for the Alley family, early settlers. The Alleys had title to land in Austin's Colony in 1824. William, the father, killed by Indians at an undetermined date, and his sons Rawson and Thomas had leagues in Brazoria County; his son John, killed by Indians at Skull Creek in 1822, held land in Fayette County (Lester G. Bugbee, "The Old Three Hundred," *SHQ*, Vol. I [1897–1898] pp. 110–117).

many signs of the depredation of that destructive animal called man"
and Gideon hurriedly took a southwest course to an open prairie where
game was scarce. Gideon would not shoot a suckling doe or a prairie
hen with young. The prairie cocks were "poor and tough" and the
jack rabbits "blue and lean and many . . . dropsical." Mesquite and
cactus thickened; rattlesnakes, wolves, and coyotes became more numerous; water and wood more scarce; the sun hotter.

In a much-used shallow ford, Gideon found moccasin tracks and
read them as those of four young Indians, going east unpursued. He
took a more northerly route after reaching a river, possibly the Nueces,
and after several days of prairie traveling arrived in the rocky hills of
what is known today as the Balcones Escarpment, the western limit of
the gulf coastal plain in Texas. After wandering among the rocks and
springs several days, Gideon decided to turn back towards "home"—
Burnham's place on the Colorado. Three days later he came out of the
rocks and was again on the plains, traveling east. At noon he stopped
at a "nice little creek" and while Ned grazed, Gideon sat on a log and
wrote in his journal, his gun propped against a stump a yard away.

While thus engaged, I felt the presence of somebody, and turning my eyes
in the direction the impression came, and near enough for me to have
reached him, stood a large nearly naked Indian having my gun and seemed
to be curiously examining the lock. For a period I was shocked—fearfully
shocked. I thought of six lone travellers that had been met and murdered at
different points in Texas during the time I had been in the country. I felt
quite lonely.[5]

Gideon spoke to the Indian in Choctaw.

I had met with a Mexican that I mistook for a Coushatta Indian at San
Felipe at the Brazos and spoke to him in Choctaw, which is the true language
of the Coushattas and he answered me in good Choctaw. On my inquiring
of him if he was a Coushatta he said no, that he was a Mexican, but had
been a prisoner with the Comanches many years—from his boyhood till he
was 27 years of age—and that he learned that language from them. They
called it the slave tongue, and that in every band or tribe of the wide-spread
prairie Indian was always to be found some who could speak the slave
tongue, by which the different tribes could and did communicate, and it

---

[5] Lincecum makes no reference to this Indian episode in his 1835 journal.

being subject to all the tribes was the reason it was called the slave tongue.[6]

The Indian understood Gideon and replied in "deep mellow-toned Choctaw." Gideon told him the gun was "doctored" and he promptly put it down. There were other Indians with him and they drew nearer as the two talked. Gideon asked where the tribe was camped and was immediately invited to visit their near-by encampment. He considered it wise to accept the invitation.

It would not do for me to show any doubt or fear, so I mounted my horse. The strip of woods did not exceed seventy yards in extent and we were soon through it. I was surprised on entering the prairie to see a large encampment. I felt completely entrapped, and to make the best of a bad condition, when about the middle of the camp I yelled out the eagle dance whoop and jumped from my horse, lay down on the grass.

Soon, two women came and unsaddled my horse and carefully laying all my things together, staked him to the grass. Directly a good looking middle-aged man came and sat beside me and asked, "From whence came ye?" "From no particular place," said I. "Whither goest thou?" said he. "To no particular place," said I. "Where is your company?" said he. I answered, "I have no company." Said he, "The chief sent me to ask you and it is best for you to speak the truth." "My tongue is not forked," I retorted. He then rose and went to the chief's tent. Soon the chief came. By this time I was sitting up. He sat down and turning his fine eyes on me continued to glare at me a minute or more. I knew his object and I returned his glare with an eye that did not quiver. Presently he said, "I want you to tell me the truth." I replied, "Speak plain then and if I understand you, the truth will come...."

"What are you doing and why alone in these wild prairies?" he asked. "I have been travelling in these prairies and mountains many moons, but did not know that any one would be offended at it," said I.

At this he arose, leaving a large red-skinned Indian standing near me with a spear in his hand. I knew then that I was a prisoner. I observed that soon after the chief entered his tent, that three men rode off in the direction I came. Night came and I slept very comfortably, the man with the spear

---

[6] The Alabama-Coushatta Indians, presently living on a reservation in Polk County, Texas, belong to the Muskhogean linguistic family, which also includes the Creeks, Choctaws, Chickasaws, Seminoles, and other branches. The dialects of the branches are so closely related as to be considered identical. The language of the Chickasaws served as a medium of commercial and tribal intercourse for all tribes along the lower Mississippi (Hodge, *Handbook of American Indians*, Vol. I, pp. 961–962).

standing over me. Early in the morning a woman brought me some roasted buffalo tongue. Nor did they neglect my horse. They took him to water and staked him in a new place. Soon my questioner of the day previous came, and after some pleasant conversation asked to see the contents of my saddlebags if I had no objection.

This was an opportunity I could not afford to let pass, for I suspected he was a medicine man. So I opened first that end that contained vials. He seemed much pleased and asked if I was a medicine man, and being informed in the affirmative he said then we were brothers, to which I assented. I soon realized that he was enlisted in my behalf. He represented me as having dropped from a storm cloud and his peoples' opinion of me was that of veneration. The children began to stand farther from me and the women spread a buffalo robe in the shade and insisted that I come out of the hot sun.

I fully appreciated the kindness, but determined to take advantage of the occasion, so taking out the vial that contained spirits of hartshorn and drawing the cork, held it to his nose. He took a pretty good snuff at it, and instantly slapping both hands to his forehead, fell over backwards exclaiming, "Sah, illish, cay." (I am dead.)

This caused great consternation among the by-standers. As soon as possible I got out the essence of peppermint and held it to his nose, dropping a little of it on his lips, and as a result he was himself again.[7]

I explained that while my medicine could kill, it could also bring to life; that to use one without having the other at hand was certain death. He was overwhelmed with wonder and astonishment. Most of the people fled to the camp, but the old man remained and calling them back said there was no danger.

He asked me for the vials that he might go and kill the chief. To this I would not consent, for, said I, if you kill him and fail to bring him to life these people will kill me. But he called up a number of prominent men and women and explained that in case he failed to restore the chief, no responsibility should rest upon me.

With this understanding, I consented. So taking the two vials and attending carefully to my instructions, he left, followed by the entire crowd, but at a respectful distance, and entered the chief's tent.

For awhile all was silence, then a little bustle, followed by the biggest

---

[7] This story is apparently one of the "Gid" legends in the Lincecum family. It was told to me as an episode in Lincecum's life by his great-grandson, Barney Lincecum, who has not read the Lincecum Papers. In another version Gideon said he applied ammonia instead of hartshorn, the antler of the hart which formerly was much used as a source of ammonia.

horse laugh I ever heard. The commotion outside was indescribable. When the old man came back with the vials he declared with enthusiasm that it was the greatest medicine in the world. . . .

Every hunter I saw come in brought with him a liver, which he would hang up, and immediately a gang of children of both sexes would be seen gathering around it, and dipping mouthfuls of the raw liver in the gall, so as to get two or three drops on it, ate it as if it was a great pleasure to them. The doctor said it was the food of the children; that it destroyed the worms, kept their bowels all right, and made them able to stand cold and fatigue longer. I tasted it; it is by no means unpleasant. For many forms of dyspepsia, in my opinion, it would be the proper diet, and it would be cleaner, nicer and less liable to adulterations than the beef-paunch soup, called "pepsin" we find in the drug stores.[8]

Gideon and the medicine man became great friends. A young girl named Nilpe, with an abundance of shining hair, wearing a skirt of woven bark and feathers and a string of odd-shaped white bone beads around her neck, was assigned as his personal servant.

Gideon taught the young boys and girls Choctaw songs and steps to the tick dance, and showed an old man how to prepare a drum by stretching a wet deerskin over the mouth of a small pot.[9] After the old man learned the rhythm of the dance, Gideon placed him in a circle of dancers. Soon the whole camp was "in a perfect frenzy of delight." Gideon promised to teach them the eagle and buffalo dance when he was allowed to go into the country and search for the plant which produced "the proper dancing medicine."

On the third day, the scouts returned and went to the chief's tent. My old friend ran to the back of the tent to eavesdrop.

Soon he came and reported that they had found three of my camps and saw but one meat stick, which proved that I had no company. The chief was satisfied, and said to let that *"hard-eye man go."*

Promising Nilpe and the old doctor that he would return with

[8] The Tanima Comanches were called Liver Eaters (W. W. Newcomb, Jr., *The Indians of Texas* [Austin, University of Texas Press, 1961], p. 157).

[9] The Choctaws in Louisiana in 1909 still remembered the tick dance although they had forgotten much of their tribal history and customs. The dancers stomp their feet "as if crushing ticks on the ground, at the same time looking down, supposedly at the doomed insects" (David I. Bushnell, Jr., "Choctaws of Bayou Lacomb," *BAE Bulletin*, No. 48 [1909], pp. 20–21).

"dancing medicine," and leaving his vials of hartshorn and pepper-mint to prove his good intentions, Gideon asked the medicine man to tell the other Indians that his "heart shook hands with them" and rode off on old Ned, with Nilpe's gift of two well-cooked buffalo tongues in his saddle bags. He left their camp about sunset.

Gideon hoped his pretense of returning would keep the Indians from following him, but to be safe he adopted a cautious course.

About dark I came to a little river. Here, thought I, they will expect to find me. I stopped, arranged my trappings, mounted and turned northward at a rapid gait. This I kept up all night, turning gradually to the right. With only a few brief stops, I continued the next day and night. When morning came, I could see thousands of buffalo and deer feeding quietly, and feeling that the danger was passed I dismounted and lay down to sleep.

So exhausted was I that it was 3 o'clock before I awoke, and to my sur-prise my horse was standing where I left him, asleep.

Being hungry, I took my gun and went to an elevation to look for deer and also to scan the prairie for Indians. After getting a deer, I returned and found my horse feeding. Not being disposed to travel, I spent the next day examining the rocks in the bed of a creek near by.

The boulders on its slaty banks were gun flint. The slate was presenting its water-worn edges with a dip of twenty degrees westwardly up the creek. I scratched some of the sand from between the edges of the slate and could distinguish particles of gold.

At a distance of ten or twelve miles to the north I could see two moun-tain peaks. I wished to climb to their summits and examine them but feared exposing myself.

In the course of ten days travel eastwardly, I reached the Colorado River at Bastrop. My clothes were about worn off and it was with difficulty that I succeeded in getting a shirt and pantaloons, and they had been used. Three days more and I was with my friend Burnham.

Gideon had been away fifty-five days. He remained another three weeks with Burnham and the two of them rode to neighboring settle-ments and looked at locations available to colonists. Gideon made an-other exploration east of the Colorado, the Little River Country, up the Brazos as far as the falls, and back through the Yegua area, where for the first time he saw the site of his future Texas home. He sought out Felix Huston, whom Gideon said was Stephen F. Austin's agent, and attempted to buy the league.[10] "He asked me $5 for it. I was not able to pay that price, but marked it, as I intended to come back. I did go thirteen years after and bought it for seventy five cents per acre."

Early in May, having fulfilled his contract with the citizens of Columbus, Gideon was ready to go back.

It was thought to be a thousand miles to my home in Monroe County, Mississippi, and most of the route was through a wild wilderness. I bought another horse, made a pack saddle and got together my clothes, specimens and cooking utensils, &c. and bid my friends an affectionate adieu.

I had promised to call at San Felipe to see Gale Boden [Borden] who had been a long time sick.[11] I got there in the evening of the second day. Boden was very much gratified that I called on him. About this time Mosely Baker was drumming up volunteers to meet the invading Mexicans.[12] All the men in San Felipe had already enrolled themselves.

I thought well of the chances it offered and added my name to the list, but George Ewing of Monroe County, Miss., Thomas Gay of Georgia and William Jack of Alabama and [William B.] Travis of Tuscaloosa, Ala., all old acquaintances of mine, opposed my joining them. Captain Baker, however, was anxious for me to go and promised his best efforts to have me appointed surgeon to the forces that would occupy Texas west of the Brazos. I thought well of it myself. I could see, should the enterprise prove successful, what permanent chaplets of wealth and glory would crown the performers. But those old friends, who were acquainted with my domestic condition opposed my becoming a volunteer more vehemently than before. George Ewing made a speech in the course of which he said, "Captain Baker no doubt thought it right, but he was not appraised of the fact that in the State of Mississippi I had a wife and ten children who would not be

---

[10] There is no known evidence that Huston, a former Natchez, Mississippi, lawyer who became a major general in the Texas Army, was Austin's agent.

[11] Borden was a surveyor and school teacher in Amite County, Mississippi, before going to Texas in 1829 (Joe B. Frantz, *Gail Borden, Dairyman to the Nation*, [Norman, University of Oklahoma Press, 1951], pp. 51–59).

[12] Moseley Baker (1802–1848) was from Montgomery, Alabama, and an ardent advocate of the Revolution. Shortly after Lincecum's encounter with him, Baker was sent to east Texas to urge volunteers to go to the defense of Gonzales, Texas, under attack by the Mexican Army, and to negotiate with Indian tribes for their support. He is best known in Texas history for burning San Felipe before Santa Anna arrived there in 1836 (*A History of Texas and Texans*, Eugene C. Barker, ed. [American Historical Society, Chicago and New York, 1914], Vol. I, pp. 274, 444).

benefited for me to bleach my bones on the prairies of Texas. It must not be. Dr. Lincecum must go home."

"But," said I, "my name is on the list and cannot be taken off." "I have the list," said Gay, "and I will show you how it can be got off." And taking a pen he erased my name.

Captain Baker was highly offended at this and they came near making a serious matter of it. But when Ewing explained the case, he, too, opposed my becoming a volunteer.

After attending one day to Gale Boden's case, I collected some meat and bread, packed up and left San Felipe at 2 P.M., the fourth day after my arrival. I crossed the Brazos on the ferry boat and went out about three or four miles to the edge of the prairie where I camped. It was a sad night for me. I felt that it would have been better for me to remain.

Lincecum seldom referred in correspondence to his early Texas travels. An exception is a letter written January 10, 1860, to John A. Rutherford, Honey Grove, Texas, in which he recalled:

You have been a citizen of Texas a long time longer than I had any knowledge of. I am acquainted with three or four, but there are but few who came to Texas in 1835 who are here now. I came and explored a large portion of Texas that year myself. I would have remained but they got up the revolution and my family were in Mississippi. So I concluded that it would not be prudent for me to engage in and risk the chances of war in a foreign nation without the knowledge of my family when I knew they were not properly provided for in case of a failure on my part. And so after being a volunteer three days in the first company that was raised at San Felipe with the prospect of being appointed surgeon general west of the Brazos, the thought of the unprotected state of my wife and children, none grown, outweighed it all; and at a meeting of the little company I stated to them the true condition of my affairs. They all voted that I must go home.

This letter offers convincing proof of Lincecum's claim that he was a volunteer in the Texas Revolution, a claim doubted by some Texas historians.

After crossing the Trinity River on a raft Lincecum stopped to nap and was awakened by the coarse voice of an officious and loquacious Texan who attached himself to Lincecum and took over the management of the expedition. At the end of each day's travel, the stranger hobbled the horses, made the fire, cooked supper, washed up, and insisted that Gideon sit by the fire and rest. Gideon found him "as good a companion as I ever saw." He was Mason Foley, who lived on the Lavaca River in Texas.[13]

At Alexandria, Louisiana, Gideon found a cholera epidemic raging; so he hurried through the town and camped in the forest.

When we struck the Mississippi River we had to travel twenty miles along the levee among the rich farms. The cholera was raging awfully. A man joined us, having his little son riding behind him. He told us that he had lost $400,000 worth of negroes, and that his wife and all his children except the one with him had died. At several places along the river all the inhabitants were dead and many unburied and the dogs were howling piteously in the yards.

At Rodney, Mississippi, Gideon wrote a letter telling his wife he would be home at 12:30 P.M., August 5. Traveling through Port Gibson, Clinton, and the Choctaw Nation, he stopped thirty miles from Columbus for the night with his brother Gabriel.

It was the last time I saw him. He told me that the month before my brother Rezin Bowie had died at Lexington, Kentucky, on his way to New York. Also that my good friend, John Pitchlyn, was dead. We reached Columbus the next day and I stopped with my brother-in-law, Jo. Bryan. I married his sister and he married my sister. My clothes were pretty badly worn and I went to Dr. A. Weirs store and got an entire new suit.[14]

At Columbus, Gideon parted with his Texas friend, Foley, and started for his home beyond Cotton Gin Port, accompanied by a neighbor, G. W. Wall, who lived fifteen miles from Gideon's house. He spent the night with Wall and after breakfast set out for home. Gideon was running ahead of schedule. When he was within a mile of his house it was only 12:00 noon. Ever a man of his word, he loitered a

---

[13] Mason B. Foley was one of the sons of Washington G. Lee Foley, who went to Texas from Alabama before 1836 and settled in Lavaca County. His son Arthur was killed with Fannin in 1836; his son James was killed by a Mexican bandit between the Nueces and Rio Grande in 1839; and his son Tucker was killed by Comanches on Ponton's Creek, Lavaca County, in 1840 (Paul C. Boethel, *The History of Lavaca County* [San Antonio, The Naylor Co., 1936], pp. 11–12).

[14] Dr. Andrew Weir later moved to Texas. Lincecum addressed letters to him, over a period of years, to Grand Bluffs, Panola County; Harmony Hill, Rusk County; and Marshall, Harrison County. In 1865 Lincecum wrote Weir: "Remember we are the last of that old gang and we should meet once more if possible, don't you think?"

while and let Ned, "the defeated race horse on the Columbus track," graze.[15] But old Ned knew the end of his long journey was just a stone's throw away and had no appetite for the tender green grass. His nudging failed to budge Gideon, who stood his ground, watch in hand. Timing his arrival to the minute, Gideon rode up to the fence at 12:30 P.M. and saw his family at dinner under a long shed in the yard.

Gideon counted his children and was relieved when they totaled the correct number, ten. The only visible change in the past seven months was that the towheads of Leonora, five, and Cassandra, three, had darkened. Gideon's old hunting dog, Hector, saw him first, raced toward him, and leaped the fence into his arms.

This attracted the attention of the family and dinner was suspended for a time. I had been absent seven months, lacking four days. I counted my money and found that I had thirty dollars more than I started with. I received for three cases of medical services two hundred and twenty dollars.

All was right at home.

A NOTE ON SOURCES

Lincecum's travel in Texas in 1835 with companions from Mississippi and his continued exploration alone when the group disbanded is told in his Journal of 1835, in his "Autobiography," and in his "Reminiscences." The Journal is apparently a somewhat sketchy contemporary account; the other two, written from memory at later dates, are more detailed. The most retrospectively important is his "Reminiscences," but he died before finishing this narrative, which promised to be an interesting document on early Texas. Writing his "Autobiography" for a grandson, Lincecum expanded his role as a lone traveler in Indian country and possibly exaggerated his exploits. Chapter IV is a composite of the three accounts.

Lincecum's Journal, edited by Andrew L. Bradford, Lincecum's great-grand-

---

15 Old Ned, a most remarkable horse, is a major character in Gideon's "Reminiscences." He was seventeen years old when Gideon rode him to Texas and back to Mississippi. Lincecum acquired Ned when his son Lycurgus rode into Columbus, Mississippi, on Gideon's small black Indian pony, an excellent hunting horse and deer-tracker, with a rapid pace, "but a poor thing to practice on." When a racing man offered to swap old Ned, then ten years old, for the pony Lycurgus agreed to the trade. Lincecum found Ned to be "a fine horse. . . . I rode him until my legs had grown to fit his back." After his return from Texas, "feeling he had done enough for me, I set him free. He had helped me to make many thousands of dollars."

son, of Marble Falls, Texas, and Dr. T. N. Campbell, chairman of the Department of Anthropology of The University of Texas, was published as "Journal of Lincecum's Travels in Texas, 1835" in the *Southwestern Historical Quarterly,* (Vol. LIII (1949–1950), pp. 180–201). See Appendix A.

J. Frank Dobie, who thought no historical novelist could ask for a richer theme than Gideon Lincecum (*Life and Literature of the Southwest* [Dallas, Southern Methodist University Press, 1952], p. 69), used Lincecum's appreciation for venison and honey in the chapter "Honey in the Rock" in his *Tales of Old-Time Texas* (Boston and Toronto, Little, Brown and Company, 1928, pp. 125, 313).

Other data in the preceding chapter are found in Lincecum's letters to John A. Rutherford, Honey Grove, Texas, January 10, 1860, to Colonel S. D. Hay, Huntsville, Texas, January 18, 1862, and to Dr. A. Weir, Harmony Hill, Rusk County, Texas, May 20, 1865.

CHAPTER FIVE

GIDEON
AND THE HEALING ARTS

I owe no man anything beyond common civility.   GID

IMMEDIATELY AFTER his return to Cotton Gin Port from his Texas trip Lincecum resumed the practice of medicine.

He had entered the profession in 1830 at the insistence of his neighbors. Since the distant days when he held the wound of his grandmother closed to stop the flow of blood, Gideon had freely exercised his natural talent for healing and caring for the sick. He had attended soldiers in the War of 1812 and among his frontier neighbors he had always been a ready and willing first-aider.

One night in August, 1830, William Wall, a Cotton Gin Port neighbor, called Lincecum in to treat his illness. During the visit Wall said: "You know more about disease than the doctors in this country and I am surprised that you don't get some medicine and set up shop."

Lincecum had been thinking the same thing, but he lacked the capital to invest in drugs. Wall gave him $100 and another neighbor, Robert Gordon, offered Gideon his credit with wholesale druggists in Cincinnati.[1] Lincecum was soon in business. Within a few months he had repaid Wall and had $300 worth of good accounts on his books.

---

[1] Robert Gordon of Scotland was in Mississippi in the early 1800's as an Indian trader. He settled on the west bank of the Tombigbee at Dundee, which he renamed Aberdeen. Later he built a mansion, Lochinvar, near Pontotoc (*Mississippi: A Guide to the Magnolia State*, Federal Writers Project, 1938, pp. 364, 462).

Gideon had no formal medical training, a situation not uncommon in the profession in those days. After he left his father's house at the age of fifteen, Gideon clerked in Eatonton, Georgia, for William Wilkins. Mason L. Weems, known as Parson Weems, an itinerant bookseller and writer credited with the invention of the story about George Washington and the cherry tree, left some of his library with Gideon to sell. Gideon's previous literary experience had been confined to the few books he could borrow, which included an old *Bible* and *The Arabian Nights*. ("I didn't know which of these books shocked my reasoning facilities the worst.")

Gideon recalled:

Here was $6000 worth of the best knowledge the world possessed. I surveyed them on the shelves and never felt so proud of anything in my life. I found many books that I had never heard of. I thought of the shortness of human life and there was not sufficient time for me to store my mind with the world's knowledge. But I was not discouraged and although I have not attained to a very profound degree of knowledge, it is a satisfaction to know that I have not lost any time in trying for it.

In his third year at Eatonton, Gideon clerked for Ichabod Thompson for $500 a year. Thompson spent a great deal of time at his Indian trading post on the Ocmulgee River and Gideon found many opportunities to read and study while Thompson was away. A friend who had a profound influence on the direction of Lincecum's life was Dr. Henry Branham of Eatonton. Dr. Branham recognized that Gideon possessed both the heart and the mind for the medical profession and urged him to read medical books.

It was probably Dr. Branham who suggested that Gideon should read Erasmus Darwin's *Zoonamia* (". . . it was the textbook of practice for the United States. I viewed the work as the finishing stroke on that subject."), *The Botanic Garden,* and *The Temple of Nature or the Origin of Society* ("all occupying a plane so far above anything I had before seen and from which . . . floods of scientific light and philosophic truths were pouring in upon my uncultivated intellect—soul food").

A year of reading books from Weems' library was a thrilling period in Gideon's young life. "Oh! this had been a glorious year for me! It tore open the windows of my abode of darkness, let in the light of science on my awakening faculties and left me with enough grand books on my shelf to nourish and feed the divine flame another year."

When he was eighteen years old Gideon, an established and responsible citizen of Eatonton, was elected tax collector. His medical studies under Dr. Branham were interrupted by the War of 1812 and indefinitely postponed by his marriage on October 25, 1813, to Sarah Bryan. His medical career, except for a brief time in Dr. Isbell's shop in Tuscaloosa, did not begin until after his years as an Indian trader and a long illness, during which time he had ample opportunity to observe at first hand the methods of doctors and their use of drugs.

Lincecum prospered in the drug-doctor business at Cotton Gin Port and his patients were pleased with his service. But Lincecum began to doubt the soundness of the prevailing medical methods. When a number of his patients died during a cholera epidemic Lincecum decided that the prescribed medication was not only ineffective but actually harmful; he even suspected that some of his patients died as a result of calomel and other "poisons" which he administered.

He confessed:

I was greatly discouraged. This, and the hundreds that were dying all around me in the hands of other physicians, convinced me that our remedies were impotent. I felt tired of killing people and concluded to quit the man-killing practice and try to procure a living by some other method. I had long felt the need of good medical works written by southern practitioners. All our books had been written by northern practitioners and their prescriptions did not suit southern complaints. So I conceived the plan to visit an Indian doctor of great reputation who resided in the Six Towns Choctaw Nation and learn what he knew of medicine and diseases.

When Gideon returned from his visit with the Indian doctor he found many of his patients complaining about his closed shop. He told them he was weary of a sham practice and that the present medical system was too uncertain. They answered that life, too, was uncertain and that no remedy would ever be found for all human ailments. But Gideon, a sincere and conscientious healer, continued his long search for better medication. He studied new medical methods as they were introduced and carefully weighed their merits. When Samuel Thomson, a New Hampshire blacksmith, published, in 1833, *A New Guide* to *Health or the Botanic Family Physician,* Lincecum was one of the first of many to scoff. He considered Thomson's cure-all of lobelia, cayenne, nervine, No. 6, and steam baths as "the most perfect tomfoolery."

Gideon declined an offer as doctor to the wealthy and large Samuel Prewitt plantation with its many slaves. The offer was made on the condition that Gideon practice the Thomsonian system. When Gideon refused, the elderly Prewitt replied: "Shut your foolish mouth! You are struggling with a big family and we want to help you."

Lincecum yielded, concocted from herbs a supply of Thomsonian medicines, which he carried in one saddlebag for the Prewitt family and slaves. The other saddlebag contained his usual supply of "old-school" drugs. At the end of the year Lincecum was a convert to the Thomsonian system of botanic medicine, a tragic death strengthening his decision to forsake the allopathic system.

He wrote of his decision:

I lost a two-year-old child under circumstances which left no grounds to doubt that death was occasioned by allopathic remedies. And whilst I was gazing on the twitching muscles of the dying child I made a solemn vow that I would never administer another dose of the poisons of the system. When I started home I emptied the old school drugs from my saddlebag in a pile on the ground.

After H. Horton Howard's *Improved System of Botanic Medicine* made its appearance, Lincecum combined it with his Indian herbal medicines and prepared his own remedies for Southern complaints.[2] Lincecum wrote accounts of his system and several case histories which "were highly commended by the editor of the journal in which they were published." These, probably Lincecum's first published works, cannot be located.

Gideon's defection from the conventional old-line practice made him a target for the "regular," or allopathic, doctors. He explained:

Because I had abandoned the allopathic system—the practice of poisons—the other doctors became highly offended. They tried every way to break

[2] Among the Lincecum Papers is an announcement, dated March 3, 1838, that Drs. M. Bailey and G. Lincecum were the legally appointed agents of the heirs of the late Horton Howard in the states of Mississippi and Alabama for the use of Howard's medicines.

me down. They told the people that the botanic system in the hands of science was a good thing, that they all understood it and practiced it when necessary; but administered by empirics it was very dangerous. As for steaming a sick person, it was truly preposterous—it was scandalous—they had known several people to die while being steamed. But this great clamor raised about me excited the attention of people far and near. Those living too far off for me to visit them, came to me and I soon saw that I must prepare rooms for them.

Gideon built a hospital near his house at Cotton Gin Port. His home, which caught the overflow, was fast turned into a tavern. When friends in Columbus urged him to move there, he followed their advice in 1841. There he was equally successful, thus again arousing the enmity of the "old school" doctors. Gideon ignored the newspaper articles directed at him, but finally, prodded by friends, inserted the following letter in the local newspaper:

Messrs. Editors:
I have noticed in your papers during the past six months numerous articles of scurrilous stuff over the signatures of M.D.s saying a great deal about a certain Steam Doctor, whom they call Aesculapian. From these low-pitched productions I cannot discover what it is that they want. However, to bring the matter at once to a focus: if any *gentleman* desires to discuss before the public, over his true signature, the merits of the two systems of medical practice, he shall be accommodated, but I have no time to waste with the loafering slangwhangers and hangers-on of the profession. That class of poor fellow will please excuse me.[3]

This "shut them up as close as an oyster."
During his seven years in Columbus Lincecum booked $51,000 in addition to cash payments. In September, 1847, Lincecum made a decision to settle in Texas. From then until March 30, 1848, he tried

[3] One of the authors of the newspaper articles which prompted Lincecum's letter was doubtless Dr. John W. Monette, a physician and geographer of Washington, Mississippi, whose anonymous writings included articles on empiricism directed against steam doctors and disciples of Samuel Thomson, Samuel Wilcox, and Horton Howard (Franklin L. Riley, "Life and Literary Service of Dr. John W. Monette," *PMHS,* Vol. IX [1906], pp. 199–237). Riley, in a footnote, stated: "A very interesting account of this system of medicine, written by a gentleman who amassed a fortune through his steam practice, is found in Vol. VIII of *PMHS*" (reference to Lincecum article). Monette and Lincecum had one thing in common—both were close friends of Colonel Caleb G. Forshey of Texas, who knew Monette when Forshey taught at Jefferson College in Mississippi.

to collect outstanding accounts, finally marking $7,500 off as bad debts.[4] He was eager to be off to a new frontier in Texas.

After settling in Long Point, Texas, Lincecum circulated printed announcements, a copy of which is in the Lincecum Papers, that he and his sons were engaged in the practice of medicine on "purely botanic principles."

In Texas he found a variety of interests to distract him from a concentrated practice and devoted more and more time to natural science, which became a consuming interest. He resented time spent in "doctoring" and frantically sought to make use of every moment left him to study plants, fossils, birds, small animals, and insects.

Gideon remained devoted to botanic medicine throughout his life and on the fifteenth anniversary of the founding of the Botanic Medical College of Memphis, Tennessee, he wrote to its president, Dr. P. C. Gale: "It is cheering to my old time-worn heart to see so many names in your faculty of the old braves who have battled so manfully for its truths, from the origin of that institution up to date."

Nor did he cease his criticism of the allopathic doctors. He once wrote to Dr. E. H. Dixon of New York, publisher of the *Scalpel*: "Now don't feel disappointed at me for not pitching into the doctors. . . . They are, to be sure, a devilish poor deceitful set, generally having short heels which enable them to rear back upon their dignity gracefully."

As he grew older Lincecum became more outspoken against the inadequacy of the medical profession. At every opportunity, in print or in private letters, Lincecum deplored the lack of sanitary conditions around the sick, the repeated failures to control epidemics, the indiscriminate use of narcotics, and the constant administration of calomel for all complaints.

By the time the Civil War started Lincecum had ceased practicing altogether. As his contribution to the war effort he treated all soldiers, including some escaping Yankees, who came by his house. Numerous old friends, unable to obtain medical care or to come to him during the war, described their complaints in letters. He prescribed by return

---

[4] A long list of patients owing Lincecum is in an account book in the Lincecum Papers. The names are in four categories—good pay, doubtful, bad, and "those in Texas."

mail. He was frequently consulted by allopathic doctors to whom he obligingly sent herbal prescriptions.

The handwriting of some of his unknown mail-order patients often told him more about their symptoms than their words.[5] To one he replied: "From an examination of your autograph I conclude that you are rather fat." Lincecum wrote to R. S. Stuart, Bell County, Texas, that his handwriting indicated "you have developed the uncontrollable nature of your animal organism. From which I am informed that you really do need assistance. . . . You must procure a physician that can aid in binding you down to strict hygienic rules a long time." Gideon recommended his son, Lucullus.

He seldom charged for advice or prescriptions and to one patient wrote: "If you are, like myself, an impoverished rebel, don't send the fee. If it is convenient, send ten dollars."

After the War he was forced to resume practice in order to support his household. A license to practice medicine in Washington County, issued by the U.S. Army, is among the Lincecum Papers. In the fall Gideon went out into the country "raking and scratching like an old gobbler in the forests and prairies" in search of his favorite medicinal plants.

After a notice of his resumption of practice appeared in the Houston *Telegraph* he complained to the editor: "It was completely obscured by that little old teacup and spoon sitting on one corner of it. Wouldn't it be more noticeable if the mortor was removed and GID in good capitals placed right above botanic medicine?"[6]

In 1866 Gideon launched his last great offensive battle against allopathic doctors. It began when a friend sent him the first issue of the *Galveston Medical Journal*,[7] about which he commented:

I have perused it with a considerable degree of satisfaction and pride. I hope it is a success and has wide circulation. I should have liked to become a sub-

---

[5] Gideon placed great reliance on his interpretation of handwriting and used it as a basis for character analysis. More than once he declined to reply to letters from strangers because their handwriting indicated they were unreliable.

[6] GID was the Lincecum cattle brand and a signature frequently used by Lincecum in signing letters and newspaper articles.

[7] The *Galveston Medical Journal* (1866–1880), the first medical periodical in Texas, was also published as the *Texas Medical Journal* and the *Galveston and Texas Medical Journal*.

scriber and perhaps contributor to it myself, but the Medical Society for which the *Journal* seems to be the organ has raised such a wall of separation betwixt themselves and me that I shall never think of crossing it.[8]

Although Gideon never crossed the wall of separation he lost no time in assaulting it:

Speaking of the Medical Society, their constitution, bylaws and code of ethics with a few exceptions are quite creditable and will, if they live up to them, do away with some of the opprobrium that has so long and so heavily hung upon the reputation of the allopathic faculty. For the sake of suffering confiding humanity I wish them well and hope that they may be able to conform to the clever rules they have laid down for themselves.

It is, however, an unnecessary alarm for the Galveston Medical Society to raise the old allopathic theme of warning against quackery and quack medicine to the unprotected foolish people so early. But the great dread of empiricism manifested by the society has not proved sufficient to prevent Dr. Greenville Dowell[9] from recommending in the case of colds and congestive fever for the patient to be rubbed over the entire surface with brandy and cayenne or with No. 6.

This treatment, Gideon pointed out, was first suggested many years before by the old allopathic enemy, Dr. Samuel Thomson of botanic medical fame,

[8] A tribute to Gideon Lincecum, probably written by Dr. F. E. Daniel, editor, with his photograph, appeared in the *Texas Medical Journal* on February 1, 1912. It called Lincecum "the most noted pioneer Texas physician and naturalist . . . The medical profession of Texas can not afford to forget this great man. We should be proud of him and cherish his memory and preserve it for future generations of doctors by some suitable monument or tablet, as an example and an incentive to those who shall come after us." The author was indebted to Walter Durham of Austin, a grandson, for the photograph and data on "this great man, one of the most remarkable men of the nineteenth century. The older members of the medical profession of Texas will remember him and recall his contributions to our knowledge of the indigenous medical plants of the state. . . . But I dare say the younger men—those of the present generation and the past one—never heard of him. Such a man and his work should not be forgotten." A copy of the *Journal* is in the possession of Gideon's great-granddaughter, Mrs. Lucille Reed, of Goliad, Texas.

[9] Dr. Greensville S. Dowell (1822–1881), owner and publisher of the *Galveston Medical Journal,* first settled in Texas in Gonzales in 1852; he served as a surgeon in the Civil War, and afterwards practiced in Galveston, where he was dean and professor of medicine at the Galveston Medical College. His operations for hernia and fixation of floating kidneys and his theory of yellow fever predate those credited as firsts (*The Handbook of Texas,* Walter Prescott Webb, ed., Texas State Historical Association, 1952, Vol. I, p. 519).

... for which he was by allopathy universally denounced as a most illiterate ignoramus and dangerous quack. The doctors even accused him of poisoning and killing his patients, imprisoned him for months, and finally tried him for his life. I was alive then and know all about it. I must look to these scientific gentlemen at Galveston and note how many *quack* remedies they incorporate in their materia medica.

When the Medical Association attempted to institute state Laws controlling medical practice, Gideon started a letter-writing campaign.[10] Among numerous letters to doctors and editors, giving his reasons for opposing such legislation, was an explanation of his position to his old friend Dr. J. C. Massie[11] of Houston:

I see from certain movements in the ranks of allopathy that they are preparing for an effort at monopoly at the first session of the legislature. . . . I see very clearly the aim of the movement is monopoly, exclusive privilege. I shall, with all my force, oppose them. Not the society, for I think well of that, but the spirit and principles of all monopoly and special privilege. . . . Equal rights is my motto.

To another old friend, Dr. Samuel G. Haynie of Austin, Lincecum expressed the opinion that "the indisputable right, possessed by every American citizen, is the choice of his blacksmith, his tailor, his doctor, his schoolteacher, or preacher."[12]

In a letter to the Houston *Telegraph* Gideon wrote:

If the allopathic faculty will conform fully to the requirements of their code of ethics it will most assuredly elevate the profession above some of the slurs and odium that is daily cast upon it by the popular voice. In the *Journal*, carefully as it has been put up, I can see the claws and teeth of their unholy designs. They say the object is to legislate to prevent *quacks* from being allowed to practice. Who are the quacks?

[10] The Medical Association of Texas was organized in January, 1853, with a membership of forty-eight. In 1869 it reorganized as the Texas State Medical Association (*ibid*, Vol. II, p. 166).

[11] Dr. Massie's textbook, *Treatise on Eclectic Southern Practice of Medicine,* published in 1854, contains many medical curiosa and remedies of the day. See Dr. Pat Ireland Nixon, *The Medical Story of Early Texas* (Lancaster, Pennsylvania, Lancaster Press, 1946), pp. 396–398. Massie was one of the allopathic doctors who sought Lincecum's advice on botanic prescriptions.

[12] Dr. Samuel G. Haynie (1806–1877) came to Texas in 1837. He and Lincecum had many mutual friends in Mississippi and Georgia, where Gideon first knew him. Haynie wrote *Chart of Phrenology* (Streeter #390).

I intend that all the various medical systems shall stand, as far as law is concerned, on an equal basis. And they shall stand, as far as the people are concerned, on the basis of preference and truth. If any physician desires to prevent quacks from being allowed to practice, let him conduct himself toward his patients with kindness, full attendance and at the same time manifesting a thorough knowledge of his profession by curing his cases, and the awful quacks will not pester him or his patients often. It will work well for every one who makes that the rule of his conduct toward his patrons and he will find that there is no necessity for calling upon the arm of the law to protect him and his patients against the terrible intermeddling, insinuating, villainous quacks.

His comments were printed in the Houston *Tri-Weekly Telegraph* of January 19, 1866 (p. 3, Cols. 4–5). Writing to Sioux Doran of the *Telegraph* staff, Gideon expressed regret that his letter had offended the doctors:

You say the M.D.s are considerably stirred up in consequence of the publication of my last articles. I should be sorry if any of them were offended at it. They can't offend me by writing pure unadulterated truth about me or anything I do. If their system is true, they ought to know that no other truth will damage it. Drs. Riddell, Hay and Massie say I have a wrong idea in regard to their intentions.[13] I am not acquainted with Dr. Hay but the other two I am, and there are but few men for whom I entertain kinder feelings and I very much regret that they have so far under-rated me as to attempt to throw off my guard in that feeble manner.

The devastating yellow fever epidemic of 1867 was proof enough to Gideon that allopathic medicine not only had not progressed but was decidedly deadly. He was certain that many died, not of the fever but from drugs. In the death of Dr. S. B. Maney, of Long Point, he was convinced that there was no evidence of yellow fever and that death was due entirely to drugs.

During this dreadful epidemic, Lincecum recorded in his diary:

Sept. 25—Everybody is frightened about yellow fever. Both the Long Point doctors are sick. I have not seen Dr. Ruff and can't say, but I know Dr. Maney's case was not yellow fever yesterday evening. I have visited

---

[13] Dr. W. P. Riddell of Houston was an old acquaintance and a frequent guest in the Lincecum Home. Gideon refers to Dr. A. J. Hay.

many sick rooms in my life but never saw such manifestations of stupid ignorance as I saw in Dr. Maney's shop and sickroom.

Sept. 26—The doctors are rearing around and talking about yellow fever, but they cure no cases. Their theories are outspoken and boldly expressed, but every case of fever dies. The plan of treatment, and they all pursue it, is to keep the patient quiet in bed, give divers powders, or morphia and quinine, one dose of castor oil, and orange leaf tea, be careful not to disturb the stomach. They add chloroform occasionally. All their cases die. None escape.

Sept. 27—Several doctors came to Long Point today and 3 or 4 nurses, one from Indianola and one from Galveston. Nobody had yellow fever, and they were not needed. Dr. Maney had a little chill and fever, lasted half an hour. It was pronounced yellow fever, and they kept him shut up in his room three days, giving him poisonous chemicals, before he had any more fever. Then it was only fever of irritation and that very slight. All the doctors cried out yellow fever then.

Lincecum went to Austin for a visit and when he returned home on October 12 found that Dr. Maney was dead. He wrote in his diary:

It is said no one would go to assist his heart broken young wife to shroud him, they were so afraid of taking the complaint that killed him. They should not have been uneasy about that, however, for they all had the complaint badly—ignorance.

Oct. 29—Yellow fever still prevails at Brenham. Dr. [John L.] Watkins, the last one of the doctors that remained in town, was buried today. The lay-still, don't-disturb-the-stomach system has killed every one upon whom it was practiced. An allopathic doctor is a dangerous animal to tamper with nowadays. They do not recognize anything as a medicine that does not bear the reputation of being a deadly poison. That which they would be afraid to give a well man is given in profusion to the sick. Do you hear?[14]

At seventy-five Lincecum still practiced, but impatiently. In his diary, June 24, 1868, he complained:

Made no collections today. Had a sick German in my house and whilst I

[14] Before 1867 epidemic yellow fever was confined to the coastal towns but in that year, because of more extensive transportation facilities, it spread rapidly inland, not only claiming a large fatality but causing panic and economic crises. The cause and cure of the disease (not discovered until 1900) caused bitter debate among doctors and laymen. No accurate account of deaths is available, but the number has been estimated at about 3,000 (Franklin W. Baldwin, *Yellow Fever in Texas in 1867* [BA thesis, Rice University, 1961]).

was physicking and nursing him I wrote a pretty long article on the habits and manner of raising its young, of the tarantula. I must not take cases of sickness any more. It confuses me & unfits me for study. I have lost all day, done nothing but measure out and administer doses.

To the end of his life Lincecum continued to render first aid wherever needed, and in 1871, in Tuxpan, Mexico, comforted an elderly neighbor, Andrews, suffering from asthma. On his lonely walks he frequently stopped in at Andrews' place, sat a while, and talked "foolishness to amuse the old man—for he is a religionist." Except for a native servant, Andrews lived alone. Lincecum, on one of his walks, found Andrews with badly swollen legs, having been unable for the past eight days to lie down.

He was doubled forward as he sat, his ribs folding over each other like an old buggy top, and it was with much difficulty that he could get his breath. I felt sorry for the old fellow, went to work with a piece of large rope, fastened to the joist overhead, brought down around under his arms as he sat in his chair; and applying just sufficient tension on the rope to open up and expand his chest to the natural pitch, thus suspending about half the weight on his body and removing the pressure from his lungs. Relief was instantaneous. The old man was soon asleep.

Lincecum was also something of a psychiatrist. When his daughter Sallie urged him to tell one of his sons how to cure himself, Gideon replied he could do nothing until the cause of his son's frustration was removed. In this case it was his son's wife. "How can a man be healthy when every plan and thought and proposition is upset by never ceasing opposition from an unlovely crack-brained idiot?"

Gideon once expressed his opinion of his profession: "I practiced medicine for 40 years. It's a humbug and does more harm to humanity than all the wars."

A NOTE ON SOURCES

Lincecum's life-long denunciation of medical practices of his day is found throughout his correspondence and writings. Lincecum's opinions and observations on the profession in this chapter include selections from his "Autobiography," his "Reminiscences," his diary of 1867, and his botanical notes.

Additional extractions have been made from numerous letters from Lincecum, including the following to: Dr. E. H. Dixon, New York City. n.d., but July, 1860; Dr. P. C. Gale, Memphis, Tennessee, October 17, 1860; Dr. W. A. Dunn, Winfield, Georgia, April 4, 1861; Mrs. E. S. Cook, Brenham, Texas, October 2, 1865; Dr. A[lva] Curtis, Cincinnati, Ohio, July 19, 1866; Sioux Doran, Houston, Texas, January 26, February 5, October 6, 1865, January 17, February 6, 1866; E. H. Cushing, Houston, Texas, n.d. but February, 1866; R. B. Hannay, Matamoros, Mexico, February 7, 1866; S. B. Buckley, Austin, Texas, January 21, 25, March 5, 1866; Parson Davis, no address, January 30, 1866; J. Lancaster, Navasota, Texas, January 31, 1866; and to Hiram H. Hill, Cincinnati, Ohio, November 21, 1865, January 1, 1866.

In opposition to a state medical bill proposed in 1866, Lincecum explained his stand and solicited support in letters, all written in 1866, to the following: Dr. A. G. ———[Lane], Lockhart, Texas, n.d.; Dr. ——— Stewart [Brenham], January 29; Dr. Ashbel Smith, Houston, Texas, January 16; Dr. J. C. Massie, Houston, Texas, January 20; Dr. S. C. Haynie, Austin, Texas, January 27; Dr. ——— Turner, Near Hog Eye, Texas, January 27, and to other doctors.

Character analyses from handwriting were made by Lincecum in letters written to Colonel S. D. Hay, Huntsville, Texas, October 26, 1861; A. G. Stobaugh, Honey Grove, Texas, April 11, 1860; Professor S. B. Buckley, Austin, Texas, June 10, 1860; Lemuel Hudson, Ferry Depot, Mississippi, November 29, 1860; R. S. Stuart, Bell County, Texas, October 6, 1861; and to others.

Free medical advice and lengthy directions for preparing prescriptions and for treatment and application are contained in Lincecum's letters to Colonel G. W. Carter, Chappell Hill, Texas, September 25, 1863; E. Durand, Philadelphia, Pennsylvania, March 12, 1861; Mrs. Rhoda Byler, Pin Oak, Texas, April 5, 1861; Mrs. Mary M. Hairgrove, Frelsburg, Texas, September 26, 1859; Carl Spencer, Brazoria, Texas, October 19, 1860; S. F. Burns, Houston, Texas, November 22, 1863; Mrs. E. H. Lewis, Anaqua, Texas, August 13, 1863; Reuben Davis, Aberdeen, Mississippi, February 13, 1867; J. V. Drake, LaGrange, Texas, May 9, 1864; P. P. Nichols, Meridian, Bosque County, Texas, December 1, 1864; Dr. J. F. Beasley, Gonzales County, Texas, February 18, 1865; J. K. Holland, Grimes County, Texas, May 12, 14, 1865; Dr. J. C. Massie, Houston, Texas, May 22, 1865; S. H. Parsons, Liberty, Texas, September 6, 1865; W. R. Baker, Houston, Texas, February 11, 1866; Emil Neumann, Brenham, Texas, May 31, July 3, 1866; and to others.

Further information on the dreadful yellow-fever epidemic of 1867 is found in Lincecum's diary for that year and in his letters to R. D. Haden, Cold Springs, Texas, September 7, 1867; R. D. Haden, Fireman's Hill, Texas, October 29, 1867; Oliver Fields, no address, September 12, 1867; George Durham, Austin, Texas, September 27, 1867; S. B. Buckley, Austin, Texas, October 21, 1867; and to James H. Caldwell, Fort Jessup, Louisiana, October 28, 1867.

Not quoted in this biography, but of possible interest to further study, is a lengthy letter in the Lincecum Papers from J. A. H. Cleveland, August 31, 1878 (probably to Sioux Doran) describing treatment of victims of the 1867 yellow fever epidemic.

A present-day evaluation of Gideon Lincecum has been made by Dr. P. I. Nixon, who wrote of him: ". . . Gideon Lincecum would have stood out in any civilization and almost in any capacity. . . . In his day and in his way, Dr. Gideon Lincecum was a great Texan" (*The Medical Story of Early Texas,* p. 384).

CHAPTER SIX

GIDEON
AND THE CHILDREN

It is a painful thing to know that the grand hope which I so
fondly cherished during the minor ages of my children has
ultimated in utter failure. Not one of them will leave a
mark that will not be obliterated by the first rude blast
that passes after they have left the mundane stage. GID

FROM HIS little patriarchy in Long Point, Texas, Gideon wrote in
1866 to an old friend: "We have lost four children, Nos. 1, 2, 3,
and 13 are dead; balance are all near and are going well enough. . . .
I used to say to you that I should never be able to bring myself into
notice, but that I hoped to shine forth in my posterity."

Gideon was rich in progeny but none of his sons and daughters
possessed personalities as sparkling as his. He and Sarah Bryan were
parents of thirteen children, all born before they came to Texas. The
children, in order of their births, were Lycurgus, Lysander M., Martha
Ann Elizabeth, Leonidas L., Leander W. C., Mary Catherine, Lachaon
Joseph, Lucullus Garland, Leonora, Cassandra, Sarah Matilde, Lysander Rezin, and Lucifer Hezekiah.

Martha Ann Elizabeth died in Columbus, Mississippi, at the age of
seventeen months. The first Lysander died in Mississippi in 1832.
Gideon once explained his death: "I, with the assistance of another
poison doctor, while I was practicing the old school of medicine, killed

III. THE FAMILY OF GIDEON LINCECUM

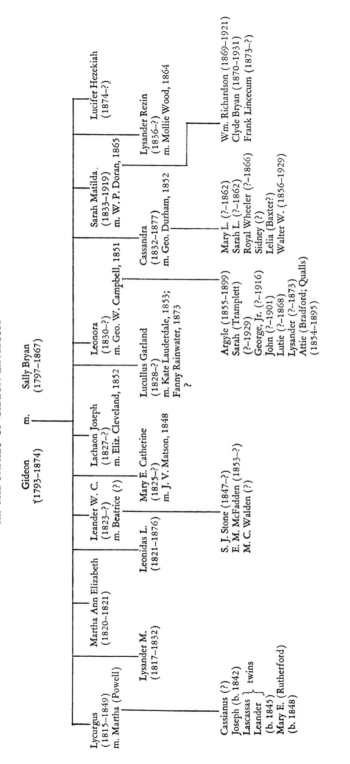

Gideon (1793–1874) m. Sally Bryan (1797–1867)

Lycurgus (1815–1849) m. Martha (Powell)
  Lysander M. (1817–1832)

Martha Ann Elizabeth (1820–1821)
  Leonidas L. (1821–1876)
    Cassianus (?)
    Joseph (b. 1842)
    Lascassas } twins
    Leander (b. 1845)
    Mary E. (Rutherford) (b. 1848)

Leander W. C. (1823–?) m. Beatrice (?)
  Mary E. Catherine (1825–?) m. J. V. Matson, 1848
    S. J. Stone (1847–?)
    E. M. McFadden (1853–?)
    M. C. Walden (?)

Lachaon Joseph (1827–?) m. Eliz. Cleveland, 1852
  Lucullus Garland (1828–?) m. Kate Lauderdale, 1853; Fanny Rainwater, 1873
    ?
      Argyle (1855–1899)
      Sarah (Tramplett) (?–1929)
      George, Jr. (?–1916)
      John (?–1901)
      Lutie (?–1868)
      Lysander (?–1873)
      Attie (Bradford; Qualls) (1854–1895)

Leonora (1830–?) m. Geo. W. Campbell, 1851
  Cassandra (1832–1877) m. Geo. Durham, 1852
    Mary L. (?–1862)
    Sarah L. (?–1862)
    Royal Wheeler (?–1866)
    Sidney (?)
    Lelia (Baxter?)
    Walter W. (1856–1929)

Sarah Matilda (1833–1919) m. W. P. Doran, 1865
  Lysander Rezin (1836–?) m. Mollie Wood, 1864
    Wm. Richardson (1869–1921)
    Clyde Bryan (1870–1931)
    Frank Lincecum (1873–?)

Lucifer Hezekiah (1874–?)

one of my children, fourteen years old, by administering the tobacco smoke injection."

The thirteenth child, Lucifer Hezekiah, was born on October 18, 1847, and on that day Gideon noted: "Born on the 64th year of American Independence. May the boy and the country ever remain free and independent." One wonders if Gideon's strange sense of humor was at work when he belatedly bestowed his father's name on one of his sons and prefaced it with the name of the fallen archangel. It is likely, however, that he was merely continuing the alliteration of the letter *L* in his sons' names, and named his last son for Lucifer, the Sardinian prelate, and not Satan. Gideon's terse statement that No. 13 was dead is the only reference to this unluckily numbered and oddly named child. The family *Bible* in which Sarah Lincecum carefully recorded the births and deaths of her children and grandchildren, cannot be located. It reportedly was given by a descendant to a Galveston, Texas, minister.

Most of the children were born in Cotton Gin Port. When the top six were old enough to go to school, Gideon bought a house in Columbus, Mississippi, where he sent them, with their mother, to be educated, while he remained in Cotton Gin Port to continue the practice he had established as a doctor.

At the end of six months he went over to Columbus to see what progress the children had made. He expected great things of them, as they were all "sprightly minded." They clamored around him excitedly chattering about all the interesting things Columbus had to offer—shows, races, fights, shootings, dances, and parties. Gideon questioned them about geography, history, and arithmetic. Their answers were vague and evasive.

"What is the longest river in the United States?"
"We didn't study that, we just study geography."
"What kind of history do you study?"
"Oh, it's just history."

Gideon suggested they ask each other questions, one of them acting the part of the teacher. They brightened at this suggestion, eager to show their newly acquired knowledge.

"Who was the first man?"
"Adam."
"Who slew his brother?"
"Cain."
"Who was the hairy man?"
"Esau."

Gideon was appalled at this catechism.

I had strained every financial nerve in getting a house at Columbus for them and had exerted my utmost powers to furnish provisions, clothing, etc., to keep them comfortable, and from the oft-repeated high reputation given the teachers in the newspapers I had hoped that I should experience the gratification of seeing signs of progress in my children. I was overwhelmed with disappointment. I felt like the whole world was a sham. My children, after six months' constant attendance at that highly praised institution could answer no question of use; but they could tell me *who was the hairy man*!

Before the day was over, Gideon peremptorily ordered them all back to Cotton Gin Port. They did not remain there long. Gideon presently moved his practice to Columbus, where his children returned to school and quickly adapted themselves to city life.

The advance of civilization, which had long been choking Gideon, was greatly evident in his children's behavior.

My children were beginning to marry off and they seemed to think of nothing but frolicking. The boys drank and dressed extravagantly and the girls dressed and danced inimitably. They spent from three to five thousand dollars a year and seemed to act as though the source from which the money came was inexhaustible. I could not get them to set their minds on any kind of business. Parties and dancing schools, shopping and "charge it to Poppa" were all they seemed to care for. The entire community of young people were similar in their habits. To remain and let them marry their equals I could plainly see would terminate in the most abject poverty and wretchedness. So I determined to carry them to a country where the surroundings and conditions would be more promising. This is the untold cause of my breaking up so abruptly the lucrative business in Columbus.

Lincecum liquidated all his Mississippi property and collected as many outstanding due bills as possible. He had decided on Texas, a three-year-old state of the Union, as the proper place for his family.

The oldest son, Lycurgus, then thirty-three, was in charge of a wagon train taking the overland route to Texas. The wagons carried the household goods, Gideon's large collection of fossils and bones, and $6,000 worth of medical supplies. With the caravan were ten slaves and ten extra horses; Lycurgus' wife, Martha, and their four children; and Leander, the third son. The trip was started in 1847, almost a year before Gideon's departure from Columbus.

On March 31, 1848, Gideon, his wife, Sarah, the remaining children, Gideon's mother, and ten additional slaves left Columbus on the Tombigbee River steamboat, New Era—Joseph Estes, captain—for Mobile, Alabama. Many years after his departure from Columbus, Gideon recalled: "Memory's pictures last longer than the objects they picture. My letters from Columbus tell me very few of the good people and friends who lined the shore the day we parted are now living; and while I write, undying memory holds up in vivid colors all the lineaments portrayed in that final sad separation."

The Lincecums reached Mobile on the third day and there transferred to another steamboat for New Orleans. There they were met by Gideon's brother Grant and his nephew John who lived in Catahaula Parish, Louisiana, where Grandmother Miriam's relatives, the Bowies, had settled in 1802 after leaving Georgia. The elderly Mrs. Lincecum and a devoted slave, Lewis, who afterwards took the surname of Lincecum, stopped in Louisiana with Grant Lincecum. Mrs. Lincecum died there the following month. Lewis, Gideon's age and a childhood playmate, after the Civil War went to Dallas, Texas, from where he corresponded with Gideon.

Gideon's family boarded the steamboat Palmetto at New Orleans for Galveston, Texas, where they arrived April 8, 1848. Three days later they were in Houston, united with Lycurgus and Leander. In six wagons they started across the prairie to Long Point, in Washington County, arriving April 22, Gideon's fifty-fifth birthday. The land he had marked thirteen years before was available. Gideon paid for it in gold and immediately started building a house.[1]

---

[1] Lincecum's assertion that he purchased Long Point land from Moses Austin Bryan, who had inherited it from Stephen F. Austin, his uncle, was doubted because Bryan was not included in Austin's will. I am indebted to Dr. Andrew Forest Muir, of Rice University, for the following information: "According to a deed from Emily M. Perry, legatee, and James F. Perry, executor, to Moses Austin Bryan, dated 14 March,

Washington County is in a section of the vast area of Texas which was settled early in the state's history as part of the original Stephen F. Austin's grant. On his trip to Texas in the colonial days of 1835, Lincecum had looked longingly at the beautiful prairie land in southeast Texas. The fertility of the black prairie soil, the post-oak belt crossing the land, the Brazos River on the east, the Colorado River southwest, and the not-too-distant Gulf of Mexico indicated to Gideon that it was a good place for farming, grazing, fishing, hunting, and pleasant living. Many small creeks drained the county—New Years, Yegua, Caney, Jackson, Rocky, Boggy, Peach, Mill, Indian, Woodward, and others. The area had changed greatly since the Mexican colonial days of Gideon's first visit. From a Mexican colony Texas had been a short-lived Republic and now was attempting to conform to its recently acquired statehood. But Washington County still retained some of the characteristics Gideon sought on a frontier, and close at hand were unmapped and almost unknown lands still inhabited by Indians where few white men dared to go.

Lincecum was equally attracted by the cultural opportunities, rare on a frontier, offered in Washington County and the near-by county of Fayette. He did not, as did many others, come to Texas seeking a fortune. From Mississippi he brought adequate worldly goods and gold to provide comfort and meet his family's needs. He wanted no more than that, and the pursuit of money had no place in his plans.

1837, and of record in Deed Records of Washington County, Texas, (Mss. in County Clerk's office, Courthouse, Brenham) D, 189–192, Stephen F. Austin's will of 19 April, 1833, contained a codicil, 8 October, 1835, in which he left Bryan the whole of League No. 5 on the La Bahía Road in Clokey's settlement (the league next to the Stephen F. Austin league, on the west, was granted to one Clokey). I had not known of this codicil and have not seen it."

On November 9, 1848, M. Austin Bryan for $1,371.00 conveyed to Gideon Lincecum the northeast corner of League No. 5, containing 1,828 acres (Deed Records, Washington County, H, 355–356). The Lincecum land was disposed of, in differing lots and acreages and over a period of time until Gideon's death, to the following (Deed Records, Washington County): Wayne S. Bishop, M, 19, 38; A. M. Dodd, M, 250; O. A. McGinnis and J. A. Denson, M, 583; J. W. Lynn, O, 533; Leonora Campbell, O, 591, U, 113, Vol. I, p. 231; Phillip Cronin, P, 181; Frederick W. Hegerman, P, 308–309; John Wilson, P, 603; Mary J. Rutherford, S, 122, U, 175, V, 46; W. J. Snelen, T, 268; R. S. Epperson, T, 439; E. J. Wood, T, 476; Henry Woods, T, 489; L. J. Lincecum, U, 80; L. W. Lincecum, U, 81; E. C. Lincecum, U, 83; L. W. C. Lincecum, U, 272; L. L. Lincecum, U, 288–289; L. R. Lincecum, U, 290; Sarah L. Doran, U, 378; Cassandra Durham, U, 519; Mary Matson, V, 57, W, 111; E. J. Neinast, V, 199; and G. W. Gentry, Vol. 4, p. 21.

Washington County offered him a refuge in his retirement. Here on his 1,828 acres of land, on an uncrowded frontier, were breathing space and freedom and, at the same time, intellectual companionship when he desired it. Lincecum planned to devote the remainder of his lifetime to a leisurely study of the natural sciences with the whole of Texas as his field laboratory. He made a token gesture of entering medical practice, announcing in a handbill, his availability as a botanic doctor, but that was intended primarily to introduce his doctor sons to Washington County and establish their practice. Except for experimenting and puttering, Gideon was free of farm work, which was performed by slaves brought with him from Columbus.

In Washington County, as a crumbling monument there today states, a nation was born. By the time Gideon arrived the original 1836 county seat had been moved from the historic old town of Washington-on-the Brazos to Brenham.

Brenham is in the center of the county, surrounded by rolling and partly timbered land producing cotton, corn, cattle, and hogs. Here the Giddings practiced law and operated stage and mail lines; the Shepards practiced law and ran for political offices; John Sayles taught school, practiced law, and wrote law books; the Bassetts established the first bank.

From Brenham, spokelike, roads led to all important settlements in the county. Ten miles east, is Chappell Hill, named for Robert Chappell, who settled there in 1841, and where presently were established Chappell Hill Female Institute and Soule University. Jacob Haller operated a stage coach inn there for the comfort of passengers on the Houston-Austin line.

Counterclockwise from Chappell Hill, and twenty miles from Brenham, is old Washington-on-the Brazos. A ferry on the river in 1825 was the beginning of a heavy traffic in Texas cotton and other products. Visiting missionaries found it a wicked town. The magistrate held court on the Sabbath and not a single professor of religion could be found in the town when Dr. Daniel Baker, Presbyterian missionary, arrived in 1838. The Reverend Robert Alexander, a Methodist there before him, had met with little success. He found the citizens "not at all religiously inclined and some . . . exceedingly wicked." Perhaps it was the memory of the laughing corpse that ultimately brought about a religious revival. At one of the mock prayer meetings, where the "recklessly wicked" Washingtonians burlesqued the many missionaries, a pistol was discharged accidentally, so it was said, killing one of the laughing spectators. Death was so sudden that the victim died laughing, and the laugh frozen on the face of the corpse was a shocking and sobering experience to some of the mourners.

Old Washington was laid out in 1835 by Dr. Asa Hoxey of Mobile, Alabama. Soon afterwards the Reverend Anderson Buffington, a Baptist preacher, arrived and started a sawmill and a newspaper called the *Tarantula*. It was here that the Texas Declaration of Independence and the Texas Constitution were drafted, the Texas Congress was assembled, the Texas peace treaty with Mexico was at last concluded, and annexation to the United States was worked out. The insignificant raw little town was visited by most prominent and notorious Texans of those days and by almost every foreign visitor who came for a brief glimpse of Texas. At Washington and near-by Barrington, the plantation of Anson Jones, a suicidal wanderer who drifted to Texas and became the last President of the Republic, the affairs of state were conducted from 1844 to 1846.

South around the circle, twelve miles north of Brenham, is Independence, the Baptist stronghold, in 1824 known as Cole's Settlement. Here was the beginning of Baylor University and its female equivalent. Sam Houston lived here for a while, near his strong-minded mother-in-law, Nancy Lea, pillar of the Baptist church established in 1839. Margaret Lea, Houston's equally strong-minded wife, persuaded him to conversion, and Rufus C. Burleson, second president of Baylor, had the honor of immersing the Big Drunk in nearby Rocky Creek. Independence was the home of Dr. Harry Lea Graves, first president of Baylor, and Moses Austin Bryan, the son of Stephen F. Austin's sister, Emily Perry.

On around the circle, eleven miles from Brenham, is Gay Hill, settled in the 1830's and named for Thomas Gay and W. C. Hill, two early settlers. Later it was the home of the Live Oak Female Seminary owned by James Weston Miller.

Still leftward around the circle, eleven miles from Brenham, was Long Point, where Gideon lived on his plantation, Mount Olympus. It was on a long point of high ground projecting northward and overlooking the valley of Yegua Creek. Toward the end of the point is a triangle of live-oak trees, all that remains today to indicate the location of Long Point.

Farther on, a few miles from Long Point and eleven miles from Brenham, is Burton, on Indian Creek, named for John H. Burton, where the Grocher family settled in 1838.

Inside and outside the periphery were other settlements: Jacksonville, three miles north of Chappell Hill, named for Terrell Jackson; Mustang, three miles east of Brenham, where Mabry (Mustang) Gray established a trading post and where William B. Travis lived and practiced law; Rock Island, on the west side of the Brazos River, named by Amos Gates, who came to Texas in 1821 with his father and four brothers, and chosen as the site for the Rock Island Academy, established in 1837; Mount Vernon Spring, six miles northwest of Brenham, laid out in 1841 by John Stamps, contractor and judge, and briefly the county seat; Glenblythe, the baronial plantation-settlement of the Scotchman Thomas Affleck, which was 7.5 miles northwest of Brenham; Union Hill, three miles northwest of Brenham, originally the Kerr Settlement, where Mrs. Lucy Kerr's brother, Alexander Thomson, held the first Methodist meeting in Texas, and where an early Indian massacre occurred; Tiger Point, six miles southwest of Brenham, where the Hensleys and Swishers lived; Turkey Creek, six miles east of Brenham, home of the Guyton family; Ayers, near Long Point, named for David Ayers; Evergreen on Waco Spring, where the Tonkawa and Waco Indians once had a savage battle; Hidalgo on a Brazos River bluff, where Dr. W. T. LeGrand collected fossils and where Dr. John G. Allen lived; Montville, where a girls' boarding school was opened in 1835 by Lydia Ann McHenry in the home of Mrs. David Ayers; Cedar Hill, where lived Henry Eichholt, the first of many Germans to settle the county; Berlin, the home of Valentine Hoffman; and Hickory Point, west of Independence, where Captain Horatio Chriesman once lived and offered his acreage as site for the capital of the Republic.

One need not go to Brenham to reach these various points. Travel between the outlying settlements, except in periods of high water, was across prairies, through post oak groves, and down numerous seasonally dry creek beds.

When Gideon arrived in Washington County the population was about 4,000, of which over half were slaves. Southern planters followed the original colonists after the Texas Revolution, bringing with them their regional customs and ways. The county had more of the feeling and character of the old South than of the new West.[2]

Lincecum became a colorful and influential citizen of the county. His influence was quiet, steady, and daily; to some it was insidious but to others, particularly to the younger citizens who sought him out, the effect was astonishingly beneficial and stimulating. Utterly unconcerned with public opinion, he was stubbornly resistant to civilization's insistence on conformity and was more pleased than offended when he was called "that old infidel Gid Lincecum."[3]

The history of Texas is rich in the lives of men who once called Washington County home—men whose power and personality determined the state's political destiny; missionaries of the faith whose power of persuasion was no less potent than that of the politicians; fighting men whose valor and love for battle made their cause appear right and glorious; slaves who rose to unexpected greatness; scientists who worked in the darkness of ignorance, indifference, and mockery; ruthless and greedy men who became giants among the quiet little gnomes now forgotten; men who became part of Texas folklore; sincere men of vision.

Even in this company Lincecum was an outstanding personality. His birdwatching, bug collecting and ant crawling made him a person of derision among some of the uninitiated, but his neighbors knew him to be a man of inherent honor with a deep regard for the dignity and rights of his fellow men, and scrupulously honest in his dealings with them.

The absence of blacksmiths and mechanics in the neighborhood

[2] Washington County sketch compiled from scattered data found in the *Texas Almanac,* (1854–1962/3); John M. Swisher, "Washington County: Remembrances of Texas and Texas People," *American Sketch Book,* IV (1879), pp. 131–136; D. W. C. Baker, *A Texas Scrap Book* (reprint of 1875 edition, by the Steck Company, Austin, Texas, 1936). Charles F. Schmidt, *History of Washington County* (San Antonio, Naylor Company, 1949); Mrs. R. E. Pennington, *The History of Brenham and Washington County* (Houston, Standard Printing and Lithographing Co., 1915).

[3] Soule Kirkpatrick of Cotton Gin Port, Mississippi, "an old gentleman of high character who was a devout Methodist" characterized Lincecum as "that old infidel, Gid Lincecum" (Dr. Samuel Wood Geiser, *Naturalist of the Frontier* [Dallas, Texas, Southern Methodist University Press, 1937], pp. 253–274).

where Gideon settled suggested to him the need for a "mechanical village," and he offered to deed half an acre to any mechanic who would settle there. The only condition imposed was prohibition of the sale of intoxicants. There were no immediate takers. The mechanics who came to investigate his offer indignantly protested and declared they would not sell their liberty for a league of the best land in Texas. Gideon, confronted with other frontiersmen as jealous of their liberty as he, chided them for calling liquor liberty. Eventually, some accepted, and at one time his acreage at Long Point had four stores and cabinet, smith, and potter shops.

Lincecum found ministers more difficult to deal with than mechanics, but far less liberty-loving. He agreed to give land for a church provided he had a hand in decorating the structure. This was acceptable to the preachers until they learned that his plan for "ornamentation" called for an arch spanning the main entrance and bearing the words "Free Discussion" in letters eighteen inches high. During the twenty years Gideon lived in Long Point there was no church, a deficiency which proved somewhat of an inconvenience when all his daughters had to go to Brenham to be married.

The marriages came fast.[4]

The first Lincecum marriage recorded in Washington County is that of Leander W. C. Lincecum, the fourth son. He was married to Miss S. J. Stone, July 20, 1847, by John P. Dupuy, justice of the peace, after having previously married a girl named Beatrice in Columbus, Mississippi. A touch of mystery in the Lincecum Papers is provided by a small account book for 1846 and 1847 expenses and purchases of the couple, paid for by Gideon. The book is labeled "Beatrice's Affairs— Keep this book entirely secret on that depends much." Following the itemized account is an unaddressed letter in Gideon's handwriting dated January 31, 1847, giving instructions for the collection of notes due and advising against the incurring of debts and any pretension to prosperity. It obviously was intended for Leander. Gideon reported to a friend in 1865 that Leander "has married his third wife and is living 15 miles on the Yegua above Long Point and has an extensive practice in a tolerable poor community. . . . What is more uncommon still, has

⁴ Marriage Records, Washington County, Texas, MSS in County Clerk's office, Courthouse, Brenham, Vols. 1–4.

become a sober, respectable man, not having been intoxicated since some time previous to the war." Leander's third wife was E. M. McFaddin, whom he married on July 21, 1853, J. R. Nunn, magistrate, officiating. The Marriage Records (Vol. 3, p. 37) also record the marriage of Leander Lincecum to M. C. Walden, September 18, 1867, Thomas Alford, justice of the peace officiating. This, however, could have been Lycurgus' son, Leander. During the early Civil War period Leander was detailed as a physician to remain in Washington County and care for the sick in the families of absent soldiers, but in 1863, at the age of forty-one, he enlisted as a private under Captain James R. Hines.[5]

Mary, the oldest daughter, and James V. Matson were married on October 5, 1848, the Reverend David Fisher, officiating. Matson, as Gideon once described him, was a "money-making man." He was a farmer and large slaveholder and his prosperity and property increased with the years. At one time he and Gideon were partners in a grain mill.

James and his brother, Richard, were sons of a Captain Matson who had brought his family to Washington County from Missouri in 1839. The Matsons settled near Burton on land purchased from Asa Mitchell, who shortly thereafter killed Captain Matson.[6] After Matson's death his widow married Captain E. M. Fuller.

James V. Matson bought 2,000 acres of the Long Point tract when Lincecum purchased his land. According to Lincecum, "Matson paid for his 2000 acres one fitified negro girl and the rest in Mexican ponies, at the same rate per acre that I paid." Captain and Mrs. Fuller died a few weeks apart in November, 1857. The Matson sons inherited their considerable property, and when Richard was killed in the Civil War, James inherited his brother's share. Lincecum never wholeheartedly approved of this son-in-law and, following a serious disagreement in 1860 over a slave, his hostility grew into bitter hatred, an emotion rare with Lincecum. Matson was the only person who ever felt the full force of Lincecum's venom. Gideon once confessed; "I shall hate to die with as bad feelings as I entertain against that man." When Lincecum divided his Long Point land among his children, Mary was left

---

[5] Confederate War Records, State Archives, Austin.
[6] Swisher, "Washington County," p. 133.

out. No deed was made to her, he explained, because of her "avaricious, plundering, trespassing, sordid-minded consort." He accused Matson of robbing the Lincecum land of valuable timbers and withholding earnings from the mill. The result was the permanent estrangement of his daughter, Mary. Twenty-three years after Mary's marriage Gideon wrote: "Damn Jim Matson. He robbed and withheld my just rights and made me poor now in my period of feeble old age." He was once delighted with news that Matson had trichinosis. "I hope he may be smitten with hemorrhoids and worms that shall loosen the flesh from his bones while he is yet alive."

Lycurgus, the first born, was the first of numerous Lincecums to be buried in Washington County. He died on February 3, 1849. Eleven years after his death Gideon was amazed to receive a letter from J. H. H. Woodward, a Houston lawyer, inquiring about Lycurgus' death in the Mexican War and mentioning the possibility that his widow and children were eligible for a pension. Gideon explained that his son enlisted in a Texas group, was discharged and paid off in Monterrey, Mexico, in August, 1847, and died two years later in Long Point. He served, Gideon recalled, with a "Captain McCullough or some such name."[7]

Gideon wrote Woodward:

I had not moved to Texas then. Col. John W. Dancy can tell all about it.[8] He resides near LaGrange. My son, from the heavy service and exposure in guarding a train of wagons on their route from Laredo to Monterrey, contracted what he denominated the Mexican bowel complaint, was never well and of which complaint he finally died. Except the pay he received at Monterrey when he was discharged I have never heard of his getting anything. He left five children who are all living. His widow married John Powell of

---

[7] Ben McCulloch, leader of a Texas Ranger spy group in the United States-Mexican War, was later a U.S. marshal, and a brigadier general in the Confederate Army. He was killed in the battle of Elk Horn Tavern, Arkansas, March 7, 1862, and buried with military honors in the Austin City Cemetery, April 10 (Victor M. Rose, *The Life and Services of Gen. Ben McCulloch* [facsimile of original ed. 1888, Austin, Texas, the Steck Company, 1958]).

[8] Colonel John Winfield Scott Dancy (1810–1866) served in the Mexican War as commander of a regiment raised by Ben McCulloch (*Handbook of Texas,* I, 463). Dancy died in 1866, not 1856, as given in the *Handbook* (Tombstone, Old City Cemetery, LaGrange). Dancy and Lincecum became good friends.

this county.[9] The children are scattered about and will not be able to procure a common school education.

The Mexican War records showed, according to Woodward, that Lycurgus Lincecum was on the company rolls of Captain Evans and was killed in action on December 22, 1847.[10] Colonel Dancy cleared the situation, remembering that Lycurgus became ill after arriving at Monterrey with the Texas volunteers and that he hired a substitute to answer his name for the remainder of his term. The unknown substitute was killed in battle.

Lycurgus' children were Cassianus, Joseph, the twins Lascassas and Leander, all born in Mississippi, and Mary Eliza, born in Washington, Texas. Lycurgus' sons, known as Cass, Jo, Lass, and Andy, all served in the Civil War. At one time, when Jo lived with the William J. Busters in Chappell Hill, Gideon wrote him that he was "fortunate to be an inmate of so good and respected a family" and urged him to protect his good name and reputation and value them throughout his life.

The second Lincecum daughter, Leonora, married George W. Campbell, a notary of Washington County, on July 5, 1851, the Reverend Fisher officiating. Campbell was from Columbus, Mississippi, where he met and fell in love with Leonora. When Gideon moved his family to Texas, Campbell followed.

Campbell was captain of Co. F, 5th Regiment, Texas Mounted Volunteers under Colonel Thomas Green of General Henry Hopkins Sibley's New Mexican Brigade. Cassianus and Joseph, Lycurgus' two oldest boys, were in his company, as were many other Washington County boys. It was mustered September 5, 1861. At this time Campbell was thirty years old and the father of seven children. He survived

[9] John A. Powell and Mrs. Martha Lincecum were married on December 28, 1855, J. G. Thomas, magistrate, officiating (Marriage Records, Washington County, Texas, Vol. 1, p. 25).

[10] Moses Evans, who served in McCulloch's spy company during the Mexican War, later became part of Texas folklore because of his association with the wild woman of the Navidad (See J. Frank Dobie, *Tales of Old-Time Texas* [Boston and Toronto, Little, Brown and Company, 1928], pp. 27–33). Lincecum refers a number of times to Evans and in a letter to J. V. Drake, of LaGrange, Texas, wrote: "We are making, as poor Mose Evans used to say, 'good licks' at the infernal Yankees in the Trans-Mississippi these times."

the battles of New Mexico and the cruel and exhausting retreat to Texas, but was too ill and dejected to continue with Green's regiment. Gideon recorded his death: "George Campbell, after returning from the Arizona campaign, drank himself to death. He dropped dead in a doggery in Brenham, leaving his wife and seven children poorly provided for." Gideon was devoted to Leonora, but his fondness for her seven children was qualified, as he told a friend, because though they were "well enough looking, [they were] tipped off with a little too much Campbell."

Cassandra, the third daughter, was married to George J. Durham, an Englishman of Austin, Texas, on December 23, 1852. The Reverend Fisher again officiated. This marriage pleased Gideon. He and Durham had been drawn together through a mutual interest in ornithology and grape culture and were friends before Durham met Cassandra.

Durham was born in 1820 in Norwich, England, and came to Texas from New Jersey with his parents in 1837. The next year, while Houston was the capital of the Republic, he was chief clerk in the comptroller's office. In 1839 he went with the government to Austin in the same capacity. In 1842, when the Mexican Army again threatened Texas, and Houston ordered the Archives removed to Houston, Durham assisted in keeping them in Austin.[11]

Durham holds something of a record in Texas history, having held a political job during the administration of every president and governor until after the Civil War. He was mayor of Austin in 1852. It is a pity he did not keep a diary. Although he frequently defied Houston, as in the Archives War, Durham apparently was well regarded by the Governor. Houston told the 1861 extra session of the state Legislature that Durham had declined an assignment the previous November as courier to Washington to take muster rolls and vouchers of U.S. troops stationed in Texas. Documents of expenditures of the Eighth Legislative session are signed by Durham as chief clerk and acting comptroller. There is no record that Durham made the trip to Washington.[12] He was one of the signers of the petition for a people's secession convention. When Captain B. F. Carter organized the Austin Light

[11] *Handbook of Texas,* Vol. I, p. 527.
[12] *Journal of the House* (1861), Special Session, pp. 18–19.

Brigade, April 24, 1861, Durham enlisted as orderly sergeant and with its seventy-five members left for San Antonio; but he was called back to Austin as state war tax collector for the Confederacy. Durham was considered as candidate for state treasurer on the 1866 coalition ticket headed by James Webb Throckmorton, but Lieutenant Colonel Mart H. Royston of Terry's Texas Rangers, "a strong Union man" and Mrs. Sam Houston's nephew, was the final choice.[13] Throckmorton, after his election, gave Durham a job as an accountant to examine Civil War Military Board records.

Durham was a talented ornithologist, an authority on Texas grapes, and an excellent marksman. In 1854 he shot and instantly killed young William H. Cleveland, son of Captain J. T. Cleveland, in front of the Metropolitan Hotel in Austin. The shooting, which followed an angry exchange of words the previous day, occurred when Durham defended himself with a quick shot from his pistol, against Cleveland's attack with a walking cane. Justice Allen ruled it justifiable homicide.[14]

Among the Lincecum Papers are invitations from the Durham Austin residence on Pecan, now Sixth, and Guadalupe, to funerals of their daughters, Sarah Lincecum, at 4:00 P.M., Thursday, April 10, 1862, and Mary Leonora, at 4:00 P.M., Friday, April 11, 1862. An explanation of this long-ago tragedy is found in the diary of Amelia E. Barr, an Englishwoman who lived for a while in Texas and was well acquainted with the Durhams:

April 9, 1862: In the evening to Mrs. Durham's. Poor little Sally, whom I suckled for two months when her mother had fever, just dead of diphtheria.

April 10, 1862: Went to see Sally for the last time. It was Ben McCulloch's funeral also. The cemetery was crowded. When we got back from Sally's funeral her sister, Leonora, was dying. She breathed her last at five o'clock.[15]

[13] Claude Elliott, *Leathercoat* (San Antonio, Standard Printing Co., 1938), p. 121.

[14] *Texas State Gazette,* Austin, April 29, 1854, Vol. V, Col. 1, p. 252.

[15] April was a month of doom for the Durhams. A son, Royal Wheeler, named for Chief Justice Royal T. Wheeler, died on April 21, 1866; George Durham's father, George Durham, Sr.[?], died on April 10, 1866; George J. Durham died of typoid fever on April 10, 1869. Cassandra Durham died on April 18, 1877, at the age of fifty-three, of pneumonia, and was buried with her husband and children in Oakwood Cemetery, Austin, Texas (Tombstones, Durham family plot, Oakwood Cemetery, Austin, Texas; sexton's records).

Mrs. Barr's Scotch husband, Robert, was an auditor for the state from 1856 to 1866 and shared a desk with Durham. Mrs. Barr wrote of Austin society in 1856:

Its leaders were Mrs. Tom Green and Mrs. George Durham. . . . Mrs. Durham was the wife of George Durham, an Englishman from my own north country and an attaché of the comptroller's office. Robert was his associate and they were excellent friends. . . . The Durhams lived in a small log house on the road to the ferry. Everyone coming into town and every one going out of town passed Mrs. Durham's. Her sitting room was as entertaining as the local news in the weekly paper. There was no restraint in Mrs. Durham's company; people could be themselves without fear of criticism. She was not pretty, not stylish, not clever, not in the least fashionable, but she was the favorite of women who were all these things. There were no carpets on the floors and there was a bed in the room wherein her friends congregated. She did not go to entertainments and I never saw a cup of tea served in her house, yet she was the most popular woman in Austin, and not to be free of Mrs. Durham's primitive log house, was to be without the hallmark of the inner circle.[16]

George and Cassandra's son, Walter W. Durham, became a prominent Austin cotton buyer and named one of his sons for his father. Another son, Sidney J. Durham, wrote (August 6, 1895) his Aunt Sallie Doran that he was in New York with the Lillian Russell Comique Opera Company, studying voice with Madame Skinner, and had become a Christian Scientist.

Gideon's youngest daughter, Sarah Matilda, always called Sallie, was married to William P. Doran, a telegrapher and newspaper man, on December 10, 1865. The Reverend Fisher was present to officiate at the marriage of the fourth and last Lincecum daughter. Again the bridegroom was one of Gideon's friends. It was Doran who was responsible for the publication of many articles and letters by Gideon in Houston and Galveston papers.

Doran, known as "Sioux" because of a by-line he used for forty-one years as a writer for Texas newspapers, was born in Rochester, New York, May 3, 1836. His first newspaper job in Texas was with Eber

---

[16] Amelia E. Barr, *All The Days of My Life* (New York and London, D. Appleton), pp. 237–238.

Worthington Cave, publisher of the Nacogdoches, Texas, *Chronicle*. He was with the Houston *Telegraph* at the beginning of the Civil War; he enlisted as a private in John P. Austin's company of the Rio Grande in March, 1861; he was honorably discharged at Fort Brown from William Christian's company A, 2nd Regiment, Texas Volunteers, because of defective hearing. Despite this handicap Doran became a war correspondent for the *Telegraph*. In a note of November 19, 1862, E. H. Cushing, publisher, directed Doran to go to Galveston and report "whatever transpires there worthy of note while it is safe to stay there. If you can purchase New Orleans or northern papers, do so at any cost." With the rank of major, Doran reported the battles of Shiloh, Vicksburg, and Galveston. One of his published accounts is that of the Battle of Sabine Pass. Doran's 1862 passes into Vicksburg and Jackson are among the Lincecum Papers. At other times Doran was editor of the Houston *Evening Star* and correspondent for the Galveston and Dallas *News*. He died on November 25, 1901, and Sallie Doran died on April 11, 1919. They had three sons—Willard Richardson, Clyde Bryan, and Frank Lincecum Doran.

Sallie was the darling of Gideon's heart. When she was a girl he taught her to play the violin and the piano, and after the family concerts were broken up by marriages, Gideon and Sallie played nightly duets in the parlor of their Long Point home. The audience was usually made up of neighbors, but, if none was present, Sarah Lincecum rocked in her chair by the fireplace and listened with constant delight as she knitted for her ever-increasing grandchildren. Sallie was with her parents on their long travels through Texas and assisted Gideon in making his extensive collection of Texas botanical specimens.

Sallie walked with him in the woods and from him learned about plants, rocks, birds, and wildlife. She enjoyed the companionship of her father and showed such an obvious reluctance to be married that Gideon was convinced she never would. She rejected numerous suitors. Even after meeting Doran she delayed her marriage a number of years to remain with her ailing mother, and a few months after her wedding returned to the old Long Point homestead to care for Sarah when her condition became critical.

Gideon educated all his children, "male and female," to be doctors, trained all of them in the botanic method. All of his sons, at times, practiced.

Leonidas, or Lon, the second son, studied botanic medicine with Dr. Alva Curtis in Cincinnati in 1844. He shared Gideon's enthusiasm for climatology and meteorology and assisted him with many projects in these fields. The Long Point Democrats, in an effort to break the power of the "old line" county politicians, named Leonidas their candidate in 1859 for the state Legislature, but he was defeated. During the Civil War he was war tax collector for Washington County but in the last months of the war joined his brothers in the Confederate Army of the Rio Grande.

Lucullus Garland, called Cul, was a practicing physician throughout his lifetime. He married Kate Lauderdale, daughter of an old family friend from Mississippi, in 1853, and practiced in Washington County until he moved to Lampasas.

Lucullus was detailed in Washington County during the war to care for families of soldiers; but on January 5, 1863, he enlisted at Brenham and became a second corporal under Captain L. N. Halbert, Company G, 23rd Brigade, commanded by Brigadier General John Sayles.[17] After the death of his first wife he married Fanny Rainwater, of Washington County, July 13, 1873, and later married a third time.

Lucullus had two notable doctor sons. John Louis Lincecum, a graduate of the University of Kentucky, practiced in Victoria, Texas and was the father of Mrs. Lucille L. Reed, of Goliad, and the grandfather of Mrs. Willie Reed Rowe, Fort Stockton, well-known Texas artist. Lucullus' younger son, Dr. Addison Lincecum, born in Long Point on April, 1874, seven months before Gideon died, is alive at this writing. There is much of the old Gid in him. He studied at Baylor and Texas University medical schools, working his way through medical school as an engineer on trains transporting granite blocks for Galveston jetties. He graduated in 1903, and acquired six additional medical diplomas. Dr. Addison was elected a vice president of the Texas Medical Association in 1912; he went to Cuba as a physician with Roosevelt's Rough Riders; he was commissioned a Texas Ranger in 1917; he served as captain with the 36th Division in World War I. In civilian life he served on the state

---

[17] Confederate War Records, State Archives, Austin.

board of health, investigating bubonic plague in Texas; and he was mayor of El Campo, Texas, where he became a public institution: developing a long practice; serving as superintendent of a hospital and as postmaster; and conducting a weekly radio current-events forum.[18] Dr. Addison and Letha Gandy were married in 1897. They had three children: Mrs. Ruth Crosby of Houston, Addison (Bill) of Brazoria, and Barney, with whom the doctor lives in the century-old Gandy house deep in the sandy swamp lands out of Morales in Jackson County on the Gandy Bend Road. The Addison Lincecums are a happy, gay, hospitable people and their household is much as Gideon's must have been. All the Lincecums are musical. Dr. Addison was regarded as the champion fiddle player in El Campo.

By his third wife Dr. Lucullus G. had a daughter, Teresa, who won considerable fame as a singer, musician, and Broadway actress.[19]

Lachaon Joseph, known as Doc, was a practicing physician for a while but preferred farming. He married Elizabeth Cleveland, February 27, 1852, the Reverend R. H. Belvin, officiating. Lachaon was a beef contractor during the war, buying up beef cattle and driving them to the Confederate Army. At one time he swam 956 head across the Mississippi at Natchez. Later he enlisted at Camp Randle under Captain Thomas L. Scott.

Lysander, the youngest son, did not marry until 1864. He remained at home, even after his marriage, learned medicine from his father, and practiced in Long Point. Lysander attempted several times to enlist in the Confederate Army, but "his asthma was so bad none of them would let him stay and the poor fellow does his wheezing at home." But the shy Lysander made himself useful at home during the war—daily cutting firewood for his sister Leonora's house while her husband was away, consuming all Gideon's shots in killing partridges for his ailing mother, and running errands for war widows. He was finally accepted for duty in 1864 and joined John S. Ford's command on the Rio Grande. A few days before he left Long Point he married Mollie Wood, daughter of Gideon's old friend, Silas Wood. From the Rio Grande he wrote Gideon an account of John S. Ford's routing Federal troops at Brownsville, and reported that Lascassus and Le-

---

[18] El Campo *Leader-News*, March 16, 1960.
[19] Interview with Dr. Addison Lincecum.

ander, twin sons of Lycurgus, were with him and "both make very good soldiers, they don't care for anything but to eat, sleep and ride a horse."

Except for Cassandra in Austin, Gideon and Sarah were able to keep their brood together. Despite his often expressed disappointment in his children and his impatience with them, Gideon enjoyed the role of a patriarch. He foresaw future generations of Lincecums occupying his Long Point domain and he opposed any plans of his children to live elsewhere. Cassandra, who yearned to live in Long Point, and George and their children were frequent visitors from Austin, especially during grouse season. Gideon was happiest when he had all his children about him and would have kept them ever so. In 1860 his children and grandchildren numbered fifty (ultimately to reach sixty-seven) and he wrote to a friend: "The old lady has the bold hardihood to get them all together sometimes; and they represent all the types of the genus. It affords one of the finest opportunities for observation on human character from the meek imbecile to the superfine hell cat."

While the Lincecum sons were away during the Civil War, the Lincecum homestead was usually full of grandchildren. On one such occasion, Gideon noted:

I had been dining with and making observations on the cerebral developments of a detachment, 15 in number, of our brood of grand dears, males and females. They sat thickly crowded on both sides of our long table, all under eight, glittering eyes and greasy lips. I was thinking of the part they were to perform in life's drama in the deep, dark, dubious future. They—with their fat, ruddy faces, laughing eyes, flowing crops of coarse black hair—will have but few reasons to praise and bless their progenitors.

Looking back to his children's formative years, Lincecum realized he was greatly negligent in parental training:

I was not fit for domestic responsibility. I was too soft. The parent must harden himself towards the child. Show no mercy. Make the child feel and know that there is no chance for anything but honesty and truth. Above all, avoid promises and falsehoods. . . . Children are all born liars, rogues and full of dissimulation. The first thing to teach them is the rights of property. In the enforcement of this rule you cannot be too rigid. Until you have this first principle thoroughly established . . . it is almost useless to teach them other precepts. If, however, you succeed in this, you have laid a platform, a permanent stage upon which you may pile up all the just and righteous instructions you are capable of.

He discussed parenthood in a letter to Judge John A. Rutherford, Lamar, Texas, in which he also assured him there was no cause to worry about the Rutherford boys, Clinton and Calvert, while they were away from home. Gideon wrote:

If I can, I always keep the inferior types at home and encourage the superior ones to go out and familiarize themselves early as possible with the performers upon the stage with whom ultimately they must act a part in life's grand drama. The weak specimens are liable to be imposed on by justice-adoring society or commit depredations themselves on the community. Hence my care and effort to keep them around me. So long, however, as society continues to permit the badly developed types of the race to multiply themselves, so long will illshaped sinners be born and parents must grieve. . . . Society itself is not yet sufficiently unfolded to recognize the remedy for the diseases that are preying upon and disorganizing the moral lifestrings of its own body.

Convinced that he would never "shine forth" in his children, Gideon looked hopefully to his grandchildren. When Sallie's first son was born, Lincecum wrote her: "May his organs of self-reliance and honesty and truth be well cultivated and highly developed. Teach him intellectual courage, so that the love of money nor the fear of hell may never be sufficient to cause him to swerve from the truth."

But, discouraged at the offspring of his children's marriages, the arrival of a new family member seldom excited him. He once wrote a friend: "The families of Leander, Lachaon and Leonora have each increased . . . but as they produce only one young at a time there has been but little said about it."

Sallie frequently sought her father's advice on raising her sons, and when she told him that her second son cried too much, Gideon wrote:

Frank wants something that he can't make you understand. . . . There are many people in the world, preachers generally, who can't get the community to stand, drill and face about in accordance with their peculiar notions of propriety, and they quarrel and berate them from day to day. It may be so with children as well as adults. People never find out really what ails the preacher and they have to put up with his bleating as long as he lives.

You'll have to do the same with Frank if you can't find out the cause of his complaint.

There was another member of the Lincecum family, a member dear to Gideon's heart and much beloved by all the Lincecums. She was Aunt Polly, one of the slaves brought from Mississippi, who had been with the Lincecum family for fifty years. The Lincecum correspondence, back to Leonidas' letters as a schoolboy in 1844 when he sent Aunt Polly his love, reflects the affection they all felt for her. She was two years younger than Gideon and died shortly before he did "with her lamp all trimmed and supplied with oil, ready for the journey."

In his later years Gideon recalled his long illness and poverty in Mississippi and, referring to his dead wife, wrote:

. . . with what fortitude, patience and courage the dear *lost one* struggled and bravely bore up during that long seven years of disease and sore poverty. Aunt Polly, too, if a history was made out, would come in as a faithful aid, performing her part thoroughly during the disastrous period. I remember her faithful services with deepest gratitude. . . . Tell Aunt Polly to hold on. She and myself are all of our gang alive now that I know of. She will run a hundred.

Among the Lincecum Papers is an unsigned poem, bearing a notation: "Written for an aged family servant who had served in the family for fifty years." The note is signed by the initials, SLD:

> Farewell, Aunt Polly, I'll see you no more,
> Though together we have spent a long life;
> A stranger I go to a far distant shore,
> To escape from the coming bloody strife.
> Then let me go to that far sunny land,
> Where the coffee and sugar cane grow
> Where the banana and orange trees stand
> With the pineapples close by the door.

At the age of seventy-five Gideon made a candid confession to an old friend:

When I was a very young man I read Dr. Franklin's works. He advised early marriage and that advice, agreeing with unchecked and misdirected amativeness, it was an easy matter for me to fall in with the old sage's directions. Accordingly, I sought out a companion and was engineering the matrimonial machinery before I was 21 years of age. The result is ten families of grown-up men and women, with their children, numbering together 61. I do not repine or regret anything about it, but I cannot avoid the recollection of the fact that in rearing this numerous brood, who average only from ordinary to middling, I lost 38 years of a life that could have been better employed. For the world is as full as it can hold of precisely the same sort of folks and there was no use in adding my brood to the already overdone business.

If Gideon ever regretted his divine divergence from the common pattern of life, he never voiced it. Only once did he indicate remorse. He was eighty years old then and his sorrow was not for himself but for his children, none of whom inherited his ability to squeeze nectar from the dry dullness of every-day life. Lincecum, at the end of his long and full life, remembered the stares of surprise on the faces of his children when he frequently attempted to instruct them in the rudiments of successful, happy, peaceful living, and their inevitable exclamation of protest: "But pappa, you aren't like other people!"

A NOTE ON SOURCES

To obtain biographical data on Lincecum's sons and daughters from the material comprising the Lincecum Papers, it was necessary to pick out scraps of relevant information and to fit them into the numerous puzzling gaps. Much of the information came from other sources.

Accounts of childhood events are found in Lincecum's "Autobiography." Some scattered references to the adult years of the Lincecum offspring were gleaned from newsy letters to old friends.

Information from the Lincecum Papers used in Chapter 6 is largely from letters to Dr. A. G. Lane, Lockhart, Texas, October 7, 1863; James Matson, no address, May 28, 1860; Jo Lincecum, Chappell Hill, Texas, March 20, April 14, 1860; Dr. W. A. Dunn, Winfield, Georgia, June 19, September 11, 1861; Dr. R. P. Hallock, New York City, 21 [March 1859]; Judge John A. Rutherford, Honey Grove, Texas, n.d., but January, 1862; Dear Brother and Sister [D. Boon and Emily Moore], Castroville, February 18, 1862; George J. Durham, Austin, Texas, August 4, 1863; Mrs. E. H. Lewis, Anaqua, Texas, August 13, 1863; Dr. A. Weir, Harmony Hill, Texas, May 20, 1865, May 4,

1866; David S. Greer, Memphis, Tennessee, November 29, 1866; and to Dr. Spencer F. Baird, Washington, D.C., December 11, 1867.

Lycurgus Lincecum's U.S.-Mexican War activity is related in Gideon's letters to J. H. H. Woodward, Houston, Texas, June 13–July [?] 1859, June 29, 1860; Haywood Lincecum, Noxubee County, Mississippi, June 13, 1859; and to J. W. Dancy, LaGrange, Texas, July 3, 1859.

CHAPTER SEVEN

GIDEON
AND THE PURIFYING KNIFE

To beget and born children in the name of the Lord has not and cannot improve the intellectual developments of our species—it must be done scientifically and philosophically before there can be any intellectual and moral advancement.

GID

GIDEON DREAMED of a perfect world inhabited by a physically superb race of men and women, morally and intellectually perfect, who selectively reproduced for even higher attainment. From 1850 to 1859 he gave much thought to the improvement of the human race and arrived at the conclusion that sexual behavior was the stimulus for the evils of the world. He did not expect to make much headway in a program which could not be effective for thousands of years but he felt that the criminal class of Texas would make a good starting place.

Gideon started a campaign for a form of criminal punishment so far advanced in theory that it created tremulous indignation among stalwart Texans who had little reason to fear its application to themselves. The hangman's noose was far more desirable and a great deal less awesome than Gideon's proposal to legalize castration and substitute it for capital punishment.

The "Memorial," as Gideon called his bill, was "suggested to my mind on examining the crania of three unfortunate specimens of humanity whom the citizens of Washington and Fayette Counties found it necessary to hang during the year of 1849." The victims were "true criminal types" and Gideon considered it fortunate that they had died before they had time in which to beget more of their kind. Yet he thought a simple operation not only would have precluded propagation but would have restored the culprits to a useful life.

Gideon mailed 676 copies of his Memorial to lawmakers, newspapers, citizens, scientists, and doctors. In it he pointed out that all forms of punishment—the gallows, branding irons, whipping posts, and penitentiaries—had failed to decrease crime:

The object and intention of the penal code is, as its framers stated, to terrify the wicked, prevent crime and improve the character of the community. Our present penalties and modes of punishment do not secure these desirable results. To hang a low-pitched criminal elevates and makes of him a hero, brings him conspicuously into notice.

Emasculation would serve as a strong deterrent to crime by others and as a check to the propagation of the criminal type.

He wrote hundreds of letters explaining his theory of selective breeding as the only method of improving the human race.[1] Defending his idea against charges of advocating mutilation, he held that the state which had the legal right to kill likewise had the legal right to emasculate. Society, he pointed out, had the right to do anything which would benefit the whole—"from sawing off the horns from the brow of the draco down to the crushing of an ant egg."

He argued:

Remove the cause of sin from the unfortunate transgressor and the proclivity to evil ceases. The truth is the intellectual developments in the human family do not sufficiently predominate to control the animal range. And so long as that is the case the whole catalogue of outrage and misrule—war, bloodshed, rapine, robberies, treachery, lies, the whole list of villainous

---

[1] The jacket of Memorial No. 147 (56-L) in the State Archives, which should contain the original Memorial, is empty except for a penciled notation on a piece of scrap paper. The memorandum records that the Lincecum petition advocating castration was "withdrawn" by Senator (Seth) Shepard and sent to him by J. F. Beall on May 7, 1874. Shepard was Lincecum's attorney during the early 1870's. The date of the withdrawal is six months before Lincecum's death.

A copy of the Memorial, dated April, 1854; a list of persons to whom a copy was sent, their replies, and a list of those failing to respond are in the Lincecum Papers.

actions—must prevail. It is the animal and not the intellectual portion of our organic structure that commits crime and does violence.

Apparently Gideon arrived at this theory independently. The only person of his acquaintance who seemed interested in the subject was W. Byrd Powell, who once questioned Gideon about his personal observation of the offspring of Indians and whites. Few of his advanced-thinking, probing, or even eccentric contemporaries agreed with Lincecum on his emasculation and selective-mating theories, and none of the esoteric periodicals he read touched upon the subject.

Gideon wrote to his friend, Dr. R. P. Hallock, of New York:

Did you never see an eunuch? I have been familiarly acquainted with five of them. One of them I made myself. He was a degraded drunken sot—in delirium tremens at the time and I did it in a kind of youthful frolic. It cured him however and made an honest . . . man of him and he often thanked me for it, telling me at the same time that I had by that act *saved his life*. He became quite industrious, religious and studious. Paid all his debts well and when I last saw him he was quite learned in religious matters. . . . They are all good useful people. . . .

In this movement you will observe that I do not propose . . . to undertake the purification of the community at the first dash. It is only aimed at the ruined specimens of society—the actually condemned criminal . . . the ramifications of the principle of this movement are traceable in all the haunts of crime from the stinking cork of the whiskey cask to the scarlet cloth that floats in the light of high heaven from the harlot's window. . . . I have had this subject under close toiling investigation during the last ten years. I *know* that *all* crime, outrages, sin, have their origin in amativeness —I mean when in excess. *All* murders, robberies, thefts, suicides; the downfall of all nations, kingdoms, cities from long before the fire and brimstone affair at Sodom and Gomorrah . . . Yea, more, extravagance in dress, every glittering gem—all the gewgaw family . . . all irregular unbecoming actions such as wiggling on the chair, frequent shifting of seats, patting and shuffling of the feet, folding and twisting a handkerchief or newspaper, gnawing the finger nails, whittling sticks, &c., &c., are the ordinary signs and manifestations of unappeased, restless, insatiate amativeness.

Gideon told Texas ranchers and farmers that if half the steps taken to improve the breed of sheep, horses, and stock cattle were applied to the human race there would be more hope for mankind.

Like begets like. The laws of hereditary transmission can not be overruled. When the horse and the mare both trot, the colt seldom paces, as the saying goes. . . . To have good honest citizens, fair acting, truthful men and women, they must be bred right. To breed them right we must have good breeders and to procure these the knife is the only possible chance. . . . Until it is demonstrated satisfactorily that man is not an animal I shall contend that the same laws will apply.

Even in language Texans could understand the idea was too shockingly new to be grasped.

The Memorial was published in part in most Texas newspapers and in full in the *Colorado Democrat* and the *Ranger*. Joseph Lancaster, editor of the *Ranger,* published in Washington, Texas, referred to it as the Lincecum Law and after printing it in full remarked that "it has received sufficient notoriety without further aid of the press." Gideon replied:

I may also remark to you that the Lincecum Law, or more properly the Lincecum proposition for the redemption and purification of mankind, can not progress as rapidly as it should without the aid of the press. . . . But the Press must have the benefit of the purifying implement itself before they can be moved to the advocacy of righteousness.

The Lincecum Memorial was presented to the Legislature in 1855 and again in 1856. Benjamin E. Tarver and John Sayles, representatives from Washington County, brought it before the house on November 16, 1855. Gideon recorded its fate:

But they did it in a manner better calculated to excite ridicule and opposition than a philosophical consideration of the matter; and had it not been for the manly interference of Dr. A[shbel] Smith of Harris County there would have been nothing done with it further than a few sarcastic remarks accompanied by a great deal of half-drunk, goggled-eyed laughter.

Dr. Smith arose midst laughter and motioned it be referred to the judiciary committee.[2] Tarver, chairman of the Judiciary Committee,

---

[2] Dr. Smith was state legislator from Harris County in 1855 and again in 1866 and 1867. When Gideon launched a campaign opposing the Texas Medical Association's proposed legislation to control medical practice he wrote Dr. Smith in January, 1865: "I am inclined to think from the active part you took when my memorial for the purification of the race was presented to that honorable body that what I shall offer now will not be offensive to you."

put it in a drawer of the committee room, where it was later found by James Shaw of Burleson County, his successor.

Elsewhere Gideon explained that after its referral to the Judiciary "one of the members, being so much frightened at the nature and claims of the Memorial, slipped into the committee room one day while the chairman was drunk and stole the document from his files of petitions and consequently it was never called up for action." Gideon was sadly puzzled over "how low highly educated men can be."

During 1856, while Lincecum continued his campaign in behalf of his Memorial, its success seemed more promising. He found unexpected support from a few outspoken women, doctors, scientists, and some lawmakers, including Dr. J. R. Beauchamp, of Cameron, Alpheus Knight, of Pilot Point in Denton County, and Judge John A. Rutherford, of Lamar.

Among those who supported his "sin-destroying and soul-purifying proposition" was F. H. Merriman of Galveston, who wrote Gideon on July 13, 1856:[3]

On the subject of your memorial, as you are in dead earnest about it, I will do what I can to aid you, especially as I have reached the shady side of life when the "heydey in the blood is tame and appetite waits on reason." But I am afraid the British boys will look upon the movement as one calculated to abridge what they conceive to be a natural right. I believe your doctrine is a sound one and has nothing in it terrible except to evil doers and that it is well calculated to extinguish bad blood more effectually than the assumption of the doubtful right of taking the life of a fellow being.

It is clear that the condition of mankind would be vastly improved and the distinction between the good and bad or those who had been bad would be as well marked and defined as the quality of the Prophet's figs described by Pindar:

> "Like Jeremiah's figs
> The good were very good indeed
> The bad too bad to give the pigs."

The law is not aimed solely at sexual sins, but starts with the hypothesis

---

[3] Franklin H. Merriman, a native Texan, was a Galveston lawyer, former state senator, state representative, and a district attorney (*Texas Almanac, 1867*, pp. 182–183). He and his wife frequently visited the Lincecum home, usually with the Durhams.

that all crime has its source in the amatory organs and by cutting off the outlet the source or fountain is dried up or turned into a useful channel.

Since I have received your letter I have conversed with several citizens on the subject of the memorial. John S. Jones, formerly chief justice of this county, said he would use his influence to get subscribers for he believed your views were right. Col. M. B. Menard said he would advocate the passage of a law giving a criminal convicted of a capital offense his choice either to be hanged or suffer the penalty of the law proposed by your memorial.[4]

In 1856 the memorial was received with the same hilarious laughter and with as little success as the year before. Gideon reported: "The second time it was presented it occasioned a smart amount of angry discussion and was finally referred to the committee on stock and stock raising." Here again it died in the committee room.

But Gideon did not cease to fight for his plan and to expound his theory of eugenics, although the word was not in his vocabulary and the science was in the minds of only a few men.

When his old friend Dr. Josiah Higgarson, of Somerville, Tennessee, asked if he had given up his project, Gideon replied:

Emphatically no. And that's not the worst of it—for so long as this old bruised heart throbs I never will. . . . I have twice presented it for the consideration of our legislature, not for the purpose or with the expectation that it would gain anything in that direction . . . but purely for the purpose of agitation.

Although the Memorial did not again come before the Legislature, Gideon enlarged his scope of propaganda and carried on voluminous correspondence with exponents of various philosophies and cults. To one of them he wrote:

It is to me a source of amusement when I, as I occasionally do, work my-

---

[4] Colonel Michel Branamour Menard died less than two months after this letter was written. Canadian-born, he was in the far west before 1820 with the American Fur Company and living with the Shawnee Indians. The company sent him to Texas to establish an agency on Galveston Island for Indian trade in deerskin. Menard found it impossible to keep up with the Indian tribal movements in Texas and the venture was unsuccessful (Paul Chrisler Phillips, *The Fur Trade* [Norman, University of Oklahoma Press, 1961], Vol. II, p. 520). Menard was in Texas in 1833; he was a signer of the Texas Declaration of Independence and one of the organizers of the Galveston City Company; he was deputy collector of customs at Galveston in 1856 and later a state representative (*Handbook of Texas*, Vol. II, p. 170).

self up to a clairvoyant condition and, dashing 10,000 or 15,000 years ahead, I find myself in the society of highly progressionists, possessing perfect knowledge of individual rights. Like the honey bees they have perfected their government; everyone knows his duty, and he will perform it or die —tall, upright, harmonious and as much alike as deer. There they stand, knife in hand, ready and by the authority of right are promptly willing to trim and prune, emasculate and purify the genus homo of every unclean thing. . . . The horns of the great beast are knocked out . . . humanity is purified, harmonized, equalized. . . . This ruin-wrecked and center-tracked little world is in *its teens* . . . and when it becomes fully mature with all its powers, capabilities and essences in full play . . . a type of beings may appear occupying a plane of intelligence as far superior to the race of genus homo that they will amuse and enrich themselves by boxing us up and exhibiting us in their menageries. Then we, like the inferior types of animality now view us, will look upon them as the gods.

Marriages seldom gave Gideon cause for pleasure. More marriages merely forecast an increase in the population of mediocrities. He replied to news of the marriages of two of his grandchildren:

G. W. Lincecum is married.[5] Society, if she knew her rights and had the courage to maintain them, would never permit such conjugal unions as that. What part of your society compact will he and that Seed gal ornament? Who will feed them?

Molly will marry day after tomorrow. Will that poor Dutchman, Jim Olds, be able to quiet her discontented spirit? If he will support her in idleness he may settle her. But why, I ask, does Society permit her to marry? Ain't she enough of that sort?

For the good of future generations, Gideon believed that only the perfect and healthy types should be permitted to procreate. "Let this rule be established and five generations will not pass until men will be found who are tall, straight and beautiful." He disregarded the moral issues and maintained that if a healthy male and female "shall come together in unforbidden wedlock, carefully observe the laws of health and decency and copulate only for the purpose of procreation,

---

[5] George W. Lincecum, Gideon's grandson, and Miss Sue A. Seed were married on March 27, 1871, D. W. Chase, deacon of the Episcopal Church, officiating (Washington County Marriage Records, County Clerk's Office, Courthouse, Brenham, Vol. 3, p. 455).

that's *clean.*" The cleanliness should be carried through pregnancy, birth, and the life of the child.

On the other hand . . . let a pair with thick necks, moist blubber lips, flat tops and ponderous jowls *rush* together, either in legal wedlock or illicitly, both minds concentrated on the genital apparatus . . . at last, the result of this reciprocal violation of the laws of health, decency and respect for posterity is pushed out on the life stage, an ill-shapen, unclean thing. . . . Often one or both parents are diseased.

Gideon frequently corresponded with his nephew John Lincecum of Bear Creek ("those healthforsaken regions"), Louisiana, whom he feared was in danger of getting religion. He once listed for John those whom he would "prune"—deceivers, liars, drunkards, praying superstitionists. But his first choice would be ministers:

Just think what consternation and wild frantic fright it would produce amongst the deceptive priesthood. It would sure enough be the day of judgment with them . . . but it would break them from sucking eggs and render their frequent visits to the houses of the pretty sisters during the absence of their husbands unnecessary, mitigatory and of no effect. The dear sisters wouldn't have the butter and eggs and honey for him after that.

When Gideon had finished his imaginary program of purification it would reveal "that the priesthood had furnished a greater number of scalps (scrotal sacs) than any other profession."

Before and during the Civil War, Gideon had many occasions to increase his "pruning" list. Early in 1861, detecting the "extensive frauds and peculations" of the state government, which were to grow to immense proportions during the War, he wrote to his friend, S. B. Buckley of Austin, Texas:

Who are we to place confidence in? Don't you think that society would greatly benefit itself in diminishing the possibility with these fellows to reproduce their kind by a free use of the knife on their genital apparatus? If I had the authority to purify that type of our species and prevent the recurrence of such filthy unreliable beings, I could go to work at it as deliberately as I would to purify and improve a spikenosed scrub breed of hogs, and the remedy that I should apply to improve the hog would be the very same that I should apply to them.

During the War he wrote to one of his many soldier-correspondents:

I do not feel surpised at the condition of affairs as I find them manifested by the genus homo. On the plane of the rights of property, reciprocal good will and peace towards our fellows he is but slightly in advance of the dog. . . . Mankind must be developed to a much more exalted plane before he can be capable of appreciating individual rights or cease to fight for unjust pretenses. Whoever is fool enough to do wrong is mean enough to quarrel and fight for it. . . . Man has progressively developed from an animal condition to his present state of intellectuality and he must be a long way further progressed before he can throw off the entire brute and become purely human.

During and after the Civil War the purifying knife was frequently and illegally applied, and some Texas citizens regretted that the Legislature had not given more consideration to the proposed Lincecum Law.

There was one time, at least, when the knife was used legally, an instance constituting something of a rarity in Texas courts. Gideon heard about the trial, and on October 25, 1864, wrote to Dr. John A. Ewing of Belton, Texas.

I understand that a rape occurred in your vicinity which was perpetrated by a negro who, after a fair and impartial examination of the case by twelve good citizens, was found worthy to suffer the penalty of emasculation. The operation being performed, I understand turned out to be a complete success and that the negro is now well and returned to his duties as a slave.

Gideon complimented the citizens of Belton on their action and asked for details. Dr. Ewing verified the rumor. The sentence of emasculation was legally passed by a jury and the operation performed by a qualified surgeon. The incident, to Lincecum, fully confirmed his theory. He sent Ewing's letter to the Houston *Telegraph* for publication.

At that time a Negro was in the Brenham jail waiting trial on a charge of attempted rape. Gideon urged Judge John Stamps "to try for a Belton verdict." Lincecum also sought the aid of the Reverend H. C. Lewis of Brenham:

I address this letter to you from having understood that you were in favour of relieving the negro of the cause of his transgression and to save his life for the use of the owner. I hope you may be able to convince the people about Brenham of the propriety, philosophy and the humanity of such a course. At present the community can not be made to understand the far-reaching benefits, the peace and protecting results to society from a judicious use of the purifying knife. If a man has a vicious bull that is hooking and gutting his stock about his lots he knows very well how to tame him and make a good docile steer of him besides stopping the increase of that breed of cattle. Man is an animal.

Despite his efforts, the Brenham Negro was acquitted. "Oh well," Gideon wrote, "It was only an *attempted* rape."

Belatedly, many people came forward to offer Gideon support for his Memorial, including E. H. Cushing of the *Telegraph,* who admitted he had always been in favor of his method for the purification of society. Chauncey Berkeley Shepard, a state senator, told Gideon he would introduce a bill in the next session of the Legislature to punish rape by emasculation instead of hanging. But at the next session, 1866, the face and the mood of the Legislature had changed and there were more pressing matters for consideration.

Many years later Edward J. Davis wrote to Sioux Doran: "I used to know Dr. Lincecum slightly before the war. The doctor was nearer right in his theory of the certain way to eradicate wrong than people were willing to give him credit for. . . . I have no doubt that if all the world could be submitted to that process for some generations we would have a better class of people."[6]

---

[6] In 1939 Dr. Pat Ireland Nixon, distinguished physician of San Antonio, read in Fort Worth before the Texas Surgical Society a paper, "A Pioneer Texas Emasculator," later printed in the *Texas State Journal of Medicine* (Vol. 36 [1940], pp. 34–38). Dr. Nixon said of Lincecum's proposal: "We of this generation are prone to believe that surgical sterilization of the mentally unfit, criminals and criminally insane is a modern day procedure." He pointed out that the state of California legalized sterilization of the feeble-minded, mentally defective, and criminally insane as early as 1909 and up to that time, 1939, twenty-seven other states, not including Texas, had similar laws.

A NOTE ON SOURCES

In "Reminiscences," which was written in the final year of his life, Lincecum continued to advocate legalized sterilization and expressed the hope that another generation would accomplish what he had failed to do in his lifetime.

In addition to the more or less form letter which accompanied a copy of the "Memorial" sent to all Texas judges and legislators, Lincecum wrote verbosely repetitious personal letters explaining or defending his theory. Random quotations from some of these letters were used in this chapter. These include letters to Dr. R. P. Hallock, New York, May 15, 1859; Dr. Josiah Higgarson, Somerville, Tennessee, May 30, 1859; Parson Lancaster, no address, June 12, 1859; R. Robertson, Poughkeepsie, New York, July 13, 1859; J. M. Taylor and J. M. Carter, Marshall, Texas, January 18, 1860; Dr. D. Lee, agricultural editor, *Southern Field and Fireside,* Augusta, Georgia, January 29, 1860; Dr. William Byrd Powell, *Journal of Human Science,* Cincinnati, Ohio, January 30, 1860; Prof. S. B. Buckley, Austin, Texas, February 17, 1861; John Lincecum, Bear Creek, Louisiana, May 22, 1859; Dr. John A. Ewing, Belton, Texas, October 25, November 18, 1864; Judge [John] Stamps, Brenham, Texas, October 25, 1864; the Reverend H. C. Lewis, Brenham, Texas, November 1, 1864; editor of the *Weekly News,* Galveston, Texas, November 20, 1864; C. B. Shephard, November 25, 1864; E. H. Cushing, Houston, Texas, December 22, 1864; Dr. E. H. Dixon, the *Scalpel,* New York, n.d., but July, 1860; Dr. Ashbel Smith, Houston, Texas, January 16, 1866; and other letters of no date to the *Weekly News* signed "Parrhesia."

CHAPTER EIGHT

GIDEON
AND THE WAW-MOUTHS

Ignorance is such a terrible, stubborn, throat-cutting thing.
GID

I N THE bitter battle between organized religion and science Gideon was not on the side of the angels.

He explained his attitude in letters written over a period of years to numerous leaders and followers of a variety of religions and cults.

When applied to myself the epithet "infidel" suits me best because that's just what I am—infidel. Not skeptic for that implies doubt. But infidel— unbeliever, scoffer at all theories, doctrinal propositions, hypothetic assertions or anything that comes in conflict with the *known* laws of the natural sciences. . . .

I have never been a religionist of any description, have always opposed it by advocating mental freedom; and on that account have always been called an infidel. Well, that's just what I am to everything that wavers or skulks away and avoids philosophic scrutiny.

. . . from my earliest recollections my mind has never felt the enthrallment of priestly influence, nor the slightest hopes or fears of anything either good or bad that might be done for me by any of the celestial gentry be them [*sic*] gods or devils. My mind requires positive knowledge of any thing or principle before it can love, fear or use it. . . . As for the *Bible* being the word of God, not only preachers but a very large portion of mankind knows that it is no such thing. . . . The *Bible* is the patchwork of many generations of lazy, ambitious, malevolent priests. . . . Moses . . . fixed up the fable of the garden of Eden, placed the tree of knowledge in it and . . . with his theological ax he assayed to cut down the secret tree, and every priest of the subsequent generations has been ruthlessly hacking at it. . . . Another half century of scientific culture will cause its wide-spreading branches to overshadow theology, extinguish the fires of hell and chase the devil with his snakes, ghosts and witches into the mountains or somewhere else for protection, for they are a type of imaginary phantasms that enjoy no hospitality among the nations or with any people where the tree of knowledge flourishes.

Gideon was proud of his pioneer ancestors and their ability to endure the great hardships of frontier life "without the slander of a single prayer." He once told a nephew that "among the Lincecums there have been but few religionists. Your Uncle Rezin and your great grandmother were all that ever I heard of, except it be true that your father has fallen into the delusion. They are generally intellectually courageous and could not be frightened by the tale of Old Mose or any man of his profession."

Lincecum believed that religion offered solace to the weak and to those without the ability to find peace of mind elsewhere. In a letter dated June 16, 1847, to the Methodist Episcopal Society of Columbus, Mississippi, Gideon wrote in behalf of a slave: "My boy Henry has applied for permission to join your church. . . . I have no objection to your receiving him as a member of your society and I hope you may be able to calm the restlessness of his disposition so that he may submit more cheerfully to the condition his creator has seen fit to place him in."

Gideon was one of a loosely organized group of Texas "infidels" who subscribed to the Boston *Investigator* and corresponded with each other. One of them was A. G. Stobaugh, of Honey Grove, who wrote Gideon that he was opposed to religious dogmas of the day and was not afraid to let it be known. Gideon told him how to be an infidel and keep the respect of his neighbors:

Stick to the truth in all things, *keep sober* and freely perform your share in all necessary public works and there is no danger. I know, for I have tried it through a long life and declare positively to you that I never had a man to make use of a rough angry word to me in my life. . . . I have always expressed myself freely and openly on all and any subject, particularly on the subject of religion, its gods, devils, holy ghosts and the whole of the ghost family. . . . We may speak freely of doctrine and principles, avoiding personalities . . . and we shall seldom offend a man whose friendship is worth cultivating.

Despite his views on religion and his low opinion of the clergy, Gideon made lifelong friendships with a number of leaders in Texas religious and educational fields. Among them were A. W. Ruter, a Methodist leader of Rutersville College, and Judge R. E. B. Baylor, a Baptist minister and educator living at Gay Hill, whose name was given to Baylor University. Gideon wrote of Baylor:

The judge is a preacher, if you recollect. I can very well stand his fiddling for he performs pretty well and knows some good pieces; but when he undertakes as he sometimes does to approach me on the subject of religion I can't stand it. That is, I can't maintain my gravity. For it looks to me that a man of his opportunities and his middling good sense ought not to talk about such foolishness, particularly when there is no one present but a single friend who is in earnest on all serious subjects.

But Gideon forgave Baylor his proselyting and wrote from Tuxpan in 1871, when Baylor was about seventy-eight years old: "And poor old Judge Baylor is trying to preach yet. He is my particular friend. Give him my respects if you should see him."

When two old minister friends from Mississippi moved to Lockhart, Texas, Gideon wrote to one of them, Dr. A. G. Lane:

My long lost but highly esteemed friend: I should be highly pleased for you and Brother Long to come down and spend some time. . . . You could, as the fates have fixed the destiny of all the people of this county long ago, dispense with the thankless duty of carrying the gospel to them and enjoy yourselves like philosophic free men.

In 1859 Gideon was successful in influencing some of the Washington County citizens to subscribe to the Boston *Investigator,* apparently a sounding board for the nation's free thinkers. He wrote to the publisher, J. P. Mendum:

I have been trying to get up an Infidel society at this place and although they are generally unbelievers they are afraid to make an open declaration of it by connecting themselves with a liberal society. So I have concluded to see if I can not bring them to a knowledge of their duty to their individual rights by distributing amongst them a few books and tracts of the kind that will afford them light and courage in that direction.

He enclosed an order for a number of books and publications which included *The Evidence against Christianity* by John S. Hittell, *Life of Thomas Paine, Infidel Text Book, Barker and Bangs Debate, Evilala or Maid of Midian, Letters to a Catholic Bishop, Gospel According to Richard Carlisle* and "such publications as you think will make the best impression amongst our intellectual cowards."

Gideon was pleased with the outcome of his campaign: "Infidelity is sure enough forming a brotherhood. It will be a brotherhood branded not by tests or oaths or creeds but *integrity* and *confidence*. It will be based on the principles inculcated by our best democratic brother, the son of Mary, 'Do unto all men as you would they should do unto you and love one another'."[1]

J. W. Chandler of Chappell Hill, in 1860, asked Gideon's support of an organization of free thinkers whose object was the achievement of mental liberty by lifting "the veil of superstition to the fact that the earth is broad, the universe unbounded and no man has yet imagined its wonders." Gideon advised that such a movement should not follow the methods used by the "waw-mouthed priesthood and their servants, the politicians" but rather: "Let us enkindle on the hilltops and the low valleys, in the fields and in the forests, in the mechanic shops, educational seminars and halls of science, brighter lights than theirs can lay claim to."

The temper of the times and the price of a free mind are demonstrated by an incident in Heidenheimer, Bell County, Texas, seventeen

---

[1] "A very considerable portion of educated German emigrants and the English workingmen who migrate to this country are Freethinkers or infidels and in many of our large as well as in the newer towns and settlements at the West they have organized Infidels or Liberal clubs and seek to bring others into their way of thinking. They have united and brought out their full strength on several occasions in the effort to have all Sabbath laws abrogated in several of the western cities. In some of the new settlements of the West they have been so largely in the majority that they have prohibited all efforts for religious worship or Sabbath observance" (Dr. L. P. Brockett, "Religious Statistics of the U.S. in 1870, *"One Hundred Years' Progress in the U.S.* [Baltimore, O. H. Elliott, 1874], Vol. 2, pp. 590–665).

Some other Texans whom Gideon regarded as infidels were C. C. Yoakum and W. T. Cole, Honey Grove; B. Beck Seat, Brenham; B. M. Seaton, Hempstead, "an apostate from the Methodist church—he used to try to preach a little"; Charles Abercrombie, C. B. Stewart, and Major Green Wood, Danville.

years after Chandler and Gideon discussed this organization. Dr. Levi Jasper [James ?] Russell, president of the Free Thinkers of Bell County, and a respected physician, was called out of his house one night and given a hundred lashes on his bare back by his neighbors. He was expelled from the Masonic Lodge and the Knights of Pythias for heresy, but the Medical Association cited him for bravery.[2]

The lynchers left a note pinned to a tree near the Little River Academy where the Freethinkers met. It read, in part:

Now a word to . . . [all the leading men of the Infidel Club]. If any of you take his [Russell's] place we will burn you out of house and home, and hang you until you are dead. If any man in this county is injured on account of what has been done, we will burn you all out. We have got 50 men to back us. Gents, we mean business: infidelity has got to stop in this county as well as horse stealing.

A young man for whom Lincecum had a deep affection was W. H. Carrington, of Austin, Texas. On September 22, 1859, Gideon wrote him:

The purest Democrat, the son of Mary, taught the priest-trampled Jews the principles of individual rights in terms that cannot be mistaken; and the then prevailing orthodoxy took him up, tried him for his infidelity, found him guilty and crucified him. It is stated that he harangued the people three years before they murdered him. How long, think you, that he could make such speeches now in Great Britain, or in New England even, before he would be taken up?

Lincecum freely expressed his opinion of the clergy, as a group, and once wrote:

The poor fellows have no sense—just propound him a few questions in natural history—in zoology, geology, botany, astronomy or any branch of science and you will find him a perfect goose—ninny. Yet he can tell all about the unseen country and you must believe or go to hell! . . . they know but little about the world they inhabit, they have not positively made themselves acquainted with the rules of common decency and reciprocal politeness which is manifested in their manner of slandering you if you chance

---

[2] Dr. P. I. Nixon, biography of Russell, *Handbook of Texas,* Vol. II, p. 519. The story of the lynching is told also by Elma Dill Russell Spencer (*Gold Country* 1828–1858, San Antonio, Naylor Company, 1958, pp. 230–232). Dr. Russell's account of the lynching was printed in the Belton *Journal,* October 31, 1877.

to differ with them in any of their views or religious dogmas . . . they are incapable of hearing the words of righteousness and truth. . . .

. . . The priesthood as a class are a badly developed type of the genus more to be pitied than blamed and in place of running together at the sound of their baptized, sanctified bells, society would do better to spend that much time in building up institutions where the poor fellows should be guided into the paths of righteousness and truth—instructed in the science of individual right, the use of existence, and that man's corn cribs and tables and wives are not by divine right made free and as a perpetual inheritance for the *holy orders*.

Religion's attitude toward Humboldt's *Kosmos* was, in Lincecum's opinion, another attempt to discourage mental freedom:

Humboldt's *Cosmos* is without doubt the most extraordinary manifestation of intellectual action that has ever emanated from the brain of humanity. Full of wisdom and useful knowledge and yet the great *Cosmos,* that noble work, that life labor of a great good man, has been almost entirely suppressed. It was offensive to theology. Theology called it "Godless Cosmos."

. . . I am an infidel and unbeliever of every proposition that ranges outside the sphere of scientific handling. All other sects, cliques, societies, churches, conventions, legislatures, courts, corporations and combinations of men are predicated on the monarchical plan.

. . . My religious sentiment enforces the discharge of my duty to my fellow being of every type—and there it ends.

Gideon thoroughly enjoyed his lengthy expositions and debates with men of all faiths:

Life is all health and music and I have a great deal of fun in many ways besides. I correspond with a great many men in all parts of the United States and with all religious sects—Jews, Catholics, Mormons and Protestants—they are all rascals.[3]

The same spirit of fun led Lincecum into a study of spiritualism which resulted in his denunciation of the popular cult. Lincecum delighted in teasing his numerous Texas spiritualist friends. He wrote Colonel S. D. Hay, Huntsville, October 1, 1861:

[3] Some of his correspondents on religion were William Byrd Powell, Cincinnati, Ohio; Caleb G. Forshey, Rutersville, Texas; M. C. Hamilton, Austin, Texas; Joseph Preat, Twenty Mile Stand, Ohio; Dr. E. W. East, Salt Lake City, Utah, formerly of Hallettsville, Texas; Dr. R. P. Hallock, New York City; Dr. Josiah Higgarson, Somerville, Tennessee; R. Robertson, Poughkeepsie, N.Y.

. . . all substance decays . . . it is the certainty of dissolution that creates in us the desire and hope that such a well-made precious organization as ourself may possibly possess some little invisible, intangible part that may possibly be invested with powers capable of resisting the universal laws of decomposition. . . . If the spirits do not find it convenient to manifest themselves to me while I am in the body it will not be long now before I shall manifest myself to them, which in the long run will be about the same thing.

Lincecum subscribed to the *Spiritual Telegraph,* published by Charles Partridge of New York, and to the *Herald of Progress,* published by A. J. Davis, who originated the spiritualist movement in the United States.[4] Gideon was revolted by Davis' philosophy: "He is a fanatical encourager of bloodshed and thieving. . . . I dismiss him and his bloody intentions." But before dismissing him entirely, Lincecum wrote Davis himself:

You give countenance to such foolish fiction as the vision of Frances Ellen Watkins, which indicates that the god you worship demands the same old-fashioned sacrifices of blood! blood! blood!—How common it is in the world's history for the founders of a new fanaticism to introduce fire and sword and blood sacrifice as a sweet savor to their gods.

In 1859 Gideon cancelled his subscription to the *Spiritual Telegraph* and wrote Partridge:

The everlasting slangwhangings and vulgar display of stupid ignorance on the subject of negrodom which is daily emanating from the northern press has at last caused us to turn our money, a good many of us, and the sentiment is growing daily, in another direction. . . . You can't let our negroes alone but we can let you alone.

The antislavery stand of the Boston *Investigator* also ended Lincecum's enthusiasm for its progressiveness. He once wrote to Mendum, the publisher, that "you have in your composition with all your attain-

---

[4] Spiritualism began in the United States in 1843 with manifestations of power by a lad of seventeen named Andrew Jackson Davis, who lived in Poughkeepsie, New York. He dictated numerous books, containing descriptions of the other world, which enjoyed a great sale. The movement reached its peak in 1858–1859 (Brockett, "Religious Statistics," pp. 590–665). In 1853 Lincecum ordered a number of books on spiritualism by S. B. Brittan from Partridge and Brittan, New York, and directed them sent to John H. Money and R. N. Gentry of Long Point.

ments a little streak of blarney. I forgive it." In 1859 Gideon had favored an increase in subscription rates to prevent the paper's suspending publication and wrote a testimonial:

There is no paper now in existence that has held to its own through thick and thin, poverty, evil reports, as has the Boston *Investigator*. Twenty-eight years, strained up to the highest note in liberty's gamut and all the time in battle array with a legion of despotism, has been no very pleasant task.

But in May, 1860, Lincecum was incensed at the paper's pro-Union stand and wrote the publisher: "Should your action in siding with the fanatic enemies of the American government get any worse I can do as all good infidel democrats would—just leave you alone."

Gideon became increasingly resentful of the editorial policies of Eastern publications, including some scientific ones he thought above controversial discussion. He chided Benjamin Silliman and James Dwight Dana, scientist-editors, for a doctrine advanced in *Silliman's Journal* that "a negro is a white man with a black skin" adding: "Progressive science favors not war, but peace. It clears away the fog of error and excites in the minds of the masses not distrust and discord but confidence in union and fraternal reciprocality."

Lincecum subscribed to a great many newspapers, "all liberal publications with the exception of the New Orleans *Delta*." Although it was not "liberal" Lincecum renewed his subscription in 1859 with $5 in coin, explaining that "paper money is of rare occurrence and of suspicious character in this portion of Texas."

He declined a subscription to a new publication started in Brenham, Texas, by Andrew Marschalk, a descendant of a man with the same name who published the first newspaper in Mississippi. On June 30, 1859, Gideon wrote Marschalk: "I am getting to be a very old man and I am already taking more papers than I can possibly read. . . . You are not a stranger to me. I also came from Mississippi." Lincecum had seen several issues of the new paper and complimented Marschalk on his "very well got-up paper" and expressed the hope that it would flourish.

The same year Lincecum cancelled a subscription to Joseph Lancaster's *Ranger*, published in Washington, Texas, and told Lancaster: "Don't send it to me anymore. . . . Some years ago I liked the *Ranger* and did what I could with my limited means to sustain it, but it has descended from the elevated position which it then occupied and is now scrambling on a much less enviable plane. I shall never take it from the P.O. again."

Lincecum frequently suspected that some newspapers, his favorite term for which was "slangwhangers," and organized religion worked together to obscure the truth. In 1860, when Professor Caleb G. Forshey of Rutersville College had a disagreement with the college board president, William Jarvis Russell, over religious and Masonic views, Lincecum wrote Forshey:

I sympathize with you and am sorry that the god-protected professors of religion and Masonry cannot get along more harmoniously. . . . Don't perplex yourself about that fellow Russell. I have heard a good many men, some of them from your section of the country, express themselves about the matter. They seemed to understand all about it and all of them spoke decidedly in your favor. . . . I think the course you pursued in abstaining from a controversy in the newspapers was proper and perfectly right. Busied as you must be if you discharge your duties in your professional occupation, you can have no time to spend in controversy with the forky-tongues, malicious, loafering newspaper slangwhangers. I hope you will pay no further attention to it but permit them as you would a filthy skunk to go on spitting out their malignant spite until they can stink no longer. . . . There are many devils even though there be no hell.

Judge Rutherford of Lamar wrote Lincecum that public opinion had compelled him to become a church goer and he apologized for his hypocrisy. Lincecum replied:

Your first and greatest wish is for universal peace—progress in knowledge and happiness of the races. If that should turn out to be a sin won't you be in a damnable pickle? . . . The stinking skunk, though he sometimes offends our olfactories is no sinner! He is a polecat: he can't be a house cat neither can he pack his sins on another. Everyone . . . must take his place in the earth life train on the merits of his own ticket. . . . It is, to be sure, right for everyone to strive to find out the use of existence, polish and improve himself all he can, and, as it makes our light more [or] less for our neighbor to light his torch [by], it would be improper to place it under a bushel. If every man was endowed with sufficient mentality and firmness to carry it into action three words would be law enough to control the world. Three omnipotent words: *Let Me Alone!*

Gideon once replied that the corn crop he had cribbed was "not fit for a preacher to eat, mean as they are" to a friend in Mississippi who had written of the excellent crops there and said that God had blessed Mississippi with plenty. Gideon wrote him: "With the same parity of nonsensical superstition we of Texas might say that he has cursed us with poverty and blight. But we don't do that for we don't think he had anything to do with either case. If he does anything at all it must be on a higher plane of action than that of smutting bread corn and killing cows."

When his sister Emily Moore reported the presence of Indians in the vicinity of Hondo, Gideon sympathized with her fright but assured her that more people were killed by scarlet and yellow fever, doctors, and each other than were victims of the red man:

Last night at Brenham a man cut off his wife's head with an ax and we hear of as many or perhaps more killings in our happy, god-serving community where the hoarse croaking prayer ceaseth not nor the sound of the church going bell quieteth never than we hear of from the Indian range. . . . as to where death shall claim me it is none of my business. So I pray not neither do I sing psalms, yet the ranting devotee in all his howling glory can never know or feel the peace that calms nor the quiet that reigns in my mind.

His peace of mind was considerably upset when his nephew John continued to show signs of breaking the Lincecum tradition, and he wrote him:

. . . to put the matter in a shape that will be easily understood by my pious nephew, so that he can make no mistake or have to guess at anything in respect to my opinions in that matter I will here state what I *know*—that all religions are false and damaging to humanity in proportion to their prevalence. . . . They are so organized that they object to all scientific and philosophic truths and tenaciously adhere to dogmas and fables that have no sense or reason in them. They will brand you as an infidel and a bad dangerous man if you refuse to acknowledge the scientific falsehood that darkness is a substance, that God had three mornings before he made the sun, that the firmament of heaven is a sheet-like glass sphere, spread out like a scroll, that half the water was put above it and by opening the windows thereof he made it rain, that the earth is foursquare having corners. . . . This is the kind of foolish falsehood that a man must have faith to believe or he is an infidel, bad man, no Christian, ought not to be entitled to legal privileges, &c."

But it was Gideon's brother Grant, John's father, who confessed, joined the church and broke the nonpraying family custom. Gideon exploded to John:

It is all nonsense to suppose that any man of any degree of common sense would fly to and lay hold of the altar, crying out to the Lord for pardon when he has done no wrong, committed no offense. When he has committed crimes for which he would send other men to hell he throws himself into the arms of the church. A man of honesty and truth has no sins to confess. Just listen to their devotional songs:

Come, humble sinner in whose breast
A thousand thoughts revolve;
Come with your guilt and fears oppressed
And make this last resolve.

Honest men have no such fears, nor do they feel like an humble frightened sinner. And when he sings, if he sings on such a subject at all, sings without fear thusly:

Let coward guilt with pallid fear
To sheltering churches fly
And justly dread the vengeful fate
That thunders through the sky.

When the Brenham Baptist Church requested a bottle of Gideon's famous mustang wine for use at sacrament on July 22, 1860, he happily obliged, sending with it the following message as a label on the bottle: "Through the agency of the weaker vessel, Satan entered, despoiled and broke up the Eden of the ancients. The same spirit is at work with the same vessels yet and often succeeds in breaking up the Eden of the families as heretofore. GID"

It was perhaps the minister of this church who sent Gideon an unidentified book and in return received this note: "To the preacher who sent me a book: If religion is true I may say without fear of successful contradiction that there is no other truth in so bad a fix! Why, it has to be argued and proved to everybody every day. GID"

To Nephew John's explanation that he joined the church because his father was dying, Gideon replied:

Death is as natural, as necessary, as common, and happens as often as life. It is only the low-pitched coward who is unwilling to take his share of it. But it is nevertheless the great bug bear that is made use of by the snob-nosed priesthood to frighten and drive prignosed ignorance into the churches with an occasional flourish of fire and brimstone.

When John pointed out the error of Gideon's ways he provoked the following reply:

If I do belong to any of the gods he must be a clever fellow as he has never pestered me in any way. He must be smart enough to know that it would not redound to his credit to send a message to me either in old musty books or proud priests. No. He must come himself and talk like a gentleman. He knows better than to send a waw-mouthed priest.

Gideon was extremely exasperated when his favorite daughter, Sallie, wrote that she was considering joining the Roman Catholic church in Brenham because of its fine new church. He was at that time living in Tuxpan, Mexico. Lincecum replied:

Well, that is in my estimation as valid a reason for joining a church as I ever heard. Weakminded people must have some invisible, intangible something upon which to rest their hopes, to lean upon in the hour of distress. The Catholic is the best superstition and much the most costly. In your forlorn condition, however, if you can not get into the Catholic church, fly to any of the churches and in the hour of your greatest distress go to the priest, confess your sins and he will not only relieve your fears but forgive your sins. . . .

Breakfast over, I went to town. Found on the plaza the usual number of people, marketable articles, etc., and at the same time I could hear the band performing music in the old stone church that fronts and overhangs the north border of the paved plaza.

The music seemed to be good. I drew nearer and found that the sanctified hosts inside were in full blast praising the Lord. The band, which was all brass instruments and ten clarinets, was performing in good style. Waltzes, marches, and other lively music were played in turn and continued for an hour. I could not forego the desire to peep in.

Every face was clothed in smiles, and joy and hope lighted up and seemed to rest on every countenance. Their cheerful voices and clear-ringing music inspired me with the thought that the Catholic superstition is on a higher plane and better calculated to fascinate and enthrall the ignorant masses than any other. . . . I am glad you have become a praying religionist. It is so much more convenient and cheaper when sent in aid of your indigent friends than any gross material means could be. My old tattered habiliments testifies to its happy results. Amen.

And for yourself my prayers that you may grow in grace until the heavenly powers may all yield obedience to your prayerful solicitations.

But it was not until after her father's death that Sallie joined a church. Among the many invitations, wedding announcements, funeral and fraternal meeting notices among the Lincecum Papers is a certificate that Mrs. Sallie L. Doran was confirmed by Bishop Alexander Gregg on Sunday, April 28, 1875, in the Episcopal parish of St. Peter's Church, established in Brenham May 2, 1848.

There is no record that Gideon ever yielded his unorthodox views. On a tattered slip of paper in the Lincecum collection in Gideon's writing appears this statement of his ethical—his religious—code: "The whole desire of my heart has always been and still is that I may in all my different stations in life steer clear of any wrong to or in anywise give offense to my fellow creatures."

His friends, however, never gave up their efforts to convert him. When Dr. A. H. Rippetoe, of Brenham, sent him some literature, Gideon wrote Sallie: "I feel very grateful to him for sending one of the religio-philosophical journals. It is a solace to me in my protracted sojourn here to be encouraged in the hope that I shall live again in the beyond. A joyous anticipation."

A few months before his death he wrote to Sallie:

You speak of the happy days that are past and fear I do not appreciate the reminiscences; but I do fully and it gives me pleasure. I think those bright days of innocent delights were only a foretaste of what is to come. It will be more exquisitely delightful and our capacity to enjoy and appreciate it will be increased to a tenfold degree when we all meet again in a higher, brighter life.

A NOTE ON SOURCES

Lincecum's most vitriolic remarks on organized religion and the ministry are in letters to his nephew John Lincecum, Bear Creek, Louisiana (May 22, 1859; June 10, August 18, October 20, December 3, 1860). The deliberately shocking and taunting letters, although addressed to John, were doubtless intended to be read by John's father, Grant Lincecum, who was not on letter-writing terms with Gideon. Oddly enough, some of these letters are signed "Thine in Christ," "Thine in Righteousness" or "In Christ I am Thine."

An example of Lincecum's frequently expressed opinion that preachers were "poor pay" is a letter to Rufus C. Burleson, Waco, Texas, October 16, 1861, pressing fulfillment of a promise to pay the Lincecum-Matson mill in flour in lieu of money. At that time Burleson was head of Waco University (later Baylor University, of which also Burleson was president). Lincecum loftily wrote to the Baptist minister: "Pray make a move in the matter."

Lincecum's views on religion quoted in this chapter are found in his letters to J. O. Illingworth, Galveston, Texas, June 28, 1860; Joseph C. Snively, Lockhart, Texas, November 14, 1861; Southwick & Sons, Galveston, Texas, October 1, 1860; Horace Seaver, Boston, Massachusetts, January 7, 1861; John A. Rutherford, Honey Grove, Texas, January 4, 1861; John A. Sanford, Tyler, Texas, March 1, 1864; T. W. Lovesa, Vincent Town, New York, n.d., but April, 1868; Richard Powell, Dripping Springs, Texas, March 6, 1861; and to W. H. [D.] Carrington, Austin, Texas, September 22, 1859.

Numerous chiding references to spiritualism are found in Lincecum's eight-year correspondence with R. B. Hannay, an Englishman who wandered over Texas during the Civil War and returned to his native country in 1867, and who was never able to convince Lincecum of the seriousness of spiritualism. Another spiritualist of Lincecum's acquaintance was Johan Reinert Reierson of Prairieville, Kaufman County, Texas, whose name and address are entered in Lincecum's address book with the notation "from Norway and is a spiritualist."

CHAPTER NINE

GIDEON
AND THE ANIMALCULUM

Texas would be a great invention if it rained a little more
often. GID

Washington County reached its prewar peak in 1859, with only slight indications of a prolonged drought, and a mere hint of the national discord which was to cloud its prosperity and happiness. It was likewise a summit for Gideon—a high point of untroubled calm. Never again was he to view life and its increasing complexities and irritations with equanimity or indifference.

Washington, a county of well-to-do farmers with large land holdings, offered little available land to newcomers. Gideon explained the scarcity of farms: ". . . to preclude the possibility of being too much crowded—nearly all of them being old Texans—will not sell off their surplus lands."

He predicted that within two years there would be no uncultivated prairie between the Brazos and Colorado Rivers, so rapidly was it being planted. This situation, he well knew, would end the open range and he was already planning to cut down the size of his herd. He told his relatives, the Moores, who had moved from the County to the western Texas frontier near Castroville: "From Brenham to Chappell Hill and from Chappell Hill to Washington and from Washington to this place and all the way to LaGrange is almost entirely under fence."

The few property sales brought $35 an acre around Chappell Hill and Gideon estimated his land would bring $25 an acre. But he had no intention of selling at any price:

It is good land and there is enough of it to sustain my posterity 100 years. And I shall leave it so that they can't sell it. I don't need money and what would the $40,000 . . . be to me compared with the comfort, health and happiness it is capable of affording to unborn generations of my posterity through the next century? You may say that with that amount of money I might settle them all off in better situations, but that's not so. There are no better situations. . . . There are no lands that can be had in this country that a man would agree to settle himself on for less than $10 per acre and these high rates are solely attributable to the fact that it is decidedly a pleasure and also a very convenient county to dwell in. People who have settled themselves here consider that they have been very fortunate and will not part with their homes.[1]

Gideon was a happy man. He had no financial worries, his well-being was not dependent on his crops, his children were all near-by, and he was under no pressure. Time moved slowly, pleasantly, and leisurely.

He had not always been so content:

I recollect when in '48 I came and set myself down in the grass on a wide-spread uninhabited Texan prairie that for several weeks I was badly beset by what I term hunter's dog hypo[2]—getting up and lying down all over the yard in the course of the day when there was no hunting to do. Indeed I continued restless, experiencing the feeling that something was lost or soon would be—until I procured sets of instruments for scientific investigation. I was troubled with the monster ennui no longer. I had "lost the pebble" and "the giant died." Ever since the arrival of my instruments the daytime is much too short for me and I impinge upon the night time on an average until $10\frac{1}{2}$ o'clock. It affords me genuine, natural, instructive, manly enjoyment, hammer in hand, to climb the rugged cliffs and gut the rock and send asunder the stone leaves of the book of the history of organized matter wherein I may read out truths and divine scientific facts which are not to be found in the manmade pasteboard and calfskin records. Or wandering over the plains, intervals on the hills or along the shaded banks of the running

[1] *The Texas Almanac, 1861,* listed average land values for 1860 in Washington County at $8.84 an acre, a price second high to that in Wharton County, $10.40 an acre.

[2] Gideon's abbreviation for "hypochondria."

brook, analyzing and reading from the gorgeous flower, leaf, stream and plant, in everything that grows

From the giant oak that waves his branches dark

To the dwarf moss that clings upon his bark

the true handwriting of ever-progressing NATURE.

Or on the serene cloudless night with telescopic eyes plunge recklessly into illimitable space and there amid shining hosts of suns, systems and constellation of suns, feel myself dwindle down to the dimensions of a mere atom—a lost atom!—but there are no lost atoms.

Then as a restorative and to relieve the feeling of insignificance I lay aside the telescope and arming myself with a large acroamatic microscope (10,000 powers) bend the spirit of the investigation downward, take a peep into the invisible world. Here, instead of relief, I find the number and the wonders greatly multiplied. Though not quite so brilliant and sparkling, the beauty and order of organic arrangement is far more pleasing and astounding. Thousands upon thousands of regularly organized, breathing, thinking beings—instinct begone—teeming from every nook and cranny of wide spread nature, all busy and all endowed with powers sufficient to meet the exigencies of existence. I have some specimens of airbreathing animalculum as perfect, perhaps more intricate, in the organic developments than any type in the visible world. One with a heart and the ascending trunk of the aorta, branching and supplying a double-lobed brain, precisely in the same manner and exactly resembling the human head. But I shrink from the attempt to describe anything further in this substantially organized, beautifully decorated but, without the aid of the microscope, invisible world of living, sensible, managing, animal forms.

The 1859 spring prospects for a cotton crop were good. Gideon did not raise cotton, the crop which accounted for the county's prosperity. His main crops were corn, sugar cane, and grapes. Washington County farmers had made "little three-cornered patch experiments" in 1858 with Chinese sugar cane, or sorgo, but Gideon was the only one to plant it again in 1859.

The first year the cane crop produced 8,820 gallons of syrup, 150 per acre, and sufficient winter forage for oxen and milk cows. The 1859 season was extremely dry and the production was only 663 gallons of syrup or 83 per acre. Gideon believed sugar cane would rank next to Indian corn as a crop "as soon as old Mrs. Grundy shall give sanction to it."[3] He found it excellent for seeing the "dried-up

³ Chinese sugar cane, or grain sorghum, in Texas today is first in acreage and

sows and pigs" through the hot months of July, August, and September. The bagasse, properly cured, was nourishing winter food for horses, mules, oxen, and cows. For preserving, the syrup was as good as brown sugar—and was cheaper. Gideon recommended cane highly as a crop, although

... there are going the rounds ... wonderful stories of its killing stock, blacking teeth, souring syrup, &c., &c., and the same poor fellows are paying me a dollar a gallon for it. ... We have used the syrup now nearly two years, boiling and cooking almost everything in it from corn meal down to the sourest grapes. Negroes and all eat it extensively to the exclusion of quantities of animal food during the hot months. Proper proportions of it poured into the vats with the bruised mustang grapes and thus passed through the first fermentative process with the grape juice produces wine of fine flavor. ... It is made into beer and beverages during the summer. ... We should now hardly know how to get along without it.

Gideon did not attempt to make sugar. He had only a wooden mill which would not press sufficiently. But at the end of the second crop he ordered an iron sugar mill from Close and Cushman of Galveston. Gideon urged that it be a sound one, as Washington County had "no good mechanics in iron to alter, improve or mend any part of such a machine."

During the year 1859, a period of accelerated mental stimulation for Lincecum, he extended his correspondence to new areas and a wider scope of topics. His letter press for the period includes the following preface:

---

second to cotton in annual money value. In both acreage and value it is first among grain crops of Texas (*Texas Almanac*, 1961–1962, p. 233). However, Gideon decided in 1864, after comparing sorghums with his neighbor, Thomas Affleck, that his was not the true Chinese sorghum. Affleck sent him four stalks of sorghum which were examined by J. B. Roberts, who stopped off at Gideon's on his way from California, where he had lived ten years, to join the Confederate Army in Louisiana. Roberts declared Affleck's sorghum to be genuine Chinese sugar cane, identical with that cultivated in California by Chinese and imported directly from China, and never seen outside California. Gideon thought the Texas variety, which was distributed by the U.S. Patent Office in 1857, came from France and was hybridized there. In a letter to Affleck, dated August, 1864, and written in the sugar house, Lincecum said: "I want to visit you and your works mighty bad, but cannot now do so, I am so jammed in the cooking establishment. I shall boil my imphee next week. I shall watch it carefully. Thine in smoke." A copy of this letter in the Texas State Archives bears an undated notation that the original is in the possession of Tom Affleck of Galveston, Texas. Affleck's letter transmitting the cane, dated August 22, 1864, is among the Lincecum Papers.

Long Point
20th March 1859

I have this day opened and commenced blotting this fine large new letter book. At this moment its pages are without stain or blemish and it is worth six dollars.

Reflection:

Shall I by filling it up with my unpolished thoughts be able to induce him, in whose hands it may chance to fall, to feel that its value is as great as when it was a blank?

Time will decide that question.

But if a sincere desire for the development of true principles from a natural basis will make it worth more, I promise myself that that desire shall not be departed from and that I shall, with all my mental strength, strive to avoid two sins which from time immemorial has almost universally obtained with that type of our species who have deemed it proper to place their thoughts on paper.

Viz., Diminution and Exaggeration.

GID

The Lincecum house was seldom without visitors and the dining table was usually a full one, especially during hunting season. Neighbors gathered nightly to listen to the family concerts in the Lincecum parlor. Gideon played his old black violin and Sallie the piano. Gideon enjoyed guests, conversation, gaiety, and music; generally, however, he was a lonely man forever seeking a congenial mind to share his own unusual interests. Alone, in the forests observing nature, he felt a superior being; in a crowd he considered himself a "perfect nullity." Lincecum once confessed: "I may not be wanting in the social circles for I can laugh, tell tales, make music, and perform antic tricks. I cannot, however, participate in the consumption of alcoholic drinks, tobacco or grease."

One photograph of Lincecum, its present location unknown, from which a number of portraits have been painted, is not a good likeness. At least he did not think so. He sat for his photograph a number of times—once for J. T. Cross and another time for the Mullen's Picture Gallery, both of Brenham, Texas. Gideon was annoyed at the results, complaining that his eyes "looked blind" and that the photographs looked flat and lifeless as though pictures of a dead man. And indeed, his eyes do look blank and expressionless. Lincecum was inordinately proud of his eyes, which never required glasses. He attributed his lasting eyesight to a daily application of a tobacco solution, the only use he had for tobacco and a remedy he frequently recommended to many of his aging friends.

Lincecum was six feet tall, with straight black hair contrasting oddly with his steel-blue penetrating eyes under heavy black brows. His physical strength and endurance were said to have been only slightly inferior to those of his father, Hezekiah, whose prowess was legendary in Georgia.

Until he was thirty-five years old Gideon kept his weight down to 195 pounds by prudent dieting. He learned the importance of diet from a sick old buck deer. On this occasion Gideon was ill, unable to work or to collect $20,000 due him from his neighbors and customers, and generally fed up with human companionship. He sought solace in the deep woods of Mississippi, where he spent his days hunting and his nights sleeping in the open. One day as he sat quietly by a lake waiting for game he saw an old buck limp painfully to the water's edge. Expecting him to slake a great thirst, Gideon was amazed to see that instead he sipped lightly of the cool water and then nibbled two or three green brier leaves. "Before I left my hiding place I supposed I had penetrated the secret of the old buck's abstemious conduct and I had formed a resolution to feed equally light and sparingly." In his later years Lincecum maintained a steady 165 pounds.

A description of him at seventy years of age is recorded in a letter to one of his correspondents:

Neck well set on the shoulders which are a little stooped—not very wide but round and muscular. Arms well-muscled—long—tipped with a splendid and most useful pair of hands and remarkably long fingers ornamented with a full set of long, clear, well-formed nails. Feet strong, size nine; toes long and generous in their action toward each other. According to my knowledge —and my acquaintance with them extends to 70 winters—there has not occurred a single instance where any one of the whole community ever attempted to ride another. Finding them so fair in their communitary deportment I could not have the heart to impose a tight shoe on them.

Temperament—sanguine, bilious and graphic. But temperament indicates no particular talent or disposition.

My hair is now nearly half-white, still covering the scalp. The beard nearly all white, nine inches in length. Eyes close but with a brow projecting almost to deformity. Large nose and high cheek bones, have rather a sunken appearance. Ears small and flat, mouth prominent, dimpled chin.

Gideon gave a detailed measurement of his head, adding: "If you are not satisfied with this, I will have the old skull left out on a stump where you can get it and measure it at your leisure."

In later years Gideon followed a routine: On awakening he made the rounds—barefooted, for he never wore shoes in warm weather nor in the mornings during winter—to check his meteorological instruments, some of them fifty yards from his house. After recording the day's reading Lincecum went to the water closet, sloshed cold well water over his body, rubbed down with a rough towel, and dressed. He was indifferent to clothes, wearing the same garments, hats, and overcoats year after year until members of his family compelled him to purchase new ones.

For breakfast he ate three ounces of corn bread, a spoonful of fresh butter, and drank a cup of coffee. For his noon meal he ate vegetables, more cornbread, and, occasionally, crisply fried bacon free of grease. His evening meal was a repetition of breakfast.

Gideon slept with his head to the north, and with windows and doors open "so that every breath taken is a new one. . . . In this manner I have conducted myself through the last ten years. And during all that time I have not enjoyed the luxury of wringing an oozy nose or suffering any disease."

In 1859, through a Houston attorney, J. H. H. Woodward, Lincecum applied for a pension rewarding his service in the War of 1812. Woodward was unable to find any record of his service. Gideon said he had enlisted and served from August to October, 1813. At the time of his enlistment Gideon was tax collector of Putnam County, Georgia, and when tax-paying time came the citizens arranged for his discharge by sending a substitute. At Camp Hope he was discharged from Captain Varner's company in Colonel Freeman's regiment, General Floyd's brigade of dragoons.

Lincecum furnished Woodward with the names of some of his company of twenty-seven men. They included James Whitfield, of Columbus, Mississippi, who was later governor of the state; William Bryan, of Ripley, Mississippi; James Abercrombie, of Mississippi and later of Danville, Texas; C. B. Strong, Greenberry Gaither, Floyd Williams, George Osbourne, William Nesbet, Richard Repass, John Todd, William B. Morgan, Washington Rose, Frank Hearn, William Marcus, William Puckett, John Taylor, Fielding Sillman, James Zachey. Other names are now illegible. Gideon recalled that during an epidemic of measles among the men he was pressed into service as a doctor.

Apparently Woodward was successful in obtaining the pension, for Lincecum wrote him in July, 1859: "I am not only satisfied . . . but am obliged to you heavily for the prompt manner and extraordinary vigilance you have exerted in ferreting out the widely scattered evidence in the establishment of my 47-year-old claim."

Lincecum opposed war and told a grandson: "The army is a bad place to form character but I thought it then a great place and to fight and slay was a great and glorious thing. I entertain a very different opinion on that subject now. I would not go into it now if fit for military duty. I should advocate the doctrine that those who raise the fuss should do the fighting."

Gideon devoted some of his leisure time to the study of phrenology, in which he had long been interested. He had been acquainted with the theory since the beginning of his long friendship with W. Byrd Powell, an eccentric and early phrenologist, whom he first met in Mississippi. In the Lincecum Papers is a penetrating character analysis of Lincecum made by Powell, dated May 4, 1839, and written in Alexander, Mississippi.

Although Powell's science is presently outdated, his reading of Gideon's personality is amazingly apt. Powell found Lincecum greatly deficient in the strongest human emotions—a desire for property and a yearning for popularity. He wrote:

Such is your spontaneous reliance upon self that in most matters of thought and feeling you find yourself without society. . . . Laws are but little advantage to you except in so far as they protect your person and property from rascals. You would act just as you do if there were no laws, for you are constituted to be a law unto yourself.

Powell thought Lincecum would have been an "ardent and warm

devotionalist" had he selected religion as a primary interest, but added he would have been "in any church mutinous." He summed up Lincecum's ability as a physician: "You are almost intuitively a doctor . . . a man born with the talent, knowing instinctively the symptoms and the remedy, and disregarding conventional medicinal practices."

Gideon's interest in phrenology often took him to Houston and Galveston, where there were frequent lectures and demonstrations.

With the Washington County Railroad partially constructed Gideon could go to Galveston in twelve hours. The rails were finished from Hempstead, the terminal for the Houston and Texas Central Railroad, to Chappell Hill, except for a bridge across the Brazos River.[4] The Austin stage from Hempstead passed six miles south of Gideon's house.[5] Washington County citizens were "all deranged on the subject of internal improvements," but Lincecum was far more interested in promoting artesian wells than the "thieving railroad projects. A great number of good wells of gushing water are greatly preferable . . . and . . . would make a paradise of our glorious state. . . . Railroads can't do that but they can make poor folks."

Generally, the citizens were pleased with their lot, the community congenial and happy. "There is but little indebtedness amongst them and they are more frugal and industrious than formerly. They are also more prudent and this year there has been less killing than heretofore."

Gideon wrote his nephew, John: "Anyone who could look upon our farms now and utter a complaint or pray for more is fit only to dwell

---

[4] The Washington County Railroad ran the twenty-one miles from Hempstead to Brenham. It was chartered February 2, 1856, and completed late in 1860. The Giddings family and William Sledge were the chief promoters. Railroad promoters received generous contributions of land, labor, money, and materials for construction from the citizens along the proposed routes. Railroad companies could borrow from the state Permanent School Fund, at 6 percent, $6,000 for every mile of completed roads. The Washington County Railroad was granted $66,000 on eleven miles of road completed in May, 1859. Additionally the state donated 112,640 acres of land (S. G. Reed, *A History of Texas Railroads* [Houston, St. Clair Publishing Co., 1941], pp. 73–74, and the *Texas Almanac, 1867,* p. 234). Gideon not only opposed railroad subsidies and the use of school funds, but knew full well that railroads erased all frontiers.

[5] The Sawyer and Risher stagecoach line, which operated four-horse coaches and connected with the Houston and Texas Central Railroad at Hempstead, left Hempstead daily at 10:00 A.M. for Austin. Passing through Chappell Hill, Brenham, La-Grange, etc., it reached Austin on the second day at midnight (*Texas Almanac, 1861,* pp. 223–225, 292, 304).

in the borders of the Mississippi swamp and be a Christian where his groans and sighs and disappointed slapping would be excusable."

In August, Lincecum asked D. Messner, a Washington County citizen visiting in New York, to bring medicines for Sarah and a new strong microscope, "One that will detect the animalculum in water and we may have some fine amusement as well as spiritual light and progress." Later he ordered a barometer and instructed Messner: "Now if the $27.50 microscope is equal in power to the $40 one—the difference in price being attributable to the difference in polish, take the cheaper one; as you know it is the use that I care for and not the shine."

Washington County farmers optimistically continued to invest in Negroes and Gideon's son-in-law Matson planned to buy more, paying the Texas market rate of $1,000 to $1,200 for good Negroes fourteen to twenty years old, more for choice hands.

Good mules were expensive—from $175 to $250. Corn at Matson's mill sold for 75 cents a bushel. Beef on foot was $2\frac{3}{4}$ to 3 cents, slaughtered, 3 to $3\frac{1}{2}$ cents; pork, 5 to 7 cents; cows and calves, $10 to $15; stock cattle, $7 to $9.[6]

Gideon was too busy watching his animalculum to pay much attention to politics, although his son, Leonidas, was a candidate that year for state representative. Lincecum had long since disfranchised himself in disgust at general political activities. He wrote his friend E. C. Stamps: "On reflection I find that I cannot conscientiously do what I half way promised the other day that I would. I cannot consent to be any longer, under existing circumstances, even a voter much less a wire puller." Apparently, Stamps had asked Lincecum's aid and influence in behalf of a relief bill, possibly for the Washington County Railroad. Gideon explained his position:

. . . my opinion of a popular government is the agreement of two or more persons not to infringe or allow any infringements or abridgement of natural individual rights. Taking this view of government you will perceive that I object to all special legislation. I have never consented that government might invoke me or my earnings in schemes of internal improvements or corporate monopolies. To these and other wrongs I never shall consent. . . . You also perceive and know that the very things I object to make up the entire business of our government. Excuse me, my dear Sir.

[6] Prices are Gideon's.

The place-seeking monopolizer may be shocked at this idea of government and think that if adopted would go by the board. To which I may say that if *their all* consists in special governmental favors they are right and as far as I am concerned they will have to go to work and earn something which is really their own, as you and I do, and not any longer live as public paupers on governmental favors.

He again explained his views to John Alexander, of Independence, Texas, who was a candidate for district attorney:

I am and *always have been* conscientiously opposed to conventions of every shape and form on the political arena. I served as a delegate in one only in my life and have been ashamed of that ever since. I am a democrat in the sense and meaning of the principles inculcated by the Son of Mary. "Call no man master" and I add, "or no set of men."

Through the many newspapers to which he subscribed Gideon was informed on national politics and "the reform movements in our declining government. Being born with the constitution I feel somewhat interested. These movements are all alike, based upon fraud coupled with a strong desire to use the means of toiling communities to enrich and place their leaders on the plane of authority—amongst the gods."

Leonidas' candidacy was an unsuccessful attempt to break the political potency of the Giddings and the Shepards. Gideon wrote:

Ever since I came to Texas there has been in this county a political clique calling themselves *the democracy* who have by the aid of the convention system managed so as to secure to themselves all the offices. Not content with that they had got up by special legislative enactments a pretty extensive thieving monopoly. Their last convention which took place in April was managed with so little regard to the opinions, rights and privileges of the working classes that they have kicked up at it. The whole community of workers has become very much incensed and disgusted at the open fraud that is and has for a long time been practiced on them and to manifest their indignation they have brought out opposition candidates.

The political issues settled for another year, the citizens of Washington County returned to their crops and settled down to their customary harmony. The fall rains failed to appear, crops were short and scanty, and Gideon gave serious thought to a solution for the water shortage. During his first five years in Texas his land had a number of running springs and branches full of water and fish.

I had no thought that water would ever be even scarce but the last six years have changed my actions on that subject extensively. All the last named time we have had no springs, the branches all dry, and were I to show a greenhorn the places where I have taken many fine messes of trout and goggle-eyed perch he would place it amongst the impossibilities.

When he first came to Texas, Gideon dug a well on his place "to get free water, not from scarcity." Four men and a horse worked four months to complete the 230-foot well. Water came up to within thirty feet of the surface and for the past eleven years the one well had been the Lincecums' only source of water for the farm, livestock, and household. Now the well was reaching an alarmingly low level and Lincecum began to think of the possibility of an artesian well on his farm.

Several years before, Lincecum had begun a study of drought cycles in Washington County as indicated by tree rings for the past 141 years. As a result of his study he was able to convince many of his discouraged neighbors who planned to move out of the county that droughts were not permanent. Unknown to him at the time, a German-born surveyor, Jacob Kuechler, made a similar study in Fredericksburg, Texas.[7] They examined the same species of oak from elevated dry lands, with almost identical findings. Gideon noted the exception:

The only difference worth naming is, in our county there occurs a greater number of medium seasons which may be, I think, attributed to our more easterly position. Our wet, very wet, and extremely wet seasons correspond with the date of his [Kuechler's] observations. That the present drought is an exception to any that has occurred within the last 141 years I may add a scrap of testimony resulting from my own observations which will, in my estimation, strengthen this opinion considerably. The pin oak (*Quercus palustris*) delights in low moist lands, is a large useful tree found in groves

---

[7] Kuechler (1823–1893) was county surveyor for Gillespie County, Texas, in 1860; commissioner of the General Land Office in 1870; chief surveyor in 1878 for the Texas and Pacific Railway Co. (*Handbook of Texas*, Vol. I, p. 975). George Durham sent Gideon a publication containing Kuechler's findings at Fredericksburg. The *Texas Almanac, 1861*, contains an unsigned article (pp. 136–137), "The Droughts of Western Texas," in which is incorporated Kuechler's table of seasons for West Texas for the past 130 years.

along the narrow bottoms of small creeks and sometimes in wider bottoms. During 1856 this species of oak in our county almost entirely died out.[8] Old trees and young and saplings all shared the same fate. Some of the largest I examined contained 143 year rings and as the old and the young alike all died together the conclusion that the present drought is an exception to any that happened within the period of time recorded by these pin oaks is, it seems to me, quite a fair one. From these unerring records the *anxious* farmer may, by examining a series of 28 years of them, form very satisfactory estimates as to the average value of his annual products. It is worth looking at.

Gideon found evidence of ancient tropical lushness while making "for the sake of amusement it affords me" an examination of the formation on the Yegua Creek slope. Deep watercuts revealed beds of solid sandstone in which he found pine knots, sycamore logs, oaks, cottonwoods, and willows whose rings showed they "flourished thousands of years before the germination of our own forests," and plants belonging to a warmer climate such as various species of cocoa trees, palms, cabbage palmetto, maguey, and yuccas.

But that they flourished here cannot be denied as in many places they are found standing erect with their roots still deeply inserted in the sandstone.

The investigation of the history of the seasons which occurred during the period in which their old undeniable stone records were written in a much warmer and much more humid atmosphere than ours would not result in any very great benefit to the practical agriculturist beyond the satisfaction of having his mind disenthralled from the disturbing influences of the unmeaning cosmogony of the ancients. But to be able to read understandingly the recorded truths which are unerringly enstamped in every tree of our living forests would be a profitable attainment to say the least of it.

Gideon left his parched land and meager corn for the Gulf Coast, accompanied by Sarah and Sallie:

We have our encampment immediately on the sea beach where the salt spray dashes into our tents and the eternal roar of the great deep frightens the uninitiated. The clean washed sanitary shore has its million varieties of glittery and gorgeously painted shells of every shape and form that imagina-

---

[8] The true pin oak is *Quercus palustris Muenchh.* Robert A. Vines (*Trees, Shrubs, and Woody Vines of the Southwest* [Austin, University of Texas Press, 1961] p. 177, states that he has "never seen the true Pin Oak in Texas outside of cultivation."

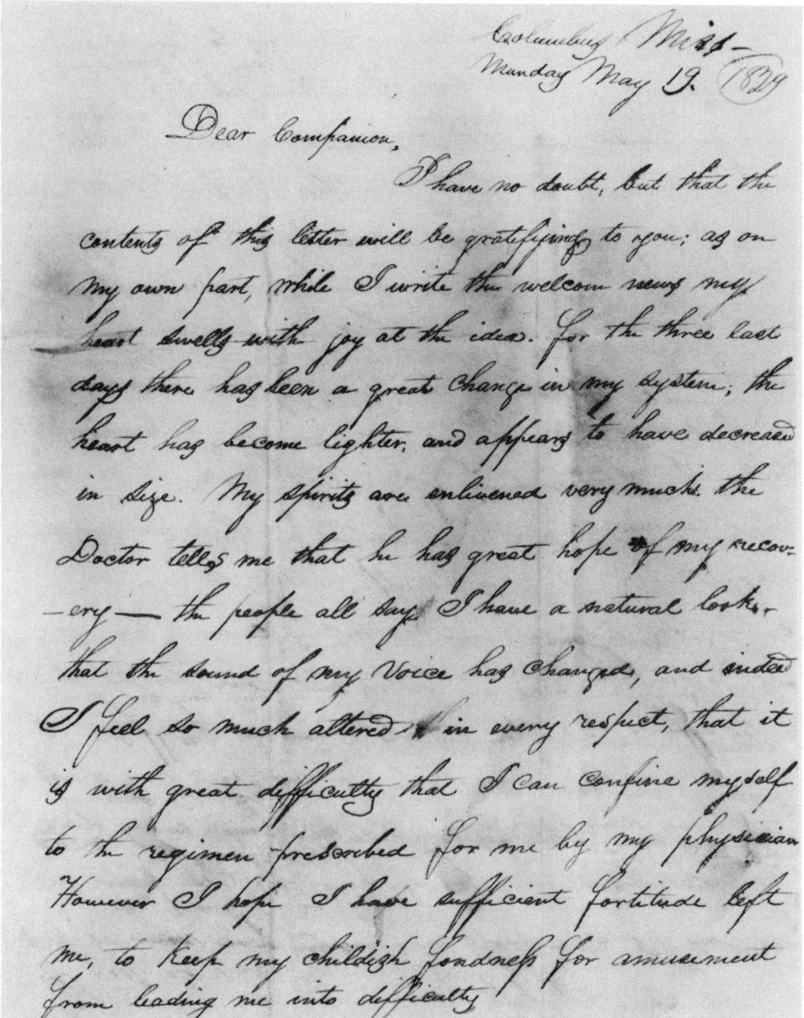
Columbus Miss—
Munday May 19. 1829

Dear Companion,

I have no doubt, but that the contents of this letter will be gratifying to you; as on my own part, while I write the welcom news my heart swells with joy at the idea. For the three last days there has been a great change in my system; the heart has become lighter, and appears to have decreased in size. My spirits are enlivened very much. the Doctor tells me that he has great hope of my recov-ery— the people all say I have a natural look, & that the sound of my voice has changed, and indeed I feel so much altered in every respect, that it is with great difficulty that I can confine myself to the regimen prescribed for me by my physician However I hope I have sufficient fortitude left me, to keep my childish fondness for amusement from leading me into difficulty

COURTESY UNIVERSITY OF TEXAS ARCHIVES

Letter from Lincecum to His Wife, May 19, 1829

Why dont you write to me, I want to hear all the little Changes, all the little things that has happened, and all the little private circumstances, which you would not like to send by word of mouth — therefore, write to me it will give me much pleasure; that is, if you write the letter yourself, I do not want a letter written by any one else, for then I should not get your ideas, it would be nothing more than another persons ideas on the Subject which you would wish to Communicate

If I continue to mend, I think I can come home in a month at least — I shall however, stay here untile I think myself entirely safe ———

Write to me how the Crop is coming on, inform me about the vining and potatoes, and dont forget the wheat ——— upon the whole, manage the affairs as well as you can, tell the boys to work and keep every thing in order, like they expected me home every day

Tell Sneed and Henry howdy. Tell Sneed that there is but few Crops as forward here now, as his was when I left home ———

(Letter to his wife, continued)

Keep all hands at work, when they have got the Crop clean set them at something, the Spring grove, wants fensing very much have that done if possible

Tell all my dear children how-dy for me, tell them not to forget me, and to act well their part, for in doing that, lies all the honor, and glory of man—

Tell Sarah, that I have not forgotten her numberless kind offices to me while I was there sick and receive for yourself all the love and affection of

a devoted Husband

Gideon Lincecum

P.S. Graybill has come back

(Letter to his wife, continued)

Lincecum's Announcement of Botanic Medical Practice,
Long Point, Texas

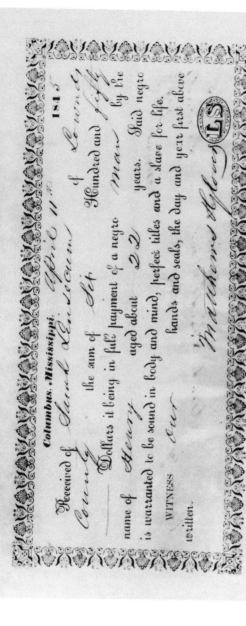

Receipt for Payment for Slave, April 11, 1845

Dried Hollyhock from Lincecum's Herbarium

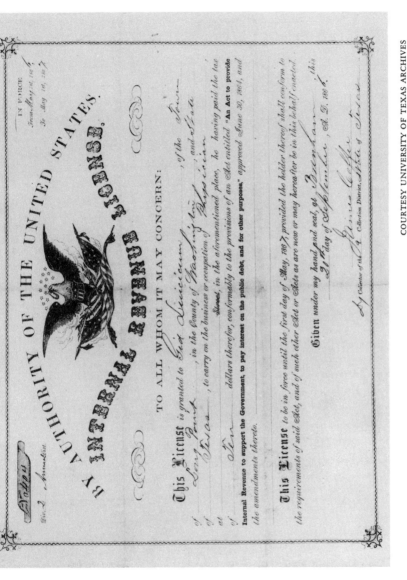

Federal License To Practice Medicine, 1867

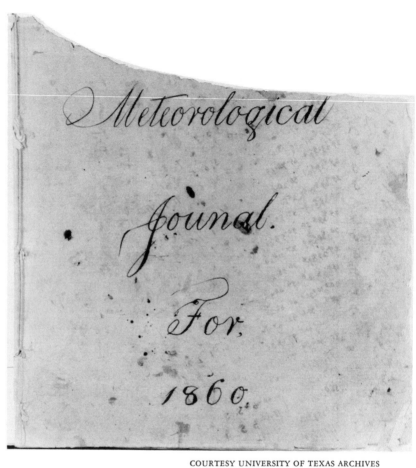

COURTESY UNIVERSITY OF TEXAS ARCHIVES

Cover for Lincecum's "Meteorological Journal, 1860"

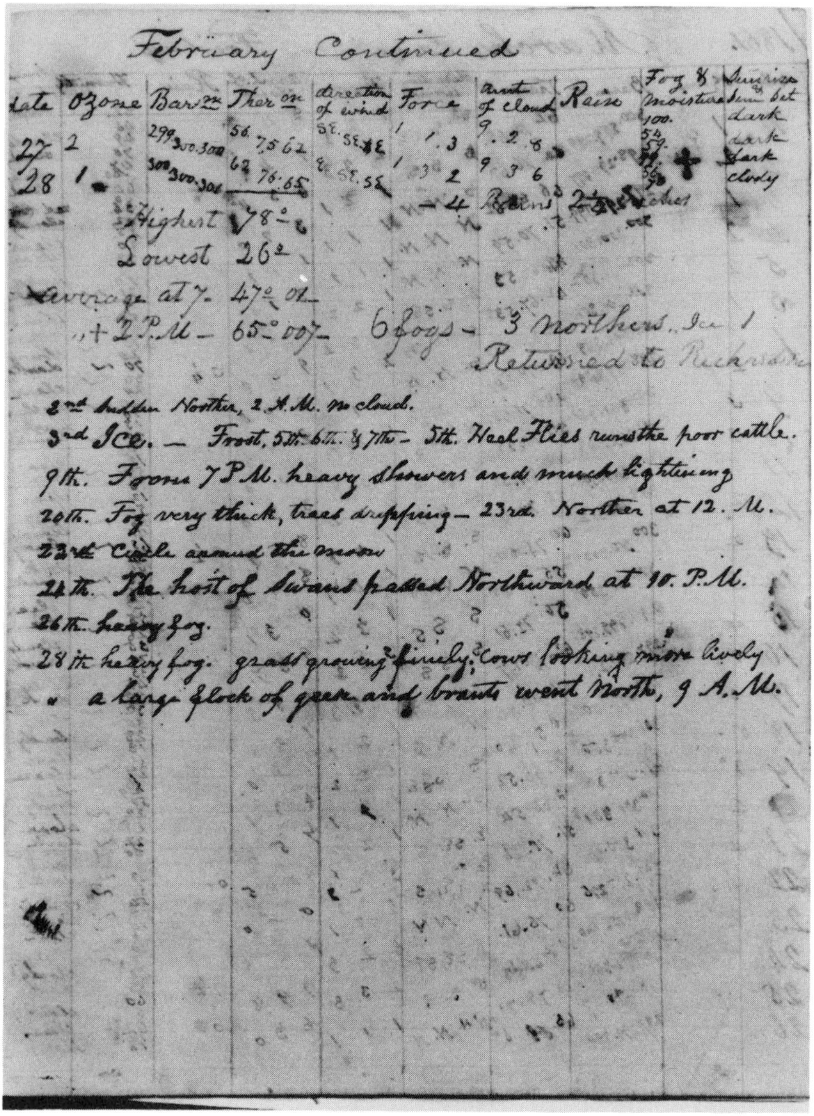
February Continued

date	Ozone	Bar.	Ther.	direction of wind	Force	Amt of cloud	Rain	Fog & moisture 100.	Sunrise & Sun set
27	2	29.9 30.0 30.0	56 75 62	SE SE SE	1 1 3	9 2 8		54 59	dark dark
28	1	30.0 30.0 30.1	62 76 65	SE SE SE	1 3 2	9 3 6		56 57	dark cloudy

— 4 Rains 2½ inches

Highest 78°

Lowest 26°

Average at 7 — 47° 01

" + 2 P.M. — 65° 007 — 6 fogs — 3 northers. Ice 1

Returned to [illegible]

2nd Sudden Norther, 2 A.M. no cloud.

3rd Ice. — Frost. 5th. 6th. & 7th — 5th. Heel Flies runs the poor cattle.

9th. From 7 P.M. heavy showers and much lightening

20th. Fog very thick, trees dripping — 23rd. Norther at 12. M.

23rd Circle around the moon

24th. The host of Swans passed Northward at 10. P.M.

26th. heavy fog.

28th heavy fog. grass growing finely, cows looking more lively

" a large flock of geese and brants went North, 9 A.M.

COURTESY UNIVERSITY OF TEXAS ARCHIVES

Page from Weather Chart for February, 1861

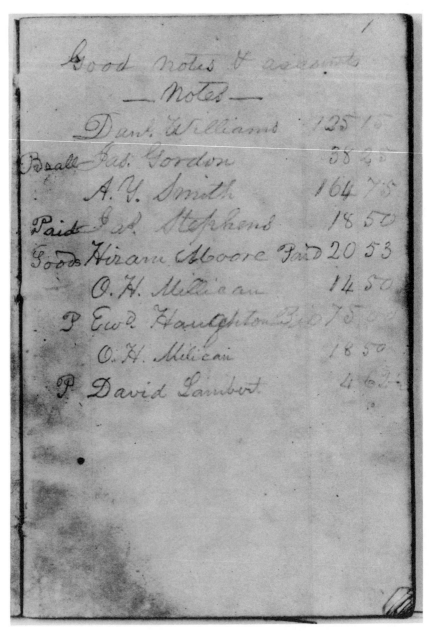

Gideon's Account Book: "Good Notes and Accounts—Notes"

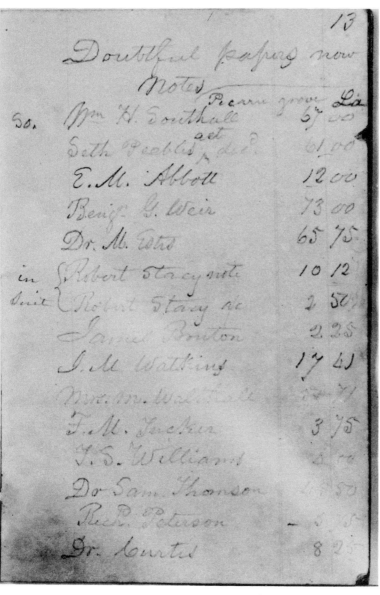

Gideon's Account Book: "Doubtful Papers, Now Notes"

COURTESY BARKER TEXAS HISTORY CENTER

Lincecum as an Old Man

tion could picture. Here on these crackling and thickly scattered conches and clams, sun cockles, and twisted helices with the foamy waves dashing surge after surge at the very feet, the curious lady [Sarah], enchanted with the rich prospect which lies so profusely strewed far and wide around her, strolls all day gathering and selecting the finest specimens until her overloaded apron gets too heavy for further progress; then she is forced to sit down on the clean dry sand and cull and reselect from her collection the most sightly; reluctantly she abandons the refused surplus and again begins the tedious search. All day she traverses the bespangled shore until welcome twilight overtakes her far down the sea-beaten beach. . . she hurries home and there displaying her well-earned trophies of the vastly deep declares to herself that tomorrow, if the day should not again turn out to be too short, she will be able to make a more beautiful selection.

Back at Long Point the drought was still the leading topic. Gideon warned his friends W. J. Gordon, of Columbus, Mississippi, who was planning a move to Long Point, of the dryness and short crops, but optimistically predicted an artesian well would not only solve the water shortage but afford irrigation for twenty-five to thirty acres. He urged Gordon to make the move and advised him to come by water, but to send his livestock overland.

If I had any favorite horses or mules that I desired to have the use of here I would procure some white man that I could trust, put in his care ten or twenty horses, three smart boys, and $200—and start them overland to Long Point fifteen days in advance of shipping myself and family and I should expect when I arrived at Long Point to find that they had been there two or three days.

Each mule and horse should be provided with a good rope halter. Three or four of them with pack saddles and sufficient number of boys to carry corn enough for one night's feed, also one good pack saddle and bags for carrying provisions, coffee pot, frying pan, &c. for camp use. And I would instruct them to camp out all the way and to lay in their supplies of corn &c. any time where they could find it convenient in the morning of each day and carry it on to a suitable camping place. In that way you can move any number of horses and as many negroes as will be required to take care of them cheaper than you could hire anyone to keep them the same length of time at one stable. In that way I had ten horses brought with three hands when I moved and it did not cost me but $142, ferryings and all.

The safest and most pleasant time to cross the Gulf is February. March is a good month; that is, the first and last weeks of it. I don't like April. There is however but little danger in the Berwick Bay route and it is a more pleasant passage. You may, if you are not detained at New Orleans, make the trip from Columbus to Long Point in 12 days. But you will have to stop with your kin folk a few days at Houston.

You may bring a carriage all the way, if you have one you like, cheaper than you can sell it there and buy another here. Fine carriages, however, have not as yet got to be the rage in the vicinity of Long Point. . . . I shall look for you anxiously. . . .

You speak of bringing with you a great deal of shrubbery. That may do if you come as early as January. Later it will be useless, except bulbs and seeds.

Forgetting the parched land and drought, Gideon described his county as he had many times viewed it:

Tell your good lady that our whole prairie is a flower garden, richly bedecked with all the shapes and various tints and colors that old Sol with his perpendicular rays and sevenfold threads of light can untwist; and that a stroll in early morn over our wide spread grassy plains and blooming lawns; viewing the flocks of sheep and herds of fat cattle; listening to the continual hum of the busy bees, the gay and gleeful notes of the pretty birds; inhaling the sweet odor of the millions of gorgeous flowers and the pure life and health-giving sea breeze would be worth more to her in solid, intellectual enjoyment than a whole year spent in an artificial lot of flowers and shrubs with a fence around it. There is no comparison, or figure than can illustrate the reality of this picture. It must be seen, breathed and traveled upon to realize and appreciate its transcendent beguilings.

If you conclude to come by land and cannot get off early in October don't try before the last of April. Everybody who has come out during winter and early spring has given most horrible accounts of their sufferings in rain, high water, mud and great difficulty and frequent delays on account of sickness, wagon breaking, hardships occasioned by the sloppy condition of the exceedingly bad roads.

James Lauderdale seemed almost worn out when he arrived last spring and he told me that he had been so worried on the way that he was sometimes almost deranged and that he had been so much troubled at moving down and broken wagon fixtures that he had done some pretty fair swearing, notwithstanding the fact that he professes to be on all ordinary occasions a penitent religionist. By land during the wet season it will require 35 to 40 days to make the trip, during May or early summer 30 days. Try water, 12 days.

Early in December the unmistakable odor of a norther was in the air: "The smell of the gray and sullen smoky norther always puts me in mind of the odor that occurs while washing a dirty gun, especially if it is with warm water that I am performing that filthy job." Sitting in his study, Gideon watched a spider which had been busily weaving a web outside the door. Suddenly it stopped its work and Gideon felt the first gentle but chilly breath of the norther. When it calmed, the spider resumed its work of measuring and tying the meshes of its net.

Soon there came a fiercer blow, he hesitated not another moment but dropping all and clinging to the thread with which he was an instant before so busily and so artistically constructing his destructive trap, cast off and letting himself down crawled into concealment amongst the tangled oak leaves. . . . "Poor fellow," thought I, "you have missed your supper but you may console yourself for it won't be long till you will be insensible to the pinching demands of a hungry stomach." . . . How many short-sighted beings in this *providence protected* world . . . will be like the spider—overtaken this night in the midst of fondly cherished anticipation, equally unprepared to meet the fierceness of the pending norther, drop the thread of their respective vocations never to be resumed again?

The temperature dropped from fifty-three degrees at 7:00 P.M., "and hominy hail falling pretty fast," to twelve degrees at 9:00 P.M. At 7:00 A.M. it was still twelve degrees with two inches of snow. After a few days of warmth another severe norther struck, catching Gideon's honeybees off guard.

"They went out to work in the afternoon today and were quite late getting in again. I think it quite likely that some of them, as they do in pleasant weather, lay out with the expectation of bringing in an early load of sweet things in the morning, but the norther came. Oh for the glory of the unerring instinct. But there is no instinct, and my bees, like erring men, must die."

The snow briefly broke the drought, but the intense cold killed the few remaining fruit trees, the wheat crop was destroyed, "a great many cows and hogs perished, [and] some horses and thirty or forty people who were caught out in the norther, unprepared, froze to death."

The unusual cold weather did not prevent all fifty-nine of the Lincecum grandchildren from visiting.

The old lady, while they were performing their gay, thoughtless whirling dances, manifested a disposition to brag a little but it would have afforded a form of higher enjoyment to me to have seen them as well pleased in something that would have called out a greater degree of intellectual action. I never did see any sense in dancing. But I never tried it, I may not know.

A few weeks later he wrote a friend: "We are all enjoying high health and good condition except the old lady. In the time of the first severe norther she got a little too smart, went out upon the ice and while sledding about with some of the youngsters fell down and dislocated her wrist. It has been a painful affair, other ways her health is good."

As 1859 closed, Gideon gave but little thought to the approaching war. He mildly expressed his views to Charles Partridge, Boston publisher:

If we cannot dwell together agreeably, separation is the only remedy. And when the two halves shall each get up their sectional splits, let them separate again and again as the office seekers and theologians may find it necessary until there is nothing left but an ugly *tale* of the sad affair. The toiling portions of these United States are all democrats, desiring liberty and peace. They form one party. Among them there would arise no national divisions. But they are ignorant illiterates, abhorring mental labor.

Gideon was never again to be so indifferent on the division of the North and the South, nor dwell so peaceably in his beloved Washington County.

A NOTE ON SOURCES

The descriptions of Washington County land values and prices are given by Lincecum in letters to W. J. Gordon, Calhoun County, Arkansas, June 14, 1859, Columbus, Mississippi, August 28, October 22, 1859; Hugh Thompson, New Orleans, Louisiana, May 27, 1859; John H. Douglas, Mason City, Illinois, January 14, 1860; and to John Lincecum, Bear Creek, Louisiana, May 22, 1859.

Lincecum's descriptions of himself and of his eating and sleeping habits are contained in letters to Dr. W. A. Dunn, Winfield, Georgia, April 4, September 11, 1861. Lincecum and Dr. Dunn became acquainted through a correspondence which began when Dr. Dunn inquired about native Texas grasses. They had never seen each other.

Gideon's observations on the spider and the bee are in letters to Caleb G. Forshey, Texas Military Institute, Rutersville, Texas, November 6, 17, December 5, 1859. These letters, and one to George Durham written September 1, 1859, describing drought cycles, mark the real beginning of Lincecum's consuming interest in natural sciences. Lincecum wrote Forshey that he regretted they could not see each other more often: "Philosophic, untrammeled natural minds are like angel visits. With me it is a lonely sad condition for I like to have someone who can think near me when I open a new volume in nature's unerring record." This interest is also revealed in a notation in Lincecum's address book: "Siegismund, Dr. August, Houston, a geologist, chemist, learned in natural philosophies and physics."

Other quotations and information on Lincecum's life and conditions in Washington County in 1859 are from Lincecum's letters, all written in 1859, to E. C. Stamps, Washington County, Texas, March 26; John Alexander, April 17; Charles Partridge, New York City, May 31; M. C. Hamilton, Austin, Texas, September 1; Cushman & Close, Galveston, Texas, April 4, 17, 21, May 30, June 19; McGowen Iron Foundry, Houston, Texas, April 4, December 18; A. Z. Rumsey, Houston, Texas, April 8, 17; E. Waller, Jr., Hempstead, Texas, June 13; Abram Close, Galveston, Texas, July 4; Hiram Close, Galveston, Texas, November 16, December 18; Messrs. Marschalk & Son, no address, August 16; D. Messner, New York City, August 10, September 7; Dr. E. W. East, Salt Lake City, Utah T., May 1.

CHAPTER TEN

GIDEON
AND THE LINCOLNITES

It would be no difficult matter to establish the doctrine
of the superiority of the white race were it not for the
occasional occurrence of distorted deviations of white manhood. GID

THE YEAR 1860 forebode hard times in Washington County. It
was a year of extended drought and heat. Gideon's weather
chart for Long Point showed a high temperature of 107 degrees for
July and an average of 101 degrees for the month. The last rain was
in April. The corn crop was a failure.

"Money is growing beautifully less and less," Lincecum wrote to a
relative in Mississippi. "We are living on short rations now and a little
more practice will show how little it takes in reality to sustain humanity. We are as poor as Job's turkey."

Lysander and the boys drove the thirsty and hungry cattle, four
hundred head bearing the GID brand, to graze near Dripping Springs
in the wild and sparsely settled county of Hays. The cattle—or what
was left of the herd—were not to come home until after the Civil
War.

The herd was left in charge of Cassianus Lincecum, Gideon's grandson, and Richard Powell, Cass's stepbrother. Gideon frequently wrote
to young Richard, because "from what Lysander tells me, you and
Cassianus are having somewhat of a lonesome time of it. . . . Sur-

rounded as you are with so large a tract of wild, romantic scenery . . . I do not think I should feel lonesome as long as there remained an unexplored gully."

Gideon urged the boys to collect rocks, fossils, and shells, and study and arrange them. He was highly pleased when Richard wrote a description of his collection.

The lonely life was not to last long. Cass was among the first Texans to volunteer for service in disarming United States troops stationed in Texas and young Richard was one of the victims of the Willis Gang, which terrorized the Texas frontier during the Civil War.[1]

On July 31, 1864, Gideon acknowledged Durham's letter of the twenty-third "announcing the rather satisfactory news of the execution of the murderers of that worthy young man, Dick Powell . . . the first instance for several years of a manifestation of justice in that unholy city [Austin]." During the next several years the stray Lincecum cattle were the subject of correspondence between Gideon and James Manor, of Manor, Texas, whom Gideon requested to pasture them; J. G. Weaver of Bastrop, who sent $100 in Confederate money for a brown and white ox branded GID; and Thomas P. Roundtree of Dripping Springs, whose sons Gideon asked to round up and brand the cattle. Lincecum wrote Roundtree: ". . . they can procure the branding iron at the ranch where Dick Powell resided at the time the Willises killed him."

But the Lincecum herd was left untended and free to roam the range.

In Washington County the creeks and streams were dry and the rivers low. The dry bed of the Yegua Creek, used as a road, soon proved to be the best route in the county. The few remaining cattle on the Lincecum farm wandered off in search of water. Gideon was reminded of his conversation with an old Indian near Goliad twenty-five years before. When Lincecum asked him why there were so many wild horses and cows on the Texas prairies the Indian explained that many years ago a seven-year drought had sent the coast Indians and their

---

[1] For the activities of the Willis family and the hanging of three of them by a mob in Austin in 1864 see Frank Brown, *Annals of Travis County*, MS, Archives Collection, University of Texas Library, Ch. 23, pp. 57–60, and J. W. Wilbarger, *Indian Depredations in Texas*, (reprint of the 1889 edition, Austin, Steck Co., 1935), pp. 536–539.

cattle inland in search of water. Finding none they continued to Mexico, abandoning their stock along the way. The horses and cows not only survived the drought but increased in number.

Gideon realized the need for an adequate and dependable water supply, not only for his family and stock, but for irrigation purposes. He dropped all other projects to start an artesian well, an experiment which caused a great deal of interest throughout Texas.

Lincecum ordered an eight-horsepower engine made by Phillip Rahm of the Eagle Machine Co. of Richmond, Virginia. The engine cost $850 and Gideon described it as a "moving thing, like a thing of life."

In November, Gideon visited Austin to check on the progress of two artesian wells being drilled by the pole process.[2] Gideon planned to use the rope process and hoped to go down 1,000 feet. Drilling began early in 1860. In late spring, answering an inquiry from J. J. Nash of Washington County, Gideon explained: "I am down ninety feet and it has cost me thus far $1600. My purpose is to procure water for our own farming and to show the community whether or not the artesian well is practical. There has been no successful experiment of this kind yet made in Texas."

In July, with no water left for operating the engine, it was necessary to haul it from the nearest source two miles away. In August the well depth was two hundred feet.

Gideon explained to an Alabama educator who was urging him to translate the Chahta Tradition from the original Choctaw:

I shall not be competent to discharge the duties of any other enterprise until I produce a satisfactory, gushing jet of water. I consider this well the last enterprise that I shall undertake while I remain in this terrain adobe and should I succeed, taking all things into consideration, it will be the greatest and most beneficial work of my life.

A new kind of trouble began to stir and, as it grew, the artesian-well experiment was indefinitely postponed. On August 18, 1860, Gideon wrote to his nephew John:

[2] One was a state well and the other was a well being bored south of Austin on the property of Swen Magnus Swenson. The state well was started in April, 1857, and when Gideon visited Austin it was down 525 feet, and Swenson's 500 feet. The *Texas Almanac, 1867* (p. 235) reported that the state well on the Capitol grounds was down 1,200 feet in 1866 and producing a small but steady stream.

We are just passing through the danger of a negro insurrection here that has worried our young men considerably. The negroes are incited to rebel by a set of northern fanatics, who are prowling about through the country preaching, selling maps, mending clocks, &c., &c. We have hung a good many of them, amongst whom were four or five preachers. As is the custom in the world's history of such matters the insurrection and the mischief they have done were all conducted in the name of the Lord. Poor Lord, he stands a bad chance to sustain a good character for the damnedest rascals perform their villainies in his name universally. In this portion of the state there was no mischief done but the negroes nearly all knew of the movement and were prevented from doing any thing by the timely interference of the white people. It seems to have been a pretty general thing throughout the state and some counties have suffered great loss from fires that occurred from the influence of the infernal plot. Five or six towns in the upper counties have been almost entirely destroyed by fire under circumstances that leave no room for conjecture in the case at all. Already 30 or 40 negroes and 10 or 12 white men have been hung or shot. Our jails are full of prisoners and vigilance committees are making daily discoveries and I have but little doubt of there being many more of the heartless scoundrels who will yet be detected. Preachers of the gospel are being looked upon with suspicion.[3]

Early fall rains brought hope for the first successful crop in seven years in Washington County. The prairies were suddenly covered with blossoms and purslane. The people were "astonished and delighted but not more so than our hogs." Gideon's gauge measured the rainfall in November at $4\frac{1}{2}$ inches; in December at $3\frac{5}{8}$ inches, and in January at 8 inches. It was a gentle rain, absorbed deeply by the thirsty soil.

When war first threatened, Lincecum earnestly hoped that Texas would secede from the United States, not to join the Confederacy but to return to an independent and permanent republic. To him the election of Lincoln gave Texas a strong reason to withdraw. He wrote:

The government of the United States has failed almost in every instance to comply with her part of the articles of annexation and we have been wishing for an excuse for separation for five or six years. We are very capable of sustaining an independent government and with our very abundantly rich resources, a very wealthy one.

Gideon viewed all the prewar activities of anti-Unionists as a move-

[3] Lincecum referred to the 1860 incendiary fires in Dallas, Denton, Gainesville, and elsewhere, after which vigilance committees were responsible for an indeterminable number of hangings. Some of the victims were ministers.

ment for an independent Texas. The war talk and ineffectual arming he considered necessary preparedness to prevent invasion. Gideon firmly believed that Texas could remain neutral while the North and the South fought their war.

When the Long Point Minute Men were organized on December 9, 1860, he viewed the Lone Star flags with pride and faith. Among them was a new one, white with a red star and a single blue stripe through the center, symbolizing that Texas could stand alone.

Gideon was scornful of "Old Sam [Houston] who has slipped his station at Austin and is now off lecturing in favor of submission" and of other Texans who advocated remaining in the Union. To a friend who worried about the men going off to war and leaving the women and children to "the mercy of the negroes" Gideon replied:

I entertain vastly more confidence in the negroes than I do in any of the infernal, fanatic, abolition race. If Texas too submits I shall declare independence within the bounds of my own domain and maintain it as long as I have life. I'll do that if the worst comes.

He was alarmed when he heard in December that Governor Houston had issued a proclamation to convene the Legislature on January 17. Gideon fervently hoped a people's convention would favor secession for an independent Texas. He wrote to his son-in-law Durham in Austin:

I shall not attempt to question his [Houston's] reason for so doing. But there is mischief in the movement. . . . I suggest that yourself, Johns, Rector, Fry, White, and as many of those clever boys as you can get together who had a hand in getting out the call for a convention, meet again and get out another.[4]

The Washington County Minute Men, anticipating a people's secession convention, met in Brenham to nominate delegates. The Long

[4] Clement R. Johns, Hays County; J. E. Rector, Travis County; James H. Fry, Webberville; George W. White, Travis County. When Governor Houston refused to convoke the Legislature to decide the secession issue, a group of secession leaders, on December 3, 1860, called on citizens of Texas to elect delegates to a people's convention in Austin, January 28, 1861. Houston then called the Legislature to meet one week before the convention (Charles W. Ramsdell, "The Secession Movement in Texas," *History of Texas,* Dr. Eugene C. Barker, comp. [Dallas, The Southwest Press, 1929], Ch. XXXIV, pp. 452–458).

Pointers assembled at Mount Vernon Springs and from here marched to the courthouse at Brenham. At the head of the long line were two elderly veterans of the War of 1812, Sam Lauderdale and Gideon Lincecum, their long white beards and blue cockades rippling in the breeze.

In an account of the Minute Men meeting, written for the Galveston *News*, Gideon identified Colonel Lauderdale as an "old warrior who during the War of 1812 and 13 with the Creek Indians was the confidant of General Jackson and the active spirit among his staff officers."[5]

Lincecum described the march to Brenham in a letter to Richard Powell:

The order was promptly obeyed and all marched with old Sam Lauderdale and myself, wearing the blue cockade, placed at the head of the company by way of ornament as we had no music . . . the long line marched into dumfounded Brenham, reaching from the lower tavern up to McIntyres where they halted and at that point sang out, three or four voices froglike, "hurra for Long Point."

The march was a stirring event and the entry into Brenham was applauded by spectators who lined the main street from the tavern to the courthouse. Gideon later reported that the citizens "slammed together with one mind like a shackling door on a windy day."

Delegates nominated for the People's Convention, and subsequently elected by Washington County voters, were Dr. Jerome Bonaparte Robertson and Williamson Simpson Oldham, with James E. Shepard and John Winfield Scott Dancy chosen as alternates.[6] They were instructed to vote for a free Texas.

[5] The Lauderdales, Sam D. and his son James, came to Texas in 1858 from Columbus, Mississippi. James, a captain in the Confederate Army, was captured, but returned home before the war ended. If the *News* published the account, a handwritten copy of which is in the Lincecum Papers, it cannot be located in the paper.

[6] Robertson (1815–1891) was a practicing physician in Washington, Texas. He came to Texas from Kentucky in 1835 with a company of volunteers to aid in the Revolution. He was a state senator in 1849, a brigadier general during the Civil War (Pat I. Nixon, *The Medical Story of Early Texas* [Lancaster, Pennsylvania, Lancaster Press, 1946], p. 355). Oldham (1813–1868) was a Brenham, Texas, lawyer. A member of the Provisional Confederate Congress, he also represented Texas in the Senate of the Confederacy (*Handbook of Texas*, Vol. II, p. 311). Shepard (1817–1894) came to Texas from Virginia in 1840 and settled in Washington County, where he was a lawyer and district judge. During the Civil War he was

Lincecum wrote to Richard Powell at Dripping Springs:

Many of our loud-talking citizens have never made their appearance at any of the public meetings—Esq. [James R.] Hines, all the [Hugh and Alfred B. F.] Kerrs and many more too mean to name on this paper. . . . None of the Regulators except John H. Dawson has had anything to do with the movement at all. The [Dr. Thomas and T. W.] Morrisses and the Union Hill gang of Regulators have all stood aloof. The whole of the Long Point folks, without exception, have enrolled their names in the company. George Gentry and [Joseph] Vincent are quite conspicuous in their patriotism and for once, when the election came on, voted with the Long Point ticket.

The Minute Men were considered by many conservatives as too militant, and in support of the organization Gideon wrote to George W. Willrich in Independence, Texas: "You ask for my opinion of the movement. If we manage it on the true basis of our reserved rights, we shall have no war. Splits in our own ranks will encourage invasion. Let us stand firm."

He answered a hold-out, Aurelius G. Ledbetter of Round Top, Texas: "My Esteemed Young Friend: Your favor enclosing the letter of Judge [Isaac Barton] McFarland was received today. What harm can there be in organization? How can it damage our cause for us to be ready to defend? Does he, McFarland, fear that it would make a *fuss*? And what are *you* afraid of?"

The People's Convention delegates, in session, January 28, 1861, went beyond instructions to vote for an independent and perhaps neu-

---

a colonel in Texas troops (*A History of Texas and Texans*, Eugene C. Barker, ed. Chicago and New York, [American Historical Society, 1914], Vol. V, p. 2294). Dancy (1810–1866) of LaGrange was Gideon's old friend about whom he once wrote: "It has long been said that a still tongue makes a wise head. It may be true. But somehow or other it has got into my mind that an empty head makes a still tongue. J. W. Dancy, who can answer almost any question contained in the world of books, is never silent—his tongue never still, all the time repeating something that has been stored up in his fine-formed and well-balanced cerebral structure from books. But J. W. Dancy is not considered a wise man. Then books are not the things from whence to gain wisdom. If they were, John would most assuredly be considered a man of consummate wisdom for he has them all set up and properly labeled on the well-arranged shelves of his stupendous intellect and his retentive powers are sufficient to take down and use them, instantly applying them on the spur of any occasion." Four delegates were elected because the people's convention suggested that citizens elect "twice as many delegates as the district had representation in the legislature." (Ramsdell, "The Secession Movement in Texas," p. 454).

tral Texas. The delegates approved a resolution to secede and also declared the annexation ordinance of 1845 void, appointed a public safety committee to disarm U.S. troops in Texas, and elected seven delegates to the convention of seceding states at Montgomery, Alabama. One of the delegates to the Confederate meeting was W. S. Oldham, a Washington County delegate to the People's Convention.

The state Legislature, meeting at the same time, was in sympathy with the Convention and recognized its legality, but won a point favoring submission of the resolutions to the voters.[7]

In disgust at the results of the People's Convention, Gideon wrote his friend, Samuel B. Buckley, a Unionist:

There is no possible chance for the people—the producing classes—to have anything like justice done for them. They are too infernal ignorant of their rights. See what the late damnable convention has done—notwithstanding the fact that it is almost diametrically in opposition to the object for which they were elected. A large majority of the people in their stultified condition cry amen, and will sanction the doings of the said hell-deserving convention at the coming election by an overwhelming majority. Well, let them all go to ruin together while I shall try to teach myself not to grieve about it.

The outcome of the election was as Gideon predicted. Texas voters approved the action of the People's Convention on February 23. The Convention, refusing to yield to the state's legal body, the Legislature, reassembled on March 2 and adopted an ordinance uniting Texas with the Confederacy, ratified the constitution of the Confederacy, voted to require state officials to take an oath of loyalty to the new affiliate, and unseated Governor Houston when he refused to take the oath.

Military action in Texas began when the Convention established a public safety committee, which functioned before the secession issue was passed by popular vote. On February 16 General David Emanuel Twiggs, commander of the Department of Texas at San Antonio, surrendered all federal forces and stores of his command to state troops under Ben McCulloch.[8] Sixty men from Washington County answered the call for volunteers to march on San Antonio. Among them was Jo Lincecum, Gideon's grandson.

[7] *Ibid.*, p. 455.
[8] *Ibid.*, p. 456.

But Gideon stubbornly held the hope that war would not come. He wrote Hiram Close, a manufacturer of Galveston:

In your letter you allude to your extraordinary success in mill making. That's something to be proud of. Something that benefits society in good earnest. A mill is the teeth of a community. And so in regard to your successful experiment in mill making we may set it down that you chew grain for the multitude. Will they thank you for it? Civil War is a ruinous affair. But if they begin it we will tell them plainly now that the seceding states will never join them again.

He was still hopeful in March, 1861, when he wrote young Richard: "My opinion is that we shall have no war. Fighting is not a very desirable occupation even to a hot-blooded southerner. And to the frigid-souled northman it is too fatiguing."

When war came Gideon threw himself wholeheartedly into the effort after making an acid remark to his spiritualist friend Colonel S. D. Hay of Huntsville: "The war came one generation too late. It would have been of great advantage to the progressive world if it had come soon enough to have destroyed the progenitors of the present thieving, faithless race."[9]

Lincecum never doubted that the South would be victorious, and he excitedly expected a successful prosecution of the war: "I am at the certain prospects of the great change in human affairs that is about to take place in a constant ecstasy of almost frantic delight, hoping all the time that I may live to see it."

The war isolated him and placed him in circumstances similar to those of his early frontier life when he had only his wits and raw material to provide the necessities of life. Gideon gloried in the blockade and urged self-sufficiency to those grown soft with the comforts of civilization. When the government appropriated all his blankets, Gideon succeeded in making a machine to spin the long Spanish moss of east Texas trees. "I am supplying my bed with a good substitute. Lincoln can't freeze me into submission so long as our forests are draped with *Tillandsia useoides*," he gloated.

---

[9] Samuel D. Hay was U.S. District Attorney for the Eastern District of Texas when John C. Watrous was judge and Ben McCulloch marshal (*Texas Almanac, 1858*, p. 103). The Legislature in 1854 authorized Hay to establish a cotton and woolen mill in Huntsville, Texas (*ibid., 1854*, p. 92).

Gideon had an idea for an iron drop shot which he thought would increase the power of a six-pound cannon, and volunteered it to Leeds & Co., Iron Foundry, New Orleans, in a letter dated June 24, 1861:

In these perilous times it behooves every one who harbors any love for human rights to think of and examine every subject that seems to promise aid or strength in resisting successfully the unholy crusade of insane robbers by whom we are daily threatened. For several months my mind has been working at a missile which would in a field fight render a six-pounder equal to a 24-pounder gun. . . . Can not iron balls, perfect globes, weighing one ounce or thereabouts, be produced in large quantities as cheaply or nearly so as ordinary castings? If they can be produced on the principle of making the leaden drop shot they would take the globular form, fly straight and on the open field or decks of vessels would, when fired from a good six-pounder, do deadly work 300 yards and would equal four six-pounders with ordinary cannon shot.

The foundry manager replied that drop shots could not be made of iron. The reply did not satisfy Gideon because he had seen the Yankee cast-iron waistcoat buttons and small buckles. He described his plan in letters to a Dr. Carter, in New Orleans, and to Judah Philip Benjamin, Secretary of War in Jefferson Davis' Cabinet, but there is no record that either replied.

Gideon relished every scrap of information about the progress of the war. Much of it was firsthand, reported by soldiers, passing in increasing numbers, and by civilian visitors to various fronts. When Leonidas went to Galveston in November, 1861, to bring back his soldier-son Billy, ill with diarrhea, he also brought detailed information on the inadequate arms, unsanitary conditions, illnesses, and low morale among the troops on the Island. There were no guns but some of the soldiers had revolvers and many had knives. Gideon shared the war news with his many correspondents. To his sister, Mrs. Boone Moore, in Castroville, he wrote:

We should doubtless feel lonesome were it not for the fact that we live where the two great thoroughfares of middle Texas cross. Few nights pass without company. They are generally soldiers and to them our house and cribs are always open, free of charge. We have fed away to them three heavy crops and, though it has reduced our means to a pretty low ebb, we are nevertheless sorry that we are not able to do more. All I have shall go free as water to sustain our cause. What would life in the south under negro equality and Yankee rule be worth? Oh, let all I have go and life too rather than see that state of affairs.

Although Gideon dropped many subscriptions to newspapers and periodicals during the war, he continued sending his $10 renewal to the Galveston *News,* then published in Houston. In one transmittal he added a note: "I have laid aside my tools and am floating down the stream of life, slowly but surely, and I am a long way past Island No. 70. I desire to keep afloat until I see the Yankee ruined. Thine, GID."

But the papers gave little information on the war and he complained about it in a letter to Durham:

The papers on our side have taken to lying as bad as the robbers beyond 36° 30′ N. We can get nothing that is reliable now except perhaps such as comes from a few responsible travelers. Our near neighbor, Mr. Fullerton, who is able to bear the expense of such a trip, returned three days ago from a visit to the Army of the Potomac. Fullerton is in high spirits; he passed through a great portion of the encampments. He is a pretty good writer and I think it likely he will publish some of the things he saw.

In a letter to the *News* in November, 1861, Gideon offered a solution to the serious shortage of pulp paper, and urged the establishment of a mill in Texas. "There are plenty of enterprising men and sufficient capital," he wrote. "In the vegetable kingdom Texas is rich in plants containing long fibre. Herewith enclosed please receive for your chemists to experiment with specimens of the bark and wood of the shrub alluded to above."[10]

When his old friend Judge Rutherford predicted that the war would retard the sciences and industries in Texas, Gideon replied: "The creative spirit that has been so long asleep from the use of northern opiates is now wide awake and we hear of wheels, looms, iron foundries, gun factories, etc., over the breadth of the Confederacy."

Hearing that a sulphur shortage hindered the manufacture of gunpowder for the Southern army, Gideon wrote to the mayor of Tuscaloosa, Alabama, telling him where he could find enough sulphur for

---

[10] It was not until 1911 that pulp paper was first successfully manufactured on a commercial scale. Today it is a prosperous industry in Texas, *ibid.* [1961–1962], p. 267).

the war demands. Lincecum had seen it forty years before and gave exact directions where the deposit could be found in a river bed eight miles below the town.

Texans found themselves almost naked in 1862, because of the scarcity of cloth, and Lincecum was one of many who tried to buy, trade, or exchange raw material for cloth manufactured at the state penitentiary in Huntsville, where a cotton and woolen factory had been established in 1854.

Gideon wrote to General John S. Besser, financial agent for the prison, on March 31, 1862:

Please be so kind as to inform me as early as convenient if there is any possible chance to obtain a supply of goods for negro clothing for summer. Our negroes will be naked in spite of all we can do if you cannot assist us. And as the good fellows are so obedient and orderly these troublous war times we are grieved to see it. Notwithstanding the fact that we have plenty of the raw material laid up in store—cotton and wool—and could and would help ourselves by spinning and weaving it if we could procure cards. Cards however are out of the question.[11]

In our family there are about 100 who will need and must have summer clothing. If you can exchange the suitable manufactured article for our raw material, be so good as to write to us what kind you will take and the price it will command as well as the price of your goods, so that we may know how much to carry over and the time for us to have it there. You will see by our promptness how bad we need it and how much you will oblige us.

Receiving no reply, Gideon went to Huntsville in June and on his return to Long Point wrote again to Besser:

For the purpose of ascertaining the truth in regard to procuring supplies from your establishment I visited Huntsville; saw you and the press by which you are daily and hourly subjected to; and from your replies to other men learned the answers to my questions. I really had not the effrontery to pester you and so left without asking you anything in favor of self. Nor do I now, except it may happen to be convenient for you.

My son, L. J. Lincecum, and Mr. G. W. Gentry will go over to your place carrying some wool and they will, if it is necessary, remain there till they can obtain some goods for family use. If by remaining they can obtain sup-

---

[11] Besser was financial agent for the Texas penitentiary from 1850 to 1863. A cotton and woolen factory had been established there in 1854 (*Handbook of Texas*, Vol. I, p. 152).

plies in turn, and if this letter be considered as an application with the date
of their arrival, it will relieve me very much and lay me under lasting obligations for you to deliver to my son *for the use of my family*, 2 ps. Osnaburgs,
1 ps. twilled woolens and 10 or 12 hank of thread. If it is not convenient
for you to do so I shall not complain, as when I was there I saw and know
that you are doing all you can.

Nothing came of this plan and in July Gideon went again to Huntsville and talked with Besser's assistant, H. Randolph. After this visit
he wrote Besser:

I had not time the day I left your office to inform you of the arrangement
I had made with Mr. H. Randolph in regard to the business entrusted to my
care by four of my neighbors. I filed their papers and you laid them at the
then bottom of the pile of applications on your office table to await their turn
in the mill. You will find my name when you get down to them, in pencil,
on the back of each of the four papers. The names and the amount each man
placed in my hands are as follows: G. W. Campbell, $50; John Carmine,
$50; W. Derrick, $20; L. G. Lincecum, $40.

A similar list with the money ($160) was placed by me in the hands of
Mr. H. Randolph of your place and when you get down to the papers of
the above-named applicants if you will be so kind as to let Mr. Randolph
know it, you will be at no further trouble. He will attend to the rest and
store the goods until the owners, furnished with an order from me, call for
them. J. V. Matson, my son-in-law, also placed his list and money in the
hands of Mr. H. Randolph to be dealt with in the same manner of which
I suppose he informed you verbally.

Gideon did not get his cloth. He wrote about his failure in a letter
to his sister Emily:

I returned two days ago from Huntsville, whence I had been trying to
procure cloth to clothe our nakedness, but failed. Notwithstanding the fact
that they weave and finish off six thousand yards per day, there were so many
people in ahead of me that the superintendent told me that it would be five
weeks before my turn could be supplied. The time set was so long that I preferred nakedness to such extraordinary detention and returned empty as I
went.

People in this country are complaining mightily and indeed some of them
are really frightened at the thought of approaching nakedness. They seem to
have no inventive force and are folding their arms in utter helplessness.

Others who were provided with a pair or two of old half-worn cotton cards are spinning and weaving long pieces of elegant jeans with which they are clothing their families quite stylish. If cards could be had they would all be at it; but the cards are outside of the region of probability even. Quite a number of people are tanning their hides and will be able to shoe themselves the ensuing winter. Numbers again have made no provisions to meet the approaching contingencies. Your humble servant belongs to the latter class. It affords a most excellent opportunity for it, and if the Lord wants to get me on his side, now is the time for it. He can hook me in now by sending me a few sides of good shoe leather, *shore.*

Gideon was not one to fold his arms. He made his own spinning wheel and carding machine and shared it with his neighbors; he experimented with dyes and sent the formulas to numerous Texas women. The ladies were delighted. When no copperas could be found for the dyes he substituted what he called vinegar of iron—old iron-scrap junk boiled in vinegar or sour beer. For black or brown he used the heart wood of the mesquite tree; for red dye, red elm bark or wild peach bark and, after boiling, a good wash in lye; for yellow, alum and acetate of lead, which was junk lead boiled in vinegar, and pecan or black-oak bark. Green moss he found produced a lovely light brown shade.

To those who complained that the blockade deprived them of ink and compelled them to write with a pencil, Gideon gave a recipe he had used all his life for making his own. The formula is included in the Lincecum Papers.[12]

Lincecum must have been in Brenham on November 1, 1862, when Sam Houston spoke against secession.[13] A county meeting to discuss ways and means of dealing with unpatriotic citizens who refused to accept Confederate currency, a topic in which Gideon was greatly interested, was in progress when Houston stopped in Brenham on his way to Huntsville. Gideon was not likely to miss such a meeting, but since his correspondence from July to mid-November, 1862, is missing, history does not have his version of this event.

---

[12] Lincecum's ink is fast fading and many pages in his papers are blank.
[13] According to Guido Ransleben (*A Hundred Years of Comfort in Texas* [San Antonio, Naylor Company, 1954] pp. 81–86), the only papers printing the Brenham speech were German language ones. It was printed in its entirety in German in the San Antonio *Freie Presse* and had great influence on the pro-Union Germans of Texas.

Although Gideon would not have admitted it, he and Houston had much in common. They both wanted Texas free of the Confederacy, opposed sending soldiers out of Texas to fight for the South, detested local military law, freely criticized the Confederate generals' conduct of the war, and deplored the muddling ineptness of the Texas state government. In later years, Sam Houston, Jr., was an inmate of the Lincecum home in Tuxpan, Mexico. But no great oak of friendship grew from these small acorns. So far as it can be determined these two old Texans never met and Gideon steadfastly refused to concede to Houston a hero's mantle.[14]

As the war progressed, Gideon's most reliable information on its conduct on various fronts came from numerous young men with whom he corresponded. Some consulted him on their growing doubts and worries about the war and Lincecum willingly projected his "unfashionable and very unpopular thoughts" onto the battlefield.

In August, 1861, Companies E and F of the 5th Regiment, under Colonel Thomas Green, were mustered in Washington County to join General Henry Hopkins Sibley's invasion of New Mexico. George W. Campbell, thirty years of age, was captain of Company F. Lieutenant B. B. Seat, twenty-eight, of Campbell's company, was one of Gideon's correspondents. On January 29, 1862, Lincecum wrote Seat in El Paso, Texas:

My Dear Young Friend: Your welcome letter of the 10th Inst. came to hand yesterday—18 days en route. You desire that I shall give you the latest war news—There have been but two battles of any importance in a long time. That took place in the Cherokee nation between Apothleyoholo,[15] the great Creek warrior, having under his command in the fight 4000 men, and some Texas rangers, an Arkansas regiment also, some Chahta and Chickasaw Indians, amounting altogether 1200 men under General McIntosh. . . . On 15th January near Prestonburg in Kentucky a severe fight took place between General Marshall with 2500 men and the Lincolnites who were 8000

[14] In all probability, Gideon was present in Columbus, Mississippi, in July, 1839, when Houston was "received with considerable attention" (Marquis James, *The Raven* [New York, Blue Ribbon Books, 1929], p. 307).

[15] History calls this warrior Hopoetholoyahola. See Stephen B. Oates, *Confederate Cavalry West of the River* (Austin, University of Texas Press, 1961), pp. 31–33, for an account of the Battle of Chustenahlaha, December 26, 1861.

strong. . . . Eight or ten days since, two of the Lincoln vessels made an attack on the little Fort Velasco, at the mouth of the Brazos. They fired 22 guns but the little guns at the fort began to pester them, as I suppose, and they made haste to take distance.

The citizens evacuated Galveston for awhile but since the arrival of the long range rifle cannon, they have all gone back again. . . . Quite a number of the citizens of Missouri and some Kentuckians are here now who, having made shift to escape with a few negroes, have brought them to Texas hoping thereby to save them. Having left their families behind they are in great haste to return. Some of them belonging to the army are here on furlough and they hire their negroes where they can, most cases however are put out for their victuals and clothes. The accounts that these men give of the state of affairs in those divided states are truly distressing. Everything that spite and malice, cherished with a natural propensity for thieving, from the midnight assassin with his incendiary box of matches to the broad daylight robbing and plundering, is performed there daily and hourly; and even more horrible deeds than these are being enacted there between men who had lived neighbors for years.

Gideon wrote of Washington County events to his son-in-law, then at Fort Thorn, New Mexico, reporting the activities of George's wife, Leonora, and their seven children; assuring him that neighbors and Lysander were making his household comfortable; and imparting the cheering news that George's little daughter, Sally, was miraculously recovering from paralysis and could walk around a chair. Gideon relayed George's war news to the Boone Moores:

We received yesterday a letter from George Campbell bearing date 25th January. They are all well . . . and are for the present stationed at Fort Thorn, New Mexico. They are three or four days march from Fort Craig, the place they set out to battle against. It was garrisoned by 1000 Federal troops and about 2000 Mexicans whom they had enlisted to join the Lincoln army. Gen. Sibley had issued a very pretty and sensible proclamation to the inhabitants of New Mexico which had the effect to discredit the tales that had been told them by the Lincolnites and Sibley's Brigade was received with open arms by the Mexicans. Thus gaining the privilege of marching his troops through their territory unmolested, he set out for Ft. Craig and had progressed to Ft. Thorn 60 or 70 miles from the Federal garrison and was waiting for all the men to come up when they received the information, as

Campbell states, that the Lincoln troops had evacuated Ft. Craig and had marched in the direction of California.[16] Sibley's Brigade, as soon as they establish a government in New Mexico, will continue their march towards Missouri. Cassianus and Jo, Lycurgus' two older boys, are in Capt. Campbell's company and George says they are soldiers of the true Lincecum stock.

Another "esteemed young friend" was John Hawkins Lewis, attached to Captain Lauderdale's regiment at Fort Hebert, Texas, located at Virginia Point, across the railroad bridge from Galveston. To Lewis on March 15 Lincecum gave further news of the situation in New Mexico:

J. E. Shepard was here today and said he saw a letter yesterday dated at Ft. Craig which was written by young Chauncy Shepard. As late as 18th February, Chauncy stated that they had approached Ft. Craig in considerable force, surprised and made prisoners of one of their advance pickets—22 in number, who were Mexicans. There is but one pass through which the fort can be approached. Sibley's forces entered that and when they had advanced to within 800 yards of the fort a long taw fight commenced which lasted an hour or two. The fort lost five men killed; our side "nobody hurt." He stated that they intended to storm the place the next day (19th). He also stated the garrison to be 5000 strong, 3000 Mexicans and 2000 regulars. The wise ones think there will be but little fighting in taking the fort but Chauncy thinks differently.[17]

Gideon remained optimistic in the face of growing defeats. While most of his neighbors suffered because of the blockade and prayed for assistance from England, he maintained that if the blockade remained three years the Confederacy would be independent of England and every other country. He believed "the spirit of liberty never has and never can receive any valuable aid from a crowned head."

[16] This optimistic rumor was false. Sibley engaged the Federals in the Battle of Valverde on February 21, 1862, and although the Confederates won the battle they did not take Fort Craig, the key fortress defending New Mexico (Martin Hardwick Hall, *Sibley's New Mexico Campaign* [Austin, University of Texas Press, 1960], pp. 83–103).

[17] Chauncey Berkeley Shepard was correct. He was the son of C. B. Shepard, state senator from Washington County, and nephew of James E. Shepard. He was eighteen when he enlisted in George Campbell's Company F, and served as Colonel Thomas Green's aide in the New Mexican and Louisiana campaigns. He was a captain when he was killed at the Battle of Mansfield, April 8, 1864 (Tombstone, Masonic Cemetery, Brenham, Texas). His name appears on most muster rolls as Charles B. Sheppard.

There was general fear of an attack on Galveston but Gideon doubted the military advantage of the town to either side; nor could he understand why the citizens of Galveston insisted on the presence of soldiers "except to drink their liquors and spend their money for their little tomfooleries." He pointed out to young Lewis, then on the Island, that even if the Confederates had sufficient arms to hold it, the carnage would only be increased. Lewis was eager for a battle and Gideon advised him against leaving Galveston "at this season" to join the army in Kentucky, Virginia, or Missouri, explaining that the abrupt change had killed more Texas troops than all the battles. Knowing Gideon's fondness for oysters, Lewis proposed to send him some. Gideon thanked him, but protested that "there are so many delays and mishaps on the railroad they would probably spoil before they could reach Long Point."

Dissatisfaction among the Confederate soldiers stationed in Texas was apparent early in the war. In February, 1862, Gideon replied to a letter from Lewis, on Galveston Island:

Your letter breathes like all the letters I receive from our boys in the army— a degree of suspicion that the heads of departments, both civil and military, are at fault somewhere. It indicates a deep-rooted dissatisfaction at the unnecessary inactivity and useless expenditures of the time and means and strength of the common soldier; while the pets and favorites of the government are luxuriating in speculations and peculations of the deepest, darkest and most damnable character. Whether this dissatisfaction amongst the common soldier arises from the fact that their position in the army precludes the possibility of taking a hand in the frauds and downright thieving or whether it swells up from the pure patriotic hearts of the true devotees of the spirit of liberty, the ultimates will be the same.

A sharp and impartial observer, Gideon believed, would be forced to the conclusion that both sides were successfully carrying out a plan to rob, plunder, and ruin the peace and happiness of inhabitants on both sides of the Mason-Dixon line, and that if the suffering people possessed intelligence and honesty they would stack their arms and return to their families.

Gideon and young Lewis exchanged long letters on their personal and, at times, private thoughts of war. Lewis, apparently, was an unusual young man to whom Gideon could safely state his "unpopular" views. Lincecum's letters to other young soldiers were generally in the nature of pep talks, in which he spurred them on to fight for the Confederacy and never yield to the Yankees. But to young Lewis he could write:

. . . I know very well that war and its bloody results, with its demoralizing ultimates, is perfectly natural and controlled by a law as regular and irresistible as is the falling rain drops or perpetual ice on the snow-capped mountains. It would seem as reasonable for me to complain at these undoubted natural phenomena as to complain at the foolish actions and unprofitable troubles so often and so eagerly entered into by the genus homo. The cause is a plain one and has almost proved itself to be out of the reach of remedial agents. Ignorance is its name. Are battle fields, cannon balls, grape shot, and Bowie knives the antidote? Do carnage and thieving promise progress?

. . . There is a general flutter, a universal breaking up of what I denominate the coagulated confederacy. This clabber has been recently pretty severely stirred, churned up; is now boiling and foaming, promising ultimates. Those ultimates at this stage of ebullition can only be guessed at. It may all turn out to be whey, or it may culminate in a fine large mass of rich butter. From the marked change in the countenance of the community I feel confident that the latter, though the boiling surges, and overwhelming waves to be encountered may oft and deeply try men's souls, will finally be awarded to the brave and daring sons of the South.

In July, 1862, the survivors of Sibley's defeated Brigade began to arrive in Washington County. On the twenty-fifth Gideon wrote to the Boone Moores:

Our family and all the connections are healthy; indeed there is no sickness in this vicinity. I might mention however that there are but few people in the county for disease to prey upon; the women and children, a few old men and soldiers who have been refused a place in the army are all that are remaining for the hydra-headed monster to sting at this time. There went from this precinct 221 volunteers. The conscript law caught a few Dutchmen who resided in the background towards the Yegua bottom and that was all it could find in this precinct. It is rather a lonely looking country about this time. Portions of Sibley's Brigade began to drop in yesterday and as they have a 60-day furlough and two companies of them went from here our society will be filled up a little during that period. This settlement has already commenced preparations for giving them a fat barbecue and a ball as soon as they all get home, which will transpire in the course of 10 or 12 days. The old lady is in for it; but she, as you know, is always in ecstasies at the thought of a big frolic of any kind. Well, let her rip, she shall not have her requirements stinted.

Another of Gideon's war correspondents was twenty-four–year–old F. M. Gaston, who enlisted in Campbell's company but returned to Washington County soon after beginning the journey to New Mexico. Early in 1862 Gideon wrote a letter in Gaston's behalf to Dr. J. Boring, Confederate Army, San Antonio, describing the soldier's deep-seated cough, adding: "It is my opinion that in a warm climate he is able to perform the duties of an average soldier. But I should not be willing to risk him during the winter and spring months in a higher latitude than he is now in."

Dr. Boring evidently agreed with Gideon's diagnosis, because a year later Gaston was in Jordan's Saline, Texas,[18] where Gideon wrote him that "everything about this vicinity is moving on in about the same style as it was when you left. No deaths or marriages, nor any recent babes that I have heard of. The war seems to have put a check upon everything. I did not expect, however, it would force a blockade upon the baby ports."

On July 27, 1863, Gaston was with Terrell's regiment at Hempstead when Gideon wrote:

It seems strange . . . that you and your officers still entertain doubts about the fall of Vicksburg! Vicksburg and Port Hudson are both in possession of the Yankees and, as I conceive, greatly to our advantage . . . we are able to keep the war up for an indefinite period and we should not think of a cessation of hostilities so long as a single principle of Southern rights is impinged on by the infernal, humanity dishonoring, damned Yankees. There is nothing right or honorable in that villainous people. . . .

Except a very large assemblage of gentlemen and ladies, negroes, children and dogs that took place at the big lake last Saturday there has been nothing to disturb the ordinary monotony of this section of the country. I was with them at the lake. There were perhaps 150 individuals there, all fine and

---

[18] Gaston consulted Gideon on the best way to produce evaporation. Jordan's Saline, now Grand Saline, was the site of a salt mine in Van Zandt County. During the war General Sterling Price ordered Colonel Rollin W. Rodgers and a company there to operate it for use by the Confederate Army (Barker, ed. *Texas and Texans,* Vol. IV, p. 1776).

bright, and having plenty of fish, which was by management of Mr. T. Affleck,[19] well prepared. They seemed to enjoy themselves exceedingly. The thing was well got up, executed in good style, having the greatest abundance of fat fish. It terminated satisfactorily, nothing occurring on the grounds to mar the good feeling that seemed to cheer every countenance. We are all well, but little fun nowadays.

Another festivity at Long Point that year, in which Gideon did not participate, was a Confederate ball arranged by the Negroes of the community. Proceeds were to go to the Texas soldiers fighting in the South. It was a financial failure according to Lincecum, not even clearing expenses, but a great social success and attended by four hundred slaves.

[19] Affleck served as chief purchasing commissioner for Texas and many army supplies came from his shops in Washington County. One soldier complained that "we have had a little trouble with our packs. The packages were put up of all shapes and sizes, and in spite of all we could do, they would not ride well, and the packsaddles made at Affleck's factory were made by men that never saw one I suppose in their lives the consequence was that already they have cut and galled our horses' backs" (*Batchelor-Turner Letters, 1861–1864,* H. J. H. Rugeley, ed. [Austin, The Steck Company, 1961], p. 30). Affleck had two sons: Isaac Dunbar, born in 1844, and John H., born in 1850. Gideon referred to the younger son when he wrote to Hannay, his stranded English friend, on October 27, 1864: "If you could get out to Brownsville you would soon meet with an opportunity to ship for Europe. Some boys who would soon be old enough to enter the Confederate service were sent off from this vicinity day before yesterday. They are on their way to Scotland via Matamoros. That countryman of yours, Thomas Affleck, had a hand in sending them off under the pretext of educating them. It was said that Affleck was going to send his 13-year-old son but I cannot say whether he did so or not. But if you had been there doubtless you might have got off as a kind of mentor with them. I did not know that any such movement was in contemplation until they were on their way." After Lincecum's death, Isaac Dunbar, called "Dunnie," was a member of a team of naturalists investigating Lincecum's theory of agricultural ants. During the Civil War Dunnie was in Major General John A. Wharton's escort company in the Louisiana and Arkansas campaigns. His was not the life of the common soldier. Not only was he well supplied with clothing from home, but he was attended by a slave, who served him coffee in bed each morning and who substituted for him for wood-chopping duty. Dunnie frequently threatened to leave the army, especially when he heard that Captain Leander H. McNelly was joining the command, and he was often piqued because family friends among the staff officers took so little notice of him. A nod of recognition from General Wharton caused Dunnie to complain that "I have never seen any one change as Genl Wharton has, since I left the company he is not the same man at all. There he would speak and shake hands with a private, but here they are beneath his notice and he is as Crabid [*sic*] as an old bear besides" ("With Wharton's Cavalry in Arkansas: The Civil War Letters of Private Isaac Dunbar Affleck," Robert W. Williams, Jr., and Ralph A. Wooster, eds., *Arkansas Historical Quarterly,* Vol. XXI, No. 3 [Autumn, 1962], pp. 247–268).

Two months after the fish fry Gaston was with Terrell's regiment in Richmond, and Lincecum, noting the errors and weaknesses of the Confederate generals, wrote that "some time ago [we] were all complaining at General Sibley for his mismanagement and drunkenness. Now it seems they are all Sibleys."

When the currency began to drop alarmingly Gideon read all the suggestions and ideas to restore it and made his own proposal in a letter to the editor of the Galveston *News*: that each man in the Confederate states deliver one-fourth of all his Confederate notes and bonds to the election precinct magistrates at the time the next war-tax payment was due and that they be publicly burned. The suggestion was too far in advance of the times and was not, of course, even considered. But, wrote Gideon, "here is an opportunity for the manifestation of the most exalted patriotism the world ever saw. I will, for one, and I own some of the money."[20]

Old Colonel Lauderdale was president and Lincecum secretary of a relief committee for Long Point and Gay Hill. Their duty was to distribute donations to the families whose men were away at war. But the day soon came when there were no donations—what the army did not take wasn't worth donating. Lauderdale and Gideon unsuccessfully petitioned the chief justice and members of the Washington County court to levy a tax to provide for the soldiers' families; but money was exceedingly scarce and few had enough to meet their war taxes.

Gideon kept an eye on home affairs and closely followed legislative and neighborhood activities. He could see the handwriting on the wall and told Major Green Wood, Danville, in February, 1863:

Despite the destructive, powerful enemy they fall short of being our worst enemy. There are those amongst us who under garb of friendship and a great flourish of patriotism are actually damaging our cause vastly more than the outspoken enemy.

At the commencement they were the greatest encouragers of the war, since which they have made shift to crawfish out of every position they took. Now, pressing every point and circumstance to amass to themselves wealth, they crush whomsoever they may. I consider the actions and desires of these characters, these blood suckers in our midst, far more damaging to our cause than

[20] Galveston *Tri-Weekly News,* October 21, 1863, p. 2, col. 4.

anything that will or can be effected against us by the machinations of the evil-hearted and accursed Lincolnites.

Don't I know that they are the very men who will become the most prominent and the first office seekers? They will mount the stump when the war is over and with the impudence of the devil declare and swear in the name of the Lord, demonstrating to the crippled on up, that all our military success with the final *happy* termination of the war in honorable peace is attributable to them. And the people will elect them!

Lincecum was a regular contributor to the *News* letters-to-the-editor column. Copies of his letters are in the Lincecum Papers. Some of them were printed; others, however, cannot be located. One discussing how to grow tobacco in Texas quoted Silas Wood of Long Point, "an old Virginia tobacco raiser." Lincecum loathed tobacco but gave advice on raising home-grown crops to ease the shortage of the plant he considered a poison. Other topics of letters included the cure of fevers and the proper treatment of gunshot wounds. Another letter was written in reply to an inquiry in the *News* on how to cultivate indigo and poppy plants. The poppy was needed as a source for opium, the indiscriminate use of which was one of his complaints against allopathic doctors. But Lincecum considered this an emergency, knowing it was opium which eased the last hours of many mutilated and mangled soldiers.

Gideon never relaxed his lively correspondence with soldiers, and one to whom he frequently wrote throughout the war and afterwards was Joseph C. Snively.[21] When Snively was with Woods' regiment at Liberty, Texas, Gideon wrote:

---

[21] Joseph C. Snively enlisted at the age of twenty-six at Camp Salado on March 18, 1863, as a private. He served under Captain James Storey, 32nd Regiment, TMV, commanded by Colonel P. C. Woods (Confederate Rolls, Texas State Archives). Apparently he was related to Lincecum and the Matsons and to Jacob Snively of Snively's Expedition fame. In 1862 Lincecum sent sympathy for the loss of Snively's brother, Dan: "Our cause has most certainly lost a courageous warrior. I will write to Dr. Culbertson in Montgomery." After the war he wrote Snively, then in New Albany, Indiana: "There have but few things transpired that would interest you except perhaps the fact that old Captain Snively did not leave Texas during the war. It turns out that he has been at Nacogdoches all the time and that he has abandoned his family and his old lady dwells alternately with her son and her daughter at Brenham where it is said she is not well treated. . . . Your kin people here consists now of only our family and J. V. Matson's."

Some of the old fellows around here have been stepping off to the old hunting ground recently, leaving me almost alone. Old Dr. [Thomas W.] Morriss and Col. A[sa] M. Lewis both took their departure a few weeks ago, leaving me no playmates now but Judge [R. E. B.] Baylor. He, to be sure, does very well, visiting me pretty often. He performs on the violin and we spend our time quite pleasantly as long as we keep from thinking of our kindred and friends who are participating in the hateful bloody strife.

The hospitable Lincecums usually had a houseful of guests—soldiers on furlough, passing travelers, and old friends. While the horses were off to the war the Lincecums had to stay at home.

Gideon wrote to his old friend Professor C. G. Fitze, of the Cold Springs Female Institute, in reply to an inquiry about native grasses, adding this personal comment:

Myself and family are great lovers of music 'tis true; but our friends in your region have greatly overrated our capacity to perform it, not one of us ever having the advantage of a lesson in music in our lives. But you'll soon discover all that when you come to see us, which we all hope you will not fail to do. Come early in the vacation, giving yourself time for a long visit. I can make good fun a long time. Sarah sends compliments and is highly pleased and very much obliged to you for the pretty music.

Gideon's worldly goods and food supply dwindled daily, but he nevertheless continued to feed the hungry soldiers and to treat the sick ones. Always his home was full of them. His neighbors were not so generous. Gideon said: "The soldiers tell us they are directed to stop here for two miles on each side of us."

Daily, Gideon walked miles in the woods seeking medicinal plants with which to treat his "dear, sacrificing soldiers." His vials of cherished specimens of dirt daubers, ants, and spiders were emptied to provide containers for medicines. Medicine, advice, opinions, and food were all given freely to soldiers who were passing in greatly increasing numbers. Occasionally a stray Yankee appeared, and he too enjoyed the hospitality of the Lincecums.

Gideon listened to the returning soldiers' complaints, not about the service and its hardships, but the depreciation of Confederate currency, war profiteering, ineptness of civil authorities, lethargy of the Southern

people, greed of individuals, traitors and speculators, and the un-
seemly behavior of Confederate officers.

Lincecum was frequently consulted by Confederates returning from
battlefields suffering a variety of ailments, the most common complaint
being hemorrhoids. One of his patients afflicted with this complaint
was Colonel George Washington Carter, of Chappell Hill, Texas,
who, additionally, had an ear ailment. Gideon wrote Carter lengthy
and complicated instructions and prescriptions for both. This was in
September, 1863, after Colonel Carter had played his major role in
April in General John Sappington Marmaduke's unsuccessful raid on
Cape Girardeau, Missouri. Lincecum considered it a rare privilege to
administer to the former Methodist minister whose rousing speech at
the People's Secession Convention he well remembered. Afterwards,
with defeat, Carter's enthusiasm for the cause collapsed, and Gideon
rued his generosity. But in 1863 Carter was a hero and Gideon ended
his letter of medical advice: "Accept, dear sir, this prescription with
my strongest wishes for your speedy good health and my hope that you
may become a terror to our insane foes and survive to participate in the
grand jubilation that is to follow our triumphant success a few years
hence."

Gideon, rejoicing when traitors to the Confederacy were arrested,
on October 22, 1863, wrote his British friend, R. B. Hannay, in Milli-
can, Texas:[22]

I was really taken by surprise when I heard that the Tories had been arrested. There are a great many more implicated in the plot. Dr. Lewis and
nine other traitors were arrested in LaGrange day before yesterday and on

---

[22] Hannay, an Englishman, visiting a brother on the lower Brazos River when the
Civil War started, was unable to return to England. Gideon frequently wrote Hannay
from 1861 through 1868. Hannay was a spiritualist, wrote poetry, hated slavery, and
had a vague business connection with E. I. Inglehart of Palestine, Texas. He was on
friendly terms with other Englishmen in Texas, among whom was J. O. Illingworth,
a shadowy figure in Texas history. Another was Henry Eeles Dresser, an eminent
British ornithologist, who came to Texas in 1863 with a cargo assigned to the Confederacy. Gideon attempted to deliver a message from Hannay to Dresser in San
Antonio, but found he was in Houston. Lincecum wrote Hannay: "I am of the
opinion from some hints that I heard among the members of that house of Englishmen that Dresser will probably remain at Houston. Their aim now seems to be to
purchase all the cotton they can get. They seem to be in funds too and as the stock
of cotton on hand will soon be exhausted and the coming crop is comparatively
nothing, this English firm is putting into action all their resources."

their way to Houston passed through Brenham yesterday evening. Many of them amassed fortunes and at the same time cracking and disparaging all Confederate efforts besides and ganging themselves into a regular system of traitors whose fortunes were to be made with the downfall of the Republic. I can feel no pity for them.

I understand a day or two ago both the Tafts were missing from Houston and the supposition is that they have been hung. Have you heard anything wrong about the Tafts? I hope the report is not true but if they are guilty I hope they may not make good their escape. I didn't like it when I heard that the old man had sent his son Jo off just at the time that the war was opening.[23]

Some Texas families who had the opportunity and the means sent their sons out of Texas, either for schooling or for evasion of conscription. Gideon wrote to the Galveston *News* in disapproval of this exodus:

On the 21st instant I notice a well-written article headed with the following question: Is it loyal or patriotic to send boys out of the Confederate States to escape the operations of the conscript laws? Four such cases have recently occurred in this county [Washington] and it has made a very unfavorable impression on the minds of the German population as well as our own citizens.

He signed the letter *Parrhesia,* a signature he occasionally used in letters to editors when he did not use his customary GID.[24]

Gideon resorted to his favorite hunting weapon—a bow and arrow —and so armed walked daily in the woods searching for game and birds to augment the dwindling bread corn of his table. He made his own gunpowder, the formula for which is in the Lincecum Papers, but this he reserved for friends who sometimes accompanied him on his hunting expeditions. Later in the war he ran out of caps and sent a package containing copper to William DeRyee, who was in charge of a Confederate munitions factory at Austin, asking that the copper be exchanged for its equivalent value in percussion caps. He explained:

[23] Gideon's address book lists a Joseph S. Taft, bookseller, Houston. Lincecum also corresponded with a P. B. Taft in Houston.

[24] The letter appeared in the Galveston *Tri-Weekly News,* January 2, 1865, p. 1, under a heading "Leaving the Country to Avoid the War." Parrhasius was a fifth-century Greek painter said to have painted grapes so perfectly that the birds tried to eat them.

"The birds are eating up my bees and for want of the caps on my part they will be able to continue their destructive work. The $M.$ $ops.$ [?] claim it as their natural rights but I dispute it on what I conceive to be just grounds and therefore need the caps."[25]

Gideon's use of the bow and arrow provoked teasing comments from his neighbors, one of whom remarked, "Once a man, twice a child."

Small moments of happiness occasionally broke the gloom of the War. One such occasion was created by the receipt of a bottle of castor oil from Ira M. Camp of Grimes County. Gideon thanked him: "I have received the bottle of pure, clarified castor oil. It is a great thing for the sick and afflicted of our portion of the state that you took that branch of manufacturing business in hand."

Disturbed continually by deserters from the Army and traitors in Texas, Gideon wrote to Durham:

I have been listening for some grand implications and developments from Austin. However much I may hope that it was unfounded there was too much of it for it to be all false. Headed as they were by such great leaders they have perhaps managed their treasonable plots in better style than the Houston and Brazos traitors.

There are Hamilton men in Austin who should, if reports are true, have been sent not out of the country but up a tree long ago. Southerners are a great deal too tender in their notions on the subject of political offenders. I should be glad to see them under present circumstances more vigilant and as snarly as a pine knot.

It would please me to hear that a company of saint catchers had been organized, armed with the lasso, and sent out to rope and haul up a tree everyone of the Lord's shepherds they could find who have no flocks and claim exemption from military service.

Young Snively, as a hospital steward with Woods' regiment, was greatly concerned about a vaccine which was causing illness of an alarming nature among the inoculated soldiers and civilians. On the march to Louisiana in March, 1864, he wrote from Cedar Bayou, Texas, asking Gideon's opinion. Lincecum replied:

In regard to the spurious vaccination our whole country is alarmed. Great

[25] Gideon probably made the exchange, because in a letter to Durham dated July 31, 1864, he wrote: "You mention that you have in your possession a box of caps for me. There, to that box of caps, hangs a nasty tale." He does not explain the tale.

numbers of the people are from its effects rendered incapable of performing any kind of labor and some of them almost helpless. I shall not express an opinion as to what its true character is for really I don't know. I have examined many of the ill-conditioned ulcers that have originated from this unholy inoculation; have thought of syphilis. . . . I am not satisfied as to its true nature and character. . . . The dissatisfaction and insubordination of your troops is a sad thing at this period of our struggle. There is something wrong somewhere.

One of a group of soldiers who deserted Woods' regiment before it reached Louisiana was Brazos Lincecum, Gideon's nephew.[26] Snively told Gideon about it in a letter from Polk County, Texas:

Poor Bras Lincecum is one of the number that went home and is now under charge of the detail left at Hempstead where a court martial met to try their case. Out of 35, but two plead guilty of desertion and they did it through ignorance. They were all found about home and many of them hunted the detail sent after them and gave themselves up to the guard. The two pleading guilty to desertion were sent to Houston, doubtless to wear a ball and chain for a period. The others will be with the regiment soon.

Sympathy for poor homesick Brazos did not diminish Gideon's contempt for deserters. He instructed his sons and grandsons with the Army of the Rio Grande:

If you can get hold of those fellows who are running off to the enemy and to Mexico there can be no impropriety in hanging them right up. I am informed by people who have received letters from the Rio Grande that Babe Irvin, Dutch Anderson, Inge and some others from this vicinity have crossed the river and gone into Mexico or to the Yankees. Anderson sold his wagon and team and a load of government cotton and took the money and went

[26] The Lincecums suffered at the hands of indifferent spellers. Brazos appears on the Confederate rolls as "Brasses Linsecone, private under Capt. John J. Myers, Lone Star Mounted Rifles, Caldwell County, 25th Brigade, TMV, enlisted July, 1861." After the war Brazos wrote from Lockhart asking Gideon's opinion of his going into the cattle business and driving a herd to market. He became a trail boss. The account of a long ride he made in 1870 is related by H. D. Gruene in *The Trail Drivers of Texas* (J. Marvin Hunter, ed. [Bandera, Texas, Frontier Times Press, 1920], p. 120). Gruene refers to him as "Brace." Brazos took a herd from Lockhart for William Green of Llano and Myers, his old brigade commander, of Lockhart. The destination was Abilene, Kansas, but there they learned the cattle were to be delivered to Cheyenne, Wyoming. At Cheyenne the purchaser wanted the herd delivered to Bear River, 110 miles above Salt Lake City, Utah, and hired Brazos as driver. In the same book (p. 399) is a picture of C. C. Lincecum (probably Cassianus) as a trail driver.

across the river. These men are not only traitors to our cause but they are damned thieves and should be stopped wherever found.

Gideon asked Lysander to watch for one of the Lincecums' runaway slaves: "Old Billy made away with a stray horse and has gone to hunt Master San. Look for him. If you find him relieve him of the cause of his dishonest proclivities by castration. Do you hear?"

In the fall of 1864 Lysander returned from the Rio Grande escorting Federal prisoners to Hempstead. He also brought back the body of John Morriss, who had died near Brownsville of typhus fever. Gideon wrote that "John was universally beliked by the Army of the Rio Grande, hence the expense they put themselves to in procuring a metallic coffin and sending him home."[27]

Late in October Gideon had another worry—the illness of his wife, about which he wrote to Hannay: "She was so unwell that we passed over the fiftieth anniversary of our union in the matrimonial tether without having any fun. It took place on the 25th instant. I hope she may get well for I should not like for her to set off to the good hunting ground before I get ready to go."

Gideon commented on one of the major Texas scandals of the Civil War in a letter to Snively, April 16, 1865. Ten days before, in the Fannin House in Houston, headquarters of General J. B. Magruder, Major General John Austin Wharton was shot and killed by Colonel George W. Baylor.

Everyone that I have heard speak of the killing that was enacted a few days since at Houston seemed to express more satisfaction than sorrow on the subject. All however that I have heard speaking were soldiers belonging to various companies of his [Wharton's] command, perhaps a hundred in all had a good many charges against him. They all mention the Yellow Bayou affair and besides several other things of less moment. They unanimously charge him with partiality and a preference in bestowing his promotions on his kinfolks. Well, soldiers will complain you know. But I never heard any of them talk that way about Gen. T. Green.[28]

---

[27] John Morriss (1833–1864) married Moina Stamps, September 10, 1857 (Tombstone, Prairie Lea Cemetery, Brenham).

[28] John Austin Wharton (1829–1865) was the only son of William Harris Wharton and Sarah A. Groce, both parents from prominent and wealthy early Texas families. He was married to Penelope, daughter of Governor David Johnson of South Carolina. Young Wharton was elected colonel of Terry's Texas Rangers after its

A rumor that Lincoln was dead was confirmed in Long Point twelve days after his assassination. Gideon wrote to Doran:

I see by the papers that came today that the story of the killing of the cold hearted tyrant, Lincoln, is no joke. I hope the man who performed that great piece of public service to the nation may make good his escape and that he may live to burst the souls of a few more despots. Wouldn't it be a glorious thing for the next news to be that some justicing spirit has sent Andy Johnson to keep company with Old Abe? The slaying of the two above named tyrants, however, will make but little difference in reference to the affairs of the southern cause if Seward is suffered to remain alive.

Lee's surrender April 9, 1865, at the Appomattox Courthouse ended the Civil War five days later—but not in Texas. The last battle of the war was fought May 12 at Palmito Ranch twelve miles east of Brownsville, where, ironically, the Federals were defeated. Texas troops continued routing out traitors and deserters, and in May Gideon reported:

Capt. McNelly is camped on Mill Creek [Washington County] near Pheare's place and has stirred up the lag-behinds and the disloyal rascals fearfully.[29] He arrested quite a number and sent them off to General Walker

---

leader, Frank Terry, was killed in Kentucky and Terry's immediate successor, Thomas S. Lubbock, died. In most contemporary accounts, Wharton is usually held in high esteem by those under his command, although later-day accounts reflect bitterness over the battle of Yellow Bayou in Louisiana, in which so many Texas soldiers were killed. A biography of Wharton is in Barker's *Texas and Texans* (p. 2275) written as a "worthy memorial to a family which is now without descendants in the Lone Star State" by Captain B. F. Weems, Wharton's assistant adjutant general. George Wythe Baylor (1832–1916) was with Wharton in the Red River campaign. After the war he was a Texas ranger (*Handbook of Texas*, Vol. I, p. 123). General J. E. Harrison, a witness to the shooting, testified at the trial that Baylor and Wharton exchanged angry words the morning of the shooting and Wharton placed Baylor under arrest for report to General Magruder. Harrison said Baylor called Wharton a demagogue and Wharton called Baylor a damned liar. Baylor was acquitted (Galveston *Tri-Weekly News*, April 7, 1865, p. 4, col. 2).

[29] Leander H. McNelly was seventeen when the war started and he left his sheepherding job with T. J. Burton, in Washington County, to enlist in George Campbell's company. After the New Mexican campaign McNelly was a scout and spy in Louisiana with Tom Green. In the Louisiana swamps McNelly's company engaged in a ten-mile running fight with Colonel Edmund J. Davis' 1st Regiment, Texas Cavalry North, U.S.A., known to the Confederates as "First Texas Traitors." According to Theo. Noel (*A Campaign From Sante Fe to the Mississippi* [reprint of the original 1865 ed., Stagecoach Press, Houston, Texas, 1961], pp. 135–136), following this fight "McNelly was not working to suit someone and he was ordered out and sent to hunting up Jayhawkers on the Calcasieu." After the war, when Davis was governor of Texas, he appointed McNelly a captain in the despised state police. McNelly later

in Houston. Amongst the number is Cordy Francis and they got William Ledbetter of Fayette County who is accused of treason and it is thought that he and Francis will be shot.[30]

May was a fretful month. Gideon wrote in his journal on the twentieth:

It is now nearly a month since we had any certain news from east of the Mississippi. We have seen some contradictory dispatches from the Yankee papers, but nothing upon which any reliable conclusions could be adduced. No one has crossed the Mississippi since Johnston's surrender, showing that the river is completely guarded. . . . Those vessels that are left on our coasts have ceased to exchange papers with us and we get not a word of news from that direction. It has been more than a month since we received news from our own people.

Gideon's fears for the Texas boys caused him to wonder whether the Yankees had "turned the negroes loose on the Confederates."

But when the soldiers began to straggle back to Texas the Lincecum home was not only a well-marked spot for a hand-out but a first-aid station as well. The condition of his community was described by Gideon in a letter to Doran in September 1865:

We are jogging on here without any perceptible change in our home affairs . . . yet with many it goes hard and they are getting along with it badly. To judge from their actions and sayings one is forced to the conclusion that their greatest trouble is the fear that somebody will think them no smarter than a nigger. . . . The community at this time really does not seem to have

---

became a Texas Ranger. For the activity of the state police during reconstruction see Walter Prescott Webb, *The Texas Rangers* (Boston and New York, Houghton, Mifflin Company, 1935), pp. 219–229. For McNelly and his rangers see Clyde Wantland, *Taming the Nueces Strip* (Austin, University of Texas Press, 1962).

[30] In a later letter Gideon amended this to read: "I just this moment heard that they did not capture Cordy Francis, Whitener and two other young men who had been concerned in robbing a Mexican train but they got William Ledbetter." William Hamilton Ledbetter, Jr., of Fayette County, was a lieutenant in George F. Flournoy's 16th Infantry Regiment, but was back in Texas in 1863. At a meeting to discuss county conditions after the surrender, held in LaGrange in May, 1865, Ledbetter made a speech interpreted as anti-Confederacy and one of those present remarked he would like to have Ledbetter at the end of a rope. Ledbetter was arrested but later released. He served as state senator in 1876 and 1878 (Leonie R. Weyand and Houston Wade, *An Early History of Fayette County* [LaGrange, *LaGrange Journal*, 1936], p. 263). Cordman Francis, thirty-nine years old, a farmer, born in Georgia, lived at Burton; his land was valued at $20,000, his personal property at $2,000 (Washington County Census, 1870).

any settled point in view. All are anxious to make money and if they had it nine-tenths of them would leave the country. They don't seem to have any other country in their minds. It is to leave here, to get away from their ruined homes, to any place, to be out of sight of their once thriving and happy situation. No one is willing to hazard an opinion as to what will be the result of this dreadful suspense and many of them have no heart to try anything. Some again, and I am one of them, have made up their minds to make the best of the bad situation, fully believing that it won't always be so.

You say you hope necessity had not caused me to go out into the woods to scrape up something to sustain life. What else could it be? And what other condition could a man be in, who had staked all he had on the great national game and kept and fed great numbers of the players and their horses four years? And it is not done yet. I am still feeding and rendering comfortable, as I am able, numbers of the poor homeless good fellows who have lost their all like I did in betting on the big game without knowing the integrity of the leaders of the play.

There is nothing strange in this matter. We gambled with experienced "black legs" and we have lost. Now all we have to do is to act like men of sense, if we can, go to work, mending our condition as fast as possible and when we all get rich again let us not make the bets and deposit the stakes until we are sure that we know all about the powers and *honesty* of the gamesters. . . . I do not look upon all this as a grievance but a blunder, a circumstance which by energetic industry and proper mental culture can all be mended up and made even better than before in a few years. Anyhow, let us not complain.

Washington County, with an almost 50 per cent slave population, experienced only minor disturbances during the War. Gideon once chided Judge Rutherford: "You say you sleep with your gun for the sake of the blacks. We have about 6000 blacks in this county and a more willing, subordinate set of negroes I have never seen anywhere. We sent hundreds and hundreds of them to throw up breast works at Virginia Point. They conducted themselves so orderly that they received high praise." Other Washington County Negroes helped build Fort Esperanza on Matagorda Island, some went to war with their masters, and others remained in charge of farms while the owners served in the Army. Gideon deeply felt his responsibility to feed and clothe his slaves during the war shortages.

After the War Gideon wrote Snively:

I told my negroes that if they remained with me they would not feel free; and I aided them in procuring good places. They have made pretty good crops. They are not satisfied, however; they say they work harder and see less satisfaction. They have all made application for the privilege of coming home next year. I can't take on that responsibility again. . . . I . . . have done very well without them . . . except I find they are about to starve I cannot think of pestering myself with the responsibility of directing their action any more. Formerly I made them keep plenty of everything to eat and wear, both for themselves and my family, too. Now they are exempt from the labor of furnishing my family and if they can't sustain themselves I don't think I can go farther than to advise them what course to pursue. I can see though that if there is no favorable change in the action of the negro bureau agents towards them that their condition will soon be an awful affair.

Lincecum made no attempt to enter into work contracts with his former slaves, thus eliminating any dealings with the Freedman's Bureau. The Lincecums, father and sons, returned to the land and began preparing the soil for new crops. Only the aging and devoted Aunt Polly refused to leave.

His son-in-law Matson, however, continued farming with Negro labor:

I can't see that the emancipation of the slaves has checked his progress a particle. . . . I suppose Matson will crib a larger crop of both corn and cotton than he ever did. He is a managing money-making man under any circumstance. He hired negroes enough to tend all three of his farms and one way and another managed to get pretty fair work out of them. They are, however a very poor dependence and but few men will employ them next year. I hear almost every body say that they have tried the experiment, and find a great deal of disappointment and vexation and no profit. They are thoroughly satisfied that free *negro* labor will not pay and most of them have abandoned the idea of using it.

Later, in a letter to Doran, Lincecum noted an improvement, but at the same time expressed grim doubts about the future:

A great change seems to have taken place in the action of the negro within the last six weeks. Having disposed of what money he had on hand he has quieted down to his acknowledged natural sphere and has gone freely to work. Those who are working for part of the crop are performing better as a general thing than those who are working for money. However, I hear of but little complaint recently from either condition and farmers are beginning to put up a little and are talking about future prospects for improvements. We have the negro here with us and to prevent him from becoming a damaging incumbrance and nuisance we must take pains and teach him the philosophy and use of existence. There is no need in curling up our noses in disgust at inevitableness. If the late political fracus at Washington doesn't interfere with the negro we shall in a very short time do well with them and for them. But I think I see in that Washington difficulty a greater and better chance for thunder and brimstone burning than that which we have just passed over. That, when it comes, will be no one-sided affair. It will grind and crush and grate over the surface of all North America, establishing for itself a character of a war worth talking about.

Although many times during the war Gideon had predicted the fate of the South in defeat, he was unprepared for the full measure of reconstruction. His determination to make the most of the situation wilted under Federal occupation; and his inherent desire for personal freedom rebelled at the humiliations daily encountered. Gideon viewed the growing evidence of retribution with amazement:

What an unscrupulous people the Yankees are! After overrunning and robbing our country of its great wealth, they still consider it a legitimate business even now, after we have all given up and quietly accepted the situation, to fraud and plunder us every time we attempt a business transaction with any of them.

Gideon, through necessity, returned to the practice of medicine, largely prescribing his own concoctions. He described his search for medicinal herbs in a letter to Doran, and in the letter gave the first indication of a yearning for a new frontier:

In the spring when everything is blooming, when singing birds, gaudy butterflies and painted flowers are filling the air and the landscape with melody, gay sights and sweet odors, is the time to go forth into nature's well-furnished laboratory and help oneself to her greatest and best bounties for the sick man. I never feel so much like a grown man as I do when I am culling and selecting choice articles of medicines from the far out, untrodden forests. . . . How pleasant it is to occupy a position where there is room enough and no signs or indications of villainy to be seen in any direction. My inner soul longs deeply for such a place now.

But Gideon still maintained his customary optimism and unbroken spirit on the first day of 1866, when he gaily recorded that "the old lady danced all night and today is no worse for it."

A NOTE ON SOURCES

In the Lincecum Papers are numerous references to Thomas Affleck (1812–1868) a remarkable Scot who came to Texas from Mississippi in 1858 and settled on 3,500 acres called Glenblythe, seven miles northwest of Brenham. He is one of the least-known and one of the most interesting Texans of that day. Although Lincecum and Affleck exchanged letters, seeds, and books, they were never good friends. Gideon regarded as much too grand Affleck's baronial Washington County kingdom, consisting of a church, a hospital, packing plants, nurseries and orchards, shops, mills, slave quarters, factories, and presses for the publication of almanacs and plantation account books, and he considered Affleck far too ambitious.

His detailed and illuminating comments on Affleck can be found in numerous letters, including those to Buckley on August (?), 1866, August 30, 1866, and September (?), 1866, and to Sallie Doran on January 22, 1868.

Lincecum's correspondence contains also material on Brigadier General (U.S.A.) Thomas J. Wood, a West Pointer, who was a friend of Durham. A letter to Joseph C. Snively, of Lockhart, on November 14, 1861, is of particular interest because of Lincecum's frankly expressed opinions of this military man.

An unknown Texan who should be the subject of further research appears periodically in the Lincecum Papers. He is J. O. Illingworth, an Englishman of fascinating background, with whom Lincecum corresponded in 1860 when Illingworth was an assistant to the publisher of the *Texas Almanac*. A letter written to R. B. Hannay on June 22, 1864, gives an interesting comment on Illingworth.

Additional interesting events and situations in Texas during the Civil War which are not included in this chapter can be found in letters from Lincecum to Christopher Gustavus Memminger, Secretary of the C.S.A. Treasury, December 4, 1861; editor, Brenham *Inquirer*, December 9, 1860; W. E. Allcorn, Brenham, Texas, April 25, 1862; editor, Galveston *News*, May 5, 1862, January 4, 1863; Richard Keene, Piedmont Springs, Texas, September 25, 1864, Jefferson, Texas, January 31, 1865; Lieutenant W. H. Hensley, Hempstead, Texas, March 5, 1865; Captain William Cooke, Post Quartermaster, 2nd District, Texas, April 20, 1865; F. M. Gaston, Mound Prairie, Texas, September 20, 1864. Lengthy discussions of a horsehair cording machine invented and sold by Hayford & Johnson of Austin County are found in Lincecum's letters to W. Richardson, Galveston *News*, January 6, 1865; Messrs. Hayford and Johnson,

Bellville, Texas, January 15, 1865; and to A. W. Moore, Bastrop, Texas, January 30, 1865.

Detailed instructions for making dyes are found in Lincecum's letters to Mrs. Mary H. Taylor, Navarro County, March 22, 1863, and to Mrs. S. P. Baber, Independence, Texas, July 13, 1863.

Further Civil War facts in the Lincecum Papers are included in the papers of Sioux Doran. These include a chatty letter from Theophilus Noel, in Chicago, to Doran, June 6, 1890, in which he details events of his personal life and reminisces about war experiences shared with Doran. The elaborate letterhead identifies Noel as an "assayer, geologist and metalurgist." Other letters to Doran containing wartime reminiscences are from Alexander W. Terrell, written from Constantinople in August, 1873, when he was minister to Turkey; James B. Simpson, Mike Carr, William Gleason, and Dr. George H. Bailey, no dates, containing their eye-witness accounts of the Battle of Sabine Pass, Texas; and from Mother St. Agnes McClellan, July 5, 1888, which contains information about Mother St. Pierre, who was Superioress of the Ursuline Academy, Galveston, during the attack by the Federals, and biographical information on a Miss Agnes B. Davis.

Other Doran papers include a handwritten copy of a speech made by Sallie Lincecum when she presented a banner to "Lt. Shepherd and Gentlemen of the Davis Mounted Riflemen" (no date); Doran's amnesty oath, No. 1693, executed in Houston on July 6, 1865; his voters' certificate, No. 12, Washington County, dated 1872 and signed by C. J. Stockbridge; and a newspaper clipping of a story by Doran, no date, in which he urged a monument be erected in Galveston for Lieutenant Commander Edward Lea, second officer of the U.S.S. *Harriet Lane* and the son of Confederate Major Albert Miller Lea, who was mortally wounded in the Battle of Galveston on January 1, 1863.

CHAPTER ELEVEN

GIDEON
AND THE HIGH LADS

How little people see of the things they are daily trampling
over. GID

LINCECUM'S EARLY interest in the natural sciences had been developed as he trotted along behind his father's ever-moving
wagon, darting into the forests in pursuit of birds, hunting small game
for pets, dawdling in wonder over a new flower, gazing in clear pools
at strange fish, and crawling on hands and knees to follow the busy
traffic of small insects. The common names of these wonderful things
were so long in his vocabulary he never remembered when he learned
them; his curiosity about such things never grew stale and dull but
remained as sharp and fresh when he was eighty years of age as in the
days of his youth.

One of his early expeditions was in an oat field in search of a
swallow's nest which Grandmother Miriam told him was fashioned of
small sticks and glue. In the field was a large white oak stump about
twenty feet high, where young Gideon had seen swallows circling and
dipping into the top. Oat bag in hand, Gideon intended to pursue his
mission of gathering grain for Hezekiah's horse, but his eagerness to
see the wonderful construction sent him shinning up the tall stump.
He saw the nest down in the hollow and poked at it with the oat bag.
The bag slipped from his fingers and fell to the bottom.

Remembering Hezekiah's wrath, Gideon attempted to retrieve the bag, easing himself down inside the stump, back rigid against one side, hands and knees against the other. Unable to maintain his balance he fell to the bottom with the bag and spent a tearful night in the stump, long-horned crickets trilling around him and large brown spiders spreading over his bare arms and legs. A rescue party found him next morning. At the age of seventy, Gideon was still climbing trees for the nests and eggs of swallow-tail hawks.

Gideon was one of the first men in the United States to recognize the importance of recording the origins of a fast-vanishing race. Before the Neanderthal skull was brought to light, he was digging up bones of another age and learning their meaning. He read the messages in strata and fossils; and from a long personal observation instinctively approached the theory of evolution before he read Darwin. Eugenics was not to Gideon a science or a theory, nor even a word, but a logical conclusion reached through daily association with his fellow men and their offspring. He once facetiously suggested the science of gerontology to Horatio Charles Wood, a young Philadelphia scientist:

... there are many energetic old fellows approximating the imbecility of the octogenarian who would feel deeply mortified to be told that he is a bore. It is therefore a good thing that some young men are endowed with sufficient investigating powers to enable them to look on the old fellow in his true colors and patience to bear without murmuring the rattle and clatter of his waning mentality. For a vigorous, accurate investigating mind the octogenarian, as a subject in natural history, would be perhaps worth the labor of serious, philosophic analysis.

Every plant, bird, insect, reptile, and fish that crossed his path was habitually given an exhaustive scrutiny. Gideon studied geological formations and mineral deposits, experimented with chemicals and explosives, considered wind currents, meteors, stars, lightning, weather phenomena, electricity, and energy. Through his knowledge of natural elements, erosion, and soil and water conservation, he predicted the day would surely come when the rich farm lands of Texas would be washed into the Gulf of Mexico.

Gideon was an avid reader, absorbing every printed word available. He read John Darby's *Botany of the Southern States,* published in 1855, and carried it with him on field trips; he was familiar with the botanical writings of Erasmus Darwin and with Alexander von Humboldt's *Kosmos,* a description of the physical universe. But he had never seen a definitive work on entomology, ornithology, or other specific natural history science, "not even a picture book," and was totally uninformed on scientific terminology.

Northern scientific friends in 1867 sent him books and journals, but Gideon was dismayed at their inadequacy. He wrote Dr. Samuel Lewis of Philadelphia: "I am closely engaged in the study of natural history. Not in books, for I find them greatly at fault, but in the field where I find specimens wearing nature's own labels. . . . Now in my old age I am forced to study the language of artificial scientific arrangements to enable me to commune with the high lads."

Soon after arriving in Texas, Gideon, his wife, Sarah, and their youngest daughter, Sallie, scheduled two annual camping trips. During the summer the three spent weeks traveling and camping in the interior and on the western frontier of Texas, and in the winter their excursion was to the Gulf Coast. Gideon's wide acquaintance among citizens of the state was made on these trips when he stopped in towns and settlements to visit.

During the journey Gideon occupied a buggy, in which he transported also his equipment, guns, and specimens; Sarah and Sallie traveled in a carriage designed and manufactured for the purpose, a forerunner of the present-day station wagon, which was convertible, as Gideon described it, into a dry house in rainy weather and a bedstead at night. Two servants usually accompanied them.

He was particularly delighted with the Texas coast, where, he observed, "the old ocean seems to be the matrix of creation. . . . All our dry land animals and vegetables have crept from beneath its waves." At the age of seventy he wrote to Nephew John that he was

. . . habitually addicted to climbing tall trees, plunging into deep waters, running and shooting when we are out in the woods. The old lady, Sallie and myself with a couple of servants make long excursions into the wildest portions of Texas we can find. Camping out all the time and sometimes as much as eight weeks at a trip. Then is when the old lady sees how I climb trees and rocky cliffs and tells me I have no business doing it.

From these excursions Gideon hauled back to Long Point wagonloads of fossils, shells, bones, rocks, and artifacts, which he dumped in the yard on top of those from Alabama and Mississippi which came with him to Texas in 1848.

After a trip in 1858 Gideon wrote a lengthy description of the volcanic hills and formations on the Colorado River and gave a geological outline of the country northwest of Austin. He described Marble Falls and added: "A company of gentlemen have recently surveyed off a town at the place and call it Marble City and organized themselves for erecting cotton and woolen mills and using power from the falls." The report, dated May 15, 1858, was addressed to Dr. W. Spillman, Columbus, Mississippi.

Lincecum was a thorough collector. He encouraged others to observe the natural history over which they daily trod and was frequently put out at those who neglected to give him tarantulas and bugs they said they had saved for him. He fumed: "Well, I think it was an indication of mental progress in them even to catch a bug. The animal developments must have been sleeping while they were catching insects."

The task of collecting was so great and time was so short that he often lamented not having helpers: "I have not as yet been able to find anybody who has sense and continuity of purpose to aid me in collecting. They are too lazy or can't think of it. They prefer sitting around and whittling sticks."

His expeditions were methodical. In preparation he wrote notes to himself:

Things to observe and collect during my summer excursion: The skulls of all mammals that are wild—Indian wolves, panthers, civet cats; skulls of rapacious fowls; skins of ivory-billed woodpeckers; rapacious birds' eggs; and other curious birds' eggs, snakes, lizards, alligators, terrapins.

Fossils of all kind that can be carried—particularly marine fossil shells and recent fresh-water shells; dry-land shells, mussel shells from all the streams, ponds, and lakes.

Let no probable place escape without a scrutinizing search. Capture and preserve all that is found. Keep the mind constantly on the subject so that not an insect shall fly or crawl in the range of vision unnoticed.

Enquire at every house for Indian remains, stone axes, spikes, and the like.

Thus it was that when he was discovered in the early 1860's by scientists of the north, he not only could supply their needs but could truthfully say: "I have examined everything belonging to Texas and preserved everything that I had the means of doing it with."

Gideon was delighted when early in January, 1860, he met Samuel Botsford Buckley.[1] The botanist-geologist stopped by the Lincecum home on a walking trip from Philadelphia and stayed four days." Buckley was "traversing the continent," studying species of forest trees and attempting to estimate their number. The old Texan showed him species of native pecans and an oak which Buckley said was new and undescribed. Gideon wrote to their mutual friend William Byrd Powell[2] that Buckley "was mightily pleased and declared he was well paid for his walk from Philadelphia." Instead of continuing his transcontinental walk, Buckley made arrangements with Dr. Benjamin Franklin Shumard, state geologist, to accompany him on an excursion to North Texas. Buckley was soon added to Shumard's staff as an assistant.[3]

___

[1] Before arriving in Texas, Buckley studied medicine at the College of Physicians and Surgeons, New York; taught in Illinois and Alabama; explored the southern states; and determined elevation of mountains in Tennessee, where one of the highest spots in the Great Smoky Mountains is named Buckley's Peak (*Dictionary of American Biography* [New York, Charles Scribner Sons, 1929], Vol. 3, pp. 232–233).

[2] Powell (1799–1866), born in Kentucky, graduate of Transylvania University, 1826; an eclectic physician whose main interest was physiology with special reference to the brain; professor of chemistry, Medical College of Louisiana (1835–1839); began a study of phrenology in 1836, and later announced that human temperament could be read by an examination of the cranium. He disappeared in 1843 for three years, touring Indian tribes and living as an Indian; founded in 1847 the Memphis Institute of Eclectic Medicine; was chairman in 1856, of cerebral physiology, Eclectic Medical Institute, Cincinnati; at the time of his death was emeritus professor at Eclectic Medical College of New York (*ibid.*, Vol. 15, p. 152, 1935).

Dr. Samuel Wood Geiser sent me to the Library of Southern Methodist University while he read the chapters on Lincecum's scientific pursuits and made comments on small pieces of yellow paper. One comment was: "I am excited with your reference to W. B. Powell. Powell was living (temporarily) in Little Rock, Arkansas, and studied the geology of the Fouke region, and published (1842) a 23-page pamphlet on the same. In 1860 he was co-editor of the *Journal of Human Science* (Cincinnati and St. Louis) and from 1856 to 1859 was professor in the Eclectic Medical Institute of Cincinnati." Dr. Geiser had researched Powell for inclusion in a publication, then in preparation, on scientists of the South.

[3] The Texas State Legislature in 1858 authorized the governor to appoint a state geologist for two years at an annual salary of $3,000. The geologist could appoint two assistants at a salary of $1,500 a year each. An appropriation of $20,000, to defray the expense of the survey, was made and the geologist was required to post an equal amount of bond. Further, he was required to take an oath he would not purchase land with a view to speculation, nor suppress nor conceal information (*Texas Almanac, 1859*, p. 23).

Buckley, a New Yorker, had studied medicine, collected botany, and worked in geology and other branches of natural science before his trip to Texas. He soon was well aware of the storehouse of knowledge and notes accumulated by Lincecum and made free use of what Gideon so generously shared.

One of Gideon's first agricultural interests in Texas was identifying and testing native grasses, always believing the best species of grasses for a Texas pasture were those nature had placed there. To prove it he enclosed a thirty-five–acre pasture and allowed the native grass to grow undisturbed by wandering animals. For ten years it produced enough fodder for his farm animals and herd.

He wrote several articles on Texas grasses, urging conservation of native pastures.[4] The best species, he said, had been destroyed by "our too numerous herds of cows and sheep" and were only to be found growing in gullies and along fences "where they have fled for protection from cattle." Lincecum carefully gathered the seeds of these sly grasses and annually sowed them in his meadow. He advised all sensible farmers to do likewise.

There it is [he said of his planted native grass] and has been for thousands of years, must continue for thousands of years to come and nothing to do to it but mow off large quantities of as good, sweet, healthy, and nutritious hay as any *reasonable* cow, horse, mule, or sheep could desire. . . .

On our widespread prairies, woodlands and extensive low grounds there are a very great number of undescribed grasses of highly useful qualities to the stock farmer, both for winter and summer pasture and also for substantial hay. When I say undescribed I do not mean that they have not been noticed by the traveling botanists who are nowadays becoming as plenty as book agents, map peddlers, spiritual mediums, and Sunday School tract dis-

---

4 "Texas Grasses," *Annual Report of the Commissioner of Patents for 1860*, Agricultural Report, U.S. Government, 1861, Vol. II, pp. 235–238; "Native or Indigenous Texas Grasses," *Texas Almanac, 1861*, pp. 139–143; "The Indigenous Texian Grasses," *ibid.*, 1868, pp. 76–77; "Grasses of Texas," *Southern Cultivator*, Augusta, Georgia, Vol. XIX, Part 1 (January, 1861), p. 33; Part 2 (February, 1861), pp. 51–52.

D. Redmond, editor of the *Southern Cultivator*, wrote in the February, 1861, issue: "We commend the article in the present and preceding number of the *Cultivator*, written by Mr. Lincecum, to the attentive perusal of our readers." Lincecum concluded his series with a description of wild oats (*Uniola*): "Surely, with all its attractive beauty and rich nutritious properties, the prudent agriculturist will not, as has been the case with many other good species of grasses, suffer this lovely one to become extinct."

tributors (and for aught I know may be disturbing our negroes in the same way). Very likely they may have collected specimens of the most of them, sent them on to some northern institution where they will be placed in scientific classification with a short description in Greek or Latin[5] of the shape of the panicles, spikes, glumes, paleas, &c., &c., all of which may be well enough in its place, but of no possible advantage to the practical agriculturist. He requires a description of its qualities, uses, the kind of soil upon which it is found to flourish best and plenty of the seed.

. . . the subject of which I speak lies strewn around them [Texans] and is trampled under foot in their yards, in their fields, and in their bright-blooming prairies. . . . Time was and not long since when the quantity and luscious quality of our endless varieties of cow fodder grasses were flourishing in such rich luxuriancy on our boundless unplowed prairies that the thought that it would ever end had never occurred to anybody. But the destructive tramp of immigration, the increasing number of farms and with them stock of all kinds, has demonstrated in a very few years the unwelcome certainty that our seemingly exhaustless meadows will soon be gone—plowed up. Now, as this is an unavoidable contingency, it behooves every one who intends to remain here to look around him and see if there is no plan whereby a portion of our waning pastures may be preserved.[6]

These articles brought inquiries from farmers throughout the South. Gideon answered them all and sent species of Texas grass with directions for planting.[7]

It is possible that Gideon discovered Coastal Bermuda grass a hundred years before it was officially known.[8] After nine years of studying native grasses he found in 1858 a grass new to him. He described it as

[5] Descriptions of plants are in Latin, never Greek.

[6] There are about 570 species of native grasses in Texas. "The pioneers in Texas and throughout the West took grass for granted. . . . In recent years, however, it has been found that grass, treated as a 'crop' often yields a greater return than that brought by such conventional crops as cotton and corn. . . . While Texas grass culture has made great strides in Texas since 1945 when it may be said that the movement began, specialists in the field think that there will be much greater development in the future" (*Texas Almanac, 1961–1962*, pp. 114–115). Benjamin Carroll Tharp lists 168 species of range and forage grasses of the greatest commercial importance for Texas ranchers in his *Texas Range Grasses* (Austin, University of Texas Press, 1952, pp. 115–124).

[7] Among the many with whom Gideon corresponded on the subject of grasses were Dr. W. A. Dunn, Winfield, Georgia; Dr. J. C. Spinks, Fort Stephens, Mississippi; B. Shropshire, LaGrange, Texas; I. A. Mitchell, Leesville, South Carolina; Professor C. G. Fitze, Coldspring, Texas; J. F. Price, Richwood's Township, Arkansas; Lucian Q. Tucker, Buck Eye, Georgia; Dr. W. Seybold, Burr's Terry, Louisiana; and V. M. Johnson, Tacaleeche, Mississippi.

[8] Dr. Geiser doubts the correctness of this statement.

related to the common variety of Bermuda, but much larger-bladed and more attractive to cattle. First noticing it near the Old San Antonio Road, he supposed it had been brought by Mexican ponies from the west. He wrote of it: "If it has come here of its own accord . . . is it not as good as a native? . . . It is a most beautiful grass and devoured by all grass-eating animals. Its roots are perennial in this latitude."

Gideon found in 1861 another newcomer, an offshoot of *Panicum obtusum*, which suddenly appeared after a rain in the cultivated bottom lands of the Colorado River near Austin. He wrote about it to the *Southern Cultivator:*" For convenience, until I am forced from the position, I shall give it a specific name. I have as good a right to name a plant as any Yankee, especially southern plants. And so in my nomenclature for its scientific name, *Panicum gibbum*, and for its common name, Austin grass."

Gideon's concern with Texas weather provides a great wealth of otherwise unrecorded data. He had long kept a personal weather journal, and after reading Matthew Fontaine Maury's *Physical Geography of the Sea*, published in 1855, Gideon volunteered his services to Maury as a weather observer. Maury, at that time superintendent of the Naval Observatory, accepted Lincecum's offer, sending him charts, instruments, and forms, and directed that Lincecum's monthly journal be sent to Commander Robert Fitzroy, Board of Trade, London. Fitzroy, commander of the *Beagle* on a voyage which Darwin made famous, then was chief of the British Meteorological Department, where he inaugurated the first weather forecasts.

Discouraged when his reports were never acknowledged, Gideon accepted an offer from Joseph Henry, the noted physicist who initiated the first United States weather-report system, to keep a record of Washington County weather for the Smithsonian Institution. He was highly pleased to add meteorology to his daily chores. For many years he provided the Galveston *News* with a monthly summary, and at the close of the Civil War was able to furnish Buckley, then state geologist, with a five-year survey.[9]

His reports not only gave detailed weather conditions but indicated the position of stars, planting and crop conditions, and the arrival of

[9] "A Preliminary Report of the Geological and Agricultural Survey of Texas," *House Journal of the Eleventh Legislature* (1866), pp. 51, 75.

grouse, sandhill cranes, Canadian geese, swans, brants, and other migratory birds.

Gideon concluded a February, 1861, report to the Galveston *News*: "The ants are cleaning out their cells, grass is growing, and cows begin to low and can look a man in the face. The southern division of swans passed northward en masse at 10 P.M. on 24th February, unusually early." And for March of the same year: "Honey abundant and fine flavored; new corn bread ever since 15th. Nobody sick." He ended the 1861 report: "And now, this last day of the year, we have green grass, flowers, butterflies, and the hum of the industrious honey bee, like spring."

He explained his pleasure in natural history in a letter of October 27, 1861, to W. A. Wilson of Caddo, Texas, who had sent a copy of Palmer's *Vindication of Secession and the South* and asked Gideon for seeds of the rain lily:

I am pleased that you have prepared and resolved to make a botanist of yourself. You will find the preparatory steps dry and of but little interest; but when you succeed in mastering the botanic language there is nothing that can afford such a mind as you possess so much real satisfaction and enjoyment. . . . In the language of the plants we converse with God himself and the answers to our questions are not such as we find in the pasteboard and calfskin records. . . . An acquaintance with the science of botany generates a taste for other branches of the natural sciences, all of which are calculated to soothe and amuse the period of dull old age.

An early and lasting friendship with Caleb Goldsmith Forshey grew out of a mutual interest in weather. Forshey, an assistant on Dr. Shumard's staff and founder of Texas Military Institute at Rutersville, kept a weather account of his vicinity for the National Observatory. Gideon and Forshey frequently compared notes, and in 1860 Forshey asked Gideon's opinion of his theory of Texas winds. In a whimsical vein Gideon replied:

I did as you asked. After working myself into a clairvoyant state, thoroughly inflating the largest balloon of my imagination, I made my ascension from a snow-capped peak in the Rocky Mountains, north, riding merrily southward on the steady sweep of the dry fogless norther. [His personification of a Texas norther continues in a gay and imaginative style for several pages and concludes:] The proud aerial navigator, your humble servant, is unceremoniously dashed and rudely tumbled, half-frozen, on the grass-clad plane below. And now the fierce norther sweeping the prairie underruns the moisture-bearing south wind from which with thirsty gorge it soon drinks up the entire burthen of the south wind.

In the first year of their friendship Buckley frequently brought Dr. Shumard on visits and hunting parties to Lincecum's Long Point home. On some visits they were accompanied by Dr. Shumard's brother, Dr. George Getz Shumard, and Dr. William Pitt Riddell, both assistant state geologists, and Riddell's brother, Dr. John Leonard Riddell.[10] Both Riddells were chemists, and John Leonard, the older, was inventor of the binocular microscope. Gideon was not overly impressed by them, dismissing them in a letter to Buckley as "like ourselves, after all, nothing but men."

Gideon knew Dr. Shumard before Buckley came to Texas and they had exchanged a number of friendly letters. Shumard sent a pamphlet, *Notice of Fossils from the Permian Strata of Texas to New Mexico*, and Gideon reciprocated with a bottle of mustang wine and the recipe for it. Lincecum was also acquainted with Dr. Shumard's other assist-

---

[10] See *Texas Almanac, 1859*, p. 187, for an unsigned article, "Sketch of the Public Life of Benjamin F. Shumard."

Dr. George Getz Shumard (1825–1867), as surgeon and geologist, accompanied Captain R. B. Marcy's 1852 exploration of the Red River. Before and after this trip he was a practicing physician in Little Rock, Arkansas. In 1854 he was geologist with Marcy and Neighbors on their tour of Texas to find suitable land for an Indian reservation. From 1855–1858 he was geologist with Lieutenant John Pope of the U.S. Topographical Corps in his unsuccessful efforts to drill artesian wells on the Llano Estacado of Texas (Colonel R. B. Marcy, *Thirty Years of Army Life on the Border* [London, Sampson, Low, Son, and Marston, 1866], pp. 374–463; W. H. Goetzmann, *Army Explorations in the American West* [New Haven, Connecticut, Yale University Press, 1959], pp. 365–356). William Pitt Riddell (1828–1872) was chemist and assistant geologist of the Texas Geological Survey from 1858–1860 (Geiser, *Naturalists of the Frontier* [Dallas, Texas, Southern Methodist University, 1948], p. 280). He taught at Rutersville with Caleb G. Forshey before joining the survey; he was in charge of a military hospital in Houston during the Civil War, and was one of the leaders in reviving the Texas Medical Association in 1869. John Leonard Riddell (1807–1865) was a graduate of Medical College, Cincinnati in 1835, and professor of chemistry in Medical College of Louisiana in 1836; in 1839 he made a trip to Texas and published his observations on the geology of the Trinity area in *Silliman's Journal* of that year (Geiser, *Naturalists*, pp. 257, 280). While he was postmaster in New Orleans during the Civil War, John T. Pickett, Confederate emissary to Mexico, entrusted to Riddell, for safe transmission to Richmond, documents of his mission. Riddell, however, sent them to Seward in Washington. "For this Dr. Riddell was a spy in the employ of the Federal government" (Burton J. Hendricks, *Statesmen of the Lost Cause* [Boston, Little, Brown and Company, 1939], p. 137).

ant, Swante Palm. Palm had sent Lincecum a copy of *Nomenclature of Clouds*, which Gideon copied in longhand before returning. Gideon sent Palm ozone paper with instructions on its use and asked for information on the use of wind instruments and the barometer.[11]

In June, 1860, Buckley was in Austin, where Gideon wrote to him:

I suppose by this time you are back from Corpus Christi and I am beginning to expect you here. Dr. B. F. Shumard told me that he intended to make a survey of this county in the course of this summer and I hope to have the pleasure of seeing him also when you pay your visit. I have preserved for his benefit some geological rarities and for your inspection only 150 specimens of trees and shrubs as yet.

In August, Buckley and Shumard spent ten days with Lincecum. After this visit Gideon wrote Shumard his thanks for Issue No. 3 of the *Transactions of the Academy of Science of St. Louis* and a copy of the *First Report of Progress of the Geological and Agricultural Survey of Texas,* adding:

. . . for which I hereby tender to you my sincere thanks and I shall not fail to reciprocate the favor on the first proper occasion that may offer. I am, however, at a loss to know to what part of my performance whilst you were with me it is that I am to ascribe the distinguished honor you did me in sending me those three precious emanations from the pen of the Rev. J. C. Ryle B.A. of seed corn notoriety.[12]

Gideon soon found an occasion to reciprocate—with a gift of a scapula of an unidentified animal found one hundred feet below ground embedded in clay and minute scraps of limestone. To Buckley he sent specimens of bitter- and sweet-fruited post oaks and a note twitting him for his inability to distinguish between them:

If you fail to discover the well-marked difference between these two oaks I shall be at a loss to know what order and species to place your holy self in.

---

[11] Swante Palm (born in Sweden in 1815; died in Austin, Texas, in 1899) was a meteorologist but appears to have made a career of local and state appointments. His great contribution to Texas was made in his role as a bibliophile. His large and fabulous collection of books was given to the University of Texas Library (*Handbook of Texas*, Vol. II, p. 326).

[12] John Charles Ryle (1816–1900) was an English author and the Bishop of Liverpool (*DAB*, Supplement 3 [1901], p. 334). Reference is probably to Ryle's stand on repeal of the Corn Laws.

I will collect the fruit of the other two post oaks as soon as the fruit matures. Post oak is equally applicable to all four of these oaks but their habits, inflorescence, fruit, and external aspect enable *me* to distinguish one from the other without hesitation or the necessity of comparison. They are, I think, entitled to as many specific names. Two of them are already named—the burr oak and the common post oak. But the sand post oak (bitter-fruited) and the basket post oak have not been placed in scientific classification.

Gideon possessed a happy gift of romanticizing his scientific pursuits. On a sunny October day in 1860 a black-oak tree in a dense thicket below Long Point stirred his imagination. He had never before observed the black oak west of the Trinity River. It was a double tree, growing from one root, each trunk thirty inches in diameter and seventy feet high. Where had the acorn come from which developed this two-trunked tree, a hundred miles from its usual habitat? A crow would not have brought it, a squirrel could not, the mallard duck doesn't eat the acorn of the black oak, but a wild pigeon does—so reasoned Gideon.

I work myself up to the clairvoyant condition and go back to 1701. 'Tis November and on a grassy prairie an immense herd of fat buffalo are grazing. There approaches a flock of wild pigeons and behind them is a keen-winged falcon. He catches and eats a pigeon and shakes the crop, containing among other things a black-oak acorn.

When Buckley disagreed with his identification, certain it was the blackjack, Gideon replied: "I know there are many varieties of the black oak, particularly in Texas. I am familiar with all of them. My black oak is distinctly different and its height is seldom attained by the blackjack."

Many Texas native oaks today bear names bestowed by Buckley. He named the basket oak for Elias Durand and bestowed Lincecum's name on the bitter-fruited post oak. When informed of this honor Gideon replied:

About naming the little post oak, do as you please. And if my name is to be placed on a monument I would prefer the bitter-fruited post oak to any other on account of its wonderful durability and its unobtrusive habits. It never pushes itself into the scrambling crowd for rich soil but modestly contents itself on the poorest beds of sand.

The classification was later changed and the only plant in Texas, so far as it can be determined, which bears Lincecum's name today is the pinewoods grape, called *Vitis lincecumi* by Buckley.

Shumard was suddenly dismissed by Governor Sam Houston in November, 1860, a month after Buckley was added to the state geological staff, and replaced by Dr. Francis Moore, Jr., who named Buckley his first assistant. When he heard the news Gideon wrote Buckley:

I knew Shumard was a rascal long ago. The brazen-faced villain had the audacity to call on me last winter to write for his paper and make collections for his academy. . . . Your judgment in such matters goes a long way with me and I am glad you have expressed your opinion on the subject of the ability of Dr. Moore to carry on the geological survey of the state. I should be sorry to know that the progress of this highly necessary work should be checked by the childish malice of our state department. If you can make it convenient, at any time, bring the doctor with you and give me a call.[13]

13 Buckley remains a man of considerable controversy among men of science. Dr. Samuel Wood Geiser made an extensive study of the Buckley-Shumard affair and believes that Buckley was the villain. A rare gentleman, Geiser hesitated to dishonor the memory of Buckley, against whom he admittedly was prejudiced from the beginning of his research, and refrained from writing anything about him for a number of years. Geiser feels that the result of his research bears out his first impression of Buckley as a man and scientist. Geiser studied the findings of an investigation of the quarrel conducted by the Philadelphia Academy of Sciences, Buckley's will, and other documents and determined that Buckley in Texas was following a personality pattern which began when he was a student of John Torrey, noted botanist and chemist, at the College of Physicians and Surgeons in New York. Torrey did most of the work on "Plants of the Appalachian Mountains," which Buckley claimed as his own. Buckley appears guilty of seriously slandering Horace Mann while Mann was president of Antioch College in Ohio. On the other hand, Shumard's career before he came to Texas as state geologist in 1858, an appointment made by Governor H. R. Runnels, and after his removal by Governor Houston, appears unimpeachable (Geiser, in interview with author). The fact that Runnels was the only person ever to defeat Houston in an election, might have influenced Houston to remove Shumard, his appointee. Houston's choice of Moore to replace him was an odd one. Moore, a surgeon in the Texas Army in 1836 and later owner of the *Telegraph and Texas Register*, often violently opposed Houston. On August 25, 1860, a month before Buckley was named an assistant geologist, Houston wrote Moore a friendly letter asking him to come to Austin as soon as convenient, as "I have determined to offer you a situation in the Geological Bureau, worth at least $1500 per annum." Houston said his mind was not entirely made up to remove Shumard "but I am inclined to think I will remove him" (*Writings of Sam Houston*, Amelia W. Williams and Eugene C. Barker, eds. [Austin, Texas, University of Texas Press, 1938–1943], Vol. VIII, p. 125). It is possible that Lincecum's dislike for Shumard was based solely on his loyalty to Buckley; however, it is more likely that he was convinced of Shumard's dereliction by Buckley's evidence in letters to Lincecum. Buckley's letters outlining charges against Shumard are unfortunately not among the Lincecum Papers. The Shumards, Moore,

Buckley and Moore accepted the invitation and for almost a month the two were in the area making a geological survey of Washington, Fayette, and adjacent counties. Early in 1861 at an extra session of the Legislature, an attempt was made to abolish the entire state survey. Gideon followed developments with interest and on February 14 wrote to the editor of the Galveston *News*:

Now, more than ever, the resources of Texas need to be developed. . . . The late discovery by the present state geologist (Dr. Moore) of an Iron Mountain in Llano County equal in quality as I understand it to the celebrated Iron Mountain of Missouri is of more value by far than the entire cost of the survey.[14]

Gideon believed the reports about Shumard's abrupt removal from office by Houston and replied on February 17 to a communication from Buckley:

Your letter of the 10th inst. has really surprised me. I have been for some time pretty certain that things were not working in accordance with the expectation of those who had placed confidence in the man [Shumard] and who took an interest in the knowledge of the developments of such an enterprise; but I have never entertained an idea of extensive frauds and peculations. . . . You say the effort Dr. Shumard and his friends made to induce the legislature to make further expenditures to relieve and sustain the *doctor's* extravagance and bad management was defeated and that report says he intends to leave soon. Is he not already gone? After the charges that were preferred against him were sufficiently established to defeat his application to the legislature and upset his plans for further peculations, can he have the face to appear in public? If he can remain in Austin now and look an honest man in the face, I must confess myself entirely ignorant of the amount of brass such unworthy faithless villains keep on hand.

While making a survey of the Fredericksburg-Fort Mason area dur-

---

and Buckley left Texas shortly after this episode; Buckley was the only one who returned.

[14] Lincecum's letter cannot be located in the *News*. The geological survey, by a joint resolution, was suspended in 1861 (*Texas Almanac, 1868*, pp. 192–193). Dr. Geiser commented to the author on the reference to the Iron Mountain: "This 'discovery' is a gross error, I believe. *There is none there.* But let it stand. I would be glad to see this in print; it shows us *what was happening behind the scenes.* Of course, it is the sheerest buncombe, but it is enlightening!" (underscoring, Dr. Geiser's).

ing March and April, Buckley accidentally shot himself in the arm. Gideon's last letter to him until after the War is dated May 12, 1861, and addressed to the Geological Rooms, Austin. His devotion to Buckley never wavered and he remained his generous and loyal friend to the end of his life. Buckley's Union sympathies and his absence from Texas during the War made little difference to the old Yankee-hater. After the War their friendship picked up where it had been interrupted.

In June, 1860, Gideon received a "very encouraging communication" from Elias Durand, a botanist and member of the Philadelphia Academy of Sciences. It was the beginning of a long and intimate correspondence between two lonely old men who, although they never saw each other, found a mutually affectionate and understanding relationship. This remarkable friendship between the foreign-born and cosmopolitan naturalist and the Texan who learned the facts of natural history from "nature's own laboratory" ended only with their deaths.

Gideon replied to this first letter:

I spend the greater portion of my time alone. I am not posted as to how much of the world knows of nature's great record. They may know it all and that which looks so fresh and beautiful to my untutored mind and which I prize so dearly may all be commonplace to the scientific investigator. You in the city and I in the woods with what intellectual powers we possess both operate in our surroundings as best we can and are perhaps equally happy.

Gideon sent Durand his notes on grasses, and the Philadelphia botanist, who also corresponded with Sallie, wrote her: "Your father's notes appear to me very important and I will try to condense them in an article under his name for the *Journal of the Pennsylvania Agricultural Society*."[15]

---

[15] Élie (but known as "Elias") Magloire Durand was born in France in 1794. He was commissioned a pharmacist in the French army, 1813, and fought in numerous battles of the Franco-Prussian War. He came to the United States in 1816 because of his Napoleonic sympathies and in 1825 opened in Philadelphia a pharmacy which became an informal clubhouse for scientists. He was elected in 1824 to the Philadelphia Academy and to the College of Pharmacy, and in 1854 to the American Philosophical Society. When his second wife died in 1851 he turned his pharmacy over to his son and devoted the remainder of his life to botanical studies. In 1868 he gave his collection of over 100,000 botanical specimens to the Jardin des Plantes, Paris. He wrote many papers on chemical and botanical subjects as well as the memoirs of François André Michaux and Thomas Nuttall. Durand died August 14, 1873, "loved and venerated" (*DAB*, Vol. 5, pp. 538–539).

When Lincecum began receiving requests for specimens from members of the Philadelphia Academy he reservedly asked Buckley: "If those fellows in Philadelphia should turn out to be of the black stripe what good reason is there why Sallie and myself should not bestow our 800 specimens on our own state?"[16] Gideon had long advocated a state collection and scientific academy in Texas. There being none, he was anxious that his work be preserved; so he presented his collection of botany from throughout Texas to the Philadelphia Academy. It was the basis for "A Collection of Plants from Texas," written by Durand and published in the *Proceedings of the Academy*, Vol. XIII (May, 1861), p. 98.

Gideon wrote Durand: "With liberal minded gentlemen anything I can do in my small way that will add a single line to the record of the natural—the only true science—shall be done as free as the water flows."

When Dr. Spencer F. Baird of the Smithsonian, who had assembled the reports on mammals, birds, and reptiles for the *United States-Mexican Boundary Survey*, published by the U.S. government in 1859, asked for a large collection, Gideon sent him, among other things, his wife's collection of Gulf Coast shells picked up on winter excursions.[7] Gideon later saw the lithographed plates of them in a government publication and could recall where and when each was found by his "dear old lady."

To Baird also went fossils and bones collected in Alabama and Mississippi; a live muskrat, which Gideon had taught to eat cornbread and nibble biscuits, on which it survived during the long journey to Washington; skins of prairie rats, grass sparrows, curlews, and plovers.

[16] To convince Gideon that the members of the Philadelphia Academy were not "black Republicans" and that they held him in high esteem despite his proslavery stand, Dr. Thomas Stewardson, corresponding secretary of the Academy, wrote Lincecum a letter of assurance in April, 1860. Upon receiving it Lincecum wrote Durand: "I am satisfied now and we are all friends."

[17] Baird (1823–1887) was the most influential and far-sighted scientist in the United States during the thirty-seven years from 1850 when he was associated with the Smithsonian Institution, first as assistant secretary under Joseph Henry and later as secretary. As a student Baird wrote a letter to John J. Audubon, who later became his close friend. Audubon's kindness in replying to his youthful letter probably accounts for Baird's unfailing courtesy to his numerous unknown correspondents (William Healey Dall, *Spencer Fullerton Baird, a Biography*, [Philadelphia and London, J. B. Lippincott Company, 1915], pp. 44–46). Gideon could not have found a more alert and appreciative recipient for his collections and specimens.

Baird was the recipient of much of Gideon's bag from hunting trips, on which young Dr. Ruff of Long Point was a frequent companion. Ruff was, according to Lincecum, "an industrious and considerably progressed young gentleman." After one hunt Gideon sent off a burrowing owl, two prairie owls, a hawk, a butcher bird, gnat bird, sapsucker, and snowbird. Lincecum had never seen a bird skinned nor did he have any instructions on the subject. He invented a system of his own, apologizing to Baird: "I have made a trial of skinning birds. I will do my best but I am, however, very fumble-fisted." Preservatives also were a problem. He experimented with carbolic acid and found that mice and small birds could be preserved whole with the injection of a few drops.

Alcohol was not only difficult to obtain but expensive. Gideon made his own out of persimmons, stealthily as he said, to avoid a state tax. This comment was made after the War. Early in the War, Gideon sold his hundred-gallon copper still to a Washington County neighbor to avoid the high tax. Others were interested in his equipment—for somewhat different purposes. In September, 1861, William H. Morris of Webberville wanted to buy it, and in October Lincecum received an inquiry from C. C. Frissel of LaGrange. To the latter he replied:

It is, however, encouraging to know in these troublous times that so many gentleman are thinking of preparing themselves for the production of the greatest and best, most popular and most loved article of which the cruel Lincoln blockade has deprived us. Let us all strive for it, let us sedulously preserve in the great work, until every little creek and ravine throughout the state shall be made perfectly redolent with the sweet savor that emanates ever from the soul-saving still house—I know of no other still in this vicinity.

Gideon reserved some birds for his son-in-law Durham. Once after hunting with his favorite bow, five feet in length, which could shoot three-ounce arrows 215 yards, he wrote to Durham: "Except the aquatic, I did not see many rare birds during my tour of the coast. I saw several pairs of whooping cranes and thinking of your desire for a skin or two, I made an effort to shoot some. Well, I didn't kill any, but speaking in the bounds of reason, I think I came in two miles of it."

Baird was genuinely fond of Gideon and had a great respect for his knowledge of Texas natural history. After the Civil War he repaid some of his obligations by sending a supply of highly desirable and hard-to-get turnip seeds to Washington County farmers at Gideon's request. When Gideon was seventy-five and Baird forty-two, the old man wrote:

You desire to maintain to advanced life your present love and enthusiasm for investigation and experimentation in the natural sciences. I can see from your autograph that your constitutional forces are good and that you may survive to a great age provided you abstain from sinning. Being naturally above the par line in the scale of humanity you must avoid all stimulants, sleep enough, rest enough and *don't fill your belly too full.* Attend to the amative developments as you do to the bowels, evacuate them only when the necessity is pressing. Herein lies the secret of longevity.

Baird died at the age of sixty-five.

When George Engelmann, the German-born Missouri physician, meteorologist, and botanist, inquired about his knowledge of the Texas grape, Gideon knowingly replied: "I have collected every species of indigenous grapes belonging to Texas." He had shared his collection with Buckley, Durham, and Durand but started another for Engelmann.[18]

When correspondence between the North and the South was halted during the Civil War, Gideon's communication with his Northern scientist friends ceased.

On December 24, 1865, Gideon wrote Durand replying to his "very kind, fraternal communication of 10th Nov. 1861, which reached me on March 11, 1862" and continued:

You express much regret at the breaking up of our agreeable, as you are pleased to call it, correspondence. No one could regret the abrupt manner in which our, as I think, quite profitable correspondence was cut short more

---

[18] Engelmann (1809–1884) came to the U.S. in 1833 and was a practicing physician in St. Louis until meteorology and botany became his consuming interests. He organized the St. Louis Academy of Sciences in 1856 and is credited with the discovery of the immunity of the American grape to the *Phylloxera* (DAB, Vol. 6 [1931], pp. 159–160). Engelmann wrote "Cactaceae of the Boundary," describing specimens collected in Texas by officers and scientists assigned to the boundary survey, which was published in William H. Emory's *Report on the United States and Mexican Boundary Survey* (Washington, D.C., Cornelius Wendell, 1859), Executive Document 135, Vol. II, Part I, pp. 1–78.

than myself. I tried, as you requested me to do, to get a letter through to you several times but as I heard no more of you I suppose they did not reach you and now I am not sure that you will ever see this.

The War left him penniless, he told Durand, and he now found it necessary to forego science and devote his time to making a living by concocting medical prescriptions from plants. But he had a few items of interest for his friend:

I have in my possession specimens of several kinds of bivalves, which I collected from the cliff of a recent landslide, that are as perfect in all their parts as they were a thousand centuries ago. . . . they were lying in their proper places and positions on what was then the bottom of the ocean. The outline of these shells is sharp and very perfect and when forced open the animal is found contracted to one side of the cavity of the shell, of a yellowish color and petrified—limey.

Buckley returned to Texas as state geologist under Governor James Webb Throckmorton and was pleased to find that his old naturalist friend had survived the war. The State Geological Survey had been re-instituted on October 30, 1866, by a joint resolution which repealed the 1861 resolution suspending the agency. Governor Throckmorton, however, found there were no funds for the project. The specimens had been removed from the Old Land Office Building to the State Library Room in the Capitol, and Buckley, appointed state geologist, December 16, 1866, was assigned to arrange and classify them. Throckmorton commended Buckley "for his industry, zeal and ability, and his fidelity in his obligations to the state."[19] Shumard was not forgotten. Lincecum wrote Buckley late in 1866:

I hope also that when you make out your report you will not fail to present the doings of that faithless Shumard in true colors. That man should not be trusted as a leader, in any kind of business that has money in it. . . . I have just got back with three of my bug-hunting boys from a whole day's entomological excursion around the Big Lake where you and Skunk Shumard and I went together on the Yegua one day. . . . Shumard didn't care a damn for the people nor the state either."

[19] James Webb Throckmorton, "Summary of the Throckmorton Administration," August 8, 1867, *Texas Almanac, 1868*, pp. 184–201.

Lincecum was highly critical of some other Texas scientists of that day, particularly William DeRyee, a Bavarian who came to Texas in 1856 and was a chemist during the war for the Confederate Nitrate and Mining Bureau, and Conrad C. Stremme, a German who came to Texas in 1853 and was assistant draftsman for the General Land Office and who had encouraged Lincecum in his artesian-well project by lending him a book on well boring. Lincecum asked Buckley:

What has become of that dishonest Frenchman, William DeRyee, state chemist? He played the devil with everything that was of any use to him and that old rotten-hearted Stremme finished it. How the rogues collect around such places, the state geologist rooms. For instance, Shumard. . . . Is there no way to make old Stremme pay for the missing apparatus? He should be sent to the penitentiary, an old thief.

Gideon, knowing Buckley's friendly interest in his personal affairs, explained his situation:

I could not think of broaching any important matter under the pressure of negro insolence and yankee bayonets. Notwithstanding the settled fact that I shall submit to these indignities in silence, it nevertheless unfits me for scientific investigation. . . . I did not suspend operation while the war was going on and even then succeeded in making a collection of some precious things, both from the geological and vegetable worlds. But I am done now. When the war broke up and I had time to look around I found I had lost everything but the homestead. It is the truth that I did not have a blanket nor horse nor mule nor jackass left to my name, nor one single dollar. I went to work and have been, as I think, doing pretty well and see that I shall soon make it go better. At this I do not repine but I tell you of it in advance to keep you from asking me questions about giving up science.

The work I am engaged in is collecting from the forests and prairies around me roots, bark and leaves, seeds, flowers, &c., from which I am manufacturing some of the most precious, pure and potent medicines that have ever been seen in Texas. It was too late in the season when I commenced. Nature had closed up nearly all her remedial agents for winter quarters and I couldn't find them, many of them. I shall wait until she opens and labels her boxes in the spring. I'll make it till then.

Gideon deplored the scarcity of known medicinal plants in Texas, especially those which could be used for emetics. He knew that somewhere there must be one, if he could only find it, because . . . there is no sense in the supposition that nature sows her diseases in one county and her remedies in another.

... I have been plowing, preparing the soil for a crop of corn, potatoes, &c., which will be needed by the time it is in the roasting ear stage as the small stock of bread stuffs we have on hand will be consumed by that time. They say I guide the plow cleverly and that my attitude and movements while doing so are quite graceful. While these remarks were being made, however, I heard no allusions in comparison to the great Cincinnatus!

Gideon's scorn of human dependence upon a watchful Providence goaded him to tease Buckley when he read an article by his friend in a Texas newspaper containing a statement that Providence, to prevent too great an increase in tarantulas, had created its mortal enemy, the wasp:

Well, I never knew that before. . . . Then the question comes up, for what purpose did providence create the spider? You never told me that you were acquainted with providence before the heavenly war we have just passed through. I was not in the war and did not get to see the mashed up bones and blood and ripped out hearts and guts that took place so often under the guidance, as it is said, of providence or I might probably have made his acquaintance too. As it is, I must confess my entire ignorance of his characteristic traits and shall not mention it in any of my notes on ants, scarabaei, doodle bugs, &c., until I am better acquainted with him.

The lethargy of Washington County resulting from the uneasy peace preceding the bitter congressional reconstruction in Texas was shared by Gideon. He wrote Durand: "I have no associates about me to encourage or keep alive the spirit of inquiry at all. Adam in the Year One, Eden, was no more alone in that respect than I am."

In March, 1866, after a day of plowing, Gideon felt the sharp pangs of what he termed "neuralgic rheumatism" which left one of his legs paralyzed from the hip down. Unable to walk for over a month, he confided to Buckley that he considered the attack the beginning of the end. When Buckley advised him to devote his time to the natural sciences instead of plowing, he replied: "That, to be sure, would be a very pleasurable thing to me *but I must have bread.*"

He was able to hobble about that summer and although his legs would last only a mile or so he set out on an excursion in June searching for medicinal plants. He went, however, only as far as Lake Creek in Montgomery County, where he found the region severely damaged by hail and the plant life destroyed.

Gideon again proposed to Buckley that he organize a scientific society in Texas:

Let me hear from you on that subject and say something about the best plan for starting it. I suppose there might be found in Texas a few men who would join it. Sufficient, perhaps, to organize and fill the offices and, I think that with proper notices and encouragement, many valuable contributions might be gotten up among them. People have now many fine specimens in geology, conchology and fossils of many kind laid up as curiosities about their houses which they would willingly contribute to an institution of that kind when it is known to be a permanent fixture. . . . I suppose you have been too busy to pay any attention to the ants this year. . . . It is a pity that the scientific institutions are always dependent on some meat-headed animal that knows nothing about its uses or principles. It seems to me that our institution might be got up and placed on a more independent plan.

In July Gideon subscribed to the *Practical Entomologist*. Then, thinking that it would benefit the local farmers, he attempted to sell subscriptions. Without success, however, for, as he wrote one of his Philadelphia friends: "I found them stone dead to everything of the kind. They tell me that if I can find a paper that will teach them how to prevent the depredations committed in our corn and cotton fields by a class of northern bugs known and distinguished as the glorious miscegenationists they will subscribe to it freely."

By November his leg had mended enough that he could return to his nocturnal prowling in the woods, and when Durand planned a trip to Europe Gideon wrote:

But at your age I can't see how you can employ your mind to give more pleasure in Europe than you can in and about Philadelphia. Yet I confess that I know but little of the resources for enjoyment of either place. My life has been spent in the wild, dark and, until recently, uncontaminated forests of America where the hooting owls, screaming panthers and howling wolves make the nights glorious as the best Italian opera or a full band of martial music. No city life or city preparations can compare even with the ringing music of the nocturnal insects as they trill their songs of love around the hunters' camp far off in the dark pathless forests. There is where the soul of the true man can expand to the dimensions of the scenery which surround it and his liberated thoughts, regardless of academic regulations or theologic anathema, dares to reach among the stars and play fearlessly with the heavenly hosts. . . . Oh! Leave me in the woods, in the far-off woods, where I may without being fettered by the tyranny of conventional rules, enjoy the full function of the perpetual mental feasts like a free man.

At Durand's request Gideon sent him notes from Gideon's Chahta Tradition, which he had translated from the original Choctaw during the war, and the botanist commented in a letter to Sallie:

I have read with great interest Gid's letter on the Choctaw Indians. It is written in a most eloquent style. . . . What a pity that such a genius as your good father be thus sequestered from the great stores of the scientific books and immense collections of natural curiosities of our great cities. It is true that his active mind finds in the forests constant employment in the study of nature, and such men as he are wanted to watch the most minute operations of nature; but what a great assistance would he not find in our large libraries and how many false deductions would he have to rectify in authors who have not had the chance, like himself, to catch on the spot the very secrets of nature. I hope the labors of your father will not be lost to the present generation and its posterity.

My health is excellent and I feel strong and alert enough to accompany your brave father in his intended excursions to hunt natural curiosities. But why do you live so far off? A trip to Texas by railroads, stages and by sea is more frightful to me than two voyages to Europe.

Gideon was in frantic haste to record all his findings in Texas natural history, and he told Durand: "When these articles I scribble are recorded in the transactions of the ancient Academy of Natural Sciences, future generations will see them and be benefited by them. They will not go for bomb fodder."

During the summer of 1867 Governor Throckmorton was removed from office by congressional reconstructionists and with him went Buckley. Gideon fulminated to Buckley:

Without any just cause Hamilton supplanted you by putting in your place a stiff, bigoted old deadhead, an enemy to liberty and to mankind generally. He pretends to great learning of so high an order that none but the illuminated are entitled to the slightest salutation. I have long looked upon that old Dutchman as not only a bad man in my Republican community but he is mean. I wrote him a letter ten or twelve years ago. I suppose he could not answer without divulging some of his learned secrets. Be that as it may it is certain that he did not reply.[20] . . . I cannot conceive why Hamilton was

[20] Lincecum does not name this person. The Texas Election Register of 1867 does not show an appointment of a state geologist to replace Buckley. Joseph Spence was appointed commissioner of the General Land Office, which assumed some of the duties previously performed by geologists. Charles Pressler and C. C. Stremme were appointed draftsmen, and Edward Ten Eyck, assistant clerk, in the Land Office. J. W. Glen appears as the next state geologist in March, 1873. Buckley was again state geologist from 1874 to 1877 (Texas Election Register, Texas State Archives).

The Buckley-Shumard controversy grew into a political issue during the Reconstruction administration of Edmund J. Davis. Although Buckley had been a Unionist before the War, he was not in sympathy with the carpetbagger and Republican faction in control of the state. Buckley was only one of the faction's many targets. The group publicized a letter supposedly written by B. F. Shumard from St. Louis on March 11, 1866, to Swante Palm in Austin, in which Shumard informed Palm that Buckley was in Philadelphia during the War and was given access to the herbarium of the Academy, where he "attempted to purloin the labors of others by removing their names from the labels and substituting his own instead, and this he did, page after page with the most unblushing impudence." Shumard denied that Buckley was connected with him in the Texas geological survey, but on the contrary he "came to me ragged and penniless, and I employed him to collect plants at one dollar per day —giving him precisely the same wages I was giving my teamsters and cooks. All the geology he knows, I taught him, and that was precious little." But when the Democrats were returned to office in the Texas election of 1873 Governor Richard Coke appointed Buckley state geologist, from which position he was able to launch his own offensive attack, contained in his *First Annual Report of the Geological and Agricultural Survey of Texas*, 1874. By comparison Buckley's charges were mild. Referring to Shumard, he wrote: "He had not the advantage of a classical education, was a poor mineralogist, and had little knowledge of the other departments of natural history." Buckley singled out the least-known member of the pre-War geological survey, Anton R. Roessler, for special criticism. Roessler wanted the appointment of state geologist in 1874, which had gone to Buckley. Buckley said of him in his *Report*: "It is due to the intelligence of the people of Texas to state that Mr. Roessler has never been employed by the state authorities as a geologist, nor has he ever added anything of importance to the geological knowledge of the state. While employed as draftsman of the survey, he was never supposed to understand geology in the least, nor was he ever requested to make independent geological examinations." Buckley accused Roessler of departing from Texas with a large number of maps of Texas counties and drawings of Texas scenes which belonged to the state. Thus it was that Roessler had the final word in the Buckley-Shumard controversy. Among many others, his last words were: "I charge him with being an ignoramus, foisted upon the people of a great commonwealth, without possessing any of the qualifications necessary to the administration of the office of State Geologist; a man of no reputation as a scientist and an individual lacking in truth, honesty and all the qualities that belong to a pure manhood. In his hideous deformity I hold him up to the gaze of the people of Texas and thus I leave him for

> "Nothing of good can come from such a source,
> Nor would we aught with him, nor now, nor ever;

sent to Washington. Was he relieved by the President or has he gone north for the purpose of stirring up mischief against Texas?[21]

Although Gideon frequently questioned Buckley's knowledge of grapes, oaks, and ants, he leaned on him for geological information. He greatly admired Buckley's talents in this field and once wrote to Doran about the geologist's maps and surveys:

Buckley's articles on the iron deposits in Texas are pretty good and will, right at this time [1866] attract attention of capitalists in this direction. I regret that he did not allude to the petroleum regions in our state. I have seen enough to satisfy me that the metallic wealth of our state is great and the coal and petroleum are almost boundless.

In preparation for an 1867 geological expedition for the Smithsonian, Gideon wrote himself a note: "Ask SBB to classify the rock series and to point out all the cretaceous and calcerous systems and any other Texas systems." To Buckley he wrote:

I have promised Professors Henry and Baird to take diagrams of the succession and character of the different strata and to pack the shell specimens so that they can be readily referred to their place in the series of rocks from whence they came. I shall need some instructions on the character of the rocks and stratification and for that reason I will go to Austin first.

Only once did the irascible Gideon show any displeasure with Buckley. That was in 1871 when he was in Tuxpan with other discouraged Democrats and wrote to Sallie:

S. B. Buckley owns a little farm in the environs of Austin upon which he raises, as he informs me, ample supplies for his family. He has been a contributor to the *Rural Carolinian* for many years. He is an industrious but

---

We leave him to himself that lowest depth
Of human baseness."
(A. R. Roessler, *Reply to the Charges Made by S. B. Buckley State Geologist of Texas, In His Official Report of 1874 Against Dr. B. F. Shumard and A. R. Roessler,* No. 83 Nassau Street, New York, n.p., February 1, 1875, 10 pages.)

[21] Lincecum referred to Andrew Jackson Hamilton, a Texas Unionist whom President Lincoln appointed military governor of Texas. He was provisional governor from June 1865, to August, 1866, when Throckmorton was elected governor. Hamilton, in 1866, was a delegate to the Loyalist Convention in Philadelphia. Throckmorton was replaced by Elisha M. Pease, whom, as a candidate of the Union party, Throckmorton defeated in the state elections of 1866 (*Handbook of Texas,* Vol. I, p. 759).

very selfish investigator. He calls on me for Mexican ants and I have collected 34 species of them but I can't say when I will send them to him.

But on his return to Texas, Gideon spent a pleasant week with Buckley in his country home, where they again exchanged knowledge and specimens.

The Department of Agriculture also used Gideon's free services and in June, 1867, while he was reading a letter from Isaac Newton, Commissioner of Agriculture, requesting a collection of agricultural specimens, Doran came to tell him he had just received a telegraphic report of Newton's death.[22] Another correspondent was Anton R. Roessler, also of the Agricultural Department and a former Texas state geologist on Shumard's staff, who wanted specimens of wool and histories of Texas sheep.[23] Letters came in from numerous sources requesting a variety of specimens from all sections of Texas, which caused Gideon to lament: "Those fellows must think I live all over Texas!"

The most hard-to-fill request came from Dr. James Aitken Meigs, who wanted the skull of a Texas Indian.[24] Gideon searched diligently for one, writing to numerous Texas Indian fighters and travelers, among them D. W. Taylor and Solomon Cox of Belton and John G. Allen of Hidalgo in Washington County.

He had heard that during 1857 an Indian had been buried near Allen's place but Allen could give him no help. Gideon replied to Allen's letter: "You speak of my intention to collect Texas Indian skulls as an onerous undertaking. Well, what the mischief is a fellow

---

[22] Newton died on June 19, 1867. He was the first U.S. Commissioner of Agriculture. Early in 1861 his good friend, President Lincoln, appointed him superintendent of the Agricultural Division of the Patent Office, which became the Department of Agriculture in 1862 (*DAB*, Vol. 13 [1934], pp. 472–473).

[23] Roessler, possibly trained in Vienna, was an excellent cartographer. He published a number of geological papers but his best work was done in mapping Texas (Geiser, *Naturalist*, p. 281).

[24] Meigs (1829–1879) was a physician, teacher, and anthropologist. From 1856 to 1859 he was librarian of the Academy of Natural Sciences, Philadelphia, and from 1857 was chairman of the Institute of Medicine at Philadelphia College. He wrote "Catalogue of Human Crania in the Collection of the Academy of Natural Sciences of Philadelphia," a supplement to *Proceedings of the Academy* for 1856 (*DAB*, Vol. 12 [1933], pp. 504–505). At the time he corresponded with Lincecum, Meigs was writing *Observations upon the Cranial Forms of the American Aborigines*, published in 1866.

to do? Here I am, 75 years old, with all the desire to learn, to accumulate a knowledge which I never had, of natural things."

So far as it is known, Lincecum failed at this assignment. The next best thing was a Mexican Indian skull, dug out of the Tuxpan River bank, which he sent to the Smithsonian.

One of Gideon's most cherished possessions was a copy of Baird's *A History of North American Birds* which the scientist sent him in 1868. When Lincecum was preparing to go to Tuxpan he sent the book to his son-in-law Durham with the message: "I am sure you would be much pleased with Professor Baird. He is one of the most ardent devotees to science, particularly your specialty and besides he is the most attentive correspondent among them all and is a thorough gentleman. Send him a few bird skins. Right at this time our sparrows interest him very much."

Gideon was both angry and dumfounded when English-born Durham belittled Baird and his book. Gideon retorted:

In reply to my letter notifying you of the fact that I had laid aside for your use Mr. Baird's work on American birds, you gave me a sufficient hint if I had noticed it to have deterred me from any further action, nor should I have recommended Mr. Baird, the *American* ornithologist, as a fitting person to correspond with you on such subjects. I regret very much that I have fallen into such an egregious blunder. It is not common with *me,* but you must recollect that I am getting a little old. With the hope that you will pardon this, my first offense of the kind, I promise that I will not again insult the dignity of your European prejudices by the obtrusion of any more such *American* trash.

If it is very much in your way you can by some favorable opportunity or some traveler send it to my grandson, George W. Lincecum, who has just commenced the study of *American* birds. It will doubtless please him and will, when he understands it, be sufficient distinction for a native-born Texan among his kind.

Gideon did not live long enough to contribute to Elliott Coues' *Fur-Bearing Animals*. Coues[25] wrote from Washington, D.C., on March 22, 1874, on stationery of the U.S. Boundary Commission:

---

[25] Elliott Coues (1842–1899), a U.S. Army surgeon who did pioneer research in ornithology and mammalogy, published *Key to North American Birds* at the age of

My Dear Sir:

Although personally a stranger to you, I am not so to your numerous interesting writings on the habits of animals, and the freedom of intercourse which all good naturalists encourage among each other will I doubt not be extended to me by you on this occasion.

To introduce the subject of this letter let me promise that I am preparing an extensive and elaborate work on the mammals of North America, to be a complete history, technical, descriptive & biographical. I shall work up the living species, while Prof. Marsh[26] will do the fossil ones—and together we hope to make a great work.

My chief deficiency is in the matter of accurate and minute information respecting the habits of the smaller animals—the rats, mice, gophers, squirrels, shrews, moles, etc., etc. Having seen *all* your publications on these subjects in the *Naturalist* and elsewhere, I am convinced that there is no one in the country who has paid more attention to these things than yourself, or who has studied more successfully. And I am very anxious to avail myself of your investigations.

Can you not, in a somewhat systematic manner, furnish me with a number of biographies—just such articles as you have so frequently communicated to the Smithsonian? Anything, however fragmentary it may be, would be welcome. I should only be too happy to incorporate all your observations in my work. I shall in any event collate and edit pretty much all you have published, but probably you would prefer to go over the points again, while it would be better on all accounts that the matter should come from you directly, rather than be transcribed from already published accounts.

I need not add how fully & very gratefully all contributions to the work would be acknowledged, and passed entirely to your credit. I hope to have an early and favorable reply from you. There is no particular hurry for the present—any time within a year would be in season for the work.

I have lately completed and am about to publish an elaborate monograph of the *Muridae,* and you need hardly be told how very valuable were the numerous specimens which I found in the Smithsonian from you.

Faithfully yours,
Elliott Coues

---

thirty. From 1873 to 1876 he was naturalist of the U.S. Northern Boundary Commission; from 1876 to 1880 he was with the U.S. Geological and Geographical Survey of Territories; he was professor of anatomy, 1882–1887, at Columbia University. His *Fur-Bearing Animals* was published in 1877 (*ibid*, Vol. 4 [1930], pp. 465–466).

[26] Othniel Charles Marsh (1831–1899) was a foremost American vertebrate paleontologist and chairman of paleontology at Yale University, which received his collection of fossils (*ibid*, Vol. 12 [1933], pp. 302–303).

This letter from the noted ornithologist and foremost scientist of his day must have been a great personal satisfaction to the old man and a fulfillment of his hope that his humble contributions would become a part of the permanent record of man's knowledge of the natural sciences. Gideon's answer to Coues is not among the Lincecum Papers; however, the letter bears a notation "answered 4 May 1874."

A NOTE ON SOURCES

The Lincecum Papers contain a number of letters from Lincecum to Powell and a few letters from Powell to Lincecum, the earliest from Powell written on June 3, 1839, from Gainesville, Alabama, and addressed to Gideon at Wall's Tanyard, Monroe County, Mississippi. Powell was a well-known phrenologist who gained considerable notice in 1836 when he made character analyses of Antonio López de Santa Anna and of Juan Nepomuceno Almonte from portraits. In a letter to Powell on February 2, 1860, Lincecum answered an inquiry concerning the whereabouts of a mutual friend, Dr. Samuel Haynie.

Learning of Powell's death in 1866, Gideon wrote to his old botanic doctor friend, Dr. Alva Curtis, in Cincinnati, on July 19, 1866, concerning a contract which he and Powell had made as to disposition of their heads after death, and the possible conflicting claim of a woman in Georgia for possession of Powell's cranium.

Sallie Lincecum Doran not only preserved most of her father's papers and those of her husband but also saved letters written to her by Elias Durand before and shortly after her marriage. These are included in the Lincecum Papers, and the sweetly sentimental letters clearly indicate that despite his age, Durand entertained romantic feelings toward Sallie. The letters are dated April 1, 1861, and February 6 and 10, and August 17, 1867. They are nostalgic relics of another day.

It is lamentable that letters to Gideon from the distinguished and pioneering scientists of his time are not extant, most particularly those from Spencer Fullerton Baird, who was in constant contact with naturalists in all parts of the world. In Texas he followed the progress of Dr. Adolphus Wislizenus, Captain George B. McClellan, Captain Stewart Van Vliet, Dr. Adolphus Lewis Heermann, John Henry Clark, Charles Wright, Duke Paul Wilhelm of Württemberg, and Lieutenant Darius Nash Couch (the latter responsible for obtaining the Louis Berlandier early Texas-Mexican collection for the Smithsonian in 1853).

Lincecum's correspondence covering his scientific interests include the letters to: Treasurer, Academy of Natural Science, Philadelphia, January 12, 1861 (transmitting 682 specimens of plants from Texas); E. Durand, Philadelphia, January 17, March 3, September 1, October 5, November 5, 1860, January 13, February 6 (transmitting 800 specimens of plants from Texas, 26 species of shells, numerous species of rock from Austin), April 11, 1861, December 25, 1865; February 1 and 22, May 2, July 15, September 30, October 16, 1866; S. F. Baird, Smithsonian Institution, Washington, D.C., February 12, October 4, December 13, 1866, December 11, July 8, November 1, 1867, January 12, 21, 27, February 24, April 1, 5, 17, 1868; Professor Stremme, Austin, Texas, October 30, 1859, September 3, 1860; B. F. Shumard, State Geologist, Austin, Texas, January 18, August 7, October 16, 1860; H. C. Wood, Jr., Philadelphia, April 17, June 22, July 3, 1866; Dr. M. L. Byrn, New York City, July 3, 1866; Townsend Glover, Department of Agriculture, Washington, D.C., March 3, 1868; George Engelmann, St. Louis, Missouri, October 20, November 25, 1867; A. R. Roessler, Washington, D.C., June 23, 1867; Professor Joseph Henry, Smithsonian Institution, June 20, 1867; J. W. Stokes, Acting Commissioner, Department of Agriculture, Washington, D.C., September 28, 1867; Dr. Samuel Lewis, Philadelphia, March 5, 1867; Professor C. D. Coffee, Philadelphia, November 24, 1867; Professor E. D. Cope, Philadelphia, November 18, 1866, February 13, 1868; Joseph Leidy, Philadelphia, July 21, 1867; W. P. Doran, Houston, February 12, 1866; S. B. Buckley, Austin, Texas, June 10, October 16, December 19, 1860, January 10, 1861, July 1, October 15, November 19, 28, 1866, January 18, February 22, June 22, October 21, December 12, 1867.

CHAPTER TWELVE

GIDEON
AND THE PISMIRES

Some people think and some have already said it that I am deranged on the subject of bugs, ants, frogs, etc. Well, it is at least a harmless derangement.   GID

GIDEON HAD learned the secrets of the entomological world and was on intimate terms with numerous species of ants, bees, bugs, and beetles before he ever saw a book on them. He knew their social life, their structure of government, their preferences in food, and details of their sex life long before he knew their scientific classifications. His knowledge surpassed that of many trained naturalists writing and teaching in the United States at that time, some of whom later claimed as their own many of his independent conclusions which he so freely passed on for the good of science.

His pursuit of bugs was an invention for mental and physical employment and personal happiness as he "sluggishly floated like an old soggy log down the time stream" he once told a friend. But Gideon's assiduous devotion to the study of insects was more than a time-passer. He recorded everything he observed as well as his conclusions, hopeful that he could contribute something lasting and worthwhile to man's knowledge of insects, which at that time was amazingly meager.[1]

---

[1] The recognized leaders in entomology at the time were Europeans. René-Antoine Ferchault de Réaumur, born in France in 1683, knew much about ants, but his manuscript written in 1742 was lost until 1925; Pierre Huber, another Frenchman, in 1810

Forty feet from his Long Point main house Gideon erected a little house of red cedar. Here he lived, away from the bustle of his gregarious wife, her constant and numerous visitors, and the many grandchildren the elderly couple called the "grand dears." Gideon referred to them as "book spoilers and paper scribblers, pictures of health and devilment." In the little house he had his bed, books, papers and pens, copying press, and gadgets. Stacked about were boxes of shells, fossils, and geological specimens. Numerous shelves held vials of specimens and double sheets of glass between which plants were carefully pressed. Outside, scattered about the high hedge of cactus, were wagonloads of petrified wood and miscellaneous bones, dried tropical plants from another country washed up on the Texas coast by the Gulf stream, and rocks, scraps, splinters, and detritus from another age.

The neat little porch was latticed and shaded by rose vines; here Gideon napped during the day on a wide cedar bench. And all about and in the little house swarmed bees, thousands of them, all on friendly terms with the old man and as playful with him as his kitten. They became entangled in his long white beard and at night shared his bed, so many at times that Gideon moved cautiously so as not to "roll upon and kill the friendly little fellows." As he sat at his writing table during the day, the bees swarmed over his bare feet. When he went into the woods the bees followed him for two miles—no more than that distance. Gideon observed that at this mileage they always turned back.

He taught his bees to swim. "They possess a splendidly organized brain and are very capable of extensive training," he remarked. Noticing that many of his hapless bees were daily drowned in a small pond in the yard, he instituted prevention measures. First he placed on the gallery floor a basin containing a small amount of water. Then, as the bees drank from it, he suddenly filled the container. They floated to the top as the water rose, and quickly scuffled out. Tirelessly, Lincecum repeated this procedure daily until many of them became good swimmers.

---

published his famous *Researches into the Natural History of Indigenous Ants,* and Auguste Forel, a Swiss, wrote his first paper on ants in 1869 and published his classic work, *Ants of Switzerland,* in 1875 (Derek Wragge Morley, *The Ant World* [Penguin Books, London, Wyman & Sons, Ltd., 1953], pp. 164–184).

He trained bees to fill churns and other containers with honey, working away from the main hive. Lincecum noted that the honeycomb in the receptacle had no bee bread in it, an indication that the bees did not intend to remain there long enough to raise young ones.

Small water beetles visited him at night as he read by his lamp and, to please them, Gideon tumbled them headlong into a glass of water where they gamboled and practiced deep diving safely away from the larger water insects, designated by him "tyrants of the pool."

Gideon watched the paper-making wasps deposit their eggs and feed wasp honey to their young. As they grew older, a small amount of "sausage meat" was added and increased gradually until the diet was entirely meat. Gideon witnessed the sausage being made, the mother wasp "cutting and mincing a nice, smooth-skinned caterpillar and making a ball of it."

He observed a dirtdauber sting into paralysis his pet tarantula and gave the species the name "tarantula killer," today called the tarantula hawk. The muddaubers, he noted, "observed the marriage institution, live and work together in pairs." Gideon cautioned a friend: "Don't kill the muddauber for were it not for them the spiders would occupy every hole and corner."

As the trap-door spider ingeniously contrived its door, hinged on one side, Gideon stood vigil until the spider left its house. He was there when it returned, saw it enter and carefully close the door by pulling it down by a cord. Among the spiders he found one he called an "aerial navigator" because "they do positively construct balloons, take in passengers and sail them perhaps half across the county in a day."

He watched the scorpions, centipedes, grasshoppers, locusts, crickets, and the cowkiller, "a lonely insect who travels quickly, seeming to be hurriedly in pursuit of something he never finds." Gideon found excitement in discovering the marvelous antics of the insect kingdom, now known as facts to every school child, but dark and doubtful fancies to many naturalists of the day.

In his small red-cedar house the patient old man hatched cotton worms in order to study their habits and determine the best method of destroying them. He repeatedly warned Washington County cotton farmers against them and in an article on their destructive power in the *Texas Almanac, 1867*, advised: "Go into the field, taking your women and children and all the force you have on the place; examine the cotton row by row, scrutinizing every stalk."[2]

Gideon's diary for 1867 records:

July 19—It has been a very hot sultry day—rain came to our relief at 5 P.M. It was a very pretty shower and beginning to be needed in the gardens, potato patches and the cotton. I told the people last year how to destroy the cotton worms. I hear them talking of the worms now but no talk of killing them. To laziness and ignorance may be attributed all our suffering.

Aug. 4—Hear a distressing account of the devastating cotton worms. . . . They say the worms are eating the entire crop, people everywhere in this region are greatly discouraged. . . . Many cotton farms are said to be already ruined and it is likely to be all lost.

Aug. 6—Polk County. In the county around, the cotton has been entirely destroyed by the worms. People . . . talk of moving away or changing their agricultural action.

Aug. 30—I put up quite a number of larvae of the cotton pest in alcohol and perhaps 100 of their pupae in a cigar box. I want to be certain that I get the true cotton moth to send to the Smithsonian.

Sept. 4—I put up some cotton moths today that hatched in my room. They hatched in six days from the rolling up of the pupae. I have many more to hatch.

Sept. 6—I put up yesterday and today a fine lot of cotton moths that . . . hatched from the winding up of the pupae in nine days, coming perfect drab colored flies. Like the silk worm, they couple, deposit their eggs, and soon die. I hear of their having been destroyed by fire and by picking them off at several farms.

Sept. 20—The quantity of moths is truly surprising this September. Hickory and cotton moths greatest.

---

2 "The Cotton Worm," pp. 195–196. The boll worm preceded the boll weevil to Texas by at least twenty-five years. To Edward Palmer (1831–1911), a botanist in San Antonio in 1879–1880, belongs the distinction of having been the first to call attention to the depredation of the boll weevil, which had previously been known to science only through a few museum specimens (Rogers McVaugh, *Edward Palmer: Plant Explorer of the American West* [Norman, University of Oklahoma Press, 1956], p. 81). In 1878 the U.S. government recognized the cotton worm as a pest and sent Eugene Amandus Schwarz to Texas to investigate it. Two years later James Parish Stelle was in charge of the cotton-worm investigation in Texas (Samuel Wood Geiser, "Notes on Some Workers in Texas Entomology, 1839–1880," *Southwestern Historical Quarterly*, Vol. XLIX [1945–1946], p. 597).

The farmers paid little heed to Gideon's warnings but for once he did not mind, explaining: "I should rejoice to know that the worms will devour the entire crop. I know of no circumstance that could frustrate Yankee arrogance so much as that would."

Officially, the cabbage worm's appearance in the United States is dated 1868; but two years earlier Gideon alerted the country to the presence and danger of the worm in a paper in the *Practical Entomologist*.[3] In it he said:

Herewith for your inspection I send a set of dead specimens of a very destructive insect that I have seen nowhere but in Texas. Mr. J. H. Hilliard says that he saw them in Louisiana and that they were confined to and destroyed his garden several times in the same manner that they are sucking my plants to death. As here, he says the Louisiana bugs touched none but the cruciform plants.

Year before last they got into my garden and utterly destroyed my cabbage, radishes, mustard, seed turnips. . . . Last year I did not plant . . . but the present year, thinking they had probably left the premises I planted my garden with radishes, mustard and a variety of cabbage. By the first of April the mustard and radishes were large enough for use and I discovered that the insect had also commenced on them. I commenced picking them off by hand and tramping them underfoot. By that means I have preserved my 484 cabbages but I have visited every one of them daily now for months, finding on them from 35 to 60 full grown insects every day.

Gideon included a detailed report of the incubation, growth, and habits of the worms.

Gideon made the Texas agricultural ant famous, if not notorious, and a subject of bitter debate among eminent naturalists of the world. This peculiar large brown ant, which lives in cities, cultivates the soil and plants, and harvests his favorite grain, was in Texas long before Austin's Old Three Hundred, but no one, until Gideon Lincecum invaded his privacy, considered him with more than passing interest.[4] Lincecum is known to all serious ant men, not because he was the first

---

[3] "The Texan Cabbage-bug," *Practical Entomologist*, Philadelphia, Vol. I, August 27, 1866, p. 110; also published in the *Prairie Farmer*, Vol. 34 (1866), p. 152.

[4] Dr. E. M. Walker, who died in 1868 in Yorktown, Texas, according to Dr. Geiser (*Naturalists*, p. 335), read a paper on the agricultural ant of Texas before the New Orleans Academy of Sciences which was published in the Academy's *Proceedings*, Vol. I (1854), pp. 47–48.

to state publicly that ants were the most social of all hymenoptera, kept slaves, harvested and stored grain, milked aphids, engaged in warfare, and mated in periodical swarmings, but, ironically, because he held that some ants planted their own favorite seed-bearing grass. Ant men have yielded to all these points except the last one and it is this point that has kept Lincecum's name alive in this particular field. While some authorities in the past have firmly closed the door on this theory it keeps opening with embarrassing persistence, especially since it has been established that some ants plant, cultivate, fertilize, and control the growth of a special type of fungus.

For twelve years he watched as the ants built their cities, planted and weeded their grain-bearing grasses, and harvested and chaffed the ricelike seeds. He spent long tiring hours on his knees in dirt and mud, year after year, during the day and at night, observing the ants store away the grain, drying it in the sun after the rain dampened it and discarding the sprouting seeds. Gideon ate the sprouting seeds to determine why they were not acceptable as food. He found the taste similar to that of the leaf of the green plant and understood why his proud, vigorous, warrior-farmers refused to eat common fodder but insisted on its being well cured.

Gideon's diligence paid off. He was witness to a rare and unrecorded scene—the swarming of male and female ants which he termed "an amative picnic." He graphically and in a most unscientific manner, described the mating convention:

There must have been at least five males to one female and all parties were rushing hither and thither over the entire area in a frantic furor. Each female would be found covered and wallowing on the ground with clusters of from four to five to twenty males and there were hundreds thickly rushing over the ground in search of females that were not to be found.

When a female becomes satisfied with her numerous lovers, by a great and violent effort, she made shift to extricate herself from their rude embrace and immediately fly away, leaving her disconsolate, exhausted lovers who made no effort to follow. Many of the males were already dead and still greater numbers lay helpless on the ground. There must have been nearly, if not quite, a bushel of the exhausted and dying male ants.

Gideon watched the female shed her wings and start boring a new home in the dirt, raise a sufficient number of neuters to assist her in her work, then retire to reproduce her millions for a new kingdom. Gideon saw the ants fighting a two-day war, during which they decapitated the enemy, formed political parties, obtained slaves, and established a police state. They were his little ant-people—intelligent, courageous and enterprising.

Totally unaware of their scientific classifications, Gideon catalogued over fifty species and named them himself. His descriptive identifications for some are interesting: red-headed tree ant; the small, black erratic ant; the servile, middle-sized brown ant; the large, black secretive ant; the small, black belligerent ant; the slow, timid ant; and the ant with a jaunty appearance.

He found in Buckley a companion who shared his interest in ants, and wrote to him soon after their meeting:

I am pleased to find that you are so industriously peeping into the secret manners and customs of that great genus of intelligent, managing, social, enterprising, commercial, agricultural, foraging, honey-gathering, aphis-milking, courageous, warlike, pillaging beings called in the holy scripture, the pismire.

I read your article on cutting ants in the *Gazette,* and will, when I meet you again, add some interesting details in reference to the private character of this great race of slave holders. . . . I shall still retain the name "agricultural" in preference to that of "stinging ant." They all sting but perhaps none of their poisons can hurt longer or be more painful than the agricultural ant. I close with a fervent prayer to the god of the great ant kingdoms that you may find out all their secrets. I shall try.

And again to Buckley: "I care nothing about describing their jaws, feelers, feet, legs, etc.; but their mode of life, governments, laws, religion, cities, confederacies, commerce, intercourse, battles, defeats and victories, slaves, prisoners, traits of character, and other peculiarities of deep interest. From them I may learn wisdom."

Buckley encouraged him in his study and suggested he write a paper on ants to which Gideon replied: "I shall continue to write down all the discoveries I may make in the ant genus and somebody will find it when I am gone to the big hunting ground. As for writing a treatise for publication, as you suggested, on the subject I do not feel competent. I have not the vanity to believe myself capable."

They frequently disagreed about ants. Lincecum, for example, did not believe as Buckley did that the ants in the slave nurseries of the cutting ants were the same species, and he thought it possible they were absconded slaves because

. . . their slaves are the same type of inoffensive, slow-moving, small, brown ant which I saw at your camp near my house last August. . . . The observations of other people do not satisfy me. They don't seem to notice their peculiar habits in a manner to appease my yearnings on that topic. I consider the ants a big subject and to do them justice would require more intellectual force than I possess.

It was obvious that the only way he was to know all about the subject was through his own observations; so he wrote to Buckley:

I have procured me a nice little spade and pickaxe for the purpose and will, ere long, pitch into the pismire kingdom. I intend to cause their oldest inhabitants to stand aghast, force their law givers and philosophers to surrender the archives of their natural arrangements and their progress in the sciences, enter their sanctum sanctorum, drag out the ministering priest and ask him questions which he *must* answer.

Late in December, 1860, Gideon read Charles Darwin's *Origin of the Species*. At that time there were few among men of science, including the more progressive ones, who shared Gideon's opinion of Darwin:

He is a good man and an earnest seeker for natural and scientific truth; has been eminently successful and in his recent work on the subject of natural selection has shocked old science and theology exceedingly. Success to him, and I shall aid him by propping him with all the little sticks I may possess that will answer the purpose. I am to a certain extent his disciple; was a disciple of his grandfather, Erasmus Darwin, during his lifetime.

Gideon wrote Darwin the first of several letters, commending him on his book and describing the agricultural ant.

In his first letter to Darwin, dated December 29, 1860, Gideon wrote:

In my journal of observations I find many cases applicable to your theory of natural selection, but in my present state of mind I feel more inclined to state some of my observations on the agricultural successes of one of our many species of Texas ants. It may interest you some. It cannot injure. Consider it. If you like it and want more, write.

The species of *Formica,* which I have named agricultural, is a large, brownish-red ant, dwells in paved cities, is a farmer, thrifty and healthy; is diligent and thoughtful, making suitable and timely arrangements for the changing seasons; in short, he is endowed with capacities sufficient to contend, with much skill and ingenuity and untiring patience, with the varying exigencies which he may encounter in the life conflict.

When he selects a situation upon which to locate a city, if it is on ordinarily dry land, he bores a hole around which he elevates the surface three, sometimes six, inches forming a low, circular mound with a very gentle inclination from the center to its outer limits, which on an average is three to four feet from the entrance. But if the location is made on a low or flat wet land, liable to inundation though the ground may be perfectly dry at the time he does the work, he nevertheless elevates his mound in the form of a pretty sharp cone, to the height of fifteen to twenty inches, sometimes even more, having the entrance near the apex. Around this . . . he clears the ground of all obstructions, levels and smooths the surface to the distance of three or four feet from the gate of the city, giving it the appearance of a handsome pavement, as it really is. Upon this pavement not a spire of any green thing is permitted to grow except a single species of grain-bearing grass. Having planted it in a circle around, and two or three feet from the center of the mound, he nurses and cultivates it with constant care, cutting away all other grasses and weeds that may spring up amongst it. . . . The cultivated grass grows luxuriantly, producing a heavy crop of small, white, flinty seeds which under the microscope very much resembles the rice of commerce. When it gets ripe it is carefully harvested and carried by the workers, chaff and all, into the granary cells, where it is divested of the chaff and packed away; the chaff is taken out and thrown beyond the limits of the pavement.

During protracted spells of wet weather, it sometimes happens that their provision stores become damp and liable, as they are invariably seeds of some kind, to sprout and spoil. If this has occurred, the first fair day after the rain they bring out the damp and damaged stores, expose them to the sun till they are dry . . . carry back and pack away all the sound seeds, leaving all that are sprouted to waste.

In a peach orchard, not far from my residence, is a considerable elevation, on the top of which there is an extensive bed of rock. In the sand beds overlying portions of this rock are five cities of the agricultural ants. They are evidently quite ancient cities and may have occupied this elevated rock for thousands of years. My term of observations on their manners and customs has been limited to the time the cattle, by the orchard enclosure, have been kept away from their rice farms—12 years. Those cities which are outside of the enclosures as well as the protected cities are, at the proper season, invariably planted with the ant rice. And we accordingly see it springing up in the farm circle about the first of November, every year. Of late years, however, . . . I notice that the agricultural ants—but no other species of ant—are locating their cities along the turn rows in the fields, walks in the garden, inside about the gates, &c., where they can cultivate their farms without molestation from the cattle. And here, if it was not for the dread I feel of offending that host of investigators who know all things and who are satisfied there is no truth beyond the range of their own observations, I should be almost wicked enough to state it as my opinion that the granivorous agriculturists had intentionally gone in and unobtrusively settled themselves in the unplowed portions of our enclosures for the purpose of escaping from the depredations of the cattle. This species of ant do no damage to the farms, however numerous.

There can be no doubt of the fact, that the peculiar grain-bearing grass, mentioned above, is intentionally planted; in farmer-like manner the ground upon which it stands is carefully divested of all other grasses and weeds during the time of its growth, and that when it is ripe and the grain taken care of they cut away the dry stubble and carrying it out of the way leave the pavement unencumbered until the ensuing autumn, when the same ant rice and in the same circle appears again, receiving the same agricultural attention as did the previous crop, and so on, year after year, as *I know* to be the case. . . . I have no theological clique to curb the play of my mind . . . and so I may here suggest that it may not exceed a few short millions of years since this now bold, healthy, thrifty, city-paving, agricultural species of emmets belonged, perhaps, to a feeble variety of hunters and herders who in the struggle for existence were entirely dependent on the natural droppings of the seeds of vegetation, such insects and worms as their hunters could master, and the aphis for subsistence.

Gideon advanced the theory that from a feeble beginning the ants grew into a strong race of warriors through their diet of nutritious rice grain, adding:

The no-corn-making, pastoral Abel had been overcome—rooted out by the vigorous, prolific agricultural Cain. Thus the transitional link between this now distinct and wonderfully developed species, and probably the well-digging species who are about the same size and color, subsisting on the foliage of vegetation, are to science forever lost.

He concluded his letter:

Old men like myself can do but little of anything and ought not to promise themselves much, but I think I will sometime when I feel in a proper condition for it, write out a short account of what I have seen during the past twelve years amongst our abundant animal and vegetable fossils, our insect kingdom and our blooming prairies.

I am a native American, born in the smoke of our first revolution; was raised and have always been a dweller in the wild border countries and now I think the chances are pretty good for me to make my exit in the turmoil and smoke of another revolution.

Gideon wrote Darwin a second letter, dated March 4, 1861, in which he said:

Your kind letter of 27th January was just one month on the way. I would not pester you again but for the question contained in it.

You speak dubiously of my "long career in wild countries." I might do the same in regard to your opportunities in the *tame* country of books and seminaries, pompous priests and legal superstition. But I don't, except your trip around the globe. If I can not have company whose minds are clearly free, I would prefer to go alone. And thus it has turned with me through my long sojourn. I have had no associates, and my observations and conclusions, be them right or wrong, are not trammeled by the sway of other minds. Except five months' schooling at a deserted log cabin in the backwoods of Georgia, by an old drunkard, my mind has not been biased by training of any kind from designing man. In the cane brakes and unhacked forests on the borders of the above-named state, with the Muscogee Indian boys for my classmates, I learned my first lessons in nature's grand seminary. Here arose my first thoughts on that subject that is now by yourself, and by me subscribed to, denominated "natural selection." Pardon this digression.

You ask, "Do you suppose that the ants plant seeds for the ensuing crop?"—I have not the slightest doubt of it. And my conclusions have not been arrived at from hasty or careless observation or from seeing the ants do something that looked a little like it and then guess at the results. I have, at all seasons, watched the same ant cities during the last 12 years, and I know what I stated in my former letter is true. I visited the same cities yesterday, I find their crop of *ant rice* growing finely; exhibiting also the signs of high cultivation, not a blade of any other kind of grass or weed to be seen in 12 inches of the circular row of the rice.

Gideon described to Darwin the horticultural or cutting ant of Texas and their inability to withstand the hot sun. For shade they planted quick-growing trees, grape vine, and Mexican poppy, and constructed tunnels to food sources, working only in the night. He concluded:

It would require a considerable volume to describe this most interesting type of our ants. I will not bore you further on that topic. I have answered your single question; you must excuse me. You may, however, say to your brother that if he feels like it and will put the proper questions to me, he will find that these little emmets can teach lessons to the genus homo even that would be profitable to imitate. You may be too much engaged, but if you feel any interest in it, this correspondence need not cease.[5]

The correspondence ceased, either because of Darwin's choice or the Civil War. However, in April, 1861, Darwin read Lincecum's letters on the Texas ants to the learned Linnaean Society of London and the following year they were published in the *Journal of the . . . Society.*[6]

Thus the agricultural ant was introduced to the scientists of the world who still doubted Solomon's ancient words on the wisdom of ants and it was received in much the same way as Darwin's theory on evolution. The eminent Dr. August Forel, an authority on Swiss ants and, later, ant psychology, sniffed: "These observations, although reported by Charles Darwin, inspire little confidence in me."[7]

Gideon was not abashed. He regarded Forel's comments as unworthy of notice: Forel had never been to Texas, had never seen an agricultural ant, and obviously didn't know what he was talking about. Gideon continued to observe the pismire.

He wrote Buckley in 1866: "Where can I find a late work on entomology? Perhaps you do not know that I never in my life saw one. I

---

[5] Darwin's reply to Lincecum's first letter is not in the Lincecum Papers. Many years after receiving it, Lincecum recalled: "To Sir Charles Darwin I am indebted for the most polite letter I ever received." Gideon could not have known that Darwin also peeped into ant beds to see for himself what was going on and that he had written a postscript to a letter to his friend, Dr. J. Hooker, in July, 1858: "I have had some fun here in watching a slave-making ant; for I could not help doubting the wonderful stories, but I have seen a defeated marauding party, and I have seen a migration from one nest to another of the slave-makers, carrying their slaves (who are *house* and not field niggers) in their mouths!" (*The Autobiography of Charles Darwin and Selected Letters*, Francis Darwin, ed., [New York, Dover Books, 1958], p. 202).

[6] "Agricultural Ant of Texas," *Journal of the Linnaean Society*, Zoology, Vol. VI (1862), pp. 29–31.

[7] Geiser, *Naturalists*, p. 212.

am, however, perhaps too far advanced in life to commence the study of natural history with any hope or prospect of success."

After the Civil War, word of the Texas insect collection got around scientific circles and requests from the North came so fast that Gideon was hard-pressed to fill all of them.

Alpheus Spring Packard, Jr.,[8] president of the Essex Institute of Salem, Massachusetts, requested a detailed description of the tarantula killer and a history of Texas scorpions. The *American Naturalist*, of which Packard was publisher, used the articles with illustrations. Vials of insects to Salem, as Gideon expressed it, "went right into the hot bed of radicalism."

George W. Peck, "a butterfly man of New York," wanted Texas species, which Gideon supplied, and in one letter he enclosed a moth, dried by the fire, which had contained 499 eggs. Dr. Samuel Lewis of Philadelphia wanted beetles and weevils, and Townsend Glover[9] of the Smithsonian wrote for "extremely small, dark and ugly moths." Horatio Charles Wood[10] wanted all insects, and asked: "Could we not work together and publish a paper on them, each taking credit and responsibility for his part? I, working on the species as I have access to the books, you the habits of the species."

To Wood's suggestion Gideon replied: "Whatever I may write as a statement of any facts in natural history may be relied upon as the unbiased results of a serious and solitary investigation with no other aim

---

[8] Packard (1838–1905) began to collect at fourteen years of age, and studied under Agassiz at Harvard; he was curator and later director of the Peabody Academy of Science, Salem, Massachusetts, professor of zoology and geology, Brown University, 1878–1905, author of *Guide to the Study of Insects* (1869), *Textbook of Entomology* (1898) (*DAB*, Vol. 14 [1934], pp. 125–126). Articles by Lincecum on subjects requested by Packard and used in the *American Naturalist* were: "The Tarantula Killers of Texas," Vol. I (May, 1867, pp. 137–141; "Scorpions of Texas," Vol. I (June, 1867), pp. 203–205; "The Tarantula of Texas," Vol. I (October, 1867), pp. 409–411.

[9] Glover (1813–1883), born in England, studied art in Germany, came to the United States in 1836 and settled in New Rochelle, New York. From 1853 to 1878 he was attached to the U.S. government's agricultural services and for the remainder of his life prepared etched plates for government scientific publications (*DAB*, Vol. 7 [1931], pp. 333–334).

[10] Wood (1841–1920) published his first paper in 1861, graduated in 1862 from the medical department of the University of Pennsylvania, where, from 1866 to 1876, he was professor of materia medica, pharmacy, and general therapeutics. He was a highly successful physician, naturalist, and neurologist (*DAB*, Vol. 20 [1936], p. 459).

or object but to arrive at truth." He sent Wood hundreds of insects and insisted:

I must have a work on entomology. I have never seen one in my life. I can't get along very well with my bugs without one. I see not why I may not during my leisure hours look into and learn the names of the great bug family before I go. I know them all, or nearly so, now with the history of their mode of life, manner of procuring food, procreating processes, and how many of them contrive to have a great deal of recreation and amusement. And all of this without having names for them.

Wood delayed sending books and Gideon, piqued, wrote him:

Books would hinder me now. I shall continue to describe nature as I see it. What I may so write will, of course, correspond with no book and therefore can be of no use to the book men. But it will remain as a curiosity and someday some *Man* will see it. . . . Cooped up as you are in a large city with time occupied perpetually, it is almost impossible for you to be anything of a field naturalist.

Gideon became disenchanted with Wood, who had agreed to pay three small boys to assist Lincecum in making the collection Wood desired but who repeatedly failed to acknowledge Gideon's request for payment for his "three little orphans." Gideon enjoyed instructing the boys and hoped: "If the little start I give them should excite the spirit of inquiry and a passion for the natural sciences, it may act as cause for higher thought and philosophic usefulness." Lincecum donated his own time, explaining to Wood that despite his seventy-five years and poverty-stricken state as the result of the War, he was nevertheless "for the sake of progress in the sciences, still able to bestow my own time and labor and I do it willingly. I desire that all the discoveries I have shall be recorded somewhere that it may not be lost from future investigators." At the end of nine months Gideon paid the boys himself, giving each ten dollars, and remarked of Wood: "He is a small man."

After Wood failed to acknowledge receipt of a large collection of butterflies and seventy-two vials of insects, other than to complain about freight charges, Gideon read in the *American Naturalist* that Wood had presented a paper entitled "Description of a New Species of Texas Myrapeda." He fumed: "But he did not go out in the deep forests, tangled vines and grassy fields, among snakes, ticks, and red bugs, and gather the specimens. He is a tacky."

Edward Drinker Cope,[11] of Philadelphia, whose interest was in the field of extinct vertebrates, herpetology, and ichthyology, wanted Gideon to send him fish—especially alligator gar and buffalo fish— and reptiles. Burt Green Wilder, of Boston,[12] inquired about the wasp that deposited eggs in paralyzed spiders. Ezra Townsend Cresson,[13] of Philadelphia, asked for bees, wasps, and ants.

Gideon, still finding time to continue his study of ants, in a letter to Durand gave him additional information on "the character, manners, customs and military action of our small, black erratic ant." In his last letter before the war, Gideon had described to Durand a battle he had witnessed:

Their wars are frightfully disastrous, particularly when it takes place between two kingdoms of the same type. I have seen not less than a gallon— 40,000—left on a single battle field. Few of them were dead; but the most of them had their legs all trimmed off, and they lay on the ground, amongst the scattered fragments of their severed limbs, doubling and gnashing their legless bodies in an agony of sullen, mad, hopeless despair.

Now, six years later, Gideon wrote:

I had written some sketches of his history, a portion of which was published in the Houston *Telegraph,* but I find that our people are not in a condition to think of anything of the kind just now and I did not send the remaining sheets of what I had written on the above-named type of ants to the press. I have clipped from the *Telegraph* the portion that was printed

[11] Edward Drinker Cope (1840–1879), born in Philadelphia, was a pioneer paleontologist who was in Texas in 1877. Among his Texas articles and publications are: "On the Zoological Position of Texas," *Bulletin of the U.S. Natural Museum,* No. 17, Washington, 1880; "Some New Batrachia and Reptilia from the Permian Beds of Texas," *Hayden's Bulletin: Verterbrate Paleontology of the Llano Estacado* [Austin, 1893]. See Geiser, *Naturalists,* pp. 25, 27, 210, 222, and *DAB,* Vol. 4 [1930,] pp. 420–421. A list of Cope's Texas writings is in the Barker Center Library, University of Texas.

[12] Burt Green Wilder (1841–1925) was professor of neurology and vertebrate zoology at Cornell from 1867 to 1910 (*Webster's Biographical Dictionary,* Springfield, Massachusetts G. & C. Merriam Co. [1943], p. 1573 .

[13] Cresson (1838–1926) published the *Practical Entomologist* at the time of his correspondence with Lincecum. He had lived in New Braunfels, Texas, in 1859, working with Lindheimer (Geiser, *Naturalists,* p. 321).

and shall enclose it and the balance of the manuscript herewith. It will, if nothing more, amuse you a little.

Durand was interested in ant battles and asked for more details. Gideon sent a report of a battle between two kingdoms of his "large black tree ant" in a letter:

Their mode of warfare aims at decapitation. They fought incessantly day and night for about forty-eight hours before they succeeded in destroying entirely the invaded city. Thousands were slain on both sides, leaving the ground pretty well covered with their heads over an area of 15 to 20 feet in diameter, looking very much like red pepper seeds which were to be seen ten days after. . . . Some species aim at the head altogether and often succeed in cutting it off; others again direct their entire force at the legs which they very dexterously cut off, while other tribes lock together until death puts an end to the struggle.

Durand often passed on to Joseph Leidy,[14] professor of anatomy and director of the biological department of the University of Pennsylvania, information contained in Gideon's numerous chatty letters. Gideon's factual account of the battle was read by Leidy before the Academy, whose members found such a tall tale beyond the realm of possibility. Leidy defended Gideon's history and when informed of his championship, the Texan wrote Durand:

Prof. Leidy stands high in my estimation. I shall allow him to laugh at any funny things he may find in any of my letters. . . . I like him anyhow for the part he took in my favor when the ant battle was read before the society. . . . Please present me respectfully to Prof. J. Leidy and tender to him my sincere thanks for defending the little history of the ant battle which I attempted. . . . Please say to him that we must not entertain any feeling on account of unbelief of these men as they perhaps have seen only the dry specimens of the ants in question and therefore could not know anything in relation to their living character and belligerent habits. These cabinet investigators have seldom felt the tick bites and stings of the warrior ants

[14] Leidy (1823–1891) was for thirty-eight years chairman of anatomy at the University of Pennsylvania; chairman of the board of curators of the Academy of Natural Sciences, and president of that body, 1881–1891. His most noted paper, written in 1847 and entitled "On the Fossil Horse of America," proved that the horse was extinct on the American continent before Columbus arrived (DAB, Vol. II [1933], pp. 150–152).

in the forests and plains traversed by the industrious and earnest examiner of nature. Let them try the experiment of going out and looking for themselves and if they seek earnestly they will find that ants do have wars and that twenty or forty thousand of some species of them engaged on a single battlefield is nothing for the initiated to wonder at.[15]

Gideon urged Buckley to name his ants or "somebody else will be naming them before long, perhaps Wood wants to be at it now." He threatened to camp near Austin and remain there until Buckley named all forty-two of them, because

I desire our catalogues be made to agree. . . . What specific name have you given our large black tree ant? He is a very important and very useful ant and I desire if he is not already named that he should have a significant name. 'Twas a scrap of the history of this ant that stirred up the boys to such a pitch at Philadelphia last fall. . . . There is your crazy little black ant— what name have you bestowed on him? He is the fellow that milks the aphid, a plant louse. He is not the only species that milks the aphid.

Gideon frequently doubted the sincerity and unselfishness of some of the Northern scientists and wrote Buckley: "If those fellows do not come up to the rack like men they will not be entitled to my ants nor any of the rest of my elaborate collection of specimens."

It was his old friend Durand who finally sent books: Agassiz' *Introduction to the Study of Natural History*, Packard's *How to Collect and Observe Insects*, Wood's *Myriapoda of North America*, Chapman's *Flora of the United States*, and Gray's *Structural Botany*.

Gideon wrote Durand:

You are surrounded with a host of highly educated and very agreeable companions whilst I am so much alone that I fall in the habit of talking to myself. And yet I see many pleasing things and have many pleasant hours and days, aye, even weeks. . . . I should have been highly pleased to have accompanied DuChaillu[16] on his African hunts. In the countries where I have traversed there has always been too little danger. I could always lie down and sleep without dread in the woods of any country through which I have traveled.

---

[15] Lincecum's paper "On an Ant Battle Witnessed in Texas" was published in the *Proceedings* of the Academy, Vol. XVIII (January, 1866), pp. 4–6.

[16] Paul Belloni DuChaillu.

I would be pleased to see the Jr. Huber's work on ants. From the little you have extracted from the *American Encyclopedia,* the younger Huber divides the ants like his father[17] did the honey bees, into males, females and undeveloped females or neuters—workers—and he makes his male and female ants copulate on the wing, precisely in the same manner that his father married the bees . . .

Durand, unabashed by the Academy's reaction to the ant battle, suggested that Gideon send a report on his agricultural ant to Leidy and enclosed a similar request from the Professor. The furor over the agricultural ant had died down since its debut in London. Gideon wrote nineteen pages on his favorite ant, condensing the history as much as possible but protesting that "it would require a snug little volume to do them justice."

Neither the reception of the London letter nor of his ant battle prepared Gideon for the hostility of the Academy members when the little paper was received. The result came in a discreet letter from Durand:

Professor Leidy is now very busy with his lectures at the University and with a paleontologic memoir of great length upon which he has been engaged for months. I met him this morning in his rooms at the Academy and we read together your history of the agricultural ants. He will communicate it to the Academy at its meeting tomorrow night; but, my dear Lincecum, I am really afraid that some will prove unbelievers in such wisdom as you attribute to this little insect. People are so accustomed to see but one being in creation endowed with reason that they will look upon you as one possessing great imaginative powers and that you make too much of what is called animal instinct. They will not exactly doubt what you relate; but they will be persuaded that you lend to your narrative your own reason, your own perspicacity and that all you imagine is nothing but illusion. . . . All that you say of the agricultural ant is certainly very wonderful and it must be in your mind exactly what you say.

It was as Durand predicted. Leidy read the Lincecum observation to the Academy and it was met with a howl of disbelief. While the controversy raged, not one of the members had enough curiosity to peer

---

[17] Francois Huber (1750–1831) was a blind French bee specialist and the father of Pierre Huber.

in an ant bed and see for himself. Gideon, informed of the reception by Durand, proved himself a peer of the academicians with his answer:

I was really pleased at that letter of yours, Durand, because I thought you had spoken like a true friend. You said what you pleased which is your right always when you speak to me. Remember that and pray let us drop that unscientific topic. Forgive you indeed! You are my dearest friend and you have done nothing to disquiet me or that I feel dissatisfied about. . . . I am pleased, highly pleased, that you had such a full meeting at the time my ant memoir was considered. It cannot now be said that it was slipped in, at the time of the next meeting. . . . I know the character of the race of beings whose history I have attempted to write and I know further that should the Academy who know nothing about them reject it, it will neither tarnish the reputation of the honest agricultural ants of Texas nor diminish my knowledge of the fact that they are a highly endowed race of *thinking, reasoning beings.* . . . I say to myself, what damage can result from the decision of a set of closeted investigators to the reasoning power of a pismire?

Despite the furor, the Lincecum paper was accepted for publication in the *Proceedings of the Academy.*[18]

Although he smarted under the criticism, which he considered a serious reflection on his integrity, Gideon continued to supply the Academy with specimens and histories, and wrote Buckley:

I am very willing and I love to contribute to academies of natural history, but I must be sure that the members are pure unselfish men. Those fellows about the Philadelphia Academy are avaricious of praise and very jealous of their reputation. They have a strong thirst for fame. There are some species of ants which stand as high intellectually, in my estimation, as the average specimen of the genus homo. . . . I have not yet thoroughly discovered the class or rather species of the genus homo to which those Philadelphia Quakers belong. I shall pet their laziness and stupid superstitions no further.

Gideon's indignation wore off somewhat and he wrote Durand:

I have largely written the history, as far as I know it, of the horticultural ant and when I get ready, or rather when I think their misdirected scholastic theology has had time to recover from the paroxysm induced by my agricultural ant letter, I will fix up the horticultural history and address it to you and you can get Leidy to communicate it.

[18] "On the Agricultural Ant of Texas," *Proceedings of the Philadelphia Academy of Natural Sciences*, Vol. XVIII (November, 1866), pp. 323–331.

Packard was one of the few who complimented him on the agricultural ant history and Gideon replied, "You brag about my paper on the agricultural ant. I think you will be better pleased with a paper I sent the boys at the Academy on the horticultural ant."

To Dr. Leidy, who sent Lincecum two copies of the agricultural ant article and acknowledged receipt of the horticultural ant paper, Gideon wrote: "I think you will find the well-digging, tunnel-making, city-building ant is more interesting than the agricultural species." He requested that if the paper was accepted the name of the ant be changed from *Myrmica texana* to *Oecodoma texana (Buckley)*. The paper was published with the name bestowed by Gideon in honor of his friend, Buckley.[19]

A number of Gideon's articles on the insects of Texas appeared in the *American Naturalist*.[20]

Just before Gideon departed for Tuxpan he wrote a farewell letter to Buckley:

I have no objections to your publishing my description of the ants you have, and you may include all my collection, which according to your suggestion I sent to Cresson. Speaking of Cresson, I am not pleased at the way he has treated me in reference to the specimens I sent him last year with all my ants. He has never written a single word to me on the subject. Don't you let him steal those ants when I am gone to Davy's locker.

Any ill feeling however, magnified or imagined, that Gideon felt toward any member of the Philadelphia Academy no doubt disappeared when he read a letter from Durand written to Doran. Durand expressed regret at Gideon's leaving Texas but also a desire to share his adventures:

---

[19] "On the Cutting Ants of Texas—*Oecodema texana buckley*," *PANS*, Vol. XIX (February, 1867), pp. 24–31. Other articles by Lincecum published in the *Proceedings of the Academy of Natural Sciences*, are: "On the Grapes of Texas," Vol. XVIII (January, 1866), pp. 4–6; "On the Small Black Erratic Ant of Texas," Vol. XVIII (March, 1866), pp. 101–106. Another paper by Lincecum, "The Cutting Ant of Texas," was published in the *Zoologist*, Vol. 3 (1868), pp. 1270–1281.

[20] "The Gregarious Rat of Texas, Vol. VI (August, 1872), pp. 487–489; "Habits of the Opossum," Vol. VI (September, 1872), pp. 555–557; "Habits of a Species of Sorex," Vol. VII (August, 1873), pp. 483–484; "The Agricultural Ant," Vol. VIII (September, 1874), pp. 513–517; "Sweet-Scented Ants," Vol. VIII (September, 1874), p. 564; "Robber Ants," Vol. VIII (September, 1874), p. 564; "The Gossamer Spider," Vol. VIII (October, 1874), pp. 593–596.

I might have proved to him that an old soldier of Napoleon was almost as nimble as an Indian hunter. I have the presumption to think that I would have been able to follow him anywhere, even to the top of a tree. When you write to him, please inform him that at the last meeting of the 26th of the month [March] he was unanimously elected a corresponding member of the Philadelphia Academy of Natural Sciences.

This was the highest honor and recognition that the members could give to an amateur, an honor not passed out indiscriminately. How proud and pleased the old man must have been when he learned so great an honor had been bestowed upon him by the oldest and most learned academy of its kind in the United States. He was, after all, an amateur, limited by lack of academic training and study, with only his determination, avid inquisitiveness, self-reliance, and native intelligence to aid him in a field requiring high skill. But strangely lacking is Gideon's reaction in either word or thought to this elevation among his "high lads."

The controversy over Lincecum's agricultural ants continued until 1877, when Gideon had been dead three years. In that year, one of the "closeted scientists" decided to go to Texas and see for himself. The expedition which established Gideon's superiority in the field of ants was financed by a religious organization and headed by a minister. He was Henry Christopher McCook, a prudish young naturalist and a Presbyterian minister in Philadelphia, who became best known for a three-volume work, *American Spiders and Their Spinning Work*.

McCook was familiar with the Lincecum controversy among his elders. He found Gideon's original letters still in the possession of Cresson. McCook had read all Gideon's printed works on insects and the agricultural ant letter printed in the *Linnaean Society Journal*. From the Academy files he dug out a paper submitted in 1860 by Buckley on "The Stinging or Mound-Making Ant," which he found to be incomplete and in some cases incorrect. For some reason not explained, McCook did not seek out Buckley or ask his aid, although he camped for several weeks outside Austin near Barton Springs.

The church in Philadelphia where McCook was minister from 1870 to 1902 financed his trip to Texas to trace the path Gideon had found so rich in natural history. In Texas he was assisted by the Reverend Edward S. Wright, pastor of the First Presbyterian Church of Austin;

Dr. M. A. Taylor and George Brush of Austin; the Reverend Warner Bradley Riggs, pastor of the Presbyterian Church of Brenham, and Isaac Dunbar Affleck, a son of Gideon's grand neighbor, Thomas Affleck.[21] It was a strange and capricious fate that arranged this team of *genus homo*, as Gideon would have said, to prove he was right about ants. Ironical, also, is it that the younger Affleck's greatest claim to Texas fame is his assistance to McCook's project on Gideon's agricultural ants.

McCook went to Long Point and poked about Gideon's old orchard, and to Brenham, where he talked with Sallie Doran, who had also witnessed the mating session of the agricultural ants and confirmed her father's description of it. McCook saw all that Gideon had seen except this event, "notwithstanding the utmost vigilance." Affleck had seen such a swarming and his description was so similar to Lincecum's that McCook did not repeat it in his book. The young naturalist accepted the "amative picnic" scene as factual, since his own observations bore out others made by Gideon.

McCook's *The Natural History of the Agricultural Ant of Texas*, published by the Philadelphia Academy of Natural Sciences in 1879, is among the least known books in Texas. McCook's explanation of the investigation is more in the nature of an apology for the disbelief of the Academy members than to Lincecum:

The venerable writer had many peculiar notions about society, religion and the genus homo generally, which he could not refrain from thrusting in the most untimely and objectionable words into the midst of his notes. The idiosyncrasies, together with some peculiarities of spelling, grammar and rhetoric more original than regular had evidently raised in the minds of the officers and members of the Academy a question, not to the integrity of the author, but as to his accuracy as an observer.

McCook made camera lucida studies of the ants and, no doubt, had

---

[21] Riggs (1849–1905), born in Wayne County, New York, was graduated from Yale in 1871; he came to Texas in 1876 where he was minister of the Presbyterian Church in Brenham until 1885 and minister of the Second Presbyterian Church in Dallas from 1888 to 1905. He died in Austin. Affleck (1844–1919) was a practicing physician in Hunt County, Texas, 1876. Later as professor in the medical department of Fort Worth University, he was known for his work on the biology of the honey bee (Geiser, "Notes on Some Workers in Texas Entomology, 1839–1880," *Southwestern Historical Quarterly*, Vol. XLIX [1945–1946], pp. 593–598).

Lincecum used this instrument the smug Presbyterian minister would never have had the occasion to come to Texas.

At least one contemporary scientist agreed with Lincecum's insistence that the ant possessed wisdom. He was Sir John Lubbock, the distinguished chancellor of the University of London, whose experiments with ants convinced him that they "have a fair claim to rank next to man in the scale of intelligence."

Lubbock noted in 1879:

A Texas ant, *Pogonomyrmex barbatus,* is also a harvesting species, storing up especially the grain of *Aristida oligantha* the so-called "ant grass," *Buchlöe dactyloides.* These ants clear disks, ten to twelve feet in diameter, round the entrance of their nest, a work of no small labour in the rich soil, and under the hot sun, of Texas. I say clear a disk, but some, though not all, of these disks are occupied, especially round the edge, by a growth of ant rice. Dr. Lincecum, who first gave an account of these insects, maintained not only that the ground was carefully cleared of all other plants, but that this grass was intentionally cultivated by the ants. Mr. McCook, by whom the subject has been recently studied, fully confirms Dr. Lincecum's claim that the disks are kept carefully clean, and that the produce of this crop is carefully harvested; but he thinks that the ant rice sows itself and is not actually planted by the ants.[22]

McCook's investigation, however, did not end the contention caused by the lowly agricultural ant in Lincecum's backyard.

William Morton Wheeler, an American zoologist, considered that McCook had failed to obtain any evidence either for or against the "Lincecum myth" that the ant actually sowed the seed of "ant rice" around the periphery of its disks or mounds and cultivated the crop in addition to harvesting and storing it in granaries. Wheeler believed that McCook had merely succeeded in extending the vogue of the myth by admitting the plausibility of Lincecum's theory. So in 1901, and again in 1903, Wheeler came to Texas to make his own observations of Gideon's "common Texas variety of Mexican *barbatus.*"

Wheeler studied the ants three years, in contrast to McCook's few months, before he found what he considered the probable source of Licencum's belief that the ants planted their crops:

[22] Sir John Lubbock, *Scientific Lectures* (London, MacMillan and Company, 1879), pp. 109–110.

If the nests of this ant can be studied during the cool winter months—and this is the only time to study them leisurely as the cold subdues the fiery sting of their inhabitants—the seeds which the ants have garnered in many of their chambers will often be found to have sprouted. . . . On sunny days the ants may often be seen removing the seeds when they have sprouted too far to be fit for food and carrying them to the refuse heap, which is always at the periphery of the crater or cleared-earth disk. Here the seed, thus rejected as inedible, often take root and in the spring form an arc or a complete circle of growing plants around the nest. Since the *Pogonomyrmex* feeds largely, though by no means exclusively, on grass seeds, and since, moreover, the seeds of *Aristida* are a very common and favorite article of food, it is easy to see why this grass should predominate in the circle.

Wheeler was more successful than McCook in observing the marriage flights of the ants described by Gideon. He witnessed them in Austin, Texas, on June 18 and 29, July 1, 1901, and July 4, 1903.[23]

Fifty years after Wheeler visited Texas, the question of whether ants plant their crops was still open. A present-day ant man, Derek Wragge Morley, who studied ants as Lincecum did—on his hands and knees in the dirt, peering into the nests—maintains that McCook cleared the mystery of Lincecum's ant, finding that it was indeed a harvester but not a planter. Morley, however, is inclined to agree with Gideon's high opinion of the ant's intelligence. He believes that while the mental abilities of ants are limited, "their mental powers should not be underrated." Like Gideon, Morley is inclined to personify his ants. He refers to the mutual feeding of ants as providing an "important emotional bond." His description of one ant's receiving food from another is pure Gideonese—"their tautly-stretched antennae quiver in apparent ecstasy." And a tired, sleeping ant will, according to Morley, "sleep the sleep of the just and be d——d to heaven and hell let loose."[24]

One fact completely overlooked by the ant men who sought to prove Lincecum wrong is that he knew the native grasses of Texas as thoroughly as he knew the ants of the state. Despite the investigation since Lincecum's death, there is no conclusive and final proof that his ants do not plant the crops of their preference, and it is yet possible that

[23] William Morton Wheeler, *Ants* (New York, Columbus University Press, 1913), pp. 286–290.
[24] Morley, *The Ant World*, pp. 16, 171, 183.

science will find his theory correct. Natural history has withheld from Lincecum a number of deserving honors, notably the credit for being the first to prove that Solomon was right when he said that ants harvested and stored grain. For the past ninety-one years that particular honor has gone to Traherne Moggeridge, whose studies were described in his book *Harvesting Ants and Trapdoor Spiders*, which was published in 1873, long after Lincecum had arrived at the same conclusion.

In another respect, science is coming around to Lincecum's wisdom theory. Science now has found that the ant's head contains a small brain but does not know what, if anything, the ant does with it. Gideon gave science his answer over one hundred years ago, but instinct and not reason still prevails in the ant kingdom.

A NOTE ON SOURCES

Quotations from Lincecum's writings on ants in this chapter are necessarily condensed. Hundreds of pages are devoted to detailed descriptions of different species of ants, day-by-day observations of activities in ant nests, migratory movements, social organizations, and general ant behavior. Written in the grandiloquent and verbose style he considered suitable when corresponding with his "high lads," the contents are saved from being tiresomely dull only because of Lincecum's delightful personification, the same unscientific approach which the academicians found so shocking.

The bulk of Lincecum's writings on entomology is contained in his letters to: Charles Darwin, Bromley, Kent, England, December 29, 1860, March 4, 1861; Ezra Townsend Cresson, Philadelphia, July 16, 1866 (transmitting an article on the cabbage bug), July 17, December 24, 1866, March 3, November 21, 1867; Aepheus S. Packard, Jr., Essex Institute, Salem, December 20, 1866, February 13, 25, June 23, November 20, 1867, January 28, February 18, 1868; H. C. Wood, Jr., Philadelphia, April 17, June 22, July 3, 8, August 31, October 8, November 8 (transmitting 85 scorpions), December 6, 1866, n.d., 1867; Dr. Samuel Lewis, Philadelphia, March 5, 1867; George W. Peck, New York, February 14, November 19, 1867; Joseph Leidy, Philadelphia, March (?), June 30, July 21, August 29, November 13, 1867; Elias Durand, Philadelphia, February 6, April 11, May 2, 1861, January 24, 29, February 22, June 27, August 13 (transmitting a history of the agricultural ant), October 16, 21, November 18, December 16, 1866, January 24, 29, February 5, March 3,

June 27, July 21, August 30, October 30, 1867; S. F. Baird, Washington, D.C., October 4, December 13, 1866, September (?), November 18, December 11, 1867, May 5, 1868; Anthony E. Marshall, Buffalo, New York, January 13, 1867; W. P. Doran, Houston, February 12, 22, 1866; B. E. Wilder, Boston, April 3, 1868.

Durand's remarks to Gideon on the academy's reception of his agricultural ant paper are found in a letter from Lincecum to H. C. Wood, Jr., Philadelphia, November 8, 1866.

CHAPTER THIRTEEN

GIDEON
AND THE OFFENDED DEMOCRATS

The embecility of old age is a dreadful thing and I have no
desire to live that long, though it may be that I have already
reached that point and am not aware of it.   GID

SARAH BRYAN Lincecum became desperately ill in January, 1867,
and Gideon's days were filled with despair and dread. His lonely,
heartbroken spirit appealed to Buckley:

Oh what shall I do if she leaves me? To whom shall I go with my little
tales of failures and successes? Will it not open a wide chasm in the chilly
evening of my existence that has been so long closed by her presence? For
53 years she has occupied the center of all my hopes and desires. I did not
know before that my old time worn heart could be afflicted with so deep a
dread of consequence.

Early in the morning on February 2 Sarah, Gideon's good companion, died in his arms, uttering no word of fear or regret. Eight of her
nine children were around her bed. The chasm in the chilly evening of
Gideon's life never closed and everything he did for the remainder of
his life was a time-passer until he could join Sarah in "the good
hunting-ground."

She was buried by the side of her first-born, Lycurgus, at the Baptist
Meeting House between Long Point and Union Hill. Afterwards
Gideon wrote to an old friend in Mississippi: "She was 70 years, 10

months and 14 days old. She was, as you know, good and harmless. . . . She served as a prudent, frugal and constant-loving wife 52 years, three months and eight days."

Many times in the years ahead he was to recall poignantly every detail of their wedding day, October 26, 1814, beginning at 9 A.M. in the yard of Benjamin Whitfield[1] on Gladys Creek, Putnam County, Georgia. Gideon and his bride rode away together in a silver-mounted double-seated gig harnessed to a "large proud black horse with a very white face and glass eyes." With ribbons flying from the gig, the couple drove through the joyful crowd, taking the rough path to Hezekiah's house in order that they could be alone. The guests took the good path to the reception at Hezekiah's, where many neighbors danced throughout the happy day and consumed a beef, goat, sheep, three hogs, two turkeys, a fat goose, a chicken, a duck, numerous pies and cakes, eighteen gallons of peach brandy and six dozen bottles of wine.

Now, for the first time in his seventy-four years, Gideon experienced real loneliness, and the ache of it was never to be eased. The bereft old man felt a great urgency to take his grief into the woods, where always before his turbulent nature had found peace. He grieved: "The soul of my house is gone, has fled from my sight and I can not content myself here."

Except for Cassandra, all his children lived nearby on land he had deeded to them the year before, 170 acres each. He had kept 350 acres and the homestead, but now he turned the house over to his youngest

---

[1] Benjamin Whitfield, a Baptist minister, later settled in Clinton, Mississippi, where in 1834 he owned 2,000 acres and 140 slaves. His estate contained 20 acres of lawn and 2½ acres of flowers. He was "a godly man who believed in music, melody, and the ministry" (Charles Hillman Brough, "Historic Clinton," *PMHS*, Vol. VII [1903], pp. 281–311). The bride, Sarah Bryan, was Whitfield's stepdaughter, a fact Gideon never mentions. He once remarked that one reason he left Georgia was to get away from his wife's relatives, who were all wealthy, thus implying that they thought Sarah had not made a promising match. Sarah's relationship to the prominent Whitfield family is revealed in a letter from William H. Sparks, author of *The Memories of Fifty Years* (Philadelphia, Claxton, Remsen and Haffelfinger, 1872; Macon, Georgia, J. W. Burke & Co., 1872), to Sallie Lincecum Doran, May 18, 1881, in which he writes: ". . . your grandmother . . . married my uncle, Benjamin Whitfield. . . . I knew your father as far back as 1808 when his father resided near Eatonton . . . and Gideon's mother still farther back." Sparks also knew Sarah Bryan Lincecum, "a grand lady," and her many nieces, nephews, brothers, and sisters (the oldest of whom married William Whitfield) and her half brothers and sisters.

son Lysander, his wife Mollie, and their baby daughter Daisy. He reserved the use of his little red-cedar house.

Gideon immediately planned his escape into the woods. Selling half his acreage, he used the money to buy a vehicle he called an ambulance, built by Epperson, his "first-rate mechanic," and a team of good grass-raised horses. The ambulance was equipped with a bed and a writing desk, as well as a large tent of his own making, and provided ample space for camping and scientific equipment.

He relinquished the role of the patriarch, which he had so long enjoyed but which now, without his good companion, was meaningless. He felt no hesitancy in leaving his sons and daughters, explaining to Durand:

It is, to be sure, a great pleasure to know that all my children are self-sustaining and laboring under no discreditable censure. I can see they are capable of maintaining their good reputation and on that account be where I may I shall suffer no uneasiness. . . . I signed up today the last deed in the distribution of my long-cherished and much-loved home. I don't care for it now. My lonely spirit longs for liberty. I am remaining here with but little consolation and shall be loath to come back again to look upon that old empty chair. . . . I can not look calmly upon the turned plate, nor upon the old empty chair on the left side of the fireplace where she so industriously worked, embroidering little presents for her very numerous grandchildren. Everything I see reminds me of the lost one. I am of no use here anyhow.

In a letter thanking Cresson for the gift of a fine pocket lens Gideon referred to a planned expedition: "As for the food needed for myself I always find plenty as soon as I find myself outside the marred and bloody tracks of unholy civilization. I shall have for company three young men, all well-armed and fish-hooked."

He very much wanted to take along a camera lucida, but since the space required for it could best be used for specimens, he decided to make his own diagrams with crayons. He asked Doran to send him crayons—black, gray, clay-colored and buff, explaining: "I can't succeed well in making diagrams with lead pencils. Enclosed you will find a specimen of pencil drawing and you will readily discover its defects."

Doran supplied the crayons and cautioned him against Indians, whose raids that winter were widespread and particularly frequent west of Austin, where Gideon planned to go. He replied: "I shall not go too far among the Indians. I have engaged to perform a certain scientific feat and I must not let the Indians or anything else kill me until that engagement is accomplished."

Lincecum planned to camp out along the way: "My objection to stopping at people's houses lies in the fleas and the chinches they harbor. I prefer a clean place in the woods alongways. Let me sleep in open air." His three companions were his two grandsons, William Lincecum and ten-year-old George Campbell and James Caldwell, of Fort Jessup, Louisiana, an amateur naturalist. William and James, "two bully soldiers," who served together in the Civil War, armed with rifles and six-shooters, rode horses, and young George rode with Gideon in the ambulance.

It was a beautiful March morning when the expedition got underway, "birds singing their songs of love and the insect world all on the wing." But it proved a false spring, a common delusion in Texas. They traveled thirty-two miles the first day before making camp. The north wind grew stronger and colder and before morning a heavy snow began to fall. Wolves howled about the camp, the horses suffered from the cold, and "poor little perishing sparrows" died, although a green-wood fire burned throughout the night and next day.

Less hardy travelers would have turned back, but the four remained in the snow for four days. Then the norther disappeared as suddenly as it had come. The birds were again singing and the sun shining when they continued to Austin, arriving there on the seventh day of their journey.

In camp near Durham's house Gideon catalogued fossils and dry land shells collected en route, and when the weather cleared he explored the Colorado River and Mount Bonnell. In the capital city of Texas he "saw one or two thinking men, but I did not bottle them up though they are very rare. I hope to find more of them." One, of course, was Buckley, and Gideon considered it great good fortune when the state geologist obtained a leave from Governor Throckmorton to accompany him on part of his expedition. Buckley was interested in locating coal, iron, and oil deposits.

They started out on March 25, going down Brushy Creek to the San

Gabriel and Little Rivers. Along the way they examined and explored creek bluffs, collecting marine fossils, insects, and everything of interest underfoot. They poked into springs, examined clays, and made diagrams of bluffs where fossils were found. On April 3 the expedition passed through Cameron, where Dr. J. R. Beauchamp[2] directed them to a deposit of coal five miles from Port Sullivan in a bluff on the north side of Little River. At the Brazos River they followed the river road toward the falls and stopped for a visit at the home of Churchill Jones.[3]

The falls of the Brazos, Gideon estimated, had moved up river at least four hundred yards during his thirty-two years' acquaintance with it. He wrote: "It is an interesting place from a geological point. The underlying stratum is blue shale or clay and is composed entirely of decomposed marine shells. The impressions of prints are plainly visible all through. The rock over which the water tumbles is of the same formation."

En route to Belton, the party stopped to examine the bluffs of Pond and Big Elm Creeks, where Gideon added a buffalo tooth and the bone of a large unidentified animal to his already overloaded ambulance. At Belton, where "they have a good courthouse and around the public square is pretty well built," Buckley and Gideon parted. Buckley returned to Austin and Lincecum and his three young companions continued toward Lampasas, stopping at a spring where they attempted to obtain swallow-tailed hawk nests and eggs, a pursuit in which Gideon seemed destined to fail. He complained: "They build their nests on the highest branch that will bear their weight, on the tallest tree they can find, beyond the reach of human ingenuity."

[2] Beauchamp, thirty-seven, a physician of Cameron, was a state representative from Milam County in 1866 (*Texas Almanac, 1867*, p. 231). He was one of the few champions of Gideon's sterilization memorial.

[3] Jones settled on the Brazos River about 1850, owned land on both sides, and operated a ferry at the site of the present Marlin bridge. His home was at the springs of Rush Creek, called Jones Spring. The trail from old Port Sullivan passed his house. He opposed secession but "went along with his state" (Lillian Schiller St. Roman, *History of Western Falls County* [Austin, Texas State Historical Association, 1951]. Gideon referred to Jones as "Churchivell Jones—an enemy of freedom." The reference might have concerned Jones' Union sympathies but more likely had something to do with Jones' knowledge of an attempt by Shumard to discredit Buckley in private letters. After Lincecum returned to Long Point he wrote Buckley: "That's what was the matter with old Churchivell Jones that morning we called on him at his home. He had heard of the Shumard letter and was in a terrible twitter."

The next few days were spent exploring Nolans and Cowhouse Creeks and Coryell County, of which Gideon wrote: "No inhabitants. It is a very beautiful country but exposed to Indian depredation. We tied up our horses til midnight fearing they might be taken away by some thieves. We were told that the white rogues were worse than the red ones."

They crossed over to the Lampasas River and twelve miles below the town visited D. W. Taylor, a stock rancher whose limestone fence Gideon admired.[4] Taylor was one of the men whom Gideon had written in his search for an Indian skull. After a "glorious thunderstorm with heavy rain and a norther" the travelers came to Lampasas Springs, which Gideon found greatly changed since his visit eleven years before:

The water is still gushing from the same places.[5] Some of them, however, have greatly diminished in the quantity discharged. The largest spring discharged then 200 barrels of water per minute. Now I do not think it discharges exceeding twenty barrels of water per minute. There are a great many springs gushing out from the banks and bed of the creek to the distance of seven miles along the creek. It is a great place and will eventually be much resorted to.

The country grew rougher and wilder as they traveled toward Burnet, across acres of solid pink granite. At Mormon Mills by the falls of Hamilton Creek,[6] Lincecum recorded in his journal:

The falls where the mill stands is 35 feet and the pool into which the water pitches has been tried with a rope 75 feet long but did not reach the bottom. In several places in the pool, quantities of some kind of gas is boiling up in considerable volume. They had no boat and I could not approach the gas

---

[4] D. W. Taylor was chief justice of Lampasas County (*Texas Almanac, 1863*, p. 32).

[5] Lampasas Springs in 1878 was "said to surpass the celebrated Virginia Springs." An article on its medicinal value, written by Lucullus Garland Lincecum, Gideon's son, appeared in the Lampasas *Leader*, May 23, 1891.

[6] Lyman Wight, one of the founders of the Reorganized Church of Jesus Christ of Latter Day Saints, and a group of followers settled at the Falls of Hamilton Creek in 1851, but abandoned it in 1853. Wight had been one of the Quorum of Twelve at Nauvoo in 1841, but did not acknowledge the leadership of Brigham Young after the assassination of Joseph Smith. Convinced in his last conversation with Smith that the new Zion was in Texas, Wight went there in 1845 (C. Stanley Banks, "The Mormon Migration into Texas," *Southwestern Historical Quarterly*, Vol. 49 [1945–1946], pp. 231–244).

spouts. Mr. Posey[7] told me that deep down in the pool the water is strongly impregnated with sulphur.

At Marble Falls, on the Colorado, Gideon and the boys collected freshwater shells, plants, butterflies, and insects and caught a fine mess of catfish for supper. He wrote of the falls: "The scenery about these falls is very fine. The whole affair has been gotten up on a grand scale. The three ledges of black marble over which the water tumbles lies in the form of a crescent, with the swag downstream near the center of the river."

A severe norther on May 5 drove them away from the falls and into the hospitable house of a Mr. Tate,[8] where they "received very kind treatment from his large and well-to-do family." His valley lands were productive in wheat, oats, and corn, and he had "plenty of everything necessary."

Leaving the ambulance to be repaired at Mr. Roper's smithy, a short distance from Mr. Tate's, Gideon went a few miles into Clear Mountain with Jacob Lacy.

The expedition continued to Doublehorn Creek, south of the Colorado River, a stony area marked with drifts of blue limestone. At the head of the creek lived Gideon's old friend Jesse Burnham, with whom he had stayed on his 1835 trip to Texas.[9] Here they stopped a few days, and then moved on several miles to visit Robert Burnham, one of Jesse's sixteen children. With Robert, Gideon visited the west side of Marble Falls and predicted: "These falls afford superior water power and when the right kind of people take possession of them it will soon be made a great place. The inexhaustible quantity and great variety of marble that is deposited here will be worked and I predict it will attract the attention of the civilized portions of the globe."

Crossing broken marble rocks, the expedition reached Shovel Mountain, a 1,500 foot elevation of marble, and traveled across it without accident to the Fredericksburg road near the Pedernales River in the heart of Indian Country. While the boys made camp, Gideon walked

---

[7] S. A. Posey is listed as a notary of Burnet County in the *Texas Almanac, 1867*, p. 232.

[8] S. M. Tate was a notary in Burnet County (*ibid*, p. 232).

[9] According to Noah Smithwick (*Evolution of a State* [fascimile of 1900 ed., Austin, Texas, Steck Co., n.d.], p. 312), who purchased and operated the Mormon Mills, Burnham and his many sons settled on the Doublehorn in the 1850's when civilization "crowded him out" of the site of his old ferry on the Colorado.

four miles to the Pedernales River and measured a drifted cypress tree —eight feet in diameter.

Gideon wanted to continue the expedition indefinitely, but next day, as they rode toward Fredericksburg, a driver of a wagon train warned that Indians were on horse-stealing raids and advised them to turn back or else keep their horses tied at night. This posed a new problem, as the driver also informed them that the nearest corn was fifty miles farther.

Gideon decided: "I could not think of starving my horses by tying them up from the grass. And besides, I came not to hunt Indians but bugs."

Reluctantly the group turned back to the road for New Braunfels and camped on Onion Creek. Next day they stopped briefly in the "neat little Dutch town" with its orderly farms. Here Gideon made his first and only contact with Ferdinand Jacob Lindheimer, a German-born botanist and editor.[10] He failed to record the visit in his journal, but later wrote Engelmann, of St. Louis:

On my spring excursion I visited Lindheimer at his office in New Braunfels. But he was so much engaged at the time, getting his paper ready for distribution, and I, being in haste that day, had but few words with him. I look upon him as an intellectual, industrious good man and was sorry that I could not have an opportunity for visiting him in his hours of leisure.

Before leaving the German settlement Gideon visited Comal Springs and found the power potential "sufficient for any amount of machinery." That night the group camped on the Cibolo Creek in Bexar County ("an inhospitable country, no grass, no corn") where even the horses refused to drink the creek water.

Gideon intensely disliked San Antonio and all of Bexar County. After a visit to San Antonio during the War he said of it in a letter to Hannay:

As to the character of the money-loving people of Texas west, it is as natural as the cactus and other thorny growth of that region. [He described the people as having] flat-top heads, twinkling eyes, nasal organ large and hook-

---

[10] Lindheimer was well known as a naturalist and many plants in Texas today bear his name. He was in Texas and Mexico in 1836, settled in New Braunfels in 1844, and died there in 1879. For many years he was editor of the New Braunfels *Zeitung* (Geiser, *Naturalists*, pp. 132–147).

ing, ample jaw and heavy back brain. The natural language . . . is, look out for No. 1., the longest stick gets the persimmons. I have no desire to visit that town anymore. There was nothing lovely to be seen in the place or on the road that goes there. The purifying knife is greatly needed in that city. . . . I never saw a more unlovely, unholy place. . . . The character of men I observed there, with few exceptions and the exceptions appeared to be straggling, were all of the same cast—all with money in their hands and begging for a chance to get more . . . it is the last stand on the broad road to perdition. The sooner I could make my escape from the hateful place— that filthy cancer on the posterior of Texas—the better it would be for me. And so at 9 P.M. of the same day I reached the place, I was ensconced in blanket 10 miles on the road towards home. A feeling of safety rested with me at my camp for I was perfectly enveloped in a vast ocean of mesquite bushes which have taken the place of the grass and placed the once bound- less prairie out of sight. . . . It might be a lovely looking place to a man of your proclivities—to pass through a large town and see piles and piles of Mexican dollars sitting on the shelves and desks in every house—hear the continual jingle of it in the hands of everybody who seems to know of no other thing or business or place in this terrain adobe—might tickle the fancy of some developments very agreeably. Therefore I pray you not to let what I have said in regard to the foul scab have any influence on your arrange- ment at all.

Gideon entered in his journal on May 18, 1867:

From Cibolo to the Guadalupe is high, dry and stony. Soil looks good but full of waterworn flintstones of a red color. It is settled with Germans who are manfully struggling with the inconveniences of a poor, dry and, except for mezquit, timberless country. We crossed Guadalupe on a good boat and camped three miles of Seguin.

May 19.—Passed through the pretty little town of Seguin. Buildings nearly all concrete which are going rapidly into a state of dilapidation. The materials are good but they did not use sufficient lime. Here I saw the Yankee soldiers drilling before the church door while prayers were going on inside. I thought of the former happy condition of the U.S. and the fable of the Garden of Eden. Man is never satisfied with his present condition.

On Wilson's Creek, in Gonzales County, Gideon visited Dr. Walker[11] and his medicinal springs, which he thought would prove

---

[11] Probably Dr. T. S. Walker, a pharmacist and doctor, who built the first dam on the Guadalupe River at Gonzales and organized the first water works. His descendants still live in Gonzales. There was no flowing hot water in the area prior to 1909, but

to be more beneficial to a greater variety of complaints than those of Lampasas. Swinging back to Austin, where they arrived on May 29, Lincecum again camped near the Durhams' and spent the next day in the state geological rooms arranging his collection. Durham insisted that his father-in-law call on Governor Throckmorton and as a result of the visit the two became friends and correspondents. Throckmorton asked Gideon to write an account of his excursion for the benefit of Texans and foreigners seeking investments, which Gideon "partly promised" to do.

After his return to Long Point on June 3 Gideon wrote a long report for Throckmorton, detailing available resources, location of springs, condition of crops and soil, and the variety of industries found on his journey, concluding: "The extensive resources will, when the right kind of people shall occupy the land, greatly increase the wealth, comfort and well-being of our widespread population. . . . Every branch of industry may find lucrative employment in this country."

Gideon's report of his three months' exploration of twenty-eight Texas counties was gratefully received by Throckmorton,[12] but before

---

an abundance of springs of varying degrees of sulphur and other chemical ingredients, as well as mud boils and quaking bogs. Gideon could not have known of the use of the hot water since 1937 by the Gonzales Warm Springs Foundation, which was of such benefit to children stricken by polio before the Salk vaccine. The flowing hot water was the result of a wildcat oil company drilling at Ottine, ten miles north of Gonzales, which at 1,600 feet yielded approximately 200,000 gallons of 106-degree water daily (Information courtesy of Joseph H. Grant, Gonzales, a member of the board of the Foundation.)

[12] James Webb Throckmorton (1825–1894), Tennessee-born, came to Texas with his father in 1841 and settled near present McKinney. He trained as a doctor, served in that capacity during the U.S.-Mexican War, but gave up medicine in 1861 to enter law and politics. He was state representative and senator, made a dramatic stand against secession but soon after Texas joined the confederacy took the oath of allegiance and intermittently served in the state and Confederate services. He won his name "Leathercoat" when he was Confederate commissioner to Indian Territory and was presented an Indian-made embroidered and beaded leather coat which he constantly wore. In 1866 he was elected governor of Texas as a conservative Unionist over the way-out Unionist candidate, E. M. Pease. He was accused in *Flake's Daily Bulletin* (May 18, 1866) of being able to sing "Dixie" and "The Flag of Our Union" at the same time. Throckmorton was sickened and discouraged by the vindictiveness of the reconstructionists, the actions of some of his fellow Texans, and his own inability to be a constructive power. His dismissal as "an impediment to reconstruction" (General P. H. Sheridan's phrase) came as a relief. While Sheridan's phrase is frequently repeated in Texas histories, seldom appears the reply of President Andrew Johnson to a newspaperman's query as to whether he thought Throckmorton had attempted to thwart Sheridan in the execution of Reconstruction laws: "No, sir, the records prove

he could make use of it he was removed from office. Gideon's faint hope for Texas collapsed and he predicted: "Everything he [Throckmorton] has done during his administration goes to prove that he is a *man*. They have not killed him yet. He will rise again with banners and dismay will fill the hearts of the now dominant usurpers."

Back in Long Point loneliness seized Lincecum immediately, and his grief for his lost one deepened in the familiar surroundings. He was eager to be away from his sad home and memories. Neighbors and friends showed their affection in many small ways. Mrs. Sallie Turly of Houston sent a fossil found in excavating a well and Samuel Hammer brought the skull of a leopard cat. Doctors Maney and Ruff, of Long Point, called and examined his specimens and Dr. J. F. Matchett of Houston frequently spent the afternoon with him.

The numerous visitors interrupted his cataloguing, and after the visit of a young man, probably one of his grandsons, Lincecum wrote in his diary:

Had company all day, in consequence of which I attended but little to entomology. I, however, made observations on the natural history of man. Found the back and basilar brain hot and much larger than the front and top head, obviously a manifestation that the poor fellow is in a twitter to get married. What a pity it is that such cases can't be relieved of such society—spoiling desires.

A few days later the visit of an obvious bore prompted him to write:

I did not go out today. Had loafering company that kept me in all day. What a dull thing a loafer is! He knows nothing that is useful and he won't try to learn. But he can eat and has pride about his raiment. Well, he must be fed or he'll die and stink about your house.

---

the reverse. The Governor of Texas placed the whole civil machinery of his state at the disposal of the military power, and aided it in every way possible, except in the manufacture of a radical majority of voters and securing Negro supremacy. That was Governor Throckmorton's sinning and for which he was arbitrarily removed by General Sheridan" (Houston *Daily Telegraph*, September 3, 1867; Claude Elliott, *Leathercoat* [San Antonio, Standard Printing Co., 1938]). In a summary of his administration (*Texas Almanac, 1868*, pp. 184–201) Throckmorton comments on Buckley's geological tour and mentions that he was accompanied by Dr. Lincecum. Buckley's account of the expedition appears in "The Mineral Resources of Texas," *Texas Almanac, 1868*, pp. 79–82.

But there were other days when he yearned for companionship and on one such day, after an illness, Gideon entered in his diary:

Went twice to town today. I sought for someone who would converse on topics of interest. They were not in town today. I returned to my room to try solitary reflections once more. I think I can work before long and then I shall not be so lonesome. My strength is returning and energy will soon follow. It will be horrible for me to remain indolent and have to pass the remainder of my life in idleness like other old men. Awful!

A visitor who was always welcome to Gideon's little cedar house was A. W. Ruter, son of Dr. Martin Ruter, for whom Rutersville College in Fayette County was named. Gideon did not mind when Ruter interrupted the work of nailing boxes of specimens for shipping, because the two always had "a very agreeable time." He found Ruter "a highly educated gentleman with a mind well-stored with profitable knowledge."

Lincecum allowed even people far removed geographically also to make demands on his time. His correspondence often indicates his willingness to give advice or to help answer questions by mail, and it reveals with equal frequency the many sides of his personality, from his cynicism in evaluation of the human race to his whimsical humor. A letter of November 29, 1866, to David S. Greer, of Memphis, Tennessee, is of this sort:

My Dear Sir:

I received today a letter from your Cousin Crawford Greer, enclosing one from you to him making certain inquiries in reference to the affairs of Dr. Thomas Hunt; and as he, Crawford, does not reside in Washington County he enclosed your letter to me with a request that I should answer your questions.

Before I commence the replies to your interrogatories I must indulge in a few remarks on my own account. I always considered the two Greer families a rather rare variety of the genus homo, and now in your letter I find sufficient testimony to confirm my opinion, *"by damn."* You and your Cousin Crawford were raised all but in the same yard and you had so far lost your dear Cousin that you were only able to state that before Morgan told it you knew Crawford lived somewhere in Texas. Texas is a broad territory. It is about 900 miles long and 700 miles wide. I can come nearer telling where every member of the Greer family is than that. But it makes no difference about that, no way. Humanity is a dang poor thing at best. . . . Your Cousin Crawford Greer's family are all well, but terribly nonsuited at the loss of the negroes. Your Cousin Dick Greer went off two or three weeks ago on an exploring tour to Brazil, S. America; he carried away with him $18,000 in gold. Your Cousin Nancy Ragsdale resides on Galveston Bay. She went there this year. She formerly dwelt at Austin and had a large farm in Brazos Bottom but since the break-up became dissatisfied and retired to the seacoast. It being 100 miles from my place she, Greer-like, never writes. I am not able to state whether her health has improved down there or not. Your Cousin Stephen Greer resides in Limestone County east of the Brazos, about 40 miles north of me.

Dr. Thomas Hunt died in 1861, I think. I know he died in the early stage of the war. I don't think anybody administered for the very good reason that there was no property found belonging to his estate. He and his old lady had, some years previous to his death, deeded his property to his son William the only child he had that was not deeply in debt; soon after which William died and his widow, who seemed to know nothing about the private nature of the conveyance, held on to the papers and the property too, and so the old doctor died insolvent.

William Hunt's widow has, since the old doctor's death, married a very clever fellow by the name of Bishop and resides about six miles from here.

There were several other of the old Dr.'s sons; they are all dead now. Albert Hunt was shot and killed in a drunken scrape; Tom died drunk; there was no other that I recollect, but had there been, he'd died drunk too.

Very Respectfully Thine
Gideon Lincecum

Nor did Lincecum begrudge the time to write to three young men whose lives doubtless were changed and influenced by their association with him. One was his nephew Grabel Huckaby, in Brooksville, Mississippi: "You desire to become a physician and to study that profession under me. Well, come on, and though I am not a doctor now you will find what you want with some of my sons. Lucullus is in the practice and will take pleasure in teaching you medicine."

In behalf of the second, young Snively, his Civil War hospital attendant friend who had entered medical college in Philadelphia, he wrote letters of introduction to his Philadelphia scientist friends.

Young James Caldwell, the third, who had returned to Fort Jessup after the expedition, decided he wanted to be a doctor and Gideon encouraged him: "I am glad you have decided to study medicine. You have the energy and character to make a good and useful practitioner. That is, if you learn and practice the natural, sanitary system of medicine. Let Howard's or Thomson's works be your guide."

On his spring expedition Gideon had talked to many old Texans who were dissatisfied and uneasy about conditions under Reconstruction and wanted to leave the country. Gideon called them "offended Democrats." Many Confederates had founded colonies in Latin America and Texas' John Henry Brown and a group had established colonies along the Tuxpan River in Mexico. Gideon began to think of going to Mexico or Honduras and wrote Durand: "The northers of another Texas winter may not find me here. Farther south as I grow older is healthier." He thought of sitting on some shady tropical river bank sipping delicious juices of tropical fruits "that are always ready for those who need them."

Daily, as Gideon saw the advances of reconstruction and retaliation which increased after Throckmorton's dismissal, he lost his resolve to make the most of things. He read Brown's book on the Tuxpan area settlements, *Two Years in Mexico or the Emigrants' Friend*,[13] and determined to go to Mexico. He wrote Engelmann: "Now society, villainous, *civilized* society has gradually thickened around me until there is no little, sacred, untramped nook to which I might retire and hide myself from the unholy gaze of meddling civilization."

Lincecum marked time by completing his collections for northern scientists but was eager to be off to his new frontier. Sallie and Doran agreed to accompany him and a small Negro boy on an expedition in the ambulance to Sour Lake.[14] They left Long Point on July 31. The

---

[13] John Henry Brown's book was printed at the New Book and Job Office in Galveston in 1867 and it is reported that 10,000 copies were printed. Considering the scarcity of the volume this seems unlikely. The University of Texas Library has a photostatic copy which is treated as rare. Recently a Dallas book dealer sold what is purported to be the only known copy for $1,200. The contents are meager and disappointing and names are handled in a most careless manner.

[14] Sour Lake in south central Hardin County was a mineral spring settled in 1835. Its pitch and oil seepage was of great medicinal value but proved more valuable when oil was discovered there in 1901. The lake and Sour Lake Springs Hotel, considered promising as a winter resort, were later purchased by the Texas Company (*Handbook of Texas*, Vol. II, pp. 638–639). F. H. Merriman of Galveston wrote Gideon in 1856 that "Col. [W. C.|] Lacy has bought Sour Lake and is keeping a hotel there and improving in health."

weather was miserably hot and their camp at Navasota the first night was a mass of mosquitoes, black gnats, cicadas, and katydids. The second night they camped a mile south of Anderson when Gideon visited Mr. Roger's sick family and "prescribed for his wife who is confined from having hurt her knee in a fall six months ago."

A mile north of Anderson[15] he saw "the unmistakable signs of the recent war in the form of bomb shells, conic, round, and all forms of missiles scattered along the road half a mile." In the sandy pine country at Coldspring, Gideon visited his old friend, Professor C. G. Fitze, who rode him out to examine his cornfield, where Gideon "captured the yellow boll worm fly."

Several days were spent exploring the magnolia forests and gathering botanical specimens and medicinal roots. They were constantly exposed to seed ticks and mosquitoes. Gideon wrote in his diary: "I do not think this is a healthy country. There are many cases of fever now."

He stopped on his journey to administer to a number of sick families, one of them the family of Dr. Anthony M. Branch[16] at the Red Fork of the San Jacinto River.

The weather continued oppressive, mosquitoes and ticks numerous. Gideon became too ill to make observations and the party turned back on August 14. Doran, Sallie, and the Negro boy were also sick. It was a miserable return, each alternating between high temperatures and long chills. Gideon administered lobelia, an emetic, which caused frequent vomiting.

Unknowingly they had entered an area where the disastrous yellow fever epidemic of 1867 had spread. It was to continue to grow and claim countless victims, a tragedy second only to the Civil War. In his diary of this period Gideon makes no reference to the yellow-fever epidemic until September 8, although he apparently had been one of the victims. Before beginning his expedition toward Sour Lake he noted the frequent showers and oppressive heat at Long Point. On July 28 the temperature at 2:00 P.M. was ninety-seven degrees. When Gideon started on his expedition the epidemic was well under way in

---

[15] During the Civil War a munitions factory was established in Anderson (*ibid*, Vol. I, p. 46).

[16] Dr. Branch died of yellow fever October 3, 1867 (*ibid*, Vol. I, p. 206).

coastal towns, but authorities had not admitted its presence. At Coldspring on August 9 Gideon noted the presence of many cases of fever. He treated the sick Branch family on August 10 and on August 12 was in Huntsville, where the town's first official epidemic death (of a total of 123) had occurred on August 9. As late as September physicians there still maintained that the disease was congestive fever. Three days after treating the Branch family, Gideon was too sick to make any collections, and on the fourth day he had a four-hour chill. He was in Navasota on the fifteenth, when the first epidemic death (of a total of 154) occurred. He made no more entries until August 26, when he wrote that he was dropsical from the use of quinine, adding: "It is very foolish to take quinine for fever."[17]

Gideon and his three traveling companions were among the survivors and the old botanic doctor attributed it all to lobelia. His illness left him "as thin and flat as a wet rag" and it was long weeks before he could return to his specimens.

It left him also restless and more than ever determined to get away. He explained his unhappiness in a letter to Durham in which he congratulated his son-in-law on the discovery of a new bird of the stork family and the resultant praise from John Cassin, the noted ornithologist:[18] "My soul is sad and seems to be satisfied with nothing so much as the anticipation of far-off adventures. I am sad and melancholy when I can find no exciting employment and that is not to be found in any of my old haunts."

John Henry Brown wrote from Tumbadero, Mexico, assuring Gideon that he would find on the Tuxpan River a rich field for explorations in geology, botany, and ornithology and that the forests and jungles abounded in medicinal roots, herbs, and gums.

Gideon decided to go to Mexico without further delay and planned

[17] Statistics from Franklin W. Baldwin's "Yellow Fever in Texas in 1867," B.A. thesis, Rice University, 1961.

[18] This was a jabiru (Mycteria americana), the head of which Durham sent to the Philadelphia Academy of Natural Sciences. It was the first ever obtained in the United States (S. W. Geiser, "Men of Science," Field and Laboratory, XXVI [1958], p. 126).

John Cassin (1813–1869), an American ornithologist, was with the Perry expedition to Japan in 1853. As a "closet naturalist" and lithographer, he arranged and identified 26,000 specimens of birds. His most notable work was illustrating The Birds of California, Texas, Oregon, British and Russian America, 1856 (DAB, Vol. 3 [1929], pp. 568–569).

to take his ambulance overland. He placed in the Galveston *News* an announcement of his plans, asking interested parties to send inquiries to him. He was bombarded with letters from offended Democrats, all wanting to join his party.[19] Groups from Montgomery and Seguin were already forming companies to go to Mexico, and each urged him to join them.

Lincecum's bout with yellow fever had left him much weaker than he realized and he fretted:

I am so old and worn out that a little sickness goes a good way with me. It is hard to be sick now when time is so precious. I desire to be well-fixed for my big exploring expedition and if I continue sick much longer I can't fix good for it. . . . I am but little account at best. I think it quite probable that my course of usefulness is about coming to a close. Well, I have done nothing to brag of, but what I have done was done in hard earnest. I have misled no one, made no misrepresentation on any serious subject, quarreled with no one, had no lawsuits nor difficulties of any kind.

By September 24 yellow fever had reached epidemic stage:

There is so much trouble about the prevailing epidemic that the mind of the investigator cannot be well brought to bear on the subject of natural history. The yellow fever has been carried out from the towns to many houses in the country and while the disease is abating in the towns it is rapidly spreading in the country. It is said there is a case here.

Long Point was emptier than during the war. Only the doctors, Mrs. Campbell and family, Mrs. Wood and four or five of her hotel boarders, and Gideon remained. Gideon left Long Point on October 1, but only to go to Austin to say farewell to the Durhams and Buckley. Buckley and his wife considered going to Tuxpan if he could collect his year's back pay from the state. Gideon urged Throckmorton to join them.

He promised to send Mrs. Buckley a present from Tuxpan. "I did not say what I would send her for I didn't know then. . . . since I parted

---

[19] Among those Gideon corresponded with on the subject of going to Tuxpan were: W. R. Hampton, J. T. Holland, H. Terrell, Jr., and Dr. M. B. Franklin of Seguin; C. E. Jones, Oakland Post Office; D. R. Wallace, Waco; E. Uzzell and his father-in-law, Dr. James A. McQueen, Anderson; Dr. H. C. Parker, Galveston, whom Gideon had known on the Noxubee River in Mississippi; S. D. Ezell, Cameron; W. H. George and B. F. Brown, Chappell Hill; and William H. Russell, Rutersville.

with her I have concluded that one of the smallest species of black monkeys would be a very appropriate and very pleasing present for her."[20]

On the way home he forgot Tuxpan long enough to observe the good grass and fat cattle in the pastures and to wonder: "Why is it that Texas cannot have a beef packing establishment and send her good fat beef to market for the world's consumption? There are beef packing houses in some countries and they make money. Such houses could be carried on in this country at less expense. . . . Average price of beef is $1\frac{1}{2}$ to 2 cents."[21]

Home again, Gideon was eager to ship his collections, "wind up his business," and be off, but: "The yellow fever continues to rage with so much violence on the route that there is no certainty in the express offices, the clerks having mostly passed away. The fever seems to be on the increase in Brenham. One hundred and fifty cases yesterday, all negroes."

The rains, the fever, and the lack of companionship depressed him: "My mind is gradually becoming more indolent and indisposed to grapple with serious or heavy propositions. It requires exciting subjects to stimulate it into action. It would become useless if I lie up in dull society. I must wander over nature's rugged fields."

In November nature sent him an excitement—a plague of grasshoppers. There were millions—eating every growing thing and covering acres with their eggs; clouds of them blown by the wind darkened the skies for weeks. Gideon came alive with interest and watched hour after hour: "People are wondering where the grasshoppers come from and what calamity will come after them. They know it is a sign if anybody could interpret it. Superstition is not dead yet. Ignorance is the cause of all our suffering. No remedy for it."

---

[20] However, finding no monkeys available when he got to Tuxpan, Gideon sent Mrs. Buckley a parrot. In the first letter Gideon wrote Buckley after the War he asked: "Do, pray, inform me how many times you have been married since I saw you?" Buckley had married only once during the War, to Libbie Myers of Elbridge, New York, in 1864. His first wife, Charlotte Sullivan, died in 1854 and his second wife, Sarah Porter, died in 1858. Both were of New York (*DAB*, Vol. 3 [1929], pp. 232–233).

[21] In 1871 D. C. Holden chilled and cured beef at Fulton but it was not until 1901 that two major meat companies established packing plants at Fort Worth (*Handbook of Texas*, Vol. II, p. 455).

At last he was able to send off his specimens: "I send them for the purpose of increasing the stock of knowledge among mankind. I am not sending them to men for their individual benefit but to their charge and guardianship for the coming generations." The shipment included fifty-two specimens of ants with their history in manuscript and other entomological items for Cresson; lizards, centipedes, tarantulas, scorpions, and spiders for Cope; fossils, shells, moths, and butterflies for the Smithsonian; hymenoptera for Packard and 2,000 butterflies for Peck. "And that," as Gideon told Buckley, "ends my attention and labors for northern naturalists. They are a small people."

On a beautiful calm day in late November he entered in his diary:

I should be proud of such weather on my journey at sea. It is a curious fact and one belonging to natural history that a certain class of people when they meet me nowadays have old rusty pistols, broken-down mules or horses which they offer to sell me. They know I am going away and thinking I may have some money they desire to get hold of it, let what may become of me in the far-off country.

November, 1867, was an unusually warm month, the temperature at Long Point averaging eighty degrees. On November 28 Gideon recalled his first winter in Texas: "This day 19 years ago the ground here was covered three inches in snow. The norther continued six days more or less, each day, till the cattle that were all very fat came very near perishing. It was the severest spell of cold I have witnessed in any country."

Gideon encountered unexpected difficulty in raising money for his journey. He offered to sell the Chahta Tradition to Cushing of the *Telegraph* for $1,000 and told him he had turned down $10,000 offered by a Union soldier who stopped at his house during the war. Cushing did not think the public was interested in Indian lore at that time, being too involved and worried by the problems of Reconstruction and poverty.

December arrived, warm and springlike and Gideon commented on the few remaining grasshoppers: "They are greatly encouraged and seem to hope that winter has passed. I saw today numbers of them coupled which indicates they think winter is over. That is what theology styles unerring instinct. Well, if we have no more frost the grasshoppers are right."

Yellow fever still lingered in the area. Gideon grew weary of the house and decided to sleep in the woods, at least for a night. "Anything for amusement. I am worn out with the confinement of the house."

He was annoyed that his friends and family were so dead-set against his going to Tuxpan and that they withheld encouragement and help in furthering his plans to get away. To placate him, some of his children agreed to go with him, but it was obvious they temporized hoping he would change his mind. Even his devoted friend, Durand, writing to Sallie opposed it:

I do not approve of this new undertaking. At our advanced age he ought not, I think, to hazard himself so far from home and the family. There are good people everywhere, but in that unsettled country there are many bad people, robbers and murderers. Scientifically disposed as your father is I have no doubt that Texas contains as many interesting subjects of inquiry as any part of Mexico.

No one, not even Sallie, fully realized Gideon's determination to leave Texas. He easily detected all the schemes and plots to trap him into remaining safely with them. His children did not understand that it was not the comfortable old life he wanted, but a new one in a strange and unsettled country which offered endless novelties to stimulate his mind and imagination. He knew only too well that he was waiting for death, an event which held no fear for him; but while he waited he wanted to live fully. Gideon often remarked that one died only once and it mattered little where—one place was as good as another.

But deeper than a desire for excitement and a new environment was Gideon's deep-rooted love of liberty, a personal thing to him, a search for which had taken him from one frontier to another. He had pushed toward new frontiers all his life and there were still new ones to be crossed. Liberty had always been to him a condition of life, and there was no liberty for him in postwar Washington County in 1867. Even at seventy-five he considered liberty worth fighting for. The battle at hand was not with the Unionists but with his own children.

He wrote Baird about his frustration:

They, now that I have got all ready for my contemplated excursion of observation, get around me and cry and grieve and cut up shines, declaring that it will never do for me to leave them. That I must not go so far away, etc., etc. They have confused me. They have shaken my heretofore strong unwavering resolution and unfitted me for future progress. I shall be compelled to abandon my Mexican exploring trip.

Gideon suspected his children were responsible for the long delay in payments of debts due him with which he hoped to finance the trip. In vexation and "a delirium of disappointment" he was determined to demonstrate that he was not the decrepit old man his children appeared to consider him. Harnessing Charlie to the ambulance, Gideon headed toward the Texas coast. James Fowler, a young man of Long Point, and George Campbell, Gideon's grandson, went with him. The flight was likely a deliberate plan to absent himself from home on his first Christmas without his good companion.

Moving leisurely toward Chocolate Bayou in Brazoria County, they stopped frequently to shoot quail, squirrel, duck, deer, and geese. Following the Bayou a short distance below Liverpool, the group arrived at the home of Gideon's old friend, Samuel Adams.[22] It was Christmas Day and the arrival of the visitors called for a big bowl of eggnog. Not wanting to offend his "dear Methodist Christian friends" Gideon sipped a teaspoon of the "frothy stinking stuff" in a merry Christmas toast and passed the remainder of his cup to his host's young daughter.

Gideon watched as she finished it off and noted: "She seemed to carry it well."

Early next morning the men and boys departed for a fishing area. Gideon and Fowler went by boat, and Adams, his son, and George went in the ambulance. Writing later of the trip to Cassandra, he described the scene:

We were looking out along the low, flat shores, anxious to discover the campfire of our friends when just at that moment the glorious sun flamed above the glittering waters. There, as if thrown by a daguerrotype, was the ambulance. . . . In the glare of the sun no land was visible, just the black

22 The 1870 census of Washington County shows that a Samuel Adams, farmer, fifty-eight, born in Virginia, lived in Chappell Hill with his wife Frances, born in Georgia, and five children, the two oldest, born in Mississippi.

carriage and the harnessed horse, seeming to hang in space in the very center of the blazing sun. . . . It was a most beautiful scene. A sweet, serene, clear morning and the sight was not only beautiful and wonderful but one that will not be presented more than once in a lifetime. It lasted but two or three minutes and then the splendor of the scene changed. The ambulance dwindled to a toy wagon—about five miles away.

Redfish and flounders were numerous. Gideon used a bow and arrow to spear the flounders. In the afternoon sun he bathed and splashed in the salt water and at night slept in the deep damp grass. On New Year's Day Gideon and the boys left Adams' house and rode over the pathless prairie to Dickinson Bayou, which flows into Galveston Bay. He wrote:

In all our coast country as far as twenty-five miles from the Gulf there are no roads or paths to be found and, except for an occasional bayou, no timber. Nothing to be seen as far as the eye could reach many times but grass, grass, grass; and it clothes the ground with a thick carpet down and in many places to the very sea beach. In all this grassy region there are but few inhabitants. I like that quiet country exceedingly.

At Dickinson Bayou, Gideon rented a little house in a good fishing and hunting area and hurried to Houston, where Sallie and Sioux had planned to meet him. They had agreed, if he could find a suitable house, to spend the winter with him on the bay—another plan, doubtless, to postpone his departure for Tuxpan. Gideon was utterly downcast when he arrived in Houston and learned that the Dorans, not hearing from him, had gone to Richmond, Texas. He felt they had dodged him and wrote to Cassandra: "They expected me to go to Richmond. But I can't fool my time away trotting after them."

The Dorans urged him to come to Richmond, where they had found a comfortable house, and told him many old Texans there were eager to see him. Gideon scoffed at the idea that any one was in the least eager to see him:

I passed through that town not long since. It was a beautiful day, people all out on the sidewalks. I passed slowly down the main street, went into a store where I found half a dozen clever looking men. Did not know any of them. Got some lead and some buckshot. Stepped out on the pavement, saw a number of strangers. Saw a crowd of men lower down the street. Went there, made enquiries about the action of their negroes, talked about yellow fever. One gentleman, after gazing intently for a moment at me asked my name. I told him: Lincecum.

He seemed to reflect a moment, but he did not go into spasms nor did he look like he had ever heard the name before. I remained in the town perhaps half an hour; saw a good many intellectual faces, but none that I recognized. Think of that! And I declare to you that after I left Brenham, although I passed through eleven towns, met many people on the road, was at many houses, I did not see but one man that I knew. No sir. Everywhere, Charlie and the fishing rods tied on top of the ambulance attracted more notice.[23]

Friends and relatives threw many lures to distract him from Tuxpan. Buckley and the Durhams invited him to Austin, Adams urged him to return to Chocolate Bayou, Lysander and Mollie worked diligently to make him happy, and Sallie pressed him to come to Richmond. He became "like a wild turkey gobbler, not wanting to roost twice in the same place" and yearned for the good companion who had always eagerly shared his excursions and who would have gaily gone off with him to Tuxpan.

Gideon attempted to make Sallie understand the urgency of his leaving Long Point:

Lysander, poor fellow, has spent his whole life in my service. And you, like Lysander, spent at least an ordinary lifetime waiting on me and your mother. For this my waning spirit feels and acknowledges the deepest gratitude. . . . But a great change has taken place. The family ties—the golden bowl—have been broken and the occupants of a long-loved and highly cherished homestead have been scattered. The fields and the houses are filled with strangers and I, as the once acknowledged head of that flourishing family, stand alone and howl like a lost dog in utter amazement at my irremedial loneliness.

He recalled how Gideon, the patriarch, under happier circumstances broke up his Mississippi home when civilization pushed him to the Texas frontier. He remembered that a compelling reason for the move

[23] The end of the war saw an increase in population and growth of Texas towns and the extension of the state's western frontier. In a letter to Hannay, Gideon reported the main street of Navasota was a "solid wall of houses continuing all the way to Gen. Blackshear's farm and they have a south Navasota rapidly going up. Old Camp is at the breast of that enterprise. They have 12 sawmills in the pinery over there and they can't do half the work called for. . . . Long Point has caught the spirit of progress and is improving smartly. Inhabitants 1500."

was to take his children from the "crushing and demoralizing civilization" of Columbus and into a new land of opportunity and sounder values. Slyly and silently he conceived a plan which offered a solution to his loneliness and relief for the ache for a new land. Lincecum's plan placed him again in the role of the patriarch, leading his flock into a new country. Again, he could be the great provider; his could be the guiding hand. Again, life would have a purpose instead of being a mere day-to-day existence of aimlessness.

There was his widowed and unhappy daughter, Leonora, with her seven children, fatherless and without guidance, growing up in the postwar violence of Texas, under the heel of the victors in an atmosphere of terror, mistrust, defeat, and despair.

To his great joy Leonora agreed to go to Tuxpan with him.

Now that his goal was closer in sight, Gideon journeyed to Richmond to visit Sallie. As always when he was with her, Gideon enjoyed life. His youngest daughter had charmed Richmond and the Doran house was a popular spot. She had a "fine-toned cabinet organ" and borrowed an excellent violin for Gideon. People dropped in every night to hear them play and it was almost like old times again except that his dear old lady was not there to rock happily to their tunes. Gideon thought his Richmond audience was not as fascinated by their music as it was amazed at a seventy-five–year–old man with a long white beard nimbly playing waltzes, cotillions, reels, and marches on a violin.

When he returned to Long Point the report that two hundred Virginians were moving into Texas spurred Gideon to be off to Tuxpan. He foresaw the "country filling up, the grass plowed under, cows starved out of existence, trees cut down and the land turned into ravines and gullies."

Fortunately he was able at long last to collect money due him and to find a buyer for Leonora's house. Leonora sold her property to Jim Holt—$5 an acre for forty-five acres of woodland, and her home place, fifteen acres, for $51 66/100 an acre. In April Lincecum wrote to Baird:

I will take the family out of the reach of the relentless tramp of radical influence with his black thieving associates. I can set them down on some wild river shore and teach them self reliance. I *must live* until this project is fully accomplished. She, Leonora, is a noble woman and her children all possess sprightly and promising developments. Taken away from the demoralizing influences by which they are now surrounded it may be that some of them will be useful. I shall do it anyhow and in performing that service for my progeny I shall traverse new fields for investigation.

On his birthday, April 23, 1868, Gideon wrote in his journal: "I am this morning going on my 76th year. My great recuperative forces got me again well as ever and we are all about ready to be off. I sold my ambulance and horses, Leonora her land. We have nothing to do now but wait for the ship."

But there was one other thing for him to do. Gideon had no will, for he had already divided his land among his children and there was little left. But he noted a few bequests:

Give Leonidas, as he is the most superstitious, the old Bible.

Give Leander, the anatomical paintings and the two books.

Give Lachaon, (this was left blank)

Give Lucullus, the Moccasin tracts (Gideon's manuscript work of botanical medicine).

Give Lysander, Howard's, Matson's and Thomson's works. The rest all having backslided do not need such books.

How I disposed of my small property. My poastoak table, cedar table and secretary head, I sold to W. P. Doran on 22nd October 1867 for cash paid $10. I am to use them till I go away.

To my granddaughter, Attilia Campbell, for her kind attentions to her suffering Grandmother I give my fine large bed, two pillows, the sheets and quilts belonging thereto.

To my granddaughter, M. E. Lincecum, the fine bedstead and woolen matress, two quilts, two sheets and one bolster. This I do for her kindness to me.[24]

Departure date by boat from Galveston was May 15. Gideon planned to travel light, carrying only clothing, axes, a grub hoe, saw, auger, chisel, draw knife, blankets, tableware, a sewing machine, and one hundred pounds of bacon. But there was another delay and disappointment. The schooner on which he was to sail to Tuxpan could not accommodate him and his brood because it was taking a large sugar mill and machinery to Mexico for Munger.[25]

[24] The daughter of Lycurgus.

[25] Probably Henry Martin Munger, one-time resident of Rutersville. His son,

The unfortunate delay gave his children time to continue their campaign to keep him at home, resulting in a bitterness which Gideon carried with him to Mexico. But his farewell message to Sallie was: "My affection for *you*, Sarah, is as fixed as fate and will only cease with my existence."

Finally, on June 6, 1868, Gideon, once more the patriarch, his daughter Leonora and her seven children—Attie, a handsome young lady; Argyle, thirteen, nicknamed Bud, the oldest son; George, John, and Lysander; and the girls, Sally and Lutie, the youngest—stood in the hallway of the family home in Long Point and said farewell to the other Lincecums and to the many neighbors who came to wish them well. Silently, Gideon shook hands with each one. As the carriage taking them to Galveston reached the top of the hill toward Brenham, he looked back briefly.

Gideon had lived this scene before. Twenty years ago it had been like this, the sad parting from loved ones, leaving the safe and familiar for an unknown new land where one was sure to find problems and hardships. Many years later he recalled the pangs of his departure from Long Point: "The scene that occurred on parting with children, grandchildren and friends was almost beyond my power to bear calmly. It was a very serious hour with me."

Three days later he stood on the deck of the schooner *San Carlos* and watched the Island of Galveston disappear in a fog. The wind rippled his long white beard and he stood tall and straight as a Moses leading his people. Leonora and her children sparkled with excitement, but Gideon, in serious conversation with Captain Kried, was calm and in control of the situation. He felt his responsibility greatly, for ahead, he well knew, were many heartaches; but he felt fully confident he was man enough and young enough to meet them. He had just solved the first one—the shock of learning that the boat fare to Tuxpan was $25 each. He negotiated with Captain Kried and was successful in getting a wholesale reduction to a total fare of $150 with luggage.

On June 16 they had their first view of the beautiful Tuxpan River. Two years later, in a letter to Sallie, he recalled their arrival: "4 P.M. At this hour two years ago we were majestically sailing up this beauti-

---

Robert Sylvester, was a pioneer manufacturer of farm machinery, especially cotton gins (*Handbook of Texas*, Vol. II, p. 249).

ful river and passing by the place I am now sitting. The thrill of gladness that swelled this old time-battered heart of mine will fully compare with the glowing sensation of delight that throbbed in the same old organ as I sailed into the mouth of Buffalo Bayou 14 April 1848."

A NOTE ON SOURCES

Much of the material in this chapter is taken from Lincecum's 1867 diary of expeditions in Texas, in which he reveals his deep love for nature and indicates a growing interest in geology. Doubtless Lincecum kept a diary for many other years, but only a few scattered pages are found in the Lincecum Papers.

The diary is written in a terse but natural and relaxed style. It is of particular value for the glimpse it affords of Gideon's personal life and private thoughts. For example, his entry for July 16 summed up his opinion of his scientist correspondents: "I consider Leidy the busiest and most liberal-minded man in the Academy of Natural Sciences. Cope is a religious fanatic. Durand is a religious pretender. Wood is a light-gutted Puritan and Cresson is a gentleman. He is a good man and wishes to improve rapidly."

There are many gems buried in the Lincecum Papers which have not been presented in this biography but which are worthy of permanent record.

Correspondence used in this chapter includes letters to: E. Durand, Philadelphia, January 24, February 5, March 3, 1867, January 29, February 16, April 25, 1868; S. B. Buckley, Austin, Texas, January 20, 1867; Reuben Davis, Aberdeen, Mississippi, February 13, 1867; Oliver Fields, Yazoo City, Mississippi, July 30, 1867; Governor James Webb Throckmorton, Austin, Texas, June 15, July 1, 27, 1867; Walter W. Durham, Austin, Texas, November 24, 1867; Frank Greer, Navasota, Texas, January 10, 1868; Cassandra Durham, January 19, April 21, 1868; W. P. Doran, Richmond, Texas, January 22, April 3, May 14, 1868; Sarah Doran, Richmond, Texas, January 31, February 8, 19, May 6, 17, June 3, 1868; D. B. Lincecum, Lockhart, Texas, April 3, 1868; R. B. Hannay, London, England, April 5, 1868; George Durham, Austin, Texas, July 17, 25, September 7, November 23, December 5, 1867, April 30, 1868; John A. Rutherford, Honey Grove, Texas, April 2, 1868; D. B. and Emily Moore, Castroville, Texas, June 4, 1868; Grabel Huckaby, Brookville, Mississippi, June 6, 1867; James Caldwell, Fort Jessup, Louisiana, October 18, 1867, April 1, 1868; Henry Hinck, Galveston, Texas, July 30, 1867; U. S. G. Owens, San Marcos, Texas, April 12, 1868; J. C. Snively, Philadelphia, December 28, 1866; Mrs. Sallie E. Ketchum (a niece) Medina County, Texas, September 7, 1866.

CHAPTER FOURTEEN

GIDEON
AND THE ANGELS

This hour 55 years ago saw an active strong young man . . .
leap into a splendid silver-mounted gig with a large black
and very fat horse in the harness; and in the gig, which was
double-seated, sat a beautiful lady . . . Miss Sally Bryan . . .
they rode off . . . Sally to the spirit land, the young man to
Mexico. GID

IF GIDEON died that cold grey February morning when his good companion went away, Tuxpan was his heaven. Perhaps another celestial home awaited, but Tuxpan was his paradise on earth.

The years there were full of hard physical labor, work that would have felled many a younger man. Wresting a livelihood from the soil with toil and sweat was the basis of life, according to Gideon's philosophy, and he believed that each man should produce not only the amount of goods he consumed, but a little extra to discharge his obligation to the helpless. His belief and determination and remarkable physical endurance carried him to impossible achievements.

He longed for his children in Texas to join him, and fretted because they would not shake off the "Yankee yoke" and share his liberty and happiness. He frequently exploded against the Yankees, turncoats, and traitors in Texas and he was often despondent over his inability to make a superrace of the small Campbells.

But Gideon's delight in the tropical richness of the Veracruz country—the bright burning sun, the cooling breeze, and the numerous new plants—was acute and intense. What more could a naturalist ask of life?

He wrote home: "Folks here just die without help when they are old enough and in this climate it rarely occurs more than once to the same individual."

There was an October morning so glorious that he had to write about it to his grandson, Bully, Sallie's son born after Gideon left Texas:

Most bright and beautiful morning. Looks like a fine spring day. Everything is growing so rapidly and the oranges look like yellow blossoms thickly set amongst the dark green leaves. And there is a small lemon tree squarely in front of the window at which I am now writing. It is a nice round-topped tree exceeding twelve feet in height, loaded with ripe lemons. The numerous scarlet flowers of a cypress vine that has twined itself around every branch of the tree seem to seek opportunity to peep out from the thick foliage, side by side with the pale yellow lemons; and, as they are in pairs, nod and blush around the pale faces of their sour-hearted companions. Two large and brilliantly appareled humming birds on quivering wings are subtly sucking their sweets. How would you like to have such a tree—such fruit and such blooms and big, glossy green humming birds in front of your window, Bully?

On such mornings his impatience melted, his annoyances became trivial, and it was an exquisite pleasure to be alive and to be a part of the wonderful new world of Tuxpan.

Cutting through the jungle with a machete to clear land for cultivation was fatiguing drudgery, and many nights Gideon was too exhausted to play his violin. But when at last the land was cleared he could write back to Texas with great pride: "We have subdued the viney jungle which surrounds us, thereby increasing our share of the light of heaven."

Cutting timber beyond the bayou and carrying it in his arms to the clearing where a sugar house was under construction, trimming boards for rafters and door posts, and shaping shingles were usual chores. But after the mill and the furnace were installed and the barrels and cooler ready, there was excitement as well as satisfaction in viewing the large sparkling crystals of the glittering heaps of sugar: "The boys finished the little patch of cane they intended to grind. There were 298 square yards of the cane ground first crop and it has produced over a thousand pounds of the most beautiful sugar. The boys are bragging mightily at their success in producing so fine an article."

Dead-tired at night, he was strengthened by the fresh mornings:

How beautiful and pleasant are our spring mornings. The pretty river, the sweet health-giving early breeze, the rain-like rattle and grand display of the bright green leaves of the luxuriant banana, the substantial promise in the wavy cornfield now in full bloom, the thick growing sugar cane full of sweetness and the ringing songs and love talk of the countless birds in the surrounding blooming forests all combine to make life agreeable—to increase the bliss of being with all who possess the soul principle.

During his first years in Tuxpan, Gideon continued his contributions to the Smithsonian, sending snakes, marsupial rats, vampire bats, boneless frogs, insects, "and perhaps a thousand butterflies" to Baird. The exceptionally fine ears of corn he raised were sent to the New York Agricultural Society by Colonel Bradford of Galveston, his upriver neighbor.

A new arrival in Tuxpan was a Dr. Naphegi, "who seems to be the superintendent of a large sugar refining company" and connected with the U.S. Department of Agriculture as a collecting agent. Dr. Naphegi offered, and Gideon accepted, $25 a month to collect for him. It is not clear how long this arrangement lasted or whether Gideon received payment. If he did it was the first time he was ever paid for his scientific efforts. Gideon wrote Sallie of meeting Dr. Naphegi: "When he was introduced to me he said he was extremely glad to see me—that through the scientific journals he had long known me."

Another arrival who proved to be a congenial companion was a T. Sault from New York, an engineer for a sugar-refining and grass-fiber manufacturing company. Gideon found Sault an "educated man and quite fond of prying into nature's secrets." They went on botanic excursions together and although Sault was "not much of a botanist" he eagerly collected and asked "sensible questions on the subject." After Sault returned to New York, Gideon sent him many new plants.

Two years and nine months after he left Long Point, Gideon wrote in his diary: "We are in full enjoyment of health with plenty of substantials on hand to meet and enjoy the beauties of the incoming spring with its flowers and butterflies."

But the first days in Tuxpan had been discouraging. The day after their arrival Gideon set out to buy a suitable house and discovered he was asked outrageous prices for land he knew sold for a dollar an acre. He was even more dismayed when strangers approached him wanting to borrow money. Borrow money, indeed! He was a poor man and would have to be extremely thrifty until he could attain self-sufficiency by the products of his land. At length he learned the demand on his money was due to a rumor that the eccentric old man with the long flowing white beard had left Texas with $20,000 in gold. He scotched the rumor and was then able to find a house at a fair price on the south side of the Tuxpan River, less than a mile below the landing at the foot of the main thoroughfare. The house was thirty-six feet long and sixteen feet wide, with the parlor in the center, and three bedrooms opening into it. The kitchen and dining room, each sixteen feet square, were detached. The main house paralleled the river, thirty-five yards away. Close by was another structure, eighteen feet square, where the boys slept.

The two acres which came with the house were planted and worked between showers and the rapid growth was a miracle to Gideon. As soon as one crop was harvested, another was planted.

All the boys worked in the field with him, and each one, down to young Lysander, had his own chores; but even the oldest was not big enough for heavy work and on Gideon fell most of the hard labor. Somehow their combined strength was sufficient to clear an additional seventeen acres of jungle land which Gideon had acquired. Three of these acres were planted in plantains, six in sugar cane, the remainder in corn and small crops.

In April, 1869, Molly Hare Lincecum, Gideon's granddaughter, arrived from Texas on the *San Carlos*. Rowing out to the bar where the schooner waited for high tide, Gideon, as he neared the boat, heard the passengers singing loudly and off key. He let out his old Indian warwhoop, which silenced the passengers; and Molly, recognizing her grandfather's call, jumped from the deck into his little boat, leaving behind two devoted admirers. They were LeRoy Alexander, whose family had settled in Tuxpan, and young Mr. Vincent,[1] whose father, Ferrell Vincent, owned a controlling interest in the *San Carlos*. Molly returned to Texas in December, 1869, still single.

Attie became engaged in May, 1869, to Miguel Mirales, an event which brought congratulations from Sioux Doran. Gideon appeared pleased with the match, describing the young man as being from an old and wealthy family engaged in wholesale business and being also "sober, industrious and very polite." But this engagement was broken.

On the twenty-third anniversary of his leaving Columbus for Texas with his family, Gideon wrote Sallie:

Oh, how much better it would have been for my family and for myself too to have brought them here instead of to Texas. The ultimates would have been so very different and so much better. . . . The captain brought me a large bundle of papers. From these I have accounts from almost every county in Texas and positively to a man who loved his country as I once did they contain nothing but oppression and the crushing tramp of aggression. How proud I am that I had the forethought and courage to leave the accursed country before they had the chance to tramp the spirit of liberty out of me. I am not organized to be a cringing sycophantic slave.

When I had settled myself and family with ample homes at Long Point I thought I should finish my course there and be buried among my children. But passing events changed the program and I did not resign my vital force at Long Point, but instead am occupying a delightful home on the banks of the beautiful Tuxpan in the land of liberty. I have not appointed my resting place yet. . . .

I am perfectly horrified at the numerous accounts of shooting, riddling, shot-him-dead, gutting, carving to death, &c., &c., &c. to the end of a long list. Then comes the untrustworthiness of the official corps—embezzlements, defalcations, robberies, woman-killing Ku Klux Klan courts, dragging hundreds of innocent citizens away from their homes in the midst of crop-

---

[1] Young Vincent, also named Ferrell, before serving four years in the Confederate Army, had farmed with his father in Brazoria County, Texas. He and his wife, daughter of a Tuxpan colonist, both died before their son, Mordelo Lee Vincent, was eight years old. Mordelo also married a daughter of a colonist and in 1912 was one of the oil developers at Tepetate, Veracruz. About 1928, Mordelo Lee Vincent and his son, Mordelo, Jr., drilled for oil in Eunice, Louisiana, and eventually were successful in striking. They called their place in Louisiana "Tepetate" and for many years the younger Mordelo maintained contact with Tuxpan (Green Peyton, *America's Heartland, the Southwest* (Norman, University of Oklahoma Press, 1948), pp. 103–110).

ping season to annoy and vex them with a perplexing sham trial on account of a dead negro found in their vicinity. And this devilment is going on at all times throughout Texas.

And this is but a short glance at the demoralized condition of that doomed country. To increase all these hardships and prolong the period of oppression such heartless beings as J. T. Whitfield, Ashbel Smith, J. D. Giddings and C. B. Shepard[2] are permitted by the people to disturb the quietude of the people's fair by their negro speeches in the holy name of Democracy, striving to excite the spirit of revolution. Damn them. I remember C. B. S. and a fine horse sent by the plunderers during the war. Does he want more plunder?

They are, however, all four bad men. They were the ranting instigators of the revolution and robbers during the time of the bloody conflict they had aided in inciting. They robbed Confederates as well as the enemy and in place of being made poor by the disastrous war they and their sort were all

[2] Gideon probably refers to Brigadier General John Wilkins Whitfield, a planter in Lavaca County, Texas, who raised a troop in the county (27th Regiment, Texas Cavalry) which became known as Whitfield's Legion. John T. Whitfield was his nephew and a colonel in the Legion (Paul C. Boethel, *The History of Lavaca County* [San Antonio, Naylor Publishing Co., 1936], pp. 69–70). Whitfield, James Shepard, D. C. Giddings, and Dr. Ashbel Smith joined a coalition group of conservative Secessionists and Unionists immediately after the War, which by 1870 was the Democratic Party in Texas.

Dr. Smith's war service was as captain of the Bayland Guards and brigadier general in command of the defense of Galveston Island. He was one of two commissioners sent to New Orleans to surrender Texas to the Union (*Handbook of Texas*, Vol. II, p. 620).

The Giddings and the Shepards were prominent early Washington County settlers. Jabez Deming Giddings (1814–1878) came to Texas in 1838 to find the body of his brother, Giles, who died of wounds received in the Battle of San Jacinto, and remained to become a lawyer, banker, railroad promoter, and member of the 1866 State Legislature. Four other Giddings brothers joined him in Texas: Dewitt Clinton (1827–1903), a lieutenant colonel in the 21st Texas Cavalry; a member of the 1866 Constitutional Convention, and in 1870 the first Southern Democrat to be seated, after a contest, in Congress; George H., a stage-line owner and mail carrier, was Lincoln's emissary to Texas in an attempt to prevent secession, and, although opposed to secession, commanded Confederate troops on the Rio Grande; and James J. and Frank Giddings (Barker, ed., *Texas and Texans*, p. 1781, 2385).

Seth Shepard (1847–1917), the son of Chauncey Berkeley, and at the age of seventeen enlisted as a private in Company F, 5th Texas Mounted Volunteers. Seth represented Washington County as a state senator, was long a political figure in state politics, and in 1905 was chief justice of the U.S. Court of Appeals (*ibid*, p. 1064.)

In a later letter Gideon summed up his opinion of the two families: "The Shepards and the Giddings—Pshaw! They possess neither honor nor honesty. Why, didn't they steal all they could from both parties all the time of the late war?" He had another complaint against the Shepards: "Chauncey owes me $23 and James E. owes me for a wagonload of corn, $15."

better off at the close than when it commenced. These are the true enemies of the people. They stir up and do all they can to excite internecine division with the hope of self-aggrandizement during the strife and confusion so raised.

Gideon's letters boil with venom against conditions in Texas, but in Tuxpan he lived calmly and at peace with his neighbors. A community fence enclosed the farms of the six American and forty Indian families in his vicinity. Most of the native farmers lived in near-by Tuxpan or at a settlement on the beach near the mouth of the river. About twenty miles upriver was Tumbadero, where John Henry Brown's American colony settled in 1866. Midway between them was another American colony, Zapatal.

Gideon had a small boat in which he sailed downriver to greet all arriving schooners, which usually had to wait at the bar for high water before entering the Tuxpan. The captains, with whom he enjoyed a most cordial relationship, brought him papers, farm equipment, and letters, thereby saving the payment of Mexican postage of twenty-five cents per half ounce regardless of the amount of postage paid at the point of origin. The high cost of communication at one time curtailed his correspondence with his scientist friends.

The *Anna D. Webber* and her "nice little sober Dutch Captain Olde" made regular trips from Galveston, as did the *San Carlos*, the *Petrel*, with Captain Cook, the *Two Brothers*, with Captain Weaver, and the *Witch of the Waves*. The schooner *Time* came from Indianola, the *Hunter*, with Captain Wilson, from Philadelphia for timber, and the *Lizzie*, with Captain Sidney Smith, from Mobile. Anchorage was about two miles out from the river's mouth, and when a strong norther blew up the schooners ran out to open sea for safety. The inhabitants of the Tuxpan area subscribed $8,000 to dredge the Tuxpan River and open a passage across the bar, the Americans pledging $7,200 and the natives the remainder. The project, however, was not accomplished during Gideon's residence there.

The ship captains brought the latest gossip and rumors from Texas and the United States, and they usually invited Gideon aboard for tea and a news session. There were times of great disappointment when no letters came from Sallie, and on one occasion the only thing for him was a parcel containing a new fur hat. He complained to Sallie: "The hat I wore a year or two before I left Texas is still pretty good yet, minus the lining."

The forty-two American families (Gideon's census for 1871), living in the Tuxpan Valley from the river's mouth to Tumbadero, were most gregarious. Entertainment was constant and considerable. Gideon seldom participated but Leonora and her entire tribe never missed an event or fiesta.

It was the custom for the Americans to gather without prearrangement in the plaza at Tuxpan every Saturday night. On one such night they were invited to the home of Mr. and Mrs. C. B. Sojourner, of Texas, who had an interest in the *San Carlos*. The fandango, much to Gideon's annoyance, and through no fault of the hosts, turned into a prayer meeting. One of the guests was Newell Crane, who formerly lived on the Bosque River in Texas and in Tuxpan operated a steam mill. Crane, whom Gideon referred to as "Parson," insisted on holding a religious service from which most of the guests, including Gideon and the hosts, fled. Gideon was delighted when Crane returned to Texas.

Captain Sidney (Gideon sometimes spelled it Sydney) Smith, of the *Lizzie*, who "somehow has got possession of our history and is very kind to us" was one of Lincecum's close friends. Gideon and all the Campbells on the night of November 3, 1872, went three miles up the river to Paso Real to attend Smith's marriage to Mark Mitchell's "last daughter."

Gideon found an agreeable companion in a near neighbor, Dr. Joel Spencer, forty-five–year–old widower, originally from Iowa but more recently from Brazoria, Texas, who lived with his young son and bachelor brother. Spencer was always free to drop by the Lincecum house at night for violin duets, their repertory consisting of about twenty old tunes. Together they sailed down the river on exploring expeditions, examining bluffs and hauling home their finds. They raked osyter beds and made soup of the oysters, which were "very large and as fat and white as a lump of curd."

Another congenial friend was Major Phillip A. Work,[3] of Wood-

---

[3] Although Gideon refers to Work as major, he was a lieutenant colonel in command of the 1st Texas Regiment under Hood. (*Chaplain Davis and Hood's Texas*

ville, Texas, a signer of the Texas ordinance of secession and an officer in the Civil War. He represented a Philadelphia lumber company. Major Work often stopped at daybreak on the river before the Lincecum house and called out to Gideon to join him in a sail to the bar, where natives were loading the company boat. While the Major supervised the loading, Gideon walked the sandy beaches gathering shells. They lunched at one of the Indian houses in the fishing village, where a "very handsome, full-blooded Indian, as clean as a new pin" served stewed pork with potatoes, boiled rice, fried eggs, hashed sausage, tortillas, frijoles hot with red pepper, and coffee. The meal over and the sea breeze blowing upriver, they hoisted sail and glided the six miles home in an hour.

Leonora and her children quickly adapted themselves to life in Mexico and became very popular members of the community. Their friends, both natives and Americans, were frequent visitors, and Leonora often went for weekend visits with families living upriver. There were group picnics on the beach, excursions up the river, and numerous fiestas in the plaza.

Unable to afford sending the children to the American school in Tuxpan, Gideon taught them himself. They picked up Spanish easily and, with their native garments and their sun-darkened skin, were often regarded as natives by new arrivals. Leonora found the Mexicans gentle, cultured, and gracious. She encouraged her children to associate with them rather than with the Americans, some of whom she found crude and unmannerly.

Their happiness the first year was marred by the death of little Lutie, the youngest of the family, a victim of a tropical fever. The thought of his own death was with Gideon daily and he wrote to Sallie: "I have laid a good foundation here which I shall, ere long, leave. And then Leonora will get along badly, she is such a poor manager. I do wish Lucullus or Lysander or both would get here before I go. It would rejoice me to see them here before that event takes place."

Sallie urged him to return to Texas, assuring him he could find happiness there. But Gideon replied: "You say you feel like we are all exiles and that it is a hard life for *me*. Exile is not the proper term.

Brigade, Donald E. Everett, ed., Principia Press of Trinity University, [San Antonio, 1962], p. 165).

We are *refugees,* fled from the land of oppression, from our ruined houses, lost freedom, heavy taxation, domineering Yankee, triumphant negro and the ugliest thing of all, the poor turncoats who joined the Loyal Leaguers."[4]

You tell me I would be so happy there. If you think what you say it shows that you have forgotten the character and status of your father's nature. Are *you* happy there? If so . . . as there is no safety outside the circle of the Loyal Leaguers, you are one of them.

Think of *me* as a member of the grand jury of Washington County sitting along side of my equals, Theodore Stamps, John W. Johnson, Lumbkin Frederick—negroes of low thieving character while in bondage—and then say what amount of happiness you would suppose me to be in the enjoyment of.[5]

It is not at the negro that my settled hatred is pointed for I know that he was placed where he is without the asking by the victorious Yankees, the enemies of human freedom, and it is upon them and the poor sordid creatures who for the sake of saving a few dollars have bent the knee to them that my curses fall. With such people I could not consent to spend my time. No, no, Sarah, you must excuse me. I can never, while possessing my common intellectuality voluntarily consent to abandon this quiet, peace-

[4] The Loyal Union League was organized by Texas Unionists and carpetbaggers to instruct Negroes in civic matters and to align them with the Republican Party. The Ku Klux Klan and the Knights of the White Camellia were organized to combat the League. G. T. Ruby, a New York-born (1841) mulatto who came to Texas after the War to establish Negro schools, was president of the Loyal Union League, member of the Constitutional Convention of 1868, and representative of the Galveston district as state senator in the Twelfth and the Thirteenth Legislatures (J. Mason Brewer, *Negro Legislators of Texas,* [Dallas, Mathis Publishing Co., 1935], pp. 26–27, 115).

[5] During the Reconstruction, Negroes found their military and political services in demand by the Texas Republican Party. Outvoting the whites, they served as jurors, public officials, and state legislators. The 1868 vote for a constitutional convention was an overwhelming victory for the Radical Republicans. There were 44,689 votes for the convention, of which 36,932 were Negro votes, and 11,440 votes against the convention, of which 818 votes were Negro votes.

Matthew Gaines (1842–1900), a Negro living in Brenham, was a state senator from Washington County, 16th District, from 1870 through 1875. Ben O. Watrous, a Negro, was one of the three Washington County delegates to the 1868 convention, which included nine Negroes. Negro state representatives from Washington County during Reconstruction were Allen Wilder, of Chappell Hill, 1873; John Mitchell, of District 17, 1874; B. A. Guy, of William Penn (a community between Independence and Washington settled by Germans before the Civil War), 1879; Andrew L. Sledge, of Chappell Hill, 1879; R. J. Moore, of Brenham, 1883–1887. Negroes and white radicals remained in numerical control of the Texas Republican Party until the late 1890's (*ibid,* pp. 125–128).

ful land of liberty and seek bondage in such a lawless country as you invite me to. I shall never cross the limits of the U.S.A. again. All who desire to see me will call on me here or not see me anymore forever.

Determined to leave the Campbells secure and safe, Gideon labored from early morning until dark. The tasks were endless—clearing a lot for planting South American grass, repairing the community fence, tarring the boat, killing hogs, harvesting the plantains, grinding corn and sugar cane, and building a well house. But there was joy in his work: "Finished the well house and we are proud of that addition of substantial property to our little stock of wealth. Oh! if we had only a little more intellectual force we could steer our ship better."

Occasional illness filled him with dread, and when he was unable to do his work and had to stand and watch the children "lift and grunt and struggle with their awkwardness," Gideon agonized.

In May, 1871, Gideon noted:

When I set out for Mexico my most sanguine expectation extended no farther than to get Lee and her children away from the negroes and settle them in a home where they might learn to sustain self by labor of their own hands. The thought that I should remain with them in the enjoyment of the sweet climate—the pretty river, the delightful seashore picnics, the glorious luscious sweet fruits and sugar cane and honey and, above all, perfect uninterrupted freedom—until I should gather six thoroughly matured crops never entered my head even in the form of a wish. I know not how much longer my special care and constitutional forces will sustain me; but while they do I have a highly furnished field for enjoyment of every moment. Oh! had I come here when I was a *man*.

One of his minor worries was his family's fondness for pork. Hogs were frequently killed and appeared almost daily on the table. Gideon once remarked that "It is to be hoped that all those who have died from the disease brought on by gormandizing on grease and fresh pork may have the privilege of going to hog heaven." He feared the young Campbells were headed for hog heaven, judging by the amount of pork they consumed. During the first year in Tuxpan, when the family supplies were purchased in the market, a pound of lard and eight pounds of beef were ample for a week, their diet supplemented by fresh and cooked fruit. Gideon considered grease as injurious to health as tobacco and whiskey.

He observed: "Now when we have plenty of pork they care nothing for the fruit but show their nature by gobbling up, Perkins like, dishes of fat meat swimming in grease. They are all animals belonging to the genus carnivora. Nothing further can be looked for from them." But he tried, and walked miles through the lovely jungles gathering fruit —oranges, lemons, mangos, avocados, papayas, and guavas. He insisted that bananas be served at every meal. He described all the beautiful fruit to Sallie and remarked: "You talk of your fruit! You have nothing there, not even in Watson's[6] horticultural garden, that would compensate for the absence of these species of forest fruit trees."

When the fish were running fat the entire family packed up for expeditions to the beach and brought the boat back loaded with their catch. Sometimes Gideon went alone, walking the sands to observe sea coast ants and Portuguese men of war. He frequently encountered a lone Indian fisherman, who for a few pennies would cast his net for Gideon and sometimes haul in as many as twenty-five fat, fine-flavored *mujeres*. He wove a basket for trapping shrimp, to be used as both family food and fish bait. Gideon's fingers were so sore from this intricate weaving that he was unable to perform on the violin when Dr. Spencer made his nightly call.

The jungles not only provided luscious fruit but were full of game, with which Gideon kept the family well supplied. At times he brought home a *chachalaca*, "about as large as a half-grown chicken and with a long tail, meat dark brown and on the plate looks like a picked chicken and about the same thing." His favorite fowl was the *perdis*, "a true partridge nearly as large as a prairie hen and certainly the greatest delicacy in the feathered kingdom." In the thickets he found the white-winged dove, "about the size and form of the turtle dove with a great white bar on the back of their wings and the naked border around the eyes of the male bird as blue as indigo, meat black like that of the turtle dove and about the same in flavor."

Squirrel meat won the approval of the family. The Tuxpan variety was, so he wrote Sallie, "larger than your fox squirrel; head, ears, back

---

6 William Watson was a pioneer Texas horticulturalist who from 1860 to 1897 owned and operated the Rosedale Nursery, the first one established in Texas, located about two miles east of Brenham (*Handbook of Texas*, Vol. II, p. 870). A number of Rosedale catalogues are in the Lincecum papers.

and tail gray; belly, throat and inner parts of the legs quite red; tender as chicken and very nicely flavored, having none of the squirrel taste belonging to that race of animals in your country." Frequently and triumphantly he returned from his hunt with a deer slung over his shoulders.[7]

Despite his worries, his little brood thrived and had few of the ailments common among the American colonists. Gideon, too, was in excellent health and on April 12, 1871, noted: "Ten more days and I shall be 78 years of age. When I look back on the two years and ten months I have resided in Mexico, it seems almost as distant in the vista of the bygone years as it does when I left Columbus, Mississippi." Letters giving news of illness among his Texan friends found little sympathy from Gideon: "In the dire contest and daily struggle you are all forced to keep up with negroes and the thieving Yankees I wonder you don't all have dyspepsia and the dry gripes too."

At dawn on his birthday, Gideon and all the Campbells and many of his neighbors sailed down the river in their boats to the south beach. With them were Mrs. [Angel] Becerra, their closest Mexican friend, her brother, and her four children and the Oliver Searcys, Lincecum's near-neighbor, and their four children.

The boys gathered firewood and the women cooked breakfast and served it on a smooth driftwood log. After breakfast Gideon and his grandson John walked the beach until it met a jungle of thorns and prickles, and here they stopped and stripped for a swim. Gideon wrote:

We played in the briney breakers for at least an hour. It is frightful to look upon the foamy breakers, full of sharks and grampi, as they come roaring and dashing their froth-capped heads on the sea-beaten sands. Yet we not only looked at them but we fearlessly plunged into even the third wave which without hesitation receives you in its briney bosom, envelopes you in its frothy vestments and whirling you shoreward, heels upward light as a feather without regard to your posture or position, casts you on the sands.

This is certainly the most amusing, delightful and healthful recreation in the world. Octogenarian as I am, I enjoy it exceedingly. While swimming and buffeting with the dashing billows of the old ocean I experience as I

---

[7] John Henry Brown, who visited Lincecum on his seventy-fifth birthday, tells in Gideon's obituary (Dallas *Morning News*, December 12, 1874) of his going hunting during this visit and bringing back a deer across his shoulders, over a distance of two or three miles.

float, the full glow of youthful vivacity and I say to myself: "Am I not a boy again?"

After the swim the old man and the young boy joined the others and found Mrs. A. M. Boyd, wife of a former Fort Bend County, Texas, doctor.[8] She had walked over from the village on the north beach, where she was staying for the sea bathing. The group accepted her invitation to lunch at her beach house. When the afternoon breeze started up they sailed home with the wind.

Gideon's writing desk was in front of a window, giving a full view of the river. One morning he described the scene: "Wind SW, clear, very pleasant. It is a beautiful morning, full of life and music. The river is clear, tranquil and smooth, reflecting the tree tops on the opposite side of the river. Here I now sit making these ill-constructed sentences." In the afternoon he added:

Well, the day's work is done and the boys gone to play and I sit at my old oaken table with mind perfectly blank. I look out upon the pretty river and behold, driven by the strong sea breeze, the big white-capped waves chasing one another hurriedly to the westward with the broken cloud shadows and shimmering sunlight racing and dancing upon its foamy bosom. And not a single thought worthy of a place here does it excite in my old brain. There is, however, from my window—taking into view the opposite shore with its street, row of grass-covered huts, the dense forest and far-off green hilltops in the background—a picture worthy of the artist's finest pencil. In the foreground on my side the orange, lemon, pomegranate and the big, flourishing mustang grape vine, the seed of which was sent in a letter by Dr. C. B. Stewart, Danville, Texas,[9] are altogether about to close the river scenery. It is as thick as my wrist, two years old, and is the only mustang vine in the country. I fear it is a male.

Gideon's life was not always so tranquil. He had his days of discouragement, as when he wrote to Sallie:

[8] Dr. A. M. Boyd, who had imported a printing press to Tuxpan, on December 29, 1871, printed the first newpaper to appear there. Dr. and Mrs. Boyd celebrated the event by inviting friends to a "grand ball."

[9] Charles Bellinger Stewart (1806–1885) was a druggist in Brazoria in 1830; later he practiced medicine in Montgomery. His first wife was Julia Sheppard, of Washington, Texas; after her death he married Mrs. Elizabeth Nichols Boyd (*Handbook of Texas*, Vol. II, p. 671). Lincecum often visited Stewart in Danville, where he had a number of close friends, among them Major Green Wood and Charles Abercrombie.

The object for which I came to Mexico has turned out a failure. I thought I could train these children to see the propriety of honest labor. They possess no capacity for self-sustaining improvement and I have failed. I have urged them incessantly two years and nine months to rise early and wash their hands and faces and have succeeded with only two of them—John and Lysander. Bud has grown to be a great, big, dirty booby and stinks so strong of tobacco smoke that you can smell him afar off. George is ill-natured with a strong strain of his father's trait in him. Lee has no controlling powers. I know not what will become of them when I—

When Porfirio Díaz launched a revolution against President Benito Juárez, the Texas papers were full of it. Lincecum's knowledge of the fighting was from verbal reports picked up in the village. He felt there was no danger to him and the Campbells and he was vexed when his children in Texas urged him to flee back to the safety of Texas. Taking advantage of his discouragement and the Revolution, both Sallie and Lysander pressed him to come home and implied that they didn't believe a word he wrote about the wonders of Mexico.

Gideon snapped back:

How little you know of my nature; and of, on all serious subjects, my unswerving veracity. For what purpose do you and Lysander suppose or imagine that my letters, extending to many quires of paper, were written? Myself, the country, its people and its products are all I have to write about; and I find that after doing the best I could for three years to post you correctly, to make you acquainted with my condition, both physically and mentally, my surroundings and prospects, good and bad, you doubt me.

Lysander invites me to go back and live with him, that I shall have everything I want and travel up the Rio Grande for several months. You do the same, only in place of the Rio Grande you will place me where I can see the railroad trains passing.

At best, a few more turns of time's great wheel will overwhelm the author and his trash, hurling them together into the lap of oblivion.

I have two or three times told you that I shall never see that accursed country again. How could you think it anything amiss if this should be the last line you ever got from

Your Father

Thereafter, Gideon seldom wrote to Sallie and not at all to Lysander. He addressed most of his letters to his grandson, Bully, obviously too young to read. This was Lincecum's way of showing his annoyance with his children for doubting the honesty of his remarks concerning the happiness he found in Tuxpan.

In the first of many communications to "My Dear Grandson," Gideon wrote: "Grandpa thinks of Bully often; and that may be because he has never seen you. Which is perhaps best. For were we to meet and I should discover that you, like the rest of my posterity, are not capacitated to aid in pushing forward the car of progress, I should count as nought."

It was not the first time the irascible old doctor had terminated correspondence with a beloved relative. He told Bully about an incident which ended his correspondence with Garland, his brother:

"Dranpa" long ago had a dear brother. He died fourteen or fifteen years ago. He came to his death from an over dose of morphine administered by the hands of a drunken scamp of a doctor. Don't you hate drunkards? You must never drink any kind of inebriating liquors. Do you hear?

But I was talking about my dearest brother. He was my oldest brother. We worked together, hunted together, played together and when we were separated we kept up perpetual correspondence. No two brothers ever loved each other more sincerely. But, notwithstanding all this familiarity and brotherly affection, he did not know me. He had never discovered that I am not a musical instrument, a thing upon which any kind of tune may be played. And so, in his ignorance of my true character, he made inquiry by letter in reference to a certain subject, of which I knew nothing and in my reply to his letter, wrote to that effect. In his answer he showed that he did not believe me. He doubted my veracity. My mortification was poignant and though he lived long after and wrote letters to me, I never penned another line to him.

Silas Wood, your uncle San's daddy-in-law, previous to my removal to this lovely land, requested me, as did many others, that as soon as I had made myself acquainted with the most prominent features of the country, to write to him. In due time I did so, and in his reply of fifteen lines he took occasion to doubt the statements I had made in my letter to him. Well, he got no more letters from me. . . .

I hope, my dear Bully, that you are organized for the love of truth; and that you may prize it highly as to enable you to recognize and appreciate the faculty wherever it may be found. I will say no more on the subject, my Bully, but will ask you to tell Uncle San that *Dranpa* thanks him very kindly for his proposition to go and live with him, do nothing, have every-thing I want and travel three months every year away out on the Rio Grande. Tell him that I would do so with pleasure were it not for the fact that I should dislike to exchange the beautiful evergreen fruitful valley of the Tuxpan with its pleasant climate, delightful scenery and my good health for the grassless ruined prairies, dried-up water courses, sun-scorched summers and terrible winter northers with its rheumatisms, croup and phthisis of Texas, to say nothing of the presence of the accursed Yankee and his thieving proclivities. Beg to be excused. The Rio Grande indeed!

Suppose your Uncle San and I were seated on its banks and my mind should fly away to the beautiful Tuxpan with its broad quiet bosom, limpid waters and picturesque shores and I could throw him into a clairvoyant con-dition, open up to his view the full glare of the Tuxpan scenery—its grand panorama. What would be his feelings comparing this with the Rio Grande —that narrow little mountain drain with its turbid waters, barren shores, wide sun-scorched wastes and drifting sands in the rainless region of Texas?

No, no. Can't consent to leave this country of good, kind, honest, decent people to go with your Uncle San amongst the robbers on the Rio Grande nor to reside with him in the interior of Texas amongst the Yankees, niggers and your Uncle J. V. Matson.

And tell your Mamma, Bully, that I thank her for her kind proposition but cannot accept. The harsh grating rumble, dust, ashes, sparks, rattle and unearthly screaching of a passing R.R. train may produce very agreeable excitement for her organisms. For me, however, and it may be attributable to the way I was raised or to my want of refined taste, I would prefer wit-nessing the action of ships and every variety of lesser water crafts with their white wings noiselessly gliding to and fro and in all directions on the pure waters of our pretty river. These sights will do for me, Bully, now that I am old, and tell your Mamma that I do not admire the reconstructing Yankees' plan for remodeling Southern society.

Fully confident that his ailing son Lysander would join him in Tuxpan, Gideon bought another farm and started cultivating it. Both Lysander and Sallie not only made plans to join him but several times informed him of their sailing schedule. Each time Gideon and the Campbells met the *San Carlos* expecting to greet them, but neither Lysander, who once went so far as to board a boat at Galveston, nor Sallie ever came. Each time old Gideon's heart broke with disappoint-ment and as late as 1872 he appealed to Sallie through her small son: "Do come, Bully, It will make me live, if not longer, at least more agreeably." The old frontiersman could not understand the timidity which kept his children anchored to Texas nor why they did not share his spirit of rebellion: "My proud Democratic *Lincecum soul,* which is the only one of that kind left, can never submit to the tyrannic rule of the thieving Yankee."

Gideon resigned himself that his children would not join him and settle down in happiness on his Tuxpan acreage. The ache in his heart for his children, whom he frequently berated but deeply loved, went with him into the fields while he labored, and into the plaza in Tuxpan, where he sipped fruit juice in the sun and talked to other old Texas rebels.[10]

[10] Some of the "Texas Rebels" mentioned by Brown were T. J. M. Richardson, Colonel, 3rd Regiment, Texas State Cavalry, of Brazoria County; James G. Montgomery, Major, 4th Texas Regiment, Company C, his family and his niece, Mary Mc-Neill, of Old Caney; William T. Townsend, of Colorado County; E. Luter and Youngs Coleman, of Goliad; Samuel Andrews and John A. King, "an old Texas surveyor past 60," both of DeWitt County; H. G. Little of Fort Bend County; Daniel Montague, for whom Montague County, Texas, was named; Joseph and H. B. Anderson, of San Antonio; Dr. and Mrs. R. M. Collins, who settled twelve miles up the Tuxpan; Judge William D. Mitchell, who died in Tuxpan in 1866, and his son, J. R. Mitchell; Captain Charles C. Linn, of Victoria; Dr. Autry, a Fort Bend County physician who married a wealthy Mexican and lived on an estate at Papantla; Major William Quayles, of Tarrant County; Albert Gallatin, a San Jacinto veteran who had been in Texas since 1832; Dr. Louis A. Ogle and son, of Bell County; George Bell, Brown's brother-in-law, and family; Alexander McAlister, Benjamin Cage, Jackson Stubbs, F. Smith, Virgil H. Phelps, Thomas and Pierre M. Brown, Henry Young, Edward Coleman, C. Stewart, General H. B. Lyons, a surveyor, and Messrs. Lambkin, Wites, Branch, Cook, and Hammock. Among the Southerners were Colonel F. T. Mitchell, a Methodist minister from Missouri, who lived between Potosí and Tampico on a five-thousand-acre haciendo; P. S. Dyer and William Albert; Platt Z. Thrush, of Mississippi; Henry Clay Jones, of Missouri; J. Wilkins, of Tennessee; and F. Porter, of South Carolina.

In addition Lincecum mentions the following: James M. Buchanan, of South Carolina, a lawyer who left Tuxpan in 1870 to join his wife in Chappell Hill, Texas. Gideon wrote letters of introduction for him to John Sayles, B. H. Bassett and J. D. Giddings, Washington County lawyers and bankers. Buchanan was traveling with his three sons. One of them was three-year-old James Paul, who grew up in Washington County and served as congressman from 1913 to 1937, part of that time as chairman of the House Appropriations Committee, and for whom Buchanan Dam in Texas is named.

Also: Miss Phoebe Barnett, in Tuxpan for her health, living with the Bradfords; Martin Glover; Mrs. Loebnitz, also seeking health and accompanied by her husband, Captain Henry E. Loebnitz of Houston; Jesse Mercer, a former state representative for whom Mercer's Gap, Comanche County, is named, and a Mr. Chisolm (Chisum?), who sought out Gideon when they arrived; a Mr. Coleman, whom he described as "a very aged man" of Grimes County and who, one of the original Tuxpan settlers, after a trip to Texas had returned.

George Bradford, a twenty-four-year-old doctor from Galveston, arrived in Tuxpan, met, and fell in love with Attilia Campbell. Gideon considered him an industrious young man "having as good a knowledge of the science of medicine as is common among doctors." It was his proud duty to accompany George and Dr. Boyd to the alcalde's office where, in accordance with Mexican custom, the bans were issued. Gideon wore a white linen shirt and trousers, of the finest material in the local market, sewed by Leonora on the machine brought with them

---

Dr. T. O. Alford practiced medicine at Ozuluama, sixty or seventy miles above Gideon's home, and came to him for prescriptions. Alford was the brother of Mrs. L. N. Halbert, one of Lincecum's Washington County neighbors.

Mr. Dalton, seventy-eight, Mrs. Dalton, fifty-six, and Mr. Daniels, seventy-four, all from Galveston, arrived in 1871. Gideon reported that when he, Dalton, and Daniels got together they "made a merry trio." One of his neighbors, a Mr. Price, died in October, 1871, and Gideon attended his funeral. He left a wife and a thirteen-year-old daughter and "no other relatives."

Dr. Franklin (apparently Dr. John A. Franklin, who practiced medicine in Columbus, Mississippi, visited Tuxpan and wrote an account of the Lincecums which was published in the Columbus (Mississippi) *Index*. A number of Gideon's old and long-lost friends read the item and wrote to him. Among them was Charles McLaren, then living in St. Louis, who had "married his second wife, an heiress" in 1853. The Charles McLaren home in Columbus, Mississippi, built several years before the Civil War, is one of the local show places. Dr. M. B. Franklin of Seguin, Texas, was in Tuxpan in 1866, but returned in November, 1867, when he wrote an account of the colony for the Lavaca *Commercial*. William H. Russell, LaGrange, who wrote a report on the progress of the Texas Boundary Survey for the *Texas Almanac, 1860,* pp. 182–187, was on the boat with Gideon on his voyage to Tuxpan.

Gideon's friend Naphegi was doubtless Gabor Naphegi, an Hungarian who had extraordinary control of the declining Santa Anna and who, according to the Mexican ex-President's son, tried to poison him. Though in exile until 1874, Santa Anna owned considerable property in Veracruz. (Frank C. Hanigher, *Santa Anna— Napoleon of the West* [New York, Coward-McCann, 1934] pp. 298–300). Gideon found Naphegi's book *Days in the Great Saraha* well-written and most interesting. Kelly, identified by Gideon as "an industrious Irishman," killed himself after a riotous drunk. Brown listed an Alfred Kelly among the 1866 settlers. Gideon's "good old friend," Dr. Alexander of Louisiana, died of dropsy. Mrs. Alexander sent for Gideon to look in on him but Gideon found his condition hopeless.

Of two other residents, apparently known to Sallie, Gideon wrote: "Mrs. Chambers has gone bravely to work and Dr. Weston thinks of getting a situation on the Railroad when old lady Chambers fails to feed and clothe him."

Others not otherwise identified are Mr. Owen, Naphegi's agent in Tuxpan; Captain Shelby of whom Gideon wrote "My good friend is gone—dead"; Paris (?) Andrews, Henry Mitchell, Jo Harrell, and Mr. Hobbs, who lived at Tumbadero; a Dr. Lelands from England; and Mr. and Mrs. Huddleston.

The Mark Mitchells, who had gone overland in 1867 to Tumbadero and then to Paso Real, were on friendly terms with Lincecum and the Campbells. They had two sons and two daughters, one of whom was Marie, "a lively, clever young lady."

from Texas. When visiting in town this was his customary garb, put on at Leonora's insistence and with many protests from him.

Gideon was joyfully optimistic about the marriage:

Fifteen days hence the nuptial ceremonies will be consummated. This will constitute him my grandson-in-law and to him I shall resign my portion of the battlefield upon which we contend for subsistence. He is a large, strong, healthy young man. Seems to be willing; and, like all willing folk, can do anything that comes to hand. . . . I feel proud of him and look upon it as a fortunate circumstance for Leonora and her children for it won't be long before I go and they would get along badly in any country.

Attie's wedding was the occasion for a big celebration among the fun-loving natives and colonists. Leonora yielded to the guests' wishes for dancing and permitted the wedding and reception to be held in town at the large home of their friends, the Becerras. Leonora killed and prepared a shoat and baked a cake and Don Angel Becerra cooked a big gobbler and provided the wine.

The civil ceremony lasted an hour, after which "the kissing and cackling went around as at an American occasion of that kind."

Attie and George divided the Lincecum parlor into two rooms "with a very neatly constructed canvas partition" and planned to live with the family until lumber for a house of their own arrived from Galveston.

Gideon predicted: "They are young and healthy and by proper course of industry and frugality may, in a short time, very easily in this glorious country establish for themselves a paradise of a home. On the other route, hunger and rags."[11]

Gideon, during his residence in Tuxpan, never ceased his scientific studies, despite the demands on his time. Ants still engaged his first attention and he found the *Bravo* ants of particular interest.[12] He welcomed these invaders and prepared for their annual visits by tucking mosquito bars under all the beds. The remainder of the house was

[11] Their son, Andrew L. Bradford, a retired marine engineer, at this writing is living in Marble Falls, Texas. With Dr. Thomas Campbell, of the University of Texas, he edited his great-grandfather's journal for the *Southwestern Historical Quarterly*. Attie, his mother, later married George S. Qualls.

[12] This was Gideon's name for the ants, probably a genera of the *Dorylinae* or army ants.

open to the visitors. The family kept out of the way and watched the ants follow their plan of invasion:

It was not only ingenious but extensive and wonderful to witness. Great numbers of them were dispatched from the main army into the house and were seen rapidly running over the walls in all directions and into the cracks and crevises and all the hiding places to be found, routing out every species of insects. While this was going on inside the house the main body in countless thousands spread themselves on the ground like a carpet in a belt three or four feet wide. Soon the frightened roaches, ants, stinking pumpkin bugs, spiders and many other creeping things were to be seen escaping from the invading foe in the house.

The ants inside did not capture many of the insects, for it seemed to be orders to drive them out to the devouring hosts who were ready to seize and devour everything that came out. By daylight they had all disappeared."

Young George Bradford took over as supervisor of farm activities. Gideon summarized:

It is all in good condition now. All clean with a fine growing crop of corn, sugar cane and one thousand hills of plantains and bananas, besides the small crops. A good horse, cart and farming tools besides a copious sugar house, mill, coolers, etc., and a pen full of fat hogs. . . . I hope they may do well on it, but go as it may I shall work no more. I have done three years hard, daily labor besides paying out $1500 to fix this substantial, pleasant home.

Gideon went on an expedition to a group of round-topped hills, visible from his front window, which he had long wanted to explore. He wrote Bully about it: "I found the scenery surprisingly beautiful and the entire view as far as I went was full of geological interest. I spent nearly all day on and amongst those singularly grouped volcanic tumors. On their tops, in their narrow deep gulches and up and down their steep sides I passed the interesting day alone."

On other days his walks took him by the houses of American colonists, where he always found a welcome. Working his way through the vines and undergrowth, Gideon came out at the house of Dr. Alexander and his son, LeRoy, where he sat and talked for an hour, and then disappeared again in the green jungle. Noon found him at the McKinney place, upriver, where he was invited to lunch. Mrs. Mc-

Kinney had just finished squeezing out twenty-five gallons of honey. He ate some of the honey, and cool clabber and fried mangoes, which he found superior to fried apples.

Homeward, he called on his old asthmatic friend, Andrews, who begged Gideon to stay the weekend. But Gideon was not given to long visits and set off again, passing through Cabello Blanco, a small Indian village paralleling the water front. Gideon was on friendly easy terms with the Mexican Indians, finding them much like those of Alabama and Mississippi: "And with these as with all the tribes I ever dwelt with they shall never have it to say that my tongue is forked. They are all friendly to me and look upon me as being one of the common sort and are willing to do anything I ask of them."[13] The women and boys ran out of the grass houses to greet the old man, examining his collection with interest and asking numerous questions. From the village Gideon walked home, arriving at sundown. He recorded his day's collection and after supper "made music" on his old violin.

When a dry spell dropped the river level, a landslide on the bluffs exposed some ancient graves. Major Work stopped by to tell him of it and show him some human bones he had picked up. The news excited Gideon who, curious about the graves, sought information on their origin from his Indian friends. The bluff, they told him, was once part of the ancient and grand city of Tabuco (or Tambuc) which had been cut away by the river. The bluff was backed by a grassy marsh which was once an extensive lake, the natives told him. The inhabitants left their crumbling city and moved to the present site of Tuxpan.

Beyond this ruin was another ancient city, Tomilco (or Tuspa), which Gideon and an Indian guide explored. Wading knee-deep in swampy water blocked by large hewn stones and stonework, Gideon found a pattern of pavement, two streets crossing at right angles and pointing to the four cardinal points of the compass. A volcanic upheaval, Gideon thought, caused the destruction of the city. He picked

---

[13] Dr. Addison Lincecum, a grandson, was greatly interested in entomology and made a special study of the fly and mosquito. In 1917 his research and curiosity took him to Tuxpan. Although it had been forty-four years since his grandfather was there, Dr. Addison found some very old Indians who remembered Gideon with reverence. They pointed out to him the exact location of his house and farm. Not a trace of Gideon remained in Tuxpan except the love for him in the memories of the Indians (Dr. Addison to the author in an interview).

up shell ornaments curiously carved, with a hole for stringing; a stone leg and foot; a human skeleton, bones folded together, arms on the thighs; broken pottery, tools, and flint knives.

Returning home Gideon was attracted by something white glittering in the bushes and vines half way up the bluff of the river. Weary as he was he climbed the bluff and was amazed to find a stalk of cotton with four bolls "puffed out fully as large as tea cups." It was superb cotton, the fiber long and snowy white and, while it was similar to other cotton plants, the stalk was a vine about ten feet long. It was the first native cotton Gideon had seen that produced mature bolls. He surmised that the seed had lodged on the bluff during a freshet and the plant had pushed its stalk out of the underbrush to the sun at the outer edge.

In his unexpected release from farm labor Gideon was often in Tuxpan seeking out new arrivals from Texas. He was seldom disappointed. Once he met Judge Munson,[14] owner of the schooner *Webber,* who had a large sugar plantation nine miles above Tuxpan. They talked several hours and Gideon reported:

I obtained from him—for he seemed to be well posted—the agricultural and political prospects of Texas. He is very interesting in conversation and his free lucid replies to my questions caused me to feel proud that I had escaped when I did. A few associates with such trained minds as Judge Munson possesses would brighten up the silent monotony of my condition very much. It would stimulate the now almost unexplored regions of thought and place the bliss of being here on a more exalted plane.

Another Munson[15] was a visitor, puttering about the garden and making himself useful. Gideon "figured Munson wasn't obligated to us but apparently he felt differently." He identified this Munson as

[14] Gideon gives every man a title—doctor, judge, captain etc. The "Judge" Munson he refers to could have been Mordello Stephen Munson, a native Texan (1825–1903), a lawyer and farmer, and a state representative, living in Brazoria in 1860 and in Columbia in 1867 (*Members of the Legislature of the State of Texas from 1846 to 1939* [Austin, n.p., 1939], pp. 35, 55).

[15] A Jesse Munson, skilled in sugar making, was overseer in 1851 and 1852 for the sugar crop at Peach Point, the Perry-Bryan plantation a few miles above the mouth of the Brazos River (Abigail Curlee, "History of a Texas Slave Plantation, 1832–1863," *Southwestern Historical Quarterly,* Vol. XXVI (1922–1923), pp. 79–127).

"overseer for J. Bryan, lived at Ceph Stamp's place . . . and is old and deaf and almost helpless."

Gideon's new freedom from farm chores provided a long-sought opportunity to make an expedition to the pyramids southeast of Papantla. Lincecum had heard many stories about them from his Indian friends, one of whom agreed to guide him to the site, deep in the jungles.

The ancient structures recalled to Gideon the tradition of the Choctaw Indians told by his long-ago friend, Chahta-Immataha. The Choctaw told Lincecum that his tribe had departed from Mexico when Cortés began his conquest.

After Gideon's exploration of the area, he wrote to Sallie:

In the numerous piles of ruined cities . . . are found ample proof of what that old Indian, Chahta-Immataha told me. It is but 75 miles from here to the place where the "three big canoes with wings" were first seen by the fishermen. They are fishing, drying and packing their fish to the big stone city yet, exactly as they were doing when the winged canoes with the thunder on board arrived and frightened them more than 300 years ago.[16]

These ruined cities which are numerous and most large and extensive are built of stone and clay in the manner of coarse concrete work and well done. Some extensive walls are still in good state of preservation. One solid mass of stonework, 100 feet square at the base, 40 feet in height, shape pyramidical. There are many flights of stairs still perfect reaching to the top which is solid and firm like the rest of the structure and near the center on top is erected a small oblong room, open at the top, about six feet wide and seven feet long and about the same in height.

Worked in the wall inside of the superstructure on opposite sides are two seats or benches. No door or place of entrance has yet been discovered to this vast pile of well-laid rocks. It is not even known that it is hollow and no conjecture has as yet been proposed as to its use or for what purpose it was constructed in the very center of an immense city. The dilapidated houses and finely paved streets are closely scattered for miles around. I happen to know what it all means well enough, for Chahta-Immataha communicated the history of these ruined cities to me long ago. These people are sun worshippers. The great stone pile I have alluded to is the Temple of the Sun.[17]

[16] Gideon apparently refers to Zempoalo, north of Veracruz, Mexico, where according to Bernal Díaz, Cortés visited before going on to present Mexico City.

[17] El Tajin, a major archaeological site in Mexico, was successfully concealed by

Another day, after a visit to the Tuxpan plaza, Lincecum wrote: "Just returned from town. I did not speak more than howdy to anyone except old drunken Jim Scott of Texas notoriety. He is not drunk today; was quite conversant showing himself to be a well-read man. He is pretty familiar with the principles of the Darwinian theory. I sat with him at least an hour and felt myself highly interested."

Cinco de Mayo began at dawn with the firing of cannons, ringing of bells and marching music from strolling bands. The noise kept up all day and at night the houses were illuminated and dancing began in the plaza. Leonora and all her children went to the fiesta but Gideon preferred to remain at home. He was feeling strangely weak and shaky. Gideon recognized the aches and pains; they were the same as those he felt on the road home from Huntsville in 1867.

The fever left him despondent and he faced the unpleasant fact that he had lived too long. He thought of his dead wife, their brothers and sisters, and old friends:

The gang that I grew up with are all gone. So there is no one to whom I can communicate the workings of my old time-shattered mind. None left to listen to my complaints or to rejoice with me at my little successes. They are all in the embrace of oblivion while I alone am left to survey the hopeless void on the plane of memory they so long and so joyously occupied. They are all dead and will be seen no more! I don't grieve but I feel very much like I wanted to speak to somebody and give vent to a suppressed volcano of smothered sentiment that must die with me as it is.

But Gideon refused to yield to time, although he knew his strength was declining. When George and Attie made a sudden decision to return to Texas, Lincecum once more was forced to return to farm work. He was sorely disappointed in the young couple, but his only comment was: "So I had to lay down my vial rack and go back to the fields."

He dug a well in the hog lot, cut 108 Spanish daggers for a "living

---

Indians for centuries. It was accidentally discovered by hunters. Apparently the first to visit and describe the ancient city, covering 2,350 acres, was an European engineer, Diego Ruiz, who was there in 1785. It was infrequently visited until the Mexican government began excavating in 1934. Much work remains to be done. One of the mural figures depicts a child undergoing cranial deformation, an ancient custom of the Choctaw (El Tajin, Instituto Nacional de Antropología e Historia, México, 1957).

fence," caught driftwood as it floated down the rising waters of the
Tuxpan and hauled it ashore, planted okra and watermelons, cut out
jungle growth and made a new clearing, cribbed bushels of corn. But
in all this toil he still found life "worth keeping in such a country and
climate" and found joy in the numerous plants and blossoms, especially the coffee bloom, "so white and beautiful and smells so
sweet."

Lincecum and the boys were loading pickets for repairs to the hog
lot fence on the cart when Charlie, hitched to the cart, without warning ran away. In his blind rush Charlie knocked the old doctor off his
feet and the cart wheels passed over his body. Lincecum suffered severe
shock and injuries to his neck, collar bones, ribs, arms, and thighs. No
doubt in great pain, Lincecum nevertheless wrote the same day to
Bully:

This is the worst hurt, Bully, Grandpa ever got during his long life. But he
will recover from it. I must and *will* get over it. I am not ready to go yet.
I have not shown my respect for posterity by planting a sufficient number
of fruit trees. . . . The time, however, is drawing nearer and knowing this I
desire to be ready—dressed and carpet bag packed . . . Be a good boy, Bully.
Use kind language to everybody. Especially to your parents and brother.
Grandpa will write again.

Lincecum began to "pack his carpet bag" in preparation for his
earthly departure. He selected his burial site and wrote about it to
Bully:

I will tell Bully of a little scheme I have planned that will prevent the unnecessary expenditure of forty or fifty dollars. Two miles below our house
and on the same side of the river is a little mountain. It is a volcanic upheaval, projecting 150 yards into the river, having a little bay above and
below, a straight perpendicular face 200 yards long and 50 to 60 feet high
on the riverside. It is composed of unstratified, rather soft yellow sandstone
and at the foot the water is 60 feet deep. Near the center of the cliff, out of
reach of the depredator, will be seen, when you come here, Grandpa's name,
date of his birth and demise cut in rock.

Immediately under this inscription, and at the bottom of the deep river,
if you will take the trouble to go down there, you will find the remains of
your Grandpa, fastened to a heavy piece of iron, being lashed to the feet,
the form standing erect.

This will not only be a cheap funeral but it will preclude the possibility of its being removed, should any one entertain such heathenish notions. Oh! Let me remain in this lovely land.

Sallie registered her objections and Lincecum replied to her protest:

You object to the place I have selected for my final resting place. That seems strange to me for I was of the opinion that it was one of the brightest thoughts that my mental apparatus had ever generated. Name and age and place of nativity emblazoned on the face of a rock 60 feet high, 200 yards long and overhanging the waters of the beautiful Tuxpan. There, out of the way of the rushing tramp of villainous humanity the old carcass, the vehicle that transported the vital spark by a tortuous route from Georgia to the Tuxpan; and the mind, the mental attribute of the living principle which made itself known to external nature, can go through the process of decomposition undisturbed. Why, the idea is not only chaste and beautiful, but it really approximates the sublime.

But Lincecum recovered from injuries sustained in the cart accident and did not pursue his plans for burial. His health returned and he soon wrote of his well-being:

I am nevertheless strong, active and healthy, can walk five or six miles with ease and facility. Am on my feet busily engaged at work the greater part of every day and may continue to remain here, like I did in Texas till everybody is tired of me. . . . It is wonderful how strong and healthy I am. Almost every one I meet are making remarks about my healthy appearance. "You are getting younger" they say.

Gideon frequently entertained friends from Mississippi as well as Texas. He spent a pleasant day with Charles H. Courier and Ed J. C. Kewes,[18] who had been members of William Walker's filibusters in Nicaragua. They had traveled widely and Gideon found them enter-

---

[18] Courier was a lieutenant in Company F, 5th Texas Regiment, and was wounded at Fort Butler, Louisiana, June, 1863 (Confederate War Records).

Kewes, who had recruited in New Orleans for William Walker, was the brother of Achilles Kewes, financial agent to the Republic of Nicaragua and Walker's devoted friend, killed in 1855 at Rivas (Lawrence Greene, *The Filibusters* [Indianapolis, New York, Bobbs-Merrill Company, 1937], pp. 122, 205, 224). Greene erroneously spells the name *Kewen*. A notation in Gideon's 1832 cash book reads: "Kewes wants to know about Oliver Woods." His address book lists Kewes' Nicaragua address.

taining and most intelligent. He had known Kewes when he edited a newspaper in Columbus.

Making his usual voyage out to meet the *Webber* shortly after noon on October 13, 1872, Gideon found one of the two passengers was young Sam Houston. The first son of the great Houston was alone, broke, and unknown in Tuxpan: "Being amongst strangers entirely I concluded to take him home with me. For which he was, or seemed to be, very grateful."

Sam left his baggage on the ship, intending to return the next day to get it. After supper the old man accompanied him on a walk in the moonlight. The broad leaves of the banana plants moved gently over-head casting weird shadows in the garden. To young Sam it was a strange new world which filled "his soul with wonder and delight" and he exclaimed: "Oh, how beautiful!"

Sam remained with Gideon until he found employment for a monthly salary of $18 on Captain Olde's farm upriver. He had been there only a few days when Gideon wrote Sallie: "I do not know what Sam's habits are. I found him sober, very polite and respectful and his conversation particularly with Leonora was chaste and intellectual. Yet it is impossible to conceal the indications of his cerebral developments. If he is not a real desperate inebriate, phrenology is not true."

Sam soon became a permanent weekend guest at the Lincecum house. After the first weekend Gideon wrote that "Sam Houston is here in bed—came home with Bud about 10 o'clock last night. They say he works well."

In November "the boys set out two rows of bananas and they and Sam made up a picnic to come off tomorrow night at the bar. I, of course, with them." Later that month Sam changed his employment, taking a job on Colonel Munson's sugar plantation. Gideon wrote Sallie on November 23:

Sam Houston stayed with us last night—left soon after breakfast this morning. He has been moulding bricks on Colonel Munson's sugar farm all last week. He is quite healthy and looks strong. He brags that he moulded a thousand bricks last Friday by 11 o'clock. He says tell Sioux that he is doing very well and has no notion of going back to Texas. He says he can live very comfortably here on the labours of his own hands, out of the reach of his *kind* associates. We showed the paragraph in your letter that had reference to him. He was highly pleased with your remarks and your hope that he may yet be the president of Mexico.

Leonora wrote on November 27, 1872, to Sioux and Sallie:

Sam Houston is up the river at work. He is a dear good boy to me. I showed him your letter. . . . He sends his love to you both and told me to tell you, Sioux, that he never drinks a drop, is changed all over. I do not think Texas will see him soon again. He has ordered a man in town to make me some snuff, says he will try and get part of the barrel Saturday night. I had gone to bed when he came. When he knocked I asked who is that? "Homefolks, old lady." He had a gentleman with him. The man said to him: "You knew Mrs. Campbell in Texas." His reply was: "I don't know when it was I did not know the old bright-eyed darling." You will think by this that I look old. But it is a way the young men and old have of calling me pet names. Some call me "Aunt," Dr. Boyd calls me "Granny," some "Sister of Charity."

Sam brought three other young men with him the week-end of December 1 and they all remained over night on their way to Tamiahua,

a great place for game about 40 miles up the Laguna. They are voyaging in a large covered canoe propelled by two sturdy Indians. They have with them their bedding, mosquito nets, fishing tackle, guns and four or five dogs. They expected me to go with them and called by for that purpose but I, having too much to do, can not allow myself the pleasure.

Julius Brown,[19] the oldest son of John Henry Brown, who had been an 1866 settler in Orizaba, came in the next day from the San Juan Mountains. Brown was sick of a fever and Leonora "gave him a lobelia emetic that surprised and relieved him." Brown and Sam Houston, Jr., became close friends and the two often came together to visit the Lincecum family.

In a May 1, 1873, letter to Bully, Gideon wrote:

---

[19] Julius Rufus Brown was born February 1, 1846, the oldest child of John Henry Brown and Mary F. Mitchell Brown, formerly of Groton, Connecticut. Julius entered the Confederate Army at the age of fifteen; he was commissioned a captain at nineteen and cited for gallantry during his service in Indian Territory. A medical student, Julius returned to Mexico intending to practice medicine there, but in May, 1873, was back at his parents' home in Dallas, where he died, June 9, 1873 (Rose, *The Life and Services of Gen. Ben McCulloch*, pp. 250–260).

Julius Brown has made shift and raised money enough to pay Sam Houston's passage and has made arrangements with the captain for him. They will go down this evening. They are both here now. Your Aunt Leonora has put herself to much trouble trying to get Sam to behave decently. All the impression she made on him was to make him feel that he had a place to go to and could indulge more freely. Being the product of an inebriated conception he can never be of any use to himself or his country. I am glad Julius has made shift to get off.

But two days later he added: "Sam Houston has given up the idea of returning on this boat and is now, sun up, soundly sleeping here in bed. The schooner will not probably get off before Monday, this last norther has disturbed the water so." At 8:00 P.M. the same day he added: "Julius Brown has just left and sure enough Sam H. remained. A lighter will go out to the schooner tonight. They will get aboard about sun-up. Julius is the only passenger. He has your Aunt Leonora's letters and a little package from me which he says he will deliver in person. May be he may."

Eight days later he wrote; "Sam H. is here all day pretty drunk. We shall have to turn him loose. Your Aunt Lee hoped to reform him and has been trying to hold him up; but he scorns all friends and delights to make them feel little. I think she will have to let him go."[20]

Gideon regretfully saw his old friend Dr. Spencer, who was going back to Texas to prospect in Concho County, off on the *San Carlos*. Another day he and Leonora sailed up the river to say goodbye to other good friends, Tom and Georganna Townsend, who were returning to Fayette County to claim an inheritance. The Townsends had come out with John Henry Brown, who had long since returned to Texas after writing his glowing account of Tuxpan. Gideon never quite forgave him his defection but was somewhat mollified when Brown sent him copies of his Indianola *Bulletin*.[21]

[20] Among the Lincecum papers is a letter written September 21, 1895, to Sallie Lincecum Doran by Margaret Belle Houston, the poetess daughter of Sam Houston, Jr., then a student at St. Mary's College, in Dallas. It begins: "Dear Aunt Sallie— Of course I remember you. . . ." Margaret Belle refers to "poor Cousin Attie—did she die of heart failure?" and mentions seeing Andrew, Attie's son, while in Brenham, with the comment "Isn't he a fine looking boy?"

Sam Houston, Jr. (1843–1886) married Lucy Anderson of Georgetown in 1875. They had three children. After his wife's death he lived with a sister in Independence (*Handbook of Texas*, Vol. I, p. 847).

[21] Doran wrote Gideon: "People are very distrustful of Mexico since J. H. Brown's

Early in 1873 Bud, the eldest Campbell, wanting independence and his own money, took a job up the river as an interpreter for the Bradfords. Gideon and the other boys continued farming but as his eightieth birthday approached the old man realized his task was too great and his time too little. He had an opportunity to sell a large part of his land and crops at a good price, keeping the house and enough land for small crops to supply the family's needs. The remaining property and money from the sale were earmarked for Leonora and her children.

Gideon spent his time collecting plants in the forest and sending them to Sallie, visiting the colonists and his Indian friends, sailing up the river with young Sally, and entertaining guests.

In this manner he introduced many alien plants to Washington County, where they flourished under Sallie's green thumb. He sent seed of a large, white, trumpet-shaped morning glory ("the world's wonder"), Roman camomile ("they are useful"), *yerba dulce* ("I hope you can get this sweet little aromatic herb to grow in your garden"), *zapatita de la reina* ("a vine of the bean family with large, very white pea blossoms"), avocado ("I do not think it will survive a Texas winter"), Juan ("a delicious fruit very much like a gooseberry"), and a cactus ("the fruit tastes like watermelon"). He sent other things: a nest of the smallest species of hummingbird ("they had just left it"), a poisonous butterfly, bonnet gourd seeds ("I have seen it in Georgia during the war of 1812 made into very good looking bonnets but its most appropriate use is as a flesh brush while in the bath") and a dwarf china ("it will require some protection during your cold northers"). He suggested that "if Watson has a greenhouse" Sallie give him some of the bean vine seed to preserve through the frost.

In return Sallie sent turnip and lettuce seeds, Parson Lewis sent cabbage seeds, and Bully sent beans, which probably introduced the Texas bean weevil to Mexico. Gideon cautioned him:

---

book was circulated and then his afterwards leaving the country." Another paper Gideon received regularly was the *Picayune,* sent by his old friend Dr. Matchett. Gideon requested Sallie: "Present me very respectfully to Dr. J. F. Matchett and thank him in my name for the *Picayune.* It gratifies me to know that he thinks of me. Tell him I am too closely engaged in the daily conflict on the battlefield for subsistence to allow me to write articles describing injurious insects. Though I am quite familiar with them and their villainous proclivities."

I am proud of the seed you sent but was sorry to find them alive and kicking. I killed all I could get my hands on but some got away for which I am sorry for we had none of that kind here and I am afraid it will introduce them to our beans. That would be a regrettable thing for at least one-fourth of the solid food of our people consists of black beans—frijoles—which is assuredly the most substantial and universally eaten article of diet we have. A few spoonsfull of well boiled frijoles, a teaspoon of chili and a tortilla makes a meal upon which one can do all day very well.

To one of his Washington County neighbors who wanted vanilla bean seed he explained: "Tell Mrs. Kavanaugh that the vanilla beans grow in the thick woods and are all picked off by the Indians before they are ripe. Consequently the seeds are never mature. They flourish only in the dense shades of the jungles and would be of no service in that country."[22]

There were rare days when he sat in the shade of his mustang vine and read books, usually on geology, or idly watched the river traffic. Once, having time on his hands and nothing else to read, he turned to Walter Scott's *The Pirate,* his first experience with the author, but "I don't think I shall ever read any more of them . . . they don't suit my mental appetite, hungry as it is for books." He read with more interest William H. Sparks' *The Memories of Fifty Years.* He told Bully that Sparks was "one of your grandma's schoolmates. I was personally acquainted with nearly all his Georgia acquaintances."

He spent more and more time in Tuxpan, attending meetings of the colony association, watching demonstrations of farm machinery, and attending local events. Once, passing the shipyard on the return from town, he and John stopped to watch the launching of a boat. The natives cheered, a band played on deck, there was the usual speech on peace, industry, and progress, and the cable was cut at last. Gideon described it to Bully:

The people applauded loudly, the ship rushed rapidly down the way and plunging head foremost into the Tuxpan, righted up like a duck and sped

---

[22] Up to the present day the Totonac Indians retain control of the cultivation of vanilla, produced by a delicate orchid which through the ages has lost the capacity of self-pollination and must be fertilized by hand. (Miguel Covarrubias, *Indian Art of Mexico and Central America,* New York, Alfred A. Knopf, Inc., 1957). The Kavanaughs were early Washington settlers. Sallie's friends were Mrs. Charles and Mrs. S. F. Kavanaugh.

away toward the opposite shore with a storm of music on her deck. As she plunged into the water the man at the prow smashed the bottle of aguardiente, crying out at the same time *"Lolita de Tuxpan"* and then the multitude shouted. It was altogether a well performed launching. Everything properly placed and she glided away to her destiny very cleverly without accident.

Each morning was a new experience for him: "Calm and clear and very pleasant. Everything ringing with life and joy and song, and the pretty river lies calm and smooth as a looking glass. How full of hope and delightful anticipation the *young* heart must feel!"

Leonora attempted to keep him out of the fields by hiding his work clothes and putting out every morning his finest white linens. Grumbling in his finery, he made straight for the plantain orchard and began cutting. Leonora pointed to a stain on his shirt and he replied: "Oh, that is just a badge of honor."

With an increasing number of eastern and northern industries locating in the Tuxpan area, immigration was heavy in 1872. That year Gideon noted that four New Yorkers came with "powerful steam engines" and that others had opened extensive sugar plantations. There was a plan by one of the sugar refining companies to open steamboat traffic from New Orleans to Tuxpan early in 1873. Gideon predicted that "then we may expect scores of Yankees. The Southerners will come in behind and do as they have always done—work for them." Tuxpan was rapidly losing its frontier character as more and more strangers appeared. Gideon watched them during the Cinco de Mayo celebration in 1873: "The natives are a happy people and seem to enjoy these frequent fiestas greatly. The Americans here look upon them as a set of ignorant gumps five hundred years behind the age whilst they, the Americans, grin in poverty and rags, trotting around in search of aguardiente."

A month later Gideon wrote:

They have the smallpox in Tuxpan. . . . They are dying at the rate of one or two a day.[23] The authorities are paying no attention to it. I smelled it passing the street yesterday. For two days there has been a large U.S. warship taking soundings off Tuxpan bar. The Mexicans are greatly alarmed and are asking

---

[23] One victim was "a young man named Avant," who had been on the boat with the Lincecums from Texas to Tuxpan.

me what it means. I tell them they have come to capture the smallpox and take it away with them. Can you contrive to send us some vaccine matter? We have had none reliable.

His eightieth birthday found him well and active: "This I attribute to the fact that I have always kept myself sober, never meddled with other people's business nor lived in fear of the devil or any of the rest of the celestial gentry."

He longed to see his children, especially Sallie and her two boys, and Leonora urged them to come: "On papa's account, come as soon as you can. You do not know how delighted papa would be, how happy he would be."

Gideon's letters from Tuxpan end in April. There is no explanation for his sudden return to Texas. Nowhere in the vast pile of papers is there a clue to his sudden departure, apparently early in June. It could not have been illness—he was not afraid of dying in Tuxpan and had planned to be buried there. He vowed he'd never return to Texas and he truly loved Tuxpan. Only his love for Sallie and an intense desire to see her before he died could have influenced him to leave his paradise.[24]

Only a short while before his departure Leonora Campbell in a letter to Sallie Doran expressed her firm belief that their father would never leave Tuxpan, even for a brief visit to Texas, and added a few comments on the irascible old man:

Oh! I wish you could see how young papa is. It pays me for all I have given up. Papa is a little childish, but sometimes I don't think it is childishness. You know how he never governed his temper at home, and he often gets in those passions. We say nothing. If we say anything he will keep on, but if we say nothing he soon gets in a good humor. We watch every move he makes. There is someone always ready to jump when he goes to do anything for himself. You know how he is—if every thing is not at hand he goes off in a fit. You would have been amused the other morning. When he

---

[24] Andrew Bradford, Lincecum's great-grandson, told the author that Gideon left Tuxpan for Texas to sell the remaining portion of his property in Long Point. Mr. Bradford gave the following information on the Campbells: Argyle, known as Bud and also as Arch, died in Conroe, Texas, in 1899; George died in Brenham in 1916; Sally [Tramplett], called Sarita, died in Brenham in 1929; John died in Austin about 1901; Lutie and Lysander, called San and Sanny, died in Tuxpan. "None of them remained in Tuxpan except Sanny and Lutie," he wrote.

took his bath I had put his towels in the wrong place and he dried on the sail. I said "You old baby you—why didn't you call for a towel?" . . . Papa does not work—only his tongue. He is our pet. Never saw him in better health.

A NOTE ON SOURCES

An item which Lincecum unfortunately abandoned when he left Texas was his letter press. Thus the only available details of his life in Tuxpan are in letters to his daughter Sallie Doran and in a few scattered fragments of miscellaneous writings. The absence of the letter press explains the total lack of letters to scientists, but existing accession records of the Smithsonian and the Academy of Natural Sciences of Philadelphia, as well as random references in letters to Sallie, indicate that Lincecum not only continued to communicate but to add to his already impressive specimen contributions. Lincecum's interest in still another science is revealed in a letter to Sallie on August 3, 1872, in which, after a lengthy explanation of electricity and atoms, he wrote: "I will start a thought for you: duration, space, matter, motion, heat, electricity—all combined —produces in my organism the idea of infinite action—energy. Call it God if you prefer that term. . . . Ye gods! What an idea! No limits! No bounds! No end! Around, above, below—all is infinite."

During his stay in Tuxpan, Lincecum wrote his "Autobiography," which is considered his most valuable contribution and one of the most important narratives of pioneer migration to the American West.

To Sallie Doran we are indebted for her apparent reluctance to discard a scrap of paper containing a phrase of writing. It is due to her habit of preservation that the Lincecum Papers also include letters written from Tuxpan by her amiable sister Leonora Campbell. However, the Lincecum Papers suffered from the heavy hands of a censor, and as a result of deliberate excision a number of incidents of promising interest and of possible historical importance remain a family secret. For example, a letter written by Gideon which would have explained his terminal dissension with the Masonic Lodge is abruptly scissored. And I am certain it is because of this unknown meddler that we are not permitted to know for a certainty that Gideon Lincecum and Sam Houston had more in common than being great Texas pioneers. In an effort to establish this suspected relationship I learned that the strongest evidence I uncovered is sheer hearsay: a statement made to me by one of Lincecum's descendants that another descendant—and the one I think to be the grandson of Gideon Lincecum and Sam Houston—had once remarked that he was related to Sam Houston but "was not proud of it."

If true, what a pity that this most historical consanguinity cannot, even at this late date, be made a public record.

CHAPTER FIFTEEN

GIDEON
AND KILLIECRANKIE

Well, I think your Grandma and I will meet again, but I look for the meeting to take place on a more exalted and brighter plane than any portion of the heaven-forsaken United States. GID

WHEN GIDEON was seventeen years old and clerking in an Indian trading post in Eatonton, Georgia, his employer, Ichabod Thompson, brought him from Savannah a black English violin as a Christmas present. It was the treasure of his life. Not being acquisitive of worldly goods, it was the only possession he cherished throughout his life.

It was at dawn on Christmas of 1810 when young Gideon answered a knock at his door and found the kindly Ichabod Thompson standing outside with the violin in his hands. Gideon, barefooted and in his nightgown, stepped outside the door to accept the wonderful instrument, the dearest Christmas present of his life. He placed the violin against his shoulder and, disregarding the cold wind, played a Mississippi popular tune, "Killiecrankie."[1]

To commemorate this momentous occasion, every Christmas dawn thereafter, for sixty-three years, Gideon arose from bed wherever the

---

[1] Gideon spelled it Gillie Crackie. The song was based on an old Scotch ballad by Robert Burns, commemorating the Battle of Killiecrankie in 1687.

day found him, and, as he was, in nightclothes and barefooted, played his Christmas tune three times.

The old violin was restrung many times. One of Gideon's most esteemed tokens of friendship was from M. A. Healy, a Brazoria hardware merchant, who, during the Civil War when strings were unobtainable, sent him some from Brownsville. Gideon acknowledged the gift: "Please accept my most sincere thanks for the kindness you have conferred on my family, myself, and many weary soldiers whose drooping spirits are to be cheered up at my house by the sound of those very superior violin strings you forwarded to me by Mr. J. Johnson."

In Tuxpan he constantly worried about the damage to the violin caused by dampness and he was frantic until he found someone who could properly repair it. Since strings were difficult to obtain in Tuxpan he once sent an urgent message to Sallie:

I can get no good strings for my violin and to me, in my isolated condition, it is a considerable deprivation. The old black violin is a source of much comfort in my lonely evenings. But now, with strings nearly all of a size, there is but little pleasure in the music. Can't you enclose a set of good Italian strings in a letter to me? I want none but the true Italian. I have a good bass, the same one I had for ten years before I came here. I only lack the three sinew strings. Get my friends E. H. or John Norton[2] to select them for me and send them by the next trip of the *Webber* if you can. My soul longs for sweet sounds and these strings fail to produce them.

In his younger days, when his house was full of visiting relatives and friends and all his musical children lived under his roof, the violin was a source of conviviality. In his old age it was a solace, a link with the happy days of his youth. In Tuxpan he once wrote of his deep loneliness:

All that mighty host of people who were with me in my childhood, boyhood, youngmanhood, and onward during my active life are every one *dead*! Gone, to be seen no more! . . . And now, when in my daily performances I achieve anything that pleases me either on the physical or moral plane and I feel a desire to communicate it, I cast around in my mind to find someone who would feel an interest in listening to an account of my successful achievements, but can find *none*. They are all silent.

[2] E. H. and John Norton were brothers in the mercantile business in Brenham.

The thought startles me with an indescribable sense of loneliness and the subject, whatever it may be that I desired to communicate, chokes back upon my senses, producing a feeling of suffocation. All, all gone and silence reigns.

Oh! it is a frightful condition for which there is no remedy. All the solace I have in such cases is to get out the old violin and saw the thoughts out on her. While doing this my spirit conjures up vast groups of the lost ones and looking upon their smiling faces I seem to pass into the joyous concourse and forget my loneliness.

The violin—Gideon seldom belittled it by referring to it as a fiddle —soothed the aches and pains of his tired old body after a day's hard work in his Tuxpan fields: "I retire to my room, get out my old violin and the stimulus of half a dozen merry tunes sets up a healthy action in all the electric currents belonging to my old machine and all pains and aches are gone."

When he returned to Texas the old black violin was one of his few possessions which Gideon took with him. Once again the sitting room of his Long Point home was the scene of concerts and musicals. He played his violin at his joyous homecoming, happily planned for him by Lysander and Mollie, who now occupied the old homestead, and Sallie and Sioux, who came over from Hempstead.

In July, Gideon went to Austin to visit Cassandra and Buckley. While there he had a pleasant duty to perform: "Bud can do what no Campbell man could ever do before him. He can whistle and sing tunes. He wants me to send him a violin. I must try to find him one." This talent, found in all the Lincecums except the Campbells, was enough to cause Gideon to forgive Bud for smoking and smelling of tobacco.

Obviously Lincecum considered his return to Texas only a temporary visit, for he wrote Sioux Doran on July 8, 1873:

I have been all the time visited and carried about to houses. All are unanimous in the expression of the opinion that I should not think of going back to Mexico. They tell me that it is a dangerous country to dwell in, full of robbers, bad society and ferocious savages. Well, as they have had a better chance than I have to know these things, they have frightened me and caused me to feel a strong inclination to go back soon and see if what they tell me is true, for it was not the case three weeks ago. . . . Cassandra and her family are all well. Cass does all the cooking herself, with Sidney's help. He supplies the wood and water, attends to setting the table, etc. Walter rises early, feeds and waters the dogs and chickens, goes to market, and then, until breakfast, fixes up anything that is out of order. That over, he goes off to the house that pays him for his services and is seen no more until dark. The little girl [Lelia] is very healthy, looks handsome and though she is beginning to help her Mamma a little, she spends half her time with Monterrey who nursed and suckled her. Professor Buckley is to call for me today, take me out to his place and keep me two days. He has no children or meddling neighbors and we shall not be interrupted during our interview. I have set the inquiry about Leonora's business under way and may remain here till the first letters return from Columbus, if Seth [Shepard] prefers that I should do so. I am keeping a daily journal for a letter to send to Leonora. I have done so from the day I left home, and have sent back to her what happened of interest up to the day I left Brenham. I desire to make her feel, during my absence, that I had rather be here than there.

Cassandra had written only one letter to her father while he was in Tuxpan—in which she told him of the death of her husband, George Durham. The last letter Durham wrote before his death was to Lincecum, who sent it back to Cassandra. Gideon grieved that he did not hear from Cassandra. In 1872 he had news of her from his friend, Major Work, who had visited Cassandra in Austin. When Work returned to Tuxpan, Gideon wrote Sallie:

Mr. Work came over to see us today and to deliver a message from Cassandra, whom he visited and spent several hours with while on business in Austin. He describes her as being very comfortably situated, in excellent health, looks to be about 28 years of age and is, according to his judgment on such subjects, the finest looking and most ladylike woman that he saw during his trip. He went from Austin to Galveston, took dinner in Brenham, but was not apprised of your residence there. He would have been willing to have spent a day with you; so that he might have an opportunity to tell you what he knew about us. I am sorry he missed you.

Sallie, knowing her father's loneliness for his children in Tuxpan, urged Cassandra to write and when Gideon learned about it, his proud old heart rebelled: "I would rather you not do that. I see no pleasure in the reception of a letter from any one when I know that the author has to be prompted and urged to write it. . . . It is not proper for you to stir up the calm, quiet frigidity of her church-going heart."

Gideon's grief and heartache because of Cassandra's neglect melted when he visited her in Austin. She was supporting herself and three children, Walter, Sidney, and Lelia, by operating a boarding house. Her father was proud of her and was pleased that every day some of George Durham's old political friends came by to see her and that Throckmorton remained her devoted friend. Gideon wrote Sallie:

Throckmorton made the inquiry privately and told her that if at any time she should need *anything* that he is always ready to serve her. I notice also that she is very popular with everybody. C[harles S.] West and [John] Alex[ander] Green—two lawyers—in the absence of their wives who are on a visit to Canada, are boarding with Cassandra till they return. They are clever, respectful gentlemen. Take two meals a day and pay her $15 a month. . . . Leonora in Tuxpan and Cassandra in Austin . . . my two widowed daughters. Both hold in the society to which they belong high positions. I don't know which of the two is most sought after or most beliked . . . Cassandra, the stately, slow moving, young looking, rather handsome Cassandra.

In Texas, Gideon communicated daily with Leonora in Tuxpan as he had with Sallie in Texas when he was in Mexico.[3] During his visit in Austin, Lincecum wrote his daughter, Leonora: "I continue to enjoy good health and walk four or five miles daily. They all quarrel at me and want to haul me about in their buggies and do often succeed in getting me in; but when I can I slip off and they find me at Cassandra's when they return." He described the bustle among the politicians at the state capital, adding: "Guffy moves more deliberately, with a hung-down head and loudly creaking shoes. He is studying politics. They had an election for two additional aldermen. Elected one negro and one radical. West says, one white negro and one black one."

Once again Gideon settled in his little red-cedar house at Long Point. He planned, or pretended to plan, to return to Tuxpan, but in his heart he must have known it was an impossible journey he could never undertake. In October he wrote to Sallie in Hempstead that Leonora was grieving over his delay in returning to Mexico but he would have to postpone the trip until May to avoid the "rubbing and chafing" of the rolling winter seas.

Gideon was pleased with Lysander's wife, Mollie, and found her to

---

[3] Unfortunately, few of these letters are in the Lincecum file.

be an exceptional housekeeper, careful, industrious, very neighborly, and extremely liberal. She was exceedingly kind to him and did everything she could to make him comfortable and happy. Lysander had a heavy practice. Gideon did what he could to be useful—mixed medicines and took care of the shop while Lysander made calls. He wrote Sallie: "Lysander is a remarkable man. He and Mollie are, I can plainly see, the most beliked and most popular family in the vicinity. . . . I am well and lonesome. I would grieve for my pretty home but I am no account nowhere, can't earn my bread. I shall encumber them wherever I go."

Late in October, 1873, Gideon renewed through correspondence an old friendship with Wilbur F. Parker, publisher of the *American Sportsman,* of West Meriden, Connecticut. It began when Gideon sent to Parker, through the mail, a horned frog, which was still in good health when Parker received it.

Parker asked Gideon to write his autobiography. Gideon told Sallie about it:

I am as dry as chaff, have no material in my pencil to manufacture a single pleasant expression. Parker called on me for some sketches of my early history. As he began the feud by giving me some of the prominent traits in his history, I could but return the compliment. So I have been writing all the time I dare sit at it for the past two weeks. I must go on now I agreed to do it. But if I had it to start again I wouldn't set my historical plow to digging. It's turning up some curious events and occurrences, beginning a century agone.[4]

Gideon wrote mostly of his hunting and fishing exploits, describing his weapons and methods of hunting, and weaving the stories into his life on various frontiers. It is a remarkable chronicle to come from the memory of an octogenarian and only once, so far as it can be determined, did his memory play him false. At one point he stated that after first reading the works of Erasmus Darwin he wrote a letter to him and received a reply. Erasmus died in 1802, when Gideon was nine years old. It is possible that Gideon intended to refer to Erasmus' son, Robert Waring Darwin, also a physician.

---

⁴ "Reminiscences of an Octogenarian" appeared in the *American Sportsman* issues of September 12, 19, 26; October 3, 10, 17, 24, 31; November 7, 14, 21, 28; December 5, 12, 19, 26, of 1874; January 2, 9, 16, 1875.

Gideon's writing did not take up all his time. He was still able to go on fishing and hunting trips and whenever possible took to the woods for camping. A page from his 1873 diary reads:

Nov. 11—we made a hard day's travel and struck camp on the edge of the Brazos bottom at 4:30 P.M. It was a pleasant night and the boys went fox hunting. Were not successful.

Nov. 12—Moved our camp three miles lower to Sand Lake. Norther blowing pretty strong, but I fished all day, caught some fine fish, had a big fish dinner. Rube Halbert[5] passed our camp last night with a wagon and forty bushels of pecans in it. They are to get seven cents a pound.

Nov. 13—Big frost. I made a good moss bed and a blanket under and two over me. Was not quite comfortable. I feel well today however.

Nov. 14—Had a fine night's rest. Had breakfast and finding it a poor hunting ground, broke up camp and set out for home. At 11 o'clock came to old Dick Sands' farm. He lives on Davidson's creek in Burleson County and is growing sugar cane finely and making very good sugar and very fine syrup. He does the work himself and it is well done. There came another company of pecan hunters with Jim Polk at their head this morning. We would have remained longer but bread gave out. We could get ducks, squirrels, and fish aplenty but without bread it was not pleasant.

January, 1874, brought heartbreaking news from Tuxpan. Leonora had been desperately ill with yellow fever and little Lysander was dead. Gideon mourned that he could not be in Tuxpan to comfort her and this devastating news marked the beginning of Gideon's decline. He opposed Sallie's plan for Leonora and her children to return to Texas. He begged her "for humanity's sake" not to urge it. "It would injure them greatly to come back to this grinding, taxing, thieving, robbing, throat-cutting, nigger-ridden, frowning community. Dry as a bone."

Gideon worried, too, about Sallie's health and in February wrote her:

I live in hopes that some intervening circumstance may turn up that will

---

[5] H. A. Halbert (1849–1926), a notable pecan breeder, originated the Alexander and Halbert varieties. He lived near Long Point but in 1886 published a newspaper in Corsicana and had a pecan orchard in Coleman County. He wrote "Edible Nuts of Texas" for the *Texas Almanac, 1904*, p. 49 (Gieser, *Horticulture and Horticulturists in Early Texas* [Dallas, Southern Methodist University, 1945], pp. 107–111).

afford me some reliable information in regard to your situation. I do not hear of you as often as I did while residing in Tuxpan.

Do you receive letters from Leonora? Do you write any to her? Mary Matson came over yesterday and she did make out to ask me if I had heard from Lee lately. I replied not since 17 December. She made no further remark.

It is a notable thing that Mary, Leander, Lachaon, Lucullus, nor any of the ½ breeds in the connection ever write a line to her. Is it any wonder that when they had the yellow fever there her reply to my letter directing her to sell out and come back should be "No, never! I have friends here, good friends and I can't consent to exchange them for the cold hearts there."

Later in February Gideon had a letter from Leonora, "full of grief for her bright-eyed boy." A letter from his friend Sidney Smith informed Gideon that Leonora was doing well and was being watched over by her many friends.

Gideon wrote Sallie of Smith's news:

When she had yellow fever she was in delirium eleven days. During some of her ravings while in that condition, she exhibited the Masonic pass of her degree. There happened to be a Mason present and saw the sign. The next day all the Masons in the valley visited her, twenty at least. Several of them travelers and entire strangers. They held a council and appointed five to see to her case every day and to see that she lacked nothing. When the strangers went away, there was money found under her pillow. *Mr. Smith tells this.* . . . Well, I may never be able to get back there, I am just now beginning to walk about after a confinement of 20 days.

In early spring Gideon lost the use of his legs and unexpectedly found the patience to endure his infirmity:

An old, superannuated octogenarian pauper like myself must be satisfied with things as they come. A week ago I got a long letter from Leonora. They are all well and doing fine. Talked of sending money for me to go home on. My tenure of life seems rather precarious at present. I must postpone the voyage a little longer to get well. . . .

I received Sioux' letter about stocking the Texas waters with foreign fish and wrote him that the day I received his letter Prof. Milner[6] had turned

---

[6] Robert Teague Milner (1851–1923) teacher, newspaperman, and state representative, was first state commissioner of agriculture in Texas and president (1908) of Texas A. & M. College (*Handbook of Texas*, Vol. II, p. 202).

40,000 young loose in the Colorado River at Austin. So there is no chance for us to get the appointment; and if there was I could not accept it. I am incapacitated to perform the labor of it. I'm nobody now. . . .

When you run into the Darwin theory in your letter, you checked yourself. You needn't be frightened. Darwin is in the main right and I find all the real scientific men sliding into the philosophy and principles of the Darwinian theory.

Gideon's mind remained clear and perceptive and he enjoyed the visits of old and new friends, especially the visit of "one of the ant killers."[7]

Gideon's last letter, dated August 22, 1874, was written to Sallie from Long Point. In it he enclosed a letter from Parker. Parker was very eager to get the Chahta manuscript but Gideon was reluctant to send it to him. He had no copy and could not undertake the task of making one. Lincecum left the decision to Sallie, but wrote:

I don't think, however, that the manuscript should go. Parker must be content with my autobiographic relics, as he calls my hunting sketches, which I have been writing and sending every time I get six pages on cap paper done. Have already sent him one hundred pages and shall continue *ad infinitum*. I think I am a little stronger than I was when I wrote before.

But Gideon grew weaker and was unable to continue his letters to Parker. The period of his old age which he had so long dreaded, had at last come and with it complete inactivity. His body rested on his bed, his hands idle, but his mind continued its constant exercise of remembering. As he waited to join his long-lost companion in their happy hunting ground, he remembered all the sixty-three Christmases he had played his happy Christmas tune on the old black violin.

He remembered the cold Christmas dawn on the Texas coast in 1867, his first Christmas without Sarah:

At the break of day I tuned up my old black violin, which I had taken along for the purpose, and having no doorway to stand in, I stepped barefooted into a little gap in the yaupon thicket and performed the Christmas tune in good style, repeating it as usual three times. And that made 57 Christmas daybreaks I have done that, without missing a single Christmas.

---

[7] Probably the Reverend E. S. Wright, Austin, Texas, Presbyterian minister who aided McCook in his ant detective work.

Gideon chuckled as he recalled that he had camped near Willbourn's place on Chocolate Bayou. Mr. Willbourn, a very religious man, came to camp to inquire about the weird daybreak music. Gideon explained he belonged to a new religious sect and that playing the tune three times at daybreak was part of the devotional. "He thought it very strange and left."

Gideon remembered the sixty-third playing of the Christmas tune, in Long Point in 1873, which was to be his last. In his night dress, barefooted, he stepped out of the door into the yard, stubbed his toe on an old white petrified cactus his hands had placed there many years before, and enjoyed

. . . the life-giving freshness of the sweet morning; the bright old moon whirling her broad yellow face down behind the western edge of this little bad-fixed world; and at the moment the last thread of her silver light disappeared, the new day was peeping out from the fractured east. Overhead the great concave dome, bespangled and adorned with glittering constellations of suns and systems of suns, making up the whole brilliant scenery of the glorious morning so grand, so magnificent and transcendently beautiful that my old tired spirit floundered and struggled to get away, to fly upward. Such was the bewildering powers of my splendid surroundings that I could no longer control my feeling, nor, at the moment, abstain from yelling out one of my big Indian whoops. For an instant the sound of the whoop reverberated down the branch and then the world rolled on as good as ever.

And in the doorway, the night-shirted old man, barefooted, stood on his weary old legs and played his violin:

> O Killiecrankie is my song;
> I sing and dance it all day long,
> From the heel unto the toe
> Hurrah for Killiecrankie O!
>
> And ye hae been where I hae been
> Ye wad na be so cantie O!
> And ye hae seen what I hae seen
> On braes of Killiecrankie O!

A NOTE ON SOURCES

The Lincecum Papers contain only meager details of the final year. One regrets that so few of Lincecum's letters to Leonora Campbell, which doubtless would provide a chronicle of daily events, are included. Several letters to Sallie and a fragment of a diary are all that remain. His writing in the closing year was devoted to "Reminiscences" and copies of this series of letters to the *American Sportsman* are not in the Papers.

John Henry Brown wrote Lincecum's obituary, which was published in the December 12, 1874, issue of the Dallas *News* and reprinted by other Texas newspapers. Brown recalled visiting Lincecum "in his own hospitable home opposite the city of Tuxpan" on Lincecum's seventy-fifth birthday. At that time Brown heard the tradition of Killiecrankie and listened to Gideon play the tune on his old black violin.

Almost half a century later the Indians of Tuxpan remembered that the white-bearded man they called "El Doctor" played his violin in the tropical moonlight and at early daybreak before a plunge in the Tuxpan River (Geiser, *Naturalists,* p. 209).

Lincecum's death was noted by most Texas newspapers but none seemed aware that his passing marked the end of an era and the last of the frontiersmen. Belatedly the *American Naturalist* (Vol. IX, [March, 1875], p. 191) published a brief obituary: "Dr. Gideon Lincecum of Long Point, Texas, died November 28, 1874, of paralysis. He was a valued contributor of this journal and his papers showed keen powers of observation. His most remarkable contributions were on the agricultural ant of Texas."

References to his old black violin and to the Christmas tune of Killiecrankie are found in Lincecum's letters to: Dr. Josiah Higgarson, Somerville, Tennessee, May 20, 1859, January 20, 1861; John H. Douglas, Mason City, Illinois, January 14, 1860; John A. Rutherford, Honey Grove, Texas, January 10, 1860, January 4, 1861; Colonel S. D. Hay, Huntsville, Texas, October 1, 1861; Colonel C. G. Fitze, Coldspring, Texas, April 9, 1861; M. A. Healy, Brownsville, Texas, April 29, 1865; Cassandra Durham, Austin, Texas, January 19, 1868; E. Durand, Philadelphia, January 29, 1868; and others.

EPILOGUE

GIDEON LINCECUM was buried by the side of his good companion in the old Mount Zion Cemetery near the Lincecum home in Washington County, Texas. Sharing his grave, at his request, was his precious old black violin.

Here, in a neglected graveyard covered with shinnery, Gideon rested for sixty-two years, forgotten but in peace. In 1936, the year of the Centennial of Texas' Independence from Mexico, there was a wholesale disinterment in commemoration of the event.

Gideon Lincecum was one of the victims.

The remains of his body and his old violin were removed to the lovely little State Cemetery in Austin, Texas, and placed in a grave in Row One of the Austin plot, so called because it is dominated by the grave of the Father of Texas.

Lincecum's grave overlooks those of some of Texas' greatest men. The Texas granite tombstone bears the official Texas Centennial emblem, and an erroneous death date—November 28, 1873. Lincecum died one year later.

Appendix A

GIDEON LINCECUM'S JOURNAL
OF A TRIP TO TEXAS, 1835

January 9, 1835
> This day Fred. Weaver, G. Lincecum, Benjm Nix, John Gwin, and Calvin Weaver, left their homes on an exploring expedition to the province of Texas. got on pretty well and camped 3 miles in the Chickasaw Nation.

10th—All mud to day, but we did not become dull, having had the pleasure of laughing all day at Mr. Gwin, who for our amusement had the politeness to turn a double Summerset in the muddyest creek we found in the day's travel—camped on Hoolky [Houlka].

11th—Had a runaway frolic with one of the horses—and camped on Natchez trace in Chocktaw Nation at Noah Wall's old place.

12th—Travelled but 3 miles to day on account of the rain and high water. Lay at Moors [Moore's].

13th—Swam 2 or 3 creeks to day—travelled but 7 miles till we were prevented progress by the pigion roost creeks, had nothing but an old sidge field to feed our horses on—

14th—travelled 9 miles today. Swam 3 creeks and the prospect bad ahead.

15th—Lay all day water bound at Big Bywiahs.

16th—went 10 miles today, after swimming 3 or four creeks. Lay at Danl. McCurtain's old place—

17th—Swam no creeks to day. Travelled 30 miles

Sunday, 18th—Travelled 27 miles, clear weather—

19th—Travelled 30 miles, Slept at Livingston—

Janry. 20th. 1835—Travelled 30 miles rained all day

21st—Travelled 30 miles

22nd—Passed through Gibson Port

23rd—This day crossed the Mississippi

24—Camped in the Miss. Swamp

Sunday 25th—This day got us out of the Swamp.

26th—This day crossed the washeta [Ouachita]. It is a very pretty River 300 yards wide, navigable for any Sized Steam boats—the lands that we passed through on this river are poor.

27—Passed over a long poor prarie to day Saw a great many geese and one bear—and camped in the long leaf pine wood.

28th—This day crossed Little river. It is about the size of Tombecbe any where above Demopolis, and is on the road 18 miles above Alexandria.

29—Crossed Red River

30—Could not make much head way. Twas so cold.

January 31st 1835—Travelled 22 miles and camped in the poorest country I ever saw

Sunday—February the 1st—Travelled 28 miles, camped in hearing of Fort Jasup [Jessup]

2nd—Came 36 miles camped in 3 miles of the Sabine river.

3rd—This day crossed the U.S. boundry, and camped 12 miles in the Spanish dominions. Land very poor.

February 4th 1835—This day brot us into the arish bayo [Ayish Bayou] Land. This is a large body of beautiful lying lands as—and the whole of it is as red as the redest clay in Monroe county Mi. It produces corn cotton &c. well, and is as healthy as any country in the world—

On the northern boundary of these good lands is situated St. Augustine a little town 25 miles East of Nacogdoches. We remained in the little Town 3 or 4 hours. It is in a great State of improvement and the inhabitants extremely kind and friendly.

Feb. 5th—From St. Augustine we turned nearly South to examine the lands on Snow river. We are now camped near the river Angeline (pronounced Ah, he, lene) We have to day seen one or two very pretty places.

Our course from home would average S. West until we turned from Augustine.

February 6th, 1835 Crossed the Angeline River. This river at low water mark is about 40 feet wide and is said to be navigable 40 miles above where we crossed it. there is some pretty places of land on the creeks of this river, the low grounds are poor and in high water are inundated to the hills on both sides Todays travel lay through pine Barrons interspersed with praries, being bounded with long leaf pine forests and not timber.

Feb 7th 1835—We were compelled to lie by to day on account of the cold. We are in Lat. 30 and 45″ and the ice is sufficient to bear a man and horse on it. But this is said to be a circumstance of rear occurance in this country

8th—Crossed the River Naches (Neches) pronounced Naish. This river is somewhat less than the Angeline, they run together and make Snow river. The land of these 2 rivers and between them is a very poor country and the low grounds to them are all inundated lands and not worth much, there are a few stock keepers settled on these rivers. On the river Naches there is an old Salt work, which has been pretty smartly worked, there is salt plenty to be seen on top of the ground now (10 days after a rain) left by evaporation. Crossed little Alabama creek and camped; on this creek the land is tolerable and the range is good.

Feb. 9th, 1835. Crossed Big Alabama Creek. The land immediately on this creek is good, as well as the water, indeed the water for the last 100 miles have been plenty and excellent. After crossing the Alabama Creeks the lands are but middling until we came to big Sandy, this is a bold running clear creek, cane fine and the land pretty good.

10th. This day passed through the thickest woods I ever saw. It perhaps surpasses any Country in the world for brush, there is 8 or 10 kinds of ever green undergrowth, privy, holly, 3 or 4 sorts of bay, wild peach tree, bay berry, &c. and so thick that you could not see a man 20 yards for miles, the soil is pretty good and the water the very best. We also crossed 2 other pretty creeks, same character, after leaving the last Creek. There is some pretty fine land which extends to the Trinity river, on which we are now camped (Coshata)

Feb. 11th Turned the Trinity.

Feb. 12th. Passed through a great deal of fine Prarie land to day—These praries surpass any thing for beauty of Scenery I have ever seen, the soil is as good as it can be, in the greater part of the prarie—There is all along the river, first from one to $1\frac{1}{2}$ miles cane land, then back swamp, sometimes considerably wide and then again not so bad, at the edge of this slash commences the prarie, and in common, gently rises to the distance, in some places of 80 rods. This slanting prarie and the level part of it next the swamp is as good as it can be.

From this sideling prarie you reach the high level prarie spread out before the wondering eye, as large as infinity. Some of the prarie is pretty good, and some excellent, some of it is sloshy and unfit for cultivation. All through is scattered, here and there, at various distances, islands of timber, some of these are sandy and dry, but a great many of them are wet, and the timber on any of them is unfit for use, except it be for firewood. There is some ash and lynn on them out of which fence rails might be made.

The people as far as we have travelled are friendly, but they will not tell the truth, they tell you that the lands are taken up, and perhaps there is not one in ten who have obtained even an order of survey for his land. Still the good lands on Trinity are covered with claims of one description or other, so that a stranger has but little chance to obtain lands, without considerably more trouble than I am or should be willing to undergo.

13th. Lay by today, got washing done, &c.

14th. Passed through Liberty and crossed the Trinidad. Liberty is a small town place situated in a large sand prarie on the east side of the Trinity river, about 3 or 4 miles from the river. The tide rises as high as this place.

15. Passed through about 5 miles of broken swampy lands and then entered the large prarie. This prarie extends from the Trinity swamps to the river San Jacinto. It rises gently to the half way ground, and then again gradually descends to the San Jacinto, to the right and left the sight is only here and there obstructed by the islands of timber which are thinly interspersed over the wide expanse. The Trinity river is a small stream not exceeding 60 or 70 yards wide at the head of tide water, it is said to be the best stream for navigation in Texas but this I cannot agree to. It is at every place I have seen it entirely obstructed with the timbers which are still, and always will be, falling in. Its banks are constantly tumbling in, which shows that to clear it out would do no good, as it would not remain so any longer than to the next high water. The San Jacinto, which we this evening forded, is in my opinion another kind of stream for navigation to the Trinity. It is a brisk running stream about 60 yards wide and seems to be at this time all alike shallow, about belly deep to a horse, with clean banks and open bed to the river. This river will once a year allow pretty good navigation for keels and small steam boats, for a considerable distance into the inland. The prarie lands on this river are beautiful.

16. Passed over an immense prarie most of which is very poor. The west side would do pretty well but no water, the water has been scarce and bad ever since we reached the Trinity river.

Feb. 17th. Crossed Cypress bayou. This is a flush running creek and pretty good water. It is a branch of San Jacinto, 45 to 50 miles long, running directly from the west. The praries on the north side of this creek are I think good. The soil is a full chocolate color and very light and dry. It is from 10 to 12 miles wide and runs west to the sea coast, nearly all good. It is bound on the north to the distance of 25 miles by Spring creek, this creek abounds with good springs and timber. The lands on Spring creek are all taken up on account of the springs, I suppose, for the lands are not as good as they are on the Cypress bayou side. This prarie is certainly a most beautiful situation, reaching from San Jacinto, a navigable stream, to the sea coast, a distance of 75 or 80 miles.

18 Feb. 1835. Passed through a vast prarie today. Sometimes we are entirely out of sight of timber, land nearly all good, what, in my judgment should

be called excellent. We came out between Cypress and Spring creek, these creeks diverge from each other, being 8 miles apart at the commencing of the good prarie and 12 to 15 miles apart at their head. Leaving the head of these creeks you enter the main prarie which is to the eye of the creeping traveller bounded by nothing but the heaven, and the soil is good as the heart could desire. Oh! what a pitty it is there is no timber. But there are none, not a stick, not even on any of the creeks. We passed 2 considerable creeks today, which had not a bush on their banks to mark their course through the vast, the boundless sea of grass. The water in the prairie is good and by digging may be had easy and plenty.

We are now stopt awhile on the Brazos low grounds to let our horses graze a little and the whole surface of the ground is covered with green grass as thick as a meadow. The Brazos low ground here is about 5 miles wide, the first $2\frac{1}{2}$ miles is what may be called Second low ground. The balance lies 2 or 3 ft. lower, but is equally good if not better soil. Fanin [Fannin] in his letter to the people of Georgia said that the Brazos lands were as good as the Red River lands. But I should say that there is no comparison between the lands of the two rivers. The Brazos has the preference in many respects. The red river low grounds are every where cut up with lagoons, slashes &c, and has deep miry back swamps. The Brazos has no back swamp, nor are the low grounds any where interspersed with lagoons, it is perfectly level without a break of any description except here and there a clear water pond which seems to be supported by springs.

19th—Crossed the Brazos at San Philipe [San Felipe]. This river is about 120 yards wide and at low water is not navigable for boats of any description. But from the signs of the high water will in my opinion be a pretty good stream for steam boats at least 3 months in the year, tho the people here say the navigation is not good—But this they have not tried in a way to ascertain satisfactorily.

San Philipe is a little town on the west side of the Brazos immediately on the bluff, and has a population of 2 or 300 of all descriptions and orders of humanity. I had forgotten to name the different kinds of timbers on the Brazos low grounds. There are plenty of elm, ash, hackberry, mulberry, some walnut, Spanish oak (of a peculiar kind), Zanthoxylum, and several other small kinds with which I am unacquainted. The soil here, like the red river bottom is red, but not near so deeply painted, that of Red river is about a Spanish brown, the Brazos somewhat more than a deep chocolate.

Feb. 20th. This day brought us through about 15 miles of sand prarie (perhaps 20 miles) this prarie is watered with numerous creeks and branches, water good, 2 or 3 of the creeks are large and deeply indented in the prarie, which produced an agreeable relief to the eye of the weary traveller. The water of these creeks is clear, gently flowing over this immense bed of sand which comparatively speaking is as white and clean as snow.

Leaving this prarie we entered a 10 mile streak of timber, soil the same as the prarie. This timber is almost entirely black jack and runner post oak from 10 to 15 feet in highth, this too is well watered. Reached the edge of the Colorado bottom and camped. The lowgrounds on this as well as the rest of the rivers are taken up, as is also the timbered spots around all the good praries. The Cypress Bayou prarie is all we have found in our rout that is timbered, and of any amount that is unoccupied and there are several leagues taken up on it. All the good land in the whole country as far as we can hear, are taken up, except high up and there all the good places are taken.

Feb. 21st 1835. Turned up the Colorado, and passed through about 15 miles of very poor timbered prarie when we turned into the low ground and after travelling over 2 or 3 miles of the best and prettiest land under the whole heavens, came to the long looked for Colorado whose swift current was rapidly rolling away its beautiful waters to the bosom of the ocean. This river is something over 100 yards wide, and at this place (110 miles above its mouth) could have been foarded. It is a shallow stream, but the water at this time is nearly at the low water mark. Crossed over and camped at Burnams. This is as hansome a situation as any man need desire. He has a well about 30 feet deep.

Sunday 22nd. Passed over a great deal of the best prarie I have seen yet, all taken up.

23st. Still good land.

24th Feb. We are now lying on the west bank of the Colorado at the San Antonio road crossing, 150 miles by land to Matagorda. The river is navagable this high up, just above this place it is said there is a shoal which is said is the head of navagation. But whether this is true or not is not for me to say, as I have not examined the shoal. At the crossing is a town which the people call Bear Strap [Bastrop]. Its proper name I believe is Mina. This place is at the extreme end of Austins Colony. Here on the west side of the river sets in Milums [Milam's] Colony, but like the rest, all the good places are selected.

Feb. 25—Lay by trying to get information, but could obtain nothing Satisfactory; the people all have two or 3 leagues of land a piece, and tell us there are no more to be had that are of any account. But they will sell theirs. We would turn out into the woods and hunt places for ourselves but were we to do so we could not know the places that are taken from those which are not. And should we find a place that would suit us and make it known, it would be claimed by some of the surveyors, clerks, commissioners, empresarios, or some of the Speculating Land officers, as premium land; which they would sell to us very reasonably—

There is a country we are told, which has not yet been explored lying from 60 to 70 miles above this place, that is said to be very good, water fine &c. But this country they have not as yet seen, nor will they see it until some body else reports to them that there is no danger. Then straitway they will all over run the country and lay their leagues again, as they have already several times done. They are very anxious that we should explore the unknown country; they are afraid of the Indians, and are desirious for some one or any one else to go and see if there is danger. If there is no danger, they are ready with surveyors and all other necessary officers to start out and select the best places before there can be surveying done for any body else. And so they have it. No Stranger, except he could remain in the country 12 months or longer can do anything advantageous for himself in this country.

26th. Lay by today on account of the severity of the cold. It was hailing, snowing & sleeting greater part of the day, wind from the north, very cold indeed. The weather in this country is the most variable that I have ever experienced in any country. Some days is so warm that you cannot keep your coat on, and perhaps a change will take place in three hours that will render you uncomfortable under all the clothes you can pack on. There appears to be a continual sesaw between the north and south winds, that is it has been so on our route ever since we crossed red river, having according to our recollection, not observed the wind to blow from any other direction than from the north or south, and what is most singular is, that you seldom experience a calm.

I have in the above mentioned the quality and so forth of the lands we have passed over. What I have said only alludes to the appearance of the soil. It does indeed look as well as land could look, the soil in some places being a fine lively color, and in others black and deep, say from 10 feet to 30. One man told us that he discovered no change in the color of the soil from the surface to the bottom, which was somewhere about 30 feet. Still the corn stalks are very small, and the specimens of cotton are very poor. I speak now altogether of the prarie lands—the bottom lands as yet almost entirely left uncultivated, owing I suppose to the frequent inundations and the labor it would take to prepare the ground for planting. We saw two experiments in the cotton plant in the swamps of the Colorado, both of which was considering the manner in which it was tended very fine. The weed was from 8 to 10 feet high, but the whole of the bottom lands on all the rivers in this country are subject to frequent overflowings.

In the praries there are two very different kinds of soil, and frequently the line of demarkation is distincly visible in one step. One kind is a dead bed of sand, and the other a black stiff crackly deep limy soil, both of which in my opinion are very dead land, one having too much sand and the other none—at any rate the crops I have seen coroberate the opinion. The corn stalks are not thicker than my thumb, nor higher than a mans head—the prarie cotton that I saw was as poor as could be.

27th. Turned back today.

Feb. 28th 1835 [blank]

Sunday March 1st. Lay at William Bartons today from information obtained from him, we ascertained from this source, and he is a great traveller, all the land that good are selected.

2nd. Lay at Criswell's.

3rd. Lay at Burnams.

March 4th. Lay all day at Burnams on account of the rain. I will here mention the prospect of those who turn their attention to cattle and other stock, the grass range in all the praries I have seen is superior for cattle to anything elsewhere of the kind on earth. The summer range is as good as it can be, consisting of all kinds of summer grass common to the Mi. praries, and there is a kind of curley grass which resembles our sedge grass which covers in some places for miles. So thick that you may lie down upon it as comfortably as you would be on a thick straw bed. And there is a kind of grass called muskeat grass which very closely resembles the blue grass, which affords good grazing for cows and horses all the winter, and in scarce years, when the other mast fails the hogs will do well on it.

There is also large tracts of wild rye which is equal in all respects in the winter for horses, cows &c. to the tame. At this time it is half leg high.

Besides all this, there is a kind of wild pea vine which is voraciously devoured by cows, horses, and almost every thing. The root of the vine is parenial and from its appearance now, as it lies spread over the prarie I think will be very hard to break. It everywhere surpasses any country for hogs I have ever heard of. The ground now in the post oak praries is litterly covered with acorns, the live oak groves also afford fine acorns for hogs, and there is a sort of oak called bur oak which bears a fine acorn. These acorns are nearly as large as hens eggs, well tasting and plenty on the Colorado bottoms. There are many other kinds of grass and fruits, pacarn &c. on which nearly all kinds of stock feed. There is a tree called the Muskeat wood which bears a pea or more properly a bean upon which stock of all kind become very fat, more particularly horse. The[y] become so fat on these peas that it is said they frequently are unfit for service. The peas produced by the vine above mentioned are also a nutricious food for cows, horses, hogs, &c. This vine very much resembles the garden pea, only it is a great deal smaller. It is no doubt a species of that plant. March 8th. Now at Burnhams ferry on Colorado. Here our company dispersed. Some took one direction and some another, as for myself I chose to remain at Burnham's. This I made my home place 55 days, or rather a place to return to from my exploring excursions. In the time mentioned I examined the land &c on the rivers Navadad [Navidad], Labacca [Lavaca], Gaulupe [Guadalupe], Rocky Creek, Harvays [Harvey], Mi [illegible], Buckners Creek, Cummins Creek and Mill Creek. After satisfying myself with these places, I on the 2nd of May set my face towards home. Spent five days examining the Brazos lands. When I arrived at San Felipe on the 8th May, when I fell in with Mr. Foley and Mr. Cope, 2 gentn. bound for the U.S. and being pretty well tired of the life woodsing it alone concluded to join company with them and return home.

. . . .

The Country which I have explored since alone is in my judgment the most desirable part of Texas. It is somewhat rolling, not broken and contains considerable very good land, with pretty plenty of tolerable good water. The grass is as good as can be, consisting of 38 varieties of grass, peas &c, all of it indiscriminately devoured by cows, horses &c. The cows are now as fat or fatter than ever I saw a stall fed beef in the U.S. I mean the milk cows and the dry cattle; It would be incredable to attempt a description. The horses too that live entirely on the prairy are as fat as there is any use for them to be. Now I have shewn that the land, the grass, the horses, the cows, and I might have added Hogs and sheep, are all fine. I will assert that they could not be better, and the water will do—the timber too in some places is pretty plenty, and almost on any league that reaches a water course the[re] can, with saving and strict economy, be found timber enough for building and firewood. There the timber is scarse and poor.

. . . .

Deer and turkey are plenty; so are the wolves and panthers, as also several of the other cat family. There are some snakes, of all sorts. There are spiders of many kinds. One species of them, which the people here call the terantula would weigh near a $\frac{1}{4}$ of a pound. This indeed is a very dangerous Spider. It is not very plenty, tho enough to cause those who camp out to use the precaution of stretching their hair ropes around their palate when sleeping at night. It is said that their bite is as painful as that of the rattlesnake. They have another very dangerous reptile here, which is called the San to fee [centipede]. This is of the scorpion tribe and is armed with stings at both ends. This very often kills when it inflicts a wound.

Besides these, there are many ugly nondescript animals. There is the horned frog, which is as ugly and as dangerous *looking thing* as any of them, but this, it is said, is inocuous. However, I was afraid to take hold of it for it is horny all over. The horns keen and sharp from a half to an inch long. Besides all this when it discovers that you are about to over take him, he will turn upon you, when he presents a very formidable appearance. Strutting out all his hundred horns, he will rais himself on his *tip toes* and spread himself as wide as your hand. In this situation he presents himself sideways, elevating the edge next to the enemy. His tail strutted out (for he has a tail) showing himself about 5 inches long, and thin and as sharp as a saw, being nicely horned and toothed on all sides but the belly. The horns on his head are much the longest, all turning back. He has good eyes which he uses like the human turning his head when he changes his object. His belly is white and smooth.

I shall now mention the insect kingdom—which perhaps exists here in as great numbers and varieties as any country on the continent of America. The most numerous tribe is the black gnat. The next in order is the musketoe. These rise in clouds so thick that when you withdraw your arm suddenly from among them you may see the hole where it came from. There is the pine gnat and the cedar gnat whose size is between the black gnat and the musketoe. The touch of these gnats is actual fire. Then comes the horse fly in all his varieties. These gall and harass the horses and cows at such a rate that they are frequently seen to fall down and bellow in agony. We will now mention the blow fly. This species of fly is the most destructive to the brutal creation of all the rest. He deposits his young (for he is viviperous) in the smallest scratch where blood is drawn, or where a tick has been mashed. They are so numerous that there is always plenty on hand when any accident happens that draws the blood to be sure to make a deposite—dogs, hogs, cows, every species of animal you may see the sign of them. The human species is not exempt from them. There are plenty of all kinds of blow flies, and every other species of flies, gnats &c. The honey bee is also very plenty. So are the wasp and yellow jacket.

Situation of the colonies

Austin's colony extends from the Gulf up the Colorado to the San Antonio crossing, a distance of 150 miles from the coast, and east to the river San Jacinto taking in the Brazos, west to Guadalupe covering the Nevadad [Navidad] and the LaVacca [Lavaca] country. The two last mentioned rivers are very pretty little streams. A league of land in this colony costs $150—90 dols. of which is imposition, but the people put up with it.

Robinson's [Sterling C. Robertson's] colony lies on the Brazos reaching north to the cross timbers, a distance of 270 miles from Austin's, which is its southern boundary. This grant embraces a vast region of first rate soil. The principal part of the colony is prarie nude of any kind of timber, except on the water courses, where there is a sufficiency for agricultural purpose and for fuel. It does not afford so great a proportion of timber as Austin's colony. But the country is higher, dryer, and not so subject to inundation as the lower colony is. It is thought that good wheat may be grown in the northern part of this colony. The chief tributary streams of the Brazos, are the Yeagua [Yegua] on the west and the Nevazott [Navasota] on the east, which mouth in this colony and the little Brazos. A league of land in this Col. cost $60—. There are about 200 settlers and upward in it. The land office for Robinson's colony is at Vista [Viesca], a little town at the falls of the Brazos.

Milam's Colony lies between the Colorado and the Guadalupe river, having Austin's and Dewitt's colonies for its southern boundary. Contains some good lands, is in a healthy region. The surface of the southern part is undulating, the northern part mountainous. The northern part of this colony is said to abound in valuable minerals. It is a well watered country. This colony is rapidly populating under the management of Robt. H. Williamson [Judge Robert M. "Three-legged Willie" Williamson]. It is said that this gentleman owns the colony although ostensibly belonging to Milam. A league of land in this colony costs $90—.

Dewitt's [Green Dewitt's] colony lies on the Guadalupe, on the west of Austin's Colorado grant. It is a pretty country and is settling fast. The office in this colony was not yet open.

Dilliom's [Martín de León] colony lies south of DeWitt's and on the same river. It is nearly all taken up by Mexicans, and emigrants from the U.S. The lands of this colony are good, though in general the bodies of rich soil are not so extensive.

The three last named colonies are better adapted to the rearing of horses and cattle. In fact the whole country surpasses all other for raising cows, horses, hogs &c.; but I make some distinction on account of Austin's and

Robinson's being better adapted to the growing of cotton, sugar cane &c., the soil being richer, in larger bodies, and better timbered.

Powell's [James Powers'] colony of Irish emigrants lies on the sea coast and the St. [San] Antonio River, south of the town of La Bahia. They are a captious, discontented, quarrelsome, drunken, riotous, bigotted, fanatical, ignorant set of Roman Catholics, incapable of self government and possessing none of the materials for making good citizens.

A New Yorker obtained a grant on the Rio Grande 2 or 3 years ago, brot on some families and then abandoned them. This grant lies in the vicinity of the San Fernando's. With that section of the country I am not intimate.

The Galveston company have obtained a grant, lying from the coast up the rivers Trinity and San Jacinto. The Galveston bay is included in this grant, and the two above named rivers disemboque in it. That country is not very valuable except as a stock country, the Southern half of it being too low and marshy, and the northern part broken and sandy though well watered and the timber equal to any country in the world. I do not wish to be understood as intimating that there is little good soil in this colony. I only speak comparatively to the territory west of that part of Texas.

Towards the source of the Trinity the lands are high, dry and fertile. This country is unsettled, nor is there much probability of its being shortly inhabited by the white man by reason of the numerous aboriginal tribes in that quarter. The remarks which I have made about Trinity will apply to the Sabine, the Southern extremity of the Naches, Angelina and Snow rivers.

Mason [John T. Mason] has obtained a grant of country which has the great road that crosses Sabine at Gaines ferry for its southern base. This grant comprehends the Ayish bayou, Toweac [Attoyac], Angelina, the country on the head of the Naches and I believe some of the Trinity and San Jacinto. The rivers Angelina and Naches makes Snow river which discharges into the western side of the Sabine bay. This river is navigable a great way up.

That part of Red river which lies in Texas is at present much spoken of by travellers. The lands on that part of the Red river are, in the cotton and corn crops very productive, and high up the river good wheat may be grown. It, like the rest of Texas, is a prarie country with wide bottom lands covered with useful timber, affording first rate prarie pastorage. This part of Texas is now, on account of the prospect which is anticipated on the opening of the raft on Red river much talked of by the Capitalists of that country and Louisiana.

There is another beautiful short river which I have neglected to mention the Barnard [San Bernard]. It rises between the Brazos and Colorado as high up as San Felipe. It runs into the gulf, is at its mouth as wide and as deep as the Brazos, and for a short distance is navigable. The timbered lands of the Barnard are very fine, producing, like the Brazos, Colorado, Oyster Bayou [Creek], Cany [Caney Bayou] and Peach creek, from 1600 to 3200 pounds of cotton pr. acre. Large plantations on these water courses often average 3000 pounds per acre.

The Guadalupe afford excellent soil. The bottoms are not wide & occasionally are subject to inundation. With the Guadalupe ends the chief Angloamerican settlements. Towards the west there are some settlements on the Noeses [Nueces]. This stream falls into Aransas bay [Nueces Bay] west of Guadalupe.

The entrance to the mouths of all the rivers are shallow. The Brazos has not at best above six feet water and is fast filling up with sand. This river makes its way to the gulf without any widening or bay, as does the Barnard. The pass into Matagorda bay has 7 feet of water. The LaVacca bay which is the western arm of Matagorda bay has a pass of 8 to 16 feet.

The greater portion of the vessels make their landing at Cox's Point up the Lavacca of late, as being more safe than any of the other landing places. The towns on the Brazos are Velasco at its mouth, at this place is kept the custom house for Austin's Colony. 12 miles above Velasco is Brazoria, the next is Columbia 12 miles above that. This place is the head of the tide water and any vessel that can enter the river, can and does run up to Columbia. The next town is San Felipe 60 miles farther up. At this place is kept the land office for Austin's Colony—25 or 30 miles up the Brazos opposite the mouth of the Navazott is situated a little town called Washington. 100 miles higher is Vista [Viesca]. At this place is kept the land office for Robinson's [Robertson's] Colony.

There are no large villages as yet on the Colorado. Matagorda is the most important in a commercial point of view. It is on a beautiful dry situation & has about 250 inhabitants. There is a raft 4 miles in length 7 miles above Matagorda which entirely obstructs the navigation of this river. But there is a project on foot for its removal, and when I left that country, there was upward of $20,000 subscribed and it is very probable that e'er this that they have obtained the amount required. When this raft is cut out the navigation of the Colorado will be equal to the Brazos and in every respect it has the ascendency. 25 miles north of Matagorda on the Colorado is Augusta, a town which was laid off this year by a gentleman from Tennessee by the name of Thomas Cayce. 80 miles higher up is another new town, named Electra, 28 miles higher is Mina, or Bastrop. This is where the San Antonio road crosses the Colorado and may become a pretty smart place for business. There is a steam mill now being erected on the east side of the Colorado between Bastrop and Electra. There are a number of families settled 35 or 40 miles above Bastrop on the river.

There are many more new towns rising at different points in Texas, all of a very late date. One 15 miles north of Coxes Point on the Nevadad, called Santa Anna [now Edna] in honor of the Mexican president, Gonzilas [Gonzales] on the Guadalupe, on the same river, Victoria. LaBahia on the St. Antonio River &c. Matamoras is a large Spanish town 25 miles of the gulf on the Rio Grande. There [are] all sorts of people here, and in a commercial point of view it is the most important place in all Coahuila and Texas. Here there are some heavy importers of goods for home consumption. This place is resorted to from many of the interior states—Durango, Chihuahua, Zacatecas, Tamaulipas, Sonora, and Santa Fe. I am told all trade to Matamoras. The population of this place is said to be 20,000. There are many other large towns on the Rio Grande.

The whole of Texas and Coahuila is a fine country and will eventually be thickly settled. The part that pleases me best is the Colorado Country. Next is the Nevadad. Then there is Oyster bayou, Caney, Peach Creek, Brazos, Barnard, Guadalupe and from information the Red river country. All delightful countries—all possessing equal advantages in regard to rearing stock of all kinds, lands as good as they can be, and pretty plenty of good water.

Thus far I have described the country in its best light—its soil, its productions, its waters, its timbers, its towns &c. I will now make a few remarks on the other side of the question.

The most serious objection to that country is the unsettled state of the government—and there is no prospect of its being better soon, but worse. There is at this time every prospect of a war, between the citizens of Texas and the other states of that restless republic.

Another objection is the injury done the citizens by the numerous wandering tribes of Indians which infest every part of the country. Their principal occupation is horse stealing. But when they find a man unarmed with a good horse they generally kill him and take his horse and clothing and whatever else he may have that they take a fancy to. There were 8 men killed and robbed in the bounds of Austin's colony during the 3 months I remained in the country. There was nothing done by the people in retaliation. But what could they do? for they might as well undertake to retaliate on the numerous tribes of ravenous beasts that inhabit the swamps of the three rivers. Still this evil may be prevented with a few hundred soldiers posted at proper stations. The other objections which might be enumerated are common to most countries.

NOTE:

The notebook in which Gideon recorded his Texas travel was originally an account book in which he entered Indian trade receipts for the years from 1821 to 1824. The accounts include those of Andrew Morrison, Judge William Cocke, Noah Wall, James Campbell, James Colbert, Major J. Pitchlynn, John Botts, Edmund Folsom, Charles Holston, Barkatubbee, Major Willis, and others.

Following the Texas Journal entries is a list of rivers with ferry fees and towns on the route from Mississippi to Texas.

On his second trip to Texas, in 1848, Gideon used the book again. Under the heading "G. Lincecum & Family, Landed at Houston, Texas, 12th April, 1848" he wrote a lengthy description of the land, crops, timber, grass, water supply, and rivers between Houston and Long Point.

The occasional ellipses in the above reproduction of Lincecum's Journal indicate portions which are omitted because they have been quoted in the main text of this account of Lincecum's life.

Lincecum's language of 1848, compared to that of the 1835 journal, indicates a direction away from colloquialism toward a more formal literary style. Already the sharply expressive vernacular of the frontier was being replaced by a vocabulary of more elegant words acquired through insatiable reading and this predicted the somewhat pedantic and florid style of Lincecum's middle years. However, the piquant speech of the pioneer was too irrevocably ingrained for permanent eradication. Its persistent encroachment adds a sparkle and freshness to otherwise dull essays in high-toned phrases. In the end the language peculiar to the frontier prevailed over Lincecum's acquired and more learned speech. Both his Autobiography and his Reminiscences are considered to be choice specimens of sustained writing in the American language.

Appendix B

MOCCASIN TRACKS FOR 1864,
or HOME MEDICINES FOR HOME DISEASES

During the Civil War, Lincecum wrote numerous letters on herbal remedies to the editors of the *Tri-Weekly Telegraph* and the *Tri-Weekly News*. Topics covered a wide range—use of tobacco solution for improved eyesight; treatment for bumps, hemorrhoids, dyspepsia, fevers, and gunshot wounds; use of wild mulberry as a cathartic; screwworms in stock; loss of hearing; and insect stings.

In 1864 he directed his letters to Edward Hopkins Cushing, publisher of the *Telegraph*, who not only encouraged him to send medical articles but proposed the publication of Lincecum's cures under the title of "Home Remedies for Home Diseases." Lincecum replied:

To put a work of that kind in such a form as to elicit public favour would require considerable systematic labor and some time. You have forgotten that I am a long way down the pull slope of my period of existence and that a fatigued, time-jarred mentality is not capable of fixing up suitable dishes for a *depraved* popular palate.

Lincecum did, however, compile a list of eighty-five botanic remedies which he called "The Moccasin Tracks, or Home Medicines for Home Diseases." While he was working on it the Civil War ended and he wrote Sioux Doran: "I wrote a long letter yesterday to Cushing on the subject of the 'book' but I am inclined to think from the tenor of the news this morning that book-making and things of like character will be suspended for awhile at least."

The book was never published but the manuscript is among the Lincecum Papers. The items below are a mere sampling and each has been condensed.

Mountain lily (*Calla palustris*)—applied to skin, good for headaches and slight burns.

Rosemary (*rosmarinus*)—oil from it good for rheumatism; few sprigs in lard tubs while it is cooling will prevent it from becoming rancid. The old women of Italy sleep on mattresses made of rosemary for the purpose of keeping them healthy.

Wild sage, cancer weed (*Salvia cyrata*)—has been used successfully by the root doctors in the cure of cancer, the extract in plasters is the mode of using it.

Fringe-tree (*Chion anthus*)—bark of the root—its greatest excellence lies in its power to control protracted gleets. For this purpose . . . the pulverized bark of the root is tinctured in a quart of gin or good whiskey and taken in half wine glass doses, 3 times a day half hour before eating . . . It seldom fails to effect a cure in 2 or 3 weeks. It is also very good in the chronic stage of gonorrhea.

Verbenaceae (*Calicarpa americana*)—the leaves placed in the headstall of the bridle will keep the flies from plaguing your horse.

White or sleek (smooth) sumac (*Rhus glabra*)—bark, leaves, fruit, gum and galls extensively used in all cases needing astringents. . . . The sumac is altogether a very valuable article answering a good purpose in many cases of disease.

Poison oak (*Rhus quinquefolia*)—the leaves . . . used by the old school doctors in paralysis. They say it produces a prickling sensation and slightly (in the doses they dare give it) opens the bowels. The patients upon which the experiments were tried recovered to a certain degree and then died. From these results they were led to conclude that the poison oak is a valuable medicine and they invited the attention of the faculty to the subject adding that there is no doubt many valuable medicines in the poison oak family. That's good hard sense for you.

Blackhaw (*Viburnum prunifolium*)—this is a pretty good medicine and may be used in any of the tonic or alterative compounds with advantage. I knew a very healthy old gentleman, 75 years of age, who used the blackhaw bark as a substitute for tobacco. He told me he had been in the habit of chewing for 30 years and that he had been very healthy all the time. The tea of the bark will relieve urgent symptoms of gonorrhea.

Virginia tobacco (*Nicotiana tabacum*)—this poisonous plant has been used a great deal as a medicine by the old school faculty and thousands have been slain by it. It is nevertheless a favorite luxury amongst all classes and I suppose will continue so, as long as old mother earth will be kind enough to produce it. . . . It is a very dangerous article and use it as you will, it always diminishes the vital energies in exact proportion to the quantity used. It may be slow but it is very sure.

Rattlesnake master (*Agave virginica*)—the root of this plant boiled in sweet milk and taken freely or chewed and swallowed so, is a certain cure for the bite of the rattlesnake. I have known it done several times. It is a Muscogee remedy.

China tree, pride of China (India?) (*Melia*)—the bark of the root. A great many people are in the habit of giving a strong decoction of the China root to their children with impunity as a vermifuge and it has become a very popular medicine for wormy complaint and they tell me that it is harmless. Of this I have my doubts. I have been called to three cases of children who were dying evidently from the effects of poison. On inquiry I found from their parents that all three of them had been treated a few hours previous pretty freely with decoction of China. . . . I have never used it.

Red-bud tree, Judas tree (*Cercis canadensis*)—I have seen the very worst cases of chronic dysentery in the last stages cured with this article. The proper way to use it is to boil the bark of the roots in sweet milk and let the patient live upon it and crackers.

Birthwort (*Aristolochiaceae*)—it is equal to the serpentaria for the same purposes and is much better in labour than ergot, as it is not poison and ergot always is.

Opium poppy (*Papaver somniferum*)—this is the opium, that deadly poison which is given profusely and with impunity to all ages, sex and conditions and, except for mercurial preparations, has destroyed more life than all other poisons taken as medicines.

Foxglove (*Digitalis purpurea*)—this plant is used in all cases of arterial excitement by the old school doctors. It has slain its millions and is still used in consumption, dropsy & slaying its victims. But let them die for die they must a long time before they will agree to think for themselves. But that day is coming and then all poisons as a curative will be rejected. I warn you against the use of the foxglove.

Bush bean—a poultice made of the leaves of the snap bean is without doubt the best application that was ever made for an inflamed wound. I have applied it to gunshot wounds which were at the very point of mortification and the relief was instantaneous.

Dandelion (*Leontodon taraxacum*)—Drs. Rush, Zimmerman, Bergins, Pemberton, Thomson, Howard, Beach and many others speak of this plant as a medicine of great powers. Being deobstruent, diuretic, hepatic, sub-tonic, aperient, &c. Very useful in liver complaints, dropsy, jaundice, hypochondria and obstructions generally.

Tomato, love apple (*Solanum lycopersicum*)—edible. This article has recently been brought into notice by the old school faculty. They made a terrible parade over it. They said and they published it in all the papers in the United States that the extract of tomatoes would answer in place of the calomel; and they rejoiced at the prospect of getting clear of the opprobrium which had been cast on the profession for several centuries on account of the deleterious and murderous effects of that particular mercurial preparation. So anxious were they and such was the feeling of relief upon the prospect of getting rid of the mercurial preparations that they had, even before many of them had ever seen the extract of tomato, begun decrying in strong terms all preparations of mercury as dangerous in the extreme, and that no rational practitioner would resort to it under any circumstance now that science had discovered so safe and innocent, so mild and pleasant a substitute. None of the doctors had the energy to go to work and prepare this invaluable extract, if they knew how—a thing very doubtful with a great many of them. But to show their confidence in the article they would eat large quantities of the raw, sometimes green, tomatoes recommending it all the while as one of the greatest and best things in the world to keep off fever. It is, said they, "a better medicine than calomel." I have seen the poor fellows cram themselves with nearly a peck at a bate and try to look wise while they were at it. But that has blown over and the dog has returned to his vomit.

Fig tree (*Ficus caria*)—this, it is said, composed the first garments of our forefathers—it was mighty rough to their new tender skins. . . . Chafe a ringworm with the rough leaf and then apply the milk of the broken stem to the affected part and it is a certain cure in two or three applications. Would not a poultice of the bruised leaves be a good application to scald heads and tetters in conjunction with constitutional remedies?

Sun dew, hyperica (*Drocera breviolia Pursh*)—slightly acrid, tonic. I do not know this plant as a medicine but it is a great curiosity both in its habits and its appearance. The scape stands erect in the center of the radical leaves which are covered with red hairs and all among these hairs are sprinkled very clear transparent drops which have the appearance of dew drops but which are in reality the very best kind of glue. These drops remain undiminished all day and the drier the weather the more limpid and enticing these drops seem. So that the little thirsty insects are enduced to approach for the purpose of slaking their thirst. Oh! horror, how terrible is the mistake. Instead of the clear limpid drop of heaven distilled dew which looked so inviting and with which he hoped to cool his parched tongue he finds himself entangled, mouth, feet and all in a strong viscid gluey substance from which there is no escape. In vain he tries his little wings; they have heretofore borne him aloft above all difficulty and danger but they avail him nothing now. He tries all his little arts, strains every sinew, plies every force. Still he sticks. Becoming exhausted at last he calmly submits to pine away in destruction when he becomes food for the sullen little treacherous plant, who still spreads forth his painted leaves and brandishes his deceptive bait.

> Oh! Shun ye insects, who pass the parching heath,
> The brilliant sundew, to taste his drop is death.

Snowball, Guelder rose (*Caprifoliaceae viburnum opulus*)—it is not for its medical properties that I have preserved this plant, for I do not know it as such, but because it is pretty.

Appendix C

TUXPAN, MEXICO

Tuxpan, on the east coast of Mexico in the northern part of the State of Veracruz, is about 350 miles below Brownsville, Texas, and 175 miles above the city of Veracruz. It is at the mouth of the Tuxpan River, its background a lush tropical jungle. After the Civil War it was settled by a large number of Confederates who chose expatriation rather than Reconstruction. Many of the original colonists went there from other sections of Mexico after the collapse of Maximilian's empire.

The exodus to Mexico of Confederate generals, other officers, and soldiers, former governors, camp followers and adventurers is a neglected but extremely interesting aspect of Texas and Southern history. Except for the march of the quixotic General Joseph Orville Shelby and his brigade through Texas and into Mexico City, the movement was not an organized one. It was a spontaneous immigration by stagecoach and horseback, and Mexico City in the summer and early fall of 1865 was crowded with thousands of Confederates, some escaping the Federals, others seeking a new land, but many looking for excitement and a postponement of the anticlimax of defeat.

Shelby, one of the wealthiest slave and landowners in Missouri before the war, refused to surrender his command and disbanded it in June, 1865, at Corsicana, Texas. Five hundred volunteers rode with him to Mexico with a vague plan of offering their services either to Juárez or to Emperor Maximilian.

General Edmund Kirby Smith, commander of the Trans-Mississippi Department, "abandoned and mortified" (Smith to Colonel J. T. Sprague, USA, May 30, 1865), found sanctuary in Mexico, where as a West Point captain in 1846 he had participated in the War with Mexico. Brigadier General Alexander Watkins Terrell, a Texas lawyer and plantation owner, with a letter of introduction to the Emperor from Governor Pendleton Murrah, of Texas, tucked in his boot, was with a group which crossed without difficulty at Roma on the Rio Grande.

John Henry Brown and his family and others leaving San Antonio were escorted to Mexico by members of Shelby's brigade. In Mexico City Brown found employment with the Imperial government, serving under Commodore Matthew Fontaine Maury, who was Maximilian's commissioner of immigration.

Before leaving Texas the Southern generals had actually planned to establish their own colony and government in Mexico, but wiser heads pointed out their folly. Crossing at various points on the border, the groups rendezvoused in Monterrey at the Paschal Hotel, operated by George Washington Paschal, who had left San Antonio during the War because of his Union sympathy. At least fifty Confederate officers were present at a July 4 banquet in Monterrey. Afterwards they viewed the Bishop's Palace, where many of them had fought in 1846.

Maury's rooms in Mexico City became Confederate headquarters. General John B. Magruder, Maximilian's colonization chief, revived the Aztec Club, which had been organized there by U.S. officers during the Mexican War. Generals B. H. Lyon, of Kentucky, and John M. McCausland, of Virginia, were Imperial surveyors. General W. H. Stevens, who had been Lee's chief engineer, was chief engineer of the Imperial Railway and Governor Thomas C. Reynolds, of Missouri, who had established Missouri headquarters in Marshall, Texas, during the war, was a railway superintendent.

Governor Henry Watkins Allen, of Louisiana, published the government's *Mexican Times* and was assisted by Major John W. Edwards, Shelby's aide. Shelby, after Maximilian declined his services, went into the freighting business. Some of his men joined the Confederate colony in Orizaba, Veracruz. John Henry Brown, after a trip to Yucatán to survey a colony site, and his family joined the Orizaba colony in October.

After Maximilian's death in June, 1867, many Confederates returned to the states, but thousands remained in Mexico. The Orizaba colony was abandoned in favor of the coastal area of Tuxpan, which John Henry Brown had previously explored on an assignment from Maury. Brown, his wife, two sons, and three daughters lived at Tumbadero, where he and his associates in 1868 bought and occupied 10,138 acres. Other Texans at Zapatal owned 7,000 acres. Immigration from Texas to the Tuxpan area was greatly stimulated by Brown's book, *Two Years in Mexico*, but shortly after its publication he returned to the United States to purchase arms in New York and New England for the Juárez government. By 1870 he and his family had resettled in Texas, first at Indianola, where he published a newspaper.

The natives of Tuxpan were well acquainted with the North Americans, particularly Texans. In 1842 the operation of the Texas Navy close to their shores was interpreted as a threat to raid the town and rout the old Texas enemy, General Martín Perfecto de Cos, from his hiding place. During the

United States-Mexican War, five years later, Commodore Matthew C. Perry led gunboats up the Tuxpan River. General Cos was still in Tuxpan but now fled inward, leaving the town to the U.S. Navy.

Despite the memory of these incursions and the knowledge that most of the Confederates had aided the Austrian against their beloved Juárez, the colonists were hospitably received by the natives. The only hostile movement directed against any of the settlements was made by Juaristas in May, 1866, before Maximilian's defeat, in a raid on a colony at Omealco founded by John Lane of Texas. No recorded retaliatory action against the colonists occurred during Juárez' or subsequent administrations.

In the Lincecum Papers is a letter from Mexican Secretary M. Romero written in Mexico City, February 25, 1872, and addressed to Otis M. Messick, formerly a colonel in the 11th Regiment, Texas Cavalry, and a resident of Tuxpan. Romero outlined the official Mexican attitude toward the colonists, assuring them that there had never been any feeling of hostility in Mexico against American colonists. Government protection had not been extended, he explained, because it had never been requested by the colonists nor had it ever been needed.

The Tuxpan colony prospered as late as 1880, but today it is vastly changed since Lincecum resided there. It is no longer his quiet lovely agricultural area, but a center of oil production and archaelogical activities.

See Alexander Watkins Terrell, *From Texas to Mexico and the Court of Maximilian in 1865,* (Dallas, Book Club of Texas, 1933); Edwin Adams Davis, *Fallen Guidon,* (Sante Fe, Stagecoach Press, 1962); John Henry Brown, *Two Years in Mexico or the Emigrants Friend,* (Galveston, New Book and Job Office, 1867). For the life of John Henry Brown see Victor M. Rose, *The Life and Services of Gen. Ben McCulloch* (Philadelphia, Pictorial Bureau of the Press, 1888).

BIBLIOGRAPHY

Unpublished Lincecum Papers

It was, of course, impossible to incorporate into this account all the rich material in the Lincecum Papers, deposited in the Archives Collection of The University of Texas Library. Much of interest and use to researchers remains unpublished. The problem is how to find it.

The bulk of the letters have been typed and placed in as nearly chronological order as possible. The typed material is bound in fifteen volumes of almost 5,000 pages, frequently unnumbered. The typing, done in 1931 and 1932 by the National Youth Administration and through the courtesy of the Texas State Medical Association, is in many cases unreliable—names are wrong, Lincecum's handwriting has been misread, addresses are omitted. Copies should be checked against originals; and the originals are difficult to locate.

Following is a description of the files of the material deposited by the Lincecum family, now contained in seven jackets:

No. 104—Letters, 1829–1870 and undated; notebooks; clippings; and pamphlets.

No. 105—Letter press and Autobiography.

No. 106—Letter press, 1860–1865; Doran correspondence; letter press; the Chahta Tradition.

No. 107—Letters; speeches; notes; botany notes.

Nos. 108, 109, and 110—botany notes.

The typed (NYA) volumes are labeled:

Diary and cash book, 1821–1873. This contains Lincecum's 1835 Texas journal.

Autobiography, dated November 3, 1871. This volume contains his letters to his grandson written from Tuxpan, Mexico.

Miscellaneous and printed writings, 1838–1869. Not all writings are Lincecum's, but no distinction is made.

Papers, 1846–1870. This volume includes Lincecum's diary, March 12–December 8, 1867; 157 pages of medicinal plants; a list of 48 species of ants; specimens found on an 1867 trip to central Texas; letters to Sallie Doran from Elias Durand, 1861–1867.

Letter press, 1854–1859.

Letter press, 1859–1865.

Letter press, 1860–1861.

Letter press, 1862–1865.

Letter press, 1865–1867.

Letter press, 1867.

Letter press, 1867–1868.

Paper and letters, 1838–1870.

Papers and letters, 1871–1887 and undated.

Two volumes, Chahta Tradition.

Published Writings by Lincecum

American Naturalist

"The Tarantula Killers of Texas," Vol. I (May, 1867), pp. 137–141.

"Scorpions of Texas," Vol. I (June, 1867), pp. 203–205.

"The Tarantula of Texas," Vol. I (October, 1867), pp. 409–411.

"The Gregarious Rat of Texas," Vol. VI (August, 1872), pp. 487–489.

"Habits of the Opossum," Vol. VI (September, 1872), pp. 555–557.

"Habits of a Species of Sorex," Vol. VII (August, 1873), pp. 483–484.

"The Agricultural Ant," Vol. VIII (September, 1874), pp. 513–517.

"Sweet-Scented Ants," Vol. VIII (September, 1874), p. 564.

"Robber Ants," Vol. VIII (September, 1874), p. 564.

"The Gossamer Spider," Vol. VIII (October, 1874), pp. 593–596.

The American Sportsman

"Personal Reminiscences of an Octogenarian," issues of September 12, 19, 26, October 3, 10, 17, 24, 31, November 7, 14, 21, 28, December 5, 12, 19, 26, 1874, January 2, 9, 16, 1875; microfilm, University of Texas Library; original in Library of Congress.

Annual Report of the Commissioner of Patents for 1860, Agricultural Report, Vol. II, U.S. Government, 1861, "Texas Grasses," pp. 235–238.

Journal of the Linnaean Society, Zoology, Vol. VI (1862), "Agricultural Ant of Texas," pp. 29–31.

Practical Entomologist, Vol. I (August 27, 1866), "The Texan Cabbage-bug," p. 110.

Prairie Farmer, Vol. 34 (1866), "The Texan Cabbage-bug," p. 152.

Proceedings of the Academy of Natural Sciences

"A Collection of Plants from Texas" (with E. Durand), Vol. XIII (May, 1861), p. 98.

"On an Ant Battle Witnessed in Texas," Vol. XVIII (January, 1866), pp. 4–6.

"On the Grapes of Texas," Vol. XVIII (January, 1866), pp. 4–6.

"On the Small Black Erratic Ant of Texas," Vol. XVIII (March, 1866), pp. 101–106.

"On the Agricultural Ant of Texas," Vol. XVIII (November, 1866), pp. 323–331.

"On the Cutting Ants of Texas—*Oecodema texana buckley*," Vol. XIX (February, 1867), pp. 24–31.

Publications of the Mississippi Historical Society

"The Autobiography of Gideon Lincecum," Vol. VIII (1904), pp. 443–519.

"Chocktaw Traditions about Their Settlement in Mississippi and the Origin of Their Mounds," Vol. VIII (1904), pp. 521–542.

"Biography of Apushmataha," Vol. IX (1906), pp. 415–485.

Southern Cultivator

"Grasses of Texas," Vol. XIX (January–February, 1861), Part I, p. 33, Part II, pp. 51–52.

Southwestern Historical Quarterly

"Journal of Lincecum's Travels in Texas, 1835" (A. L. Bradford, T. N. Campbell, eds.), Vol. LIII (1949–1950), pp. 180–201.

Texas Almanac

"Native or Indigenous Texas Grasses" (1861), pp. 139–143.

"Botany—Directions by Which the Poisonous Plants of Texas May Be Readily Recognized" (1861), pp. 143–144.

"The Cotton Worm" (1867), pp. 195–196.

"Texas Marble" (1868), pp. 87–8.

"Medicated Waters of Texas" (1868), pp. 88–90.

"The Indigenous Texian Grasses" (1868), pp. 76–77.

"Gypsum in Texas" (1868), pp. 85–86.

"The Water Power of Texas" (1868), pp. 90–91.

Zoologist

"The Cutting Ant of Texas," Vol. 3 (1868), pp. 1270–1281.

Works Utilizing Lincecum's Writings

The Lincecum material has been used by a few notable writers and in some distinguished publications:

American Ethnology Bulletins

John Constantine Pilling, "Bibliography of the Muskhogean Language," No. 9, p. 53.

John R. Swanton, "Source Material for the Social and Ceremonial Life of the Choctaw Indians," No. 103, pp. 12–26.

Frederick W. Hodge, Biography of Apushmataha, "Handbook of the American Indian," No. 30, Vol. II, pp. 329–330.

T. N. Campbell

"The Choctaw Afterworld," *Journal of American Folklore*, Vol. 72, No. 284, (1959) pp. 146–154.

"Choctaw Subsistence: Ethnographic Notes from the Lincecum Manuscript," *Florida Anthropologist*, Vol. XII, No. I (1959), pp. 9–24.

"Medicinal Plants used by the Choctaw, Chickasaw, and Creek Indians in the Early Nineteenth Century," *Journal of the Washington Academy of Sciences*, Vol. 41, No. 9 (September, 15, 1951), pp. 285–290.

J. Frank Dobie

Life and Literature of the Southwest, Southern Methodist University Press, Dallas, 1952, p. 69.

Tales of Old-Time Texas, Little, Brown & Co., Boston, 1928, pp. 125–313.

Samuel Wood Geiser

"Gideon Lincecum," *Dictionary of American Biography*, Vol. XI (1933), pp. 241–242.

"Gideon Lincecum," *Naturalists of the Frontier*, Southern Methodist University Press, Dallas, 1937, pp. 253–274; 1948, pp. 199–214.

"Men of Science in Texas, 1820–1880," *Field and Laboratory*, Vol. XXVI (1958), pp. 86–139.

"Naturalists of the Frontier: IV. Gideon Lincecum," *Southwest Review*, Vol. XV (Autumn, 1929), pp. 93–111.

"Notes on Some Workers in Texas Entomology, 1839–1880," *Southwestern Historical Quarterly*, Vol. XLIX (1945–1946), pp. 593–598.

Pat Ireland Nixon

Medical Story of Early Texas, Lancaster Press, Inc., Lancaster, Pennsylvania, 1946, pp. 376–384.

"A Pioneer Texas Emasculator," *Texas State Journal of Medicine*, Vol. XXXVI (May, 1940), pp. 34–38.

William A. Love

This Mississippi historian, born in 1848 in Lowndes County, Mississippi, made extensive use of the Lincecum material in articles printed in early issues of the *Publications of the Mississippi Historical Society*.

INDEX

ing house of, 294; mentioned, 52, 68, 229

Durham, George, Sr.: 83 n.

Durham, George J. (son-in-law of Gideon): marriage of, 82; birth of, 82; political career of, 82–83, 140; military record of, 83; as ornithologist, 83, 188–189, 198; as Texas grape authority, 83; homocide by, 83; deaths of children of, 83 n., death of, 83 n., 293; Gideon's vexation with, 198; Gideon's visits to, 231, 237, 244; discovery of stork species by, 243 and n.; mentioned, 129 n., 146, 162 and n., 250, 294

Durham, Lelia (granddaughter of Gideon): 293, 294

Durham, Mary Leonora (granddaughter of Gideon): 83

Durham, Royal Wheeler (grandson of Gideon): 83 n.

Durham, Sarah Lincecum ("Sally"; granddaughter): 83

Durham, Sidney J. (grandson): 292, 294

Durham, Walter W. (grandson): 61 n., 84, 293, 294

Dyer, P. S.: 292 n.

Eagle Lake: 41

Eagle Machine Company, of Richmond, Va.: 138

East, Dr. E. W.: 109 n.

Eatonton, Ga.: 18, 19, 55, 56, 290

Eclectic Medical College of New York: 176 n.

Eclectic Medical Institute of Cincinnati: 176 n.

Edgefield District, S.C.: 8

"Edible Nuts of Texas": 296 n.

Edwards, Maj. John W.: 324

Egypt (Texas settlement): 42

Eichholt, Henry: 76

Elbridge, N.Y.: 245 n.

El Campo, Texas: 87

Electra, Texas: 315–316

Elk Horn Tavern, battle of: 80 n.

El Paso, Texas: 150

El Tajin: 278 n.

emasculation. SEE Lincecum, Gideon; Lincecum Memorial

Engelmann, George: 189 and n., 235, 241

England: 82, 152, 160, 214, 273

entomology: Gideon's studies and observations in, 59, 65, 77, 133, 173, 202–226 and nn. *passim,* 232, 234; Gideon's pleasure in, 202; Gideon's articles on, 213–222 and nn. *passim,* 328–329; Gideon's cataloging in, 238; Addison Lincecum's work in, 276 n., Gideon's observations in, in Mexico, 274–275. SEE ALSO ant; Lincecum, Gideon; natural science; Philadelphia Academy of Natural Sciences; scientists; Smithsonian Institution

—, Gideon's contributions to, with: aphid, 207, 218; bean weevil, 286; bee, 203–204, 216, 219, 223 n.; beetle, 214; boll weevil, 205 n.; boll worm, 205 n.; *Bravo* ant, 274 and n.–275; butterfly, 214, 234, 246, 257; cabbage worm, 206 and n.; cotton worm, 204–205 and n.; cowkiller, 204; dirtdauber, 204; grasshopper, 245, 246; hymenoptera, 246; moth, 205, 214, 246; muddauber, 204; sea-coast ant, 266; scorpion, 214, 246; spider, 133, 204, 216, 246; tarantula, 65, 246; tarantula hawk (tarantula killer), 204, 214; wasp, 204, 216; water beetle, 204; weevil, 214; yellow boll worm fly, 242

epidemics. SEE disease

Episcopal Church: 99 n.

Episcopal parish of St. Peter's Church (Brenham, Texas): 116

Epperson, ——— (of Texas): 230

Epperson, R. S.: Long Point property of, 73 n.

Essex Institute of Salem, Mass.: 214

Estes, Joseph: 72

ethnology. SEE Chahta Tradition, Choctaw Indians, Indians

eugenics: 93–102 and nn. *passim,* 173. SEE ALSO evolution; Lincecum, Gideon

Eunice, La.: 259 n.

Europe: 156 n., 193, 194, 202

Evans, Capt. Moses: 81 and n.

Evergreen, Texas: 76

Evidence against Christianity, The: 107

Evilala or Maid of Midian: 107

evolution: 173, 213, 279, 298

Ewing, George: 49–50

Ewing, Dr. John A.: 101

expeditions of Gideon Lincecum: to Texas in 1835, 35–52 and nn., 303–316; to Gulf Coast of Texas, 130–131, 174, 248–251; in Texas interior, 174,

138 and n., 191; in improvisation during Civil War, 144–149 and nn. *passim*; in manufacturing gunpowder, 161–162; in interest in others, 175, 180, 239–241; in grief for loss of wife, 228–230, 250, 255; and opinion on loafers and bores, 238; in longing for new frontiers, 241, 247, 250–251; and superstition, 245; and ignorance, 245; in celebrating Christmas, 245, 290–291, 298–299, 301; and interest in Texas development, 237, 245 and n.; in philosophy toward work, 255; on swimming, 267–268; with his black violin, 290–292 *passim,* 298–299, 301; in writing autobiography, 295 and n., 298

—, children of: teaching theories and experiments with, 20, 70–71, 78, 263; and deprivations of, 30, 49–50; in medical practice, 60, 74, 86, 240; descriptions of, 68–72 *passim,* 78–88 and nn.; deaths of, 68, 70, 80–87 *passim*; marriages of, 71, 78–88 *passim*; and bequests, 72 n., 79–80, 229–230, 252; in military service, 80–82; and parenthood, 88–91 *passim;* in patriarchy, 88–91, 250–251, 253

—, grandchildren of: 89–91, 133–134, 137, 203, 231, 252, 255, 263

— and the Indians: knowledge of Indian tongues, 24–30 *passim,* 42, 44–45 and n.; friendship between, 25–30, 113, 276 and n.; and Gideon's nicknames, 26, 29–30; and Gideon's writings of, 27–28; and Indian medicine, 27–28, 56; travelling show of, 29; and Gideon as prisoner, 45–47; songs and dances of, 47; and relic collecting, 175, 197. SEE ALSO Chahta Tradition, Choctaw Indians, Indians, Tuxpan

— at Long Point, Texas: death of, 3, 298–299; plantation of, 48–49, 72–78 and nn. *passim*; position of, in Washington county, 77 and n.–78; as cattleman and farmer, 118, 120 and n.–121, 136–137 and n., 192; temporary paralysis of, 192–193; departure of, for Tuxpan, 241–245 *passim,* 252–253; financing move to Tuxpan by, 246, 247, 251; obituary of, 267 n.; return of, 288, 292–293; planned return to Tuxpan by, 292–294 *passim,* 297; care of, by children, 294–295; final activities

of, 294–299; decline of, 296–298; last Christmas of, 299; grave of, 301. SEE ALSO Long Point; Washington County; Texas

— as physician: of botanic medicine, 6, 17, 21, 28 n., 35, 54–65 and nn. *passim,* 70–71, 190, 242–243; with Texas expedition of 1835, 35–39, 52; search of, for medical improvements, 56–65 and nn. *passim*; and Thomsonian system of botanic medicine, 56–57; and Howard system of botanic medicine, 57 and n.; on plantation, 57; criticism of, by medical profession, 57–58 and n., 63 and n.; medical writings by, 57, 252, 318–322; mail-order patients of, 59–61; honored in medical journal, 61 n.; opinion of, on medical legislation, 62–63; and yellow fever, 63–64 and n., 242–245 and nn., *passim;* and psychiatry, 65; in Tuxpan, 65, 288; and son's death, 57, 68, 70; and inoculation, 162–163; encouragement of would-be doctors by, 240; request of, for vaccine, 288. SEE ALSO botany, healing arts, medicine

—, attitude of, toward the Negro: slaves of, 19, 72, 74, 105, 147–149, 164, 168; and Aunt Polly, 90, 168; and abolitionists, 110, 140; and Negro insurrection, 139 and n.; and postwar Negro problems, 167–169; after War, 264, 265, 267, 271. SEE ALSO Civil War, Negro, Reconstruction, secession movement, slavery, slaves, Yankee

— and politics: in Texas Revolution, 49–50; in War of 1812, 124, 141; philosophy of, 127–128, 134, 143, 157–158, 194–196 and nn.; as secessionist, 134, 139–143, 149–150; and dislike of Yankees, 139, 155, 169, 255, 264, 271, 272; as anti-Lincolnite, 139, 144, 146, 165; and Sam Houston, 140, 149–150; and blockade, 144; and Civil War, 144–145, 151–158 and nn. *passim,* 164 and n.; and kindnesses to soldiers, 145–146, 159, 291; on patriotism, 153–162 *passim,* 156 n.; Gideon's advice sought on salt processing by army, 155 n.; proposal of, regarding Confederate currency, 157; on war relief committee, 157; and medical services during Civil War, 158–166; on traitors and deserters, 160–165 and